Introducing Sociology

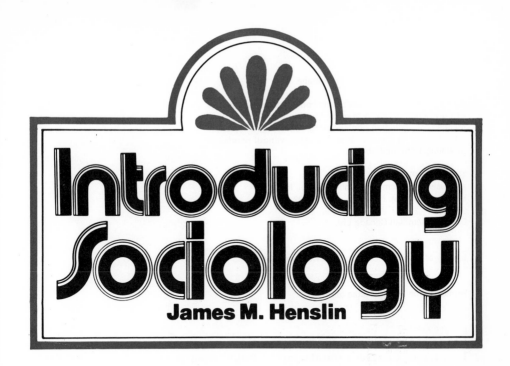

Introducing Sociology

James M. Henslin

Toward Understanding Life in Society

THE FREE PRESS

A Division of Macmillan Publishing Co., Inc.

NEW YORK

Collier Macmillan Publishers

LONDON

THE FREE PRESS
A Division of Macmillan Publishing Co., Inc.
866 Third Avenue, New York, N.Y. 10022

Collier–Macmillan Canada Ltd.

Library of Congress Catalog Card Number: 74–12595

Printed in the United States of America

printing number
1 2 3 4 5 6 7 8 9 10

Library of Congress Cataloging in Publication Data

Henslin, James M
    Introducing sociology.

    Bibliography: p.
    Includes index.
    1. Sociology.   I.   Title.
HM51.H3977 1975   301   74-12595
ISBN 0-02-914430-2

Contents

Preface

Teaching the introductory course in sociology is difficult at best. Students enter the class with a wide variety of backgrounds, interests, and expectations. A sort of tightrope must be walked between presenting theoretical orientations vital to contemporary sociology and making readily understandable applications of those orientations. Too far in either direction and one becomes either too vague and abstract or one fails to provide an adequate conceptual framework for a sociological understanding of social life. In this book I try to present a balanced position for walking this tightrope.

Major models, or theoretical orientations for interpreting human behavior, are presented within a context which applies those models to everyday life situations. Materials which might otherwise appear abstract, and perhaps vacuous, are applied to concrete situations with which students already have some familiarity. The "familiar" then takes on a different interpretation, allowing the student to see the value of the sociological approach to understanding human behavior.

Contemporary sociology is both rich and diverse in its scope and in its research. While this bounty is to the credit of the discipline, it can also present problems for teaching the introductory course. How does one attain the goal of teaching major sociological research findings and yet not fall into the trap of presenting mere fragments? Where is the unifying framework which allows the instructor to present both the richness and the diversity of sociology without letting it seem as though sociology is merely a bunch of unconnected parts? This is a major problem with which each sociology instructor struggles and which too often goes unresolved, as the usual texts present only bits and pieces of sociology. The social institutions, for example, are usually treated separately, with socialization confined to one section, social problems to another, and so on. Consequently, in spite of the instructor's efforts, students frequently end up seeing sociology as a disconnected array of fragmented topics.

It is hoped that through its three unifying themes this text presents a solution to this central problem in teaching the introductory course. As substantive sociological topics are covered in the text they are tied together by the twin themes of socialization and the symbolic nature of human life. Intertwined in their analysis is the symbolic nature of human beings living their lives together in society, being socialized into general culture and yet working out their own adjustments to life. Emphasized within the themes of socialization and symbolic interaction is an aspect of society which we all personally experience on a day-to-day basis, the role of the symbols into which we are socialized in both constraining us by channeling our behavior and freeing us by providing a choice as we adapt to the demands of our social world. This ongoing tension between social control and the individual working out his or her own life situation is present throughout this text.

The third major theme which integrates the materials of this text is the sociological imagination. The opening chapter presents the major ideas of the sociological imagination, and the following chapters apply the sociological imagination to a variety of situations. Analyzing human behavior within this basic framework emphasizes the structural context of human behavior, while simultaneously focusing on people as they work out their own life situations assures that those who live within that context are not neglected. As Mills suggested we do, the social-cultural-historical factors that establish the context for what people do are applied to the concrete situations in which individuals find themselves. This application enables the introductory student to understand human behavior within a sociological context, not merely to see the importance of vague "social forces," but to see how structural factors apply to concrete, everyday life situations. This approach takes sociology away from academic abstractions and lets the student directly apply the sociological perspective to his or her own situation in life.

The traditional topics of sociology are presented, such as social class, social institutions, culture, values, and racism. Material on the social institutions is interwoven throughout the text, with, for example, education, the family, and economics being covered as they apply to the specific topics treated, while separate chapters draw out the social-control implications of the legal and political systems, integrating materials previously presented. Additionally, topics not ordinarily covered in introductory texts are analyzed which rate high student interest and provide an excellent format for teaching sociology. These include interpersonal and intergroup games, homosexuality, mental illness, juvenile delinquency, slavery, and the women's liberation movement. The concluding chapter picks up major strands of thought that have run through the preceding chapters. It weaves these strands into a whole by focusing them on the question of how society manages to stay together in spite of its many conflicting groups.

In their initial introduction to sociology, students sometimes stumble badly over sociological terms. Some report that they spend most of their time struggling to learn a cumbersome vocabulary. If most introductory students went on to further study in sociology, this effort would be worthwhile, as it would provide a valuable tool. For the majority of students, however, the introductory course is the only formal exposure they receive to sociology. This creates a dilemma for the instructor, since acquiring a working knowledge of sociological terms is essential for grasping the perspective which the discipline offers.

When students have complained to me about the difficulty of learning the sociological vocabulary, I have found that they have little difficulty in learning it if the terms are explained in clear language, placed within a relevant context, and illustrated by example. To use jargon to explain jargon, however, as is typically done in texts, presents a frustrating task for everyone concerned. Accordingly, I have made this part of learning sociology easier by introducing each sociological term within a context which explains it. Each term is presented in a straightforward fashion and is then immediately applied. Further clarification is provided by the profuse use of examples. Additionally, the terms are cumulative, building upon one another as the student progresses through the book. Consequently, the student will learn most of the terms simply by reading the text, acquiring them from their context. This helps the student overcome one of the major barriers in the introductory course, allowing him to go beyond a mere learning of vocabulary to a fuller understanding of what sociology is all about.

I would suggest that the *Student's Guide* I have written to accompany this text be used. The *Guide* not only contains further examples and explanations of what is covered in the text, but also presents for each chapter in the text detailed suggestions on how the student can apply the material. The *Guide* also contains a cross-indexed glossary of the terms explained in the text, keyed to the text pages on which each term is initially (and in some cases subsequently) defined, and a chapter comparing sociology with the other social sciences. The instructor will find that many of the suggestions made in the *Guide* for applying the sociological topics analyzed in the text will make good term-paper topics, group projects, and shorter in-class reports.

Students may also find it helpful to use the matched volume of readings which I have edited to accompany this text. *Introducing Sociology: Selected Readings* provides a key selection for each chapter of the text. Used in combination with the text, this book of readings should further aid students' introduction to a sociological understanding of life in society.

If this text accomplishes its purpose, I owe a great debt to the students in my many introductory classes who allowed me to pre-test the materials with them. From them I have also learned much about teaching sociology. This is an ongoing debt I have too often left unacknowledged.

The usual types of sources on which I have depended in writing this book are acknowledged in the appropriate places in the text. But it is impossible to document in traditional forms of citation those sources of ideas (especially ideas originating from conversations with students, friends, and colleagues, as well as those absorbed from wide reading) that are so elusive that they remain beyond positive recall. I cannot therefore express adequately my appreciation and debt to those whose ideas have penetrated my consciousness and have become a part of my basic orientations. This insufficient note must suffice.

In working on the various stages of the manuscript, I have also incurred innumerable other debts. I wish to specifically acknowledge the various contributions of Jane Altes, Peter M. Blau, Jane Haegele, Maureen J. Hart, Jim Hayes, Art Iamele, Lynn Krieger, Ed Maguire, Al McCurry, Dave McDermott, Irv Naiburg, Kathy Oller, George Rowland, Ed Sagarin, and Martin S. Weinberg. Chapter 7 is based primarily on the various analyses presented by Erving Goffman. Because it would be so repetitious, no referencing to his particular works is given in that chapter, but the reader is referred especially to Goffman's *The Presentation of Self in Everyday Life.*

I also wish to specifically acknowledge the great debt of love, patience, and understanding which I owe my wife, Linda, to whom this book is respectfully and admiringly dedicated.

James M. Henslin

List of Figures and Tables

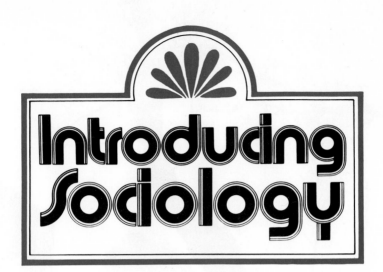

1
The Sociological Imagination

chapter 1

The Sociological Imagination

Fred and Janet met six years ago at a New Year's Eve party. They were immediately attracted to each other. Fred had finished college the year before, and Janet was just entering her last semester. They discovered that they were both concerned about social issues, that they enjoyed similar sports and recreation, and that each had been quite active in religious affairs. They began to date and grew increasingly attracted to each other. Within a couple of months they began to "get serious." Both were interested in marriage, but each felt that marriage was something that should not be rushed into. They talked over goals in life and continued to date. Their interest in each other did not diminish but grew, and they resolved that when Janet graduated they would become husband and wife. They anxiously looked forward to the day that they could begin leading a meaningful life together.

Upon Janet's graduation they were married. It was a June wedding, just as Janet had dreamed about since her childhood. The local newspaper ran their pictures and carried an article on their wedding. They honeymooned in an idyllic setting, and all their friends agreed that theirs was a perfect match. After living in an apartment for the first year of their marriage, they moved to a recently developed subdivision. The payments on their suburban home were somewhat steep, especially with the payments on their new car and the furniture with which they had "tastefully decorated" their new home; but with both working, they managed well.

Janet became pregnant during their second year of marriage, somewhat ahead of schedule, but their daughter, Susan Anne, was a wel-

Born into a particular society at a historical point in time, we live out our lives within confines established by our social groups. Although we experience our intimate relationships as intensely personal, even these are patterned by larger social forces surrounding us. (Photo by Laima Turnley)

come addition to their family. Fred didn't want Janet to work after she became a mother, and Janet agreed not to, but reluctantly. With the added expense of their child and the loss of Janet's income, things were rougher financially, and Fred took a job which he liked less but which paid more.

Fred became increasingly dissatisfied with his work, while Janet grew less satisfied with her position at home. She began complaining about staying home all day and not having anyone but a child to talk to. He became more irritable upon returning home after work, and their quarrels became more frequent. They had always quarreled somewhat, just as they knew their married neighbors and friends quarreled, but their quarreling now not only became more frequent but also took on an added note of bitterness. They began to blame each other for their dissatisfactions, for their feelings of lack of fulfillment. For the first time, they began to seriously question why they ever married in the first place.

With their neighbors continuing to demonstrate affluence, they began to feel poor. Fred agreed that Janet could take on a part-time job. They bought a boat, from which they derived great enjoyment the summer before last. During that summer they even began to forget about some of their problems and felt that they had successfully handled a difficult period of adjustment.

Janet became dissatisfied with her part-time job, however, and began searching for a full-time position. To her surprise, she found that even though she had completed college and had work experience no one would hire her. Employers now had their pick of college graduates. She blamed Fred for her situation, as it had been his idea that she give up her full-time job in the first place. Quarrels flared anew, and this time both Fred and Janet realized that the past few months had been not a solution to their difficulties but merely an interlude. When Fred was unexpectedly laid off during an "operational cut-back," their income between his unemployment compensation and Janet's part-time job was insufficient to make all their payments, and their boat was repossessed. Both Janet and Fred felt deeply humiliated at this unexpected turn of events, and their quarreling further increased. Each blamed the other for the position in which they found themselves, and it was at this point that they decided they no longer loved each other.

Six months ago Janet and Fred's marriage collapsed in tears, accusations, and counter-accusations. In court proceedings, Janet was awarded the divorce and granted custody of their daughter. Janet still works only part time because she feels that she must spend more time with Susan Anne now that Fred is only a visitor in their home. Fred has

Our lives come under the control of customs long established before we arrive on the social scene, customs which influence us from the cradle to the grave. (Photo by Laima Turnley)

secured a full-time job, but with his alimony and child support payments he can afford only a small apartment and a used car. Both are bitter.

What went wrong? Fred and Janet perceived that their marital difficulties were due to problems of some sort, but they saw these problems as rooted in the personal level: She was not doing what he wanted, he felt unable to meet her expectations, she felt unfairly treated, financial difficulties plagued them, and they were continually arguing. Their perspective was primarily limited to their immediate situation, and they failed to see the broader historical or social context of their particular problems. They left marriage "wondering what went wrong," but they did not connect their personal situation with the social milieu that led to their appearance in divorce court and now straps their incomes with legal bills, alimony and child support payments, the expense of two cars, and separate dwellings.

What they failed to see was that their marital difficulties, although played out on a personal level, resulted from historical forces impinging on them. Cultural changes have taken place, for example, which have changed the shape of American families. From the **extended family,** in which several generations live together, not only the parents and their children but also the grandparents and unmarried aunts and uncles, we have moved to the **nuclear family,** in which parents and their unmarried children form the typical family unit. This basic structural change in the family places tremendous strain on the adjustment of each married couple. In the nuclear family, the married couple must depend on each other for a larger proportion of their personal satisfactions. Physical and emotional needs are not shared among so many persons as in the extended family, yet these needs remain extremely insistent. Happiness has now become perhaps the primary goal of marriage; if one partner begins to feel unhappy, the marriage tends to be blamed, or, more specifically, the marital partner on whom such high expectations have been lodged.

Married couples have been shaped by pervasive cultural forces of which they are themselves only vaguely aware. Each member of society has a vast number of wants, needs, and expectations, which greatly extend beyond physical subsistence. They have learned these needs by growing up in particular social groups at a distinct historical point in time. These learned needs add increasing strain to a marriage. Janet felt the need for "liberation," a desire to change from the wife's traditional role of cooking, cleaning, and child care to a more active role in society—to enjoy a career and to receive recognition in her own right. She chafed at her situation. But Fred expected her to play a role similar to the one his mother had played and to remain content with life at

In the extended family typical of agrarian cultures several generations live together. As our economic patterns changed from agrarian to industrial, our family units also underwent modification.   (Courtesy of Lorimar Productions, Inc. Photo furnished by CBS Television Network.)

home. Their perception of the source of their difficulties remained on the personal level, on a feeling of "psychological incompatibility." They did not see the social and historical forces which led to such sweeping changes in what they expected from marriage and in the roles they expected each other to play within marriage.

When Janet and Fred were first plagued with financial problems, they placed blame on incorrect budgeting. They did not perceive these problems as rooted in the economic forces driving Americans to consume evermore. Beyond their perception, but directly impinging on their lives, was the need of a capitalistic form of economy to maintain increasing production and increased consumption, especially the pervasive forces of advertising which led Fred and Janet to feel that they needed a new car, a color television, the latest in kitchen gadgetry and recreational playthings, "a home that is a step upwards," and on and on. They did not see that installment payments are a corollary of our economic system, allowing greater immediate consumption, the spending of income yet unearned. They saw, rather, that installment purchases allowed easier access to the material goods they so frantically desired, that they could possess now and not have to wait as long as their parents had waited to own fine things.

When Fred lost his job and fell behind in their payments, they blamed his unemployment on company mismanagement and even on fate or bad luck. What they failed to see was that the economy had been perceived by governmental leaders as "too hot," the resulting inflation viewed as dangerous, and a new policy of "tight money" initiated in order to "cool down" the economy. They did not understand that a certain rate of unemployment is considered acceptable and normal by political leaders and that Fred had been caught on the negative end of an impersonal economic decision that had not too gently squeezed him out of his job and placed the final strain on their marriage. Although they were on the receiving end of large-scale events, Fred and Janet perceived their situation in much more personal terms.

In looking for the causes of just a single instance of a marriage which "failed," the sociological imagination takes all these **variables** or factors into account: historical changes in family structure, changing expectations of the purposes and goals of marriage, changing expectations of the roles or parts that husbands and wives play in marriage, and such economic aspects of social life as employment and material consumption. Although these variables make their impact felt on the individual level, that is, they are played out within the personal marital relationship, when one uses the sociological imagination, or perspective, divorces are not seen in isolation. They are not viewed in the sociological imagination as simply individual matters, but as part of much broader historical patterns. Although any particular marital break-up might be due to unique factors of one sort or another, roughly figured, in the United States on the average from 1943 to 1968 one couple has obtained a divorce for each four couples getting married. From 1968 to 1972, however, divorce underwent a dramatic increase of 44 percent, going from 582,000 in 1968 to 839,000 four years later. During this same period, marriages in the United States increased from 2,059,000 to 2,269,000, an increase of only 10 percent. Currently in the United States, one couple is getting divorced for every three couples getting married. (See Figure 1.1.) For a broader understanding, then, one must look beyond any particular divorce to search for the social forces making divorce such a common event in our contemporary society.

Perceiving this vital interconnection between biography and history, between the self and the social world, between what happens to an individual and the social forces surrounding him, is the **sociological imagination** at work.

The sociological imagination is not by any means used only to understand marital difficulties and divorce. It is, rather, the basic perspective of sociologists in their approach to understanding human behavior. Central to the sociological imagination, or sociological perspective, is

Figure 1.1   U.S. Marriages and Divorces, 1940–1972

Total

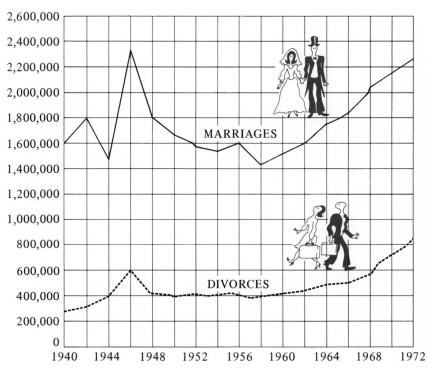

Sources: Monthly Vital Statistics, 17, March 12, 1969; 19, September 21, 1971; 21, January 27, 1973; Vital Statistics of the United States, 1966, 3, Marriage and Divorce.

applying large-scale events in society to the more personal situations of individuals. By following the sociological imagination and placing what happens to individuals into a broader social context, one attains a different understanding of individual lives.

C. Wright Mills, who developed the concept of the sociological imagination, stressed that one can understand neither an individual life nor a society without understanding both the individual and his society. Mills emphasized that change in society exerts direct and profound effects upon the people living in it. For example, when a feudal society undergoes industrialization, peasants become workers, and feudal lords are either liquidated or become businessmen. When the economics of an industrialized society undergo change, a person may have a wide choice of jobs or become unemployed. When war breaks out, a student is drafted out of college; a teacher carries a rifle; a chicken farmer becomes an administrator; the boy next door travels to a distant country whose name he did not even know, he is killed, his wife lives alone, and his child grows up without a father (Mills 1959b). In order to adequately understand people, it is essential to understand the historical milieu in which they live out their lives.

Yet people do not ordinarily grasp this interplay between the individual and society, this vital interconnection between a person's biography and what is happening in history. People's ideas of what is happening to them are usually limited to their private orbits. They usually see events in their lives as being connected to events on a much smaller scale, such as to what is happening at work, within the family, and with friends and relatives. Most people hold down a very small corner in life, and their limited experiences in society have a limiting effect on how they perceive themselves and what is happening to them. It is as though their particular experiences within their own small world place blinders over their eyes, preventing them from seeing the connection between their own biography and history. To use the sociological imagination means to remove these blinders, to become able to see that what is happening to an individual is both intimately and intricately connected with larger-scale events in society.

Central to the sociological imagination is the idea that people can understand their own experiences and gauge their own fates only by locating themselves within their own historical period. They can understand their own places in life only by becoming aware of the life chances of other individuals in similar circumstances. Every individual lives out a biography within some particular society, within a historical sequence that has far-reaching consequences for him. To relate the consequences of social and historical events to the lives of individuals is to apply the sociological imagination.

Not only are people affected by their society, by its "historical push and shove," but also by their own living they contribute to the shaping of their society and the course of its history. The sociological imagination or perspective is an understanding of these reciprocal relationships, these intersections within a society of biography and history. The sociological imagination is the capacity to shift from one perspective to the other: to see the individual within the broader framework of his social world, but also to see the effects of individuals on their world.

According to the sociological perspective, then, history is not determined. Although there are many trends built into history, people are able to change historical events. Alternatives do face people, and people make decisions that change what happens to them and, in some cases, to what happens to large populations of the world. There are generals as well as uniformed privates; heads of state as well as ordinary citizens; corporate executives as well as hourly production workers. People are not inert objects, but as an ordinary part of their daily lives they make moral choices between the alternatives they confront (Mills 1959b:116–117; 174).

Few persons, however, are in a position to make decisions that drastically affect the course of history, as do some generals, some heads of state, and some corporate executives. The vast majority play a much lesser role in history. Most people are limited to making decisions that entail only small-scale consequences for themselves and a few others. History shapes many people vastly more than most people shape history. Consequently, an understanding of the social or historical forces that shape people is basic to the sociological imagination.

Three major types of questions are asked by one who possesses the sociological imagination (Mills 1959b:6–7). (1) Regarding the *structure of society:* What are its essential components, and how are they related to one another? (2) Regarding the particular *historical period:* What are its major characteristics, and how are they changing? (3) Regarding *kinds of people:* What type of people live in the historical period and society you want to understand, and how are these people shaped by their society and their historical period?

Possessing the sociological imagination means that one traces linkages between what is happening to an individual and what is happening within society and within history. Troubles that may appear only personal, such as Fred and Janet's marital and employment difficulties, are then seen to be both intimately and inherently related to what is happening in broader segments of society. The sociological imagination emphasizes that what happens to an individual is vitally related to *structural* aspects of society, that is, to the way society is put together, to how its social institutions are interrelated—to its **social structure.**

When Janet became discontent with housecleaning, child care, and playing the traditionally female subservient role to a husband, she was not simply reacting in an idiosyncratic manner to her life situation. Her feelings, ideas, attitudes, and desires were intimately related to what was happening in society. Social forces of which she was herself but vaguely aware were shaping the way she saw the world and her place in the world. We have now arrived at a particular historical point where people in our society are increasingly coming to perceive that we are marked by disparities between our ideas of equality and the ways that the sexes are dealt with in formal law, in traditional institutional arrangements, and in informal interaction. Out of such perceived disparities has arisen the women's liberation movement, which has so vociferously forced increased attention to the relative positions of males and females in our society, to disparities in laws and practices concerning employment and salaries, and which has pressed and won such practical issues as whether it is lawful to have separate help-wanted ads for males and females.

Within this changed social matrix people have become increasingly sensitized to male-female disparities, and a heightened awareness of sexual inequality has begun to pervade individual consciousness. As a result, Janet, like so many other contemporary women, began to feel dissatisfied with her lot in life. She became discontent with a position of differential sexual treatment which previous generations had accepted as "normal." She at first began to experience vague stirrings within her, feelings that something was wrong in her life. After troubledly searching her life situation, she finally concluded that she was not being dealt with as a whole person. Yet Janet's mother did not share these feelings. She was unable to understand her daughter's discontent because she had been raised within a different social matrix, a milieu which had imparted to her different ideas and attitudes. Through their varying experiences in contrasting periods in the same society, mother and daughter had attained contrary perspectives on life. Each viewed events in life from her own perspective, and each consequently arrived at different interpretations of those same events. By understanding changes in society as they bear upon more intimate scenes and experiences, writes Mills (1959b:162), "we are able to understand the causes of individual conduct and feelings of which (people) in specific milieux are themselves unaware."

Fred and Janet's problems with their conflicting ideas and expectations of their marital roles were their personal troubles. As we have seen, however, this part of their marital trouble was interconnected with the larger social issue in American society of changing expectations of relationships between men and women. **Troubles** are private matters having to do with biography. They are perceived threats to an individual's social or personal life. **Issues** are public matters that arise when values cherished by many people are felt to be threatened. Troubles, though often seen only in personal terms, are intimately connected with larger social issues. To see this relationship between personal troubles and public issues is to directly apply the sociological imagination.

The following example further illustrates this interconnection between troubles and issues. Fred and Janet's daughter once came down with what they thought was a serious illness. Susan Anne's temperature suddenly shot up one morning, and she began to cough and experience severe difficulty in breathing. Janet at once called their family doctor, but he was dealing with an emergency case at the hospital. She frantically called others, but no doctor would come to their home. Fred and Janet finally rushed Susan Anne to a doctor's office some distance from their home where they had to wait two hours in a packed waiting room. When they finally were able to see the doctor, he was extremely hurried. After a cursory diagnosis, he gave Susan Anne a shot, wrote a prescription, told them to put her to bed, and sent them home. Fred and Janet later received a bill for twenty-five dollars for the doctor's services.

Their difficulty in obtaining adequate medical care for their child was a personal trouble, but it is only a small part of the larger social issue of an inadequate medical delivery system facing the United States today. We are currently experiencing a drastic shortage of doctors combined with rapidly escalating medical costs. We can readily see that part of this problem is the high demand for medical services and the long, arduous, and expensive training our physicians undergo. Not so readily apparent, however, are the social forces that have created an artificial shortage of medical personnel. In 1932 the average income for American physicians was about $3700 a year. Though not extremely bountiful, this was not an inadequate income when measured by the standards of that period. But our physicians are members of a society in which a high premium is place on income and by which both personal and professional worth is commonly measured. Consequently, American doctors felt that this income was far from satisfactory. The American Medical Association's Council on Medical Education then studied the matter. They concluded that the reason their incomes were not higher was because the medical schools in the United States were producing more physicians than the country needed. The American Medical Association then resolved to reduce the output of our medical schools. By 1933 the Association of Medical Colleges began reducing its enrollment. By 1935 the Council reported the encouraging sign that there was a decrease of 584 future doctors in freshman classes throughout the country (Warren Brown 1970).

The sociological perspective or imagination looks beyond the individual in his immediate situation, his individual circumstances or private orbit, and examines the larger historical context which affects his life situation. In this example we not only become aware of historical events that have created a shortage of physicians in this country, but we also gain an understanding of some factors that have contributed to our ranking nineteenth in the world in the ratio of doctors to population, fifteenth in infant mortality rates, and twenty-third in life expectancy (*Statistical Year Book of the United Nations*, 1972; *World Health Statistics Annual, 1969, 1; World Health Statistics Reports, 24,* 1971). Though the American Medical Association's decision contributed to the needless deaths which these rankings represent, it was effective for its intended purpose. Our physicians' incomes have increased handsomely indeed. General practitioners now average $37,450 a year, while obstetricians and gynecologists enjoy the fantastic average annual income of $50,000 (*Statistical Abstracts of the United States,* 1973, Table 103). By using the sociological imagination, then, we attain a startlingly different perspective on even such a small but common scene as a family waiting for medical care in an overcrowded doctor's office.

The life of an individual cannot be adequately understood without understanding the social institutions within which one's biography is lived out. To understand what happens to an individual in this life, we must understand the significance and meaning of the roles he plays. But to understand these roles, we must understand the institutions of society because they largely determine what happens to people. Because we live in particularized and limiting small segments of society, however, few of us gain an adequate over-all picture of the forces affecting us. Most of us are so tied up with some small part of society that it is extremely difficult for us to obtain an adequate grasp of the whole. The goal of learning the sociological imagination is to expand our small-scale, segmented vision of social events in order to perceive biographical events in terms of broader historical changes in society. Grasping biography in relation to history allows us to transcend the restricted and limiting milieu in which most of us live out our lives.

A person who takes this approach to understanding people is also able to develop new insights into what is happening to himself. By examining the intersections between the events of one's own biography and what is happening in history and society, one can attain a different self-consciousness. Applying the sociological imagination to the self allows a person to view oneself as an outsider to society and history and yet see oneself as intimately involved in history and society. This approach enables a person to take a different view of even intimate aspects of his own biography by "mentally standing apart" from the events and scrutinizing their social context. One's own problems then are viewed as personal troubles that are also part of larger social issues. A person sees that the various problems or troubles he is experiencing in living his life are intimately related to large-scale factors in society played out on the individual level. One then perceives that one's own troubles are also not simply individual matters due to idiosyncracies of personality, but part and parcel of what is occurring in the society at large. This applies not only to one's troubles and frustrations but also to one's joys and satisfactions of life.

In applying the sociological imagination to the self, one searches relevant social milieux in order to determine the significant larger-scale influences on one's own available alternatives, the choices one has made between these alternatives, and the influence of these choices and alternatives on subsequent events of one's life. By doing this, one is attempting to view the self in the context of the three major areas of the sociological imagination, that is, one examines (1) the structure of one's own society and (2) the characteristics of one's own historical period in order to see (3) how the self has been shaped by history and society. In this way, the sociological imagination yields both a heightened awareness of self and a new way of thinking about the self.

Understanding the individual by seeing how history and society intersect with his biography is central to exercising the sociological imagination. The sociological imagination is the search for the causes and meanings of human behavior within "the big picture," an attempt to understand the intimate realities people experience by examining their connection with larger social realities. Through the sociological perspective one can perceive the larger forces that affect human life and thus not be limited to seeing individual experience as isolated from the broader aspects of society.

Using the sociological perspective allows us to grasp this vital interconnection between history and biography—even when that biography is our own. Going beyond individual situations, however, this approach yields new insights into many areas of life. As we apply the sociological imagination to contemporary events in our era of rapid social change, we are able to better perceive and understand the far-reaching effects on people of revolutions, the abrupt rise and fall of political authority, the sharp ascendance of capitalism, the deeply-rooted, culturally-based conflicts between the industrialized nations and the "under-developed" nations, both the endemically bitter and the merely pretentious contentions among those who aspire to leadership within the industrialized world, the noxious effects on people of continual uncertainty, ghetto violence, bureaucracy, pollution, perceived rising crime rates and unsafe city streets, and the baneful effects of a thawing cold war in the midst of the continuing threat of a hot war that holds the terrifying potential of nuclear annihilation (Mills 1959b).

Acquiring a new perspective on life in society by learning to exercise the sociological imagination can be taken as the goal of this book and the goal for most introductory courses in sociology. Applying the sociological imagination will yield startlingly different understandings of

> . . . pressure groups and boys' gangs and Navajo oil men; air forces pointed to demolish metropolitan areas a hundred miles wide; policemen on a corner; intimate circles and publics seated in a room; criminal syndicates; masses thronged one night at the crossroads and squares of the cities of the world; Hopi children and slave dealers in Arabia and German parties and Polish classes and Mennonite schools and the mentally deranged in Tibet and radio networks reaching around the world. Racial stocks and ethnic groups are jumbled up in movie houses and also segregated; married happily and also hating systematically; a thousand detailed occupations are seated in businesses and industries, in governments and localities, in near-continentwide nations. A million little bargains are transacted every day, and everywhere there are more "small groups" than anyone could ever count.
>
> The human variety also includes the variety of individual human beings; these too the sociological imagination must grasp and understand. In this imagination an Indian Brahmin of 1850 stands alongside a pioneer farmer of Illinois; an eighteenth-century English gentleman alongside an Australian aboriginal, together with a Chinese peasant of one hundred years ago, a politician of Bolivia today, a feudal knight of France, an English suffragette on hunger strike in 1914, a Hollywood starlet, a Roman patrician. To write of "man" is to write of all these men and women, also of Goethe, and of the girl next door (Mills 1959b:132–133).

In the following chapters we shall explore various aspects of social life and emphasize the intersections of biography and history within social structure. We shall especially focus on how people construct their worlds of reality and how they live within those worlds they construct (Mills 1959b:134).

The Culture Context

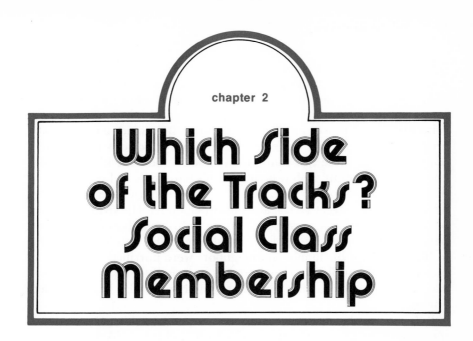

chapter 2

Which Side of the Tracks? Social Class Membership

A twenty-two-year-old man, whom I shall call Bob Smith, was shot by a security guard in the Altgeld Gardens Housing Project in Chicago. After the shooting, Smith was charged with battery, "reckless conduct," failure to possess a firearm owner's identification, and failure to register a firearm. Although the guard claimed that his gun accidently went off, eyewitnesses to the event stated that the guard shot Smith after he had handcuffed him. Three weeks after being shot and arrested, Bob Smith was charged with stealing two quarts of beer from a drug store. He supposedly had committed this crime just before his arrest. All but the theft charges were dismissed at his trial (*The Brief,* May 1971).

Bill Robertson, a fictitious name, was born twenty-four years ago in Chicago. Bill's father had enjoyed a highly successful career in real estate, building upon a fortune his father had acquired through land and stock speculation. Several years ago Bill's father was elected president of the Chicago Real Estate Board. Bill attended Lake Forest and recently completed his Master's in Business Administration at Harvard. He is now first vice-president of his father's real estate firm and has been elected to the Board of Directors of a major insurance company. Bill's engagement to Miss Kathleen Roundtree Abernathy, the only child of John Singleton Abernathy III and Marian Prescott Abernathy née Roundtree, was extensively covered by the *Chicago Tribune,* as will be his wedding. They plan on spending their first two months of marriage in Paris, Geneva, Brussels, and London, where Bill will also solidify contacts for his father, who has plans for internationally expanding his extensive industrial holdings. The Police Commissioner's son is a frequent visitor at Bill's home in Park Forest, as are an alderman's son and Preston McNarry Lodge, whose father, in addition to his other holdings, is one of the chief stockholders in Swift and Company.

It does not take a highly developed sociological imagination to perceive major differences in life styles between Bob Smith and Bill Robertson. Similarly, major differences in the ways persons in authority react to each of these two young men, based upon their life styles, are also readily apparent. Bob is poor, and his parents have lived their entire lives in abject poverty. Some of his first memories are of hunger, welfare workers, street gangs, and court personnel. His vivid memories of firearms directed against people living in his neighborhood, by both neighbors and uniformed policemen, also reach back to his early years in life. Although his family and neighbors were horrified by this latest incident in "the projects," they were not surprised that it occurred as it was not the first or the last time that something similar has happened among them.

Bill, on the other hand, is obviously extremely wealthy. He was born into wealth, he lives in the midst of wealth, and it is unlikely that until his death he will be anything but a wealthy and powerful man. Some of his first memories are of a governess, riding lessons, dancing classes, tutors, private schools, and high-ranking political visitors at his home. He has literally received the best education money could buy, and his interconnected business and social contacts continue to multiply. Most of Bill's honeymoon expenses will be written off for tax purposes as business expenditures. His marriage, his planned European travel, his expanding investments, and his accumulating power are not surprises to his neighbors, as this was not the first or the last time that something like this has happened to "one of theirs."

Analyzing such drastically differing **life chances,** the probabilities as to the fate one may expect in life (Berger 1963:79), is part of the study of social stratification, the way society is divided into strata or social classes. People in every society are characterized by inequalities of some sort. Some people are stronger, learn more quickly, are swifter, shoot weapons more accurately, or *according to whatever criteria are considered important in that particular society* have more of what counts than do others. Natural or biological inequalities in life are a normal part of living in human society. Other inequalities in whatever counts in a society may appear more contrived, such as distinctions of social rank based on wealth, but no system of ranking people is "a part of some natural and inevitable order of things" (Bottomore 1966:10). All systems of social ranking are the result of human endeavor; they are all based on ranking people according to the criteria considered important in that particular society. Studying **social stratification,** the ways people are ranked in a society and the resulting consequences for their life chances, is an essential part of exercising the sociological imagination.

The bases for social ranking are almost endless. Societies around the world have used such differing criteria as beauty, courage in battle, ancestry, scarification, birth marks, birth order, skill in hunting, and piety. The Northwest Pacific Indians, inhabiting the region from Oregon to Alaska, even used ostentatious generosity as their basic criterion for claiming and awarding social rank. A person claiming hereditary rights, such as the right to be known by a certain ancestor's name or the right to celebrate traditional rituals such as the singing of lineage-associated songs, would give a **potlatch,** a large feast at which the person claiming hereditary rights would bestow lavish gifts on the gathered guests. In one form of the potlatch, the individual seeking the disputed status would invite his or her kinsmen to the feast, as well as members of other tribes and lineages and rivals to the claimed rights. By ostentatiously giving away or destroying property, the individual would stake his or her claim to the disputed rights. The greater the value of the gifts bestowed on the guests or ceremoniously destroyed, the greater the legitimacy granted the claim. If a rival to the disputed rights was not able to reciprocate with a potlatch in which even more valuable gifts were given away or destroyed, the first became the winner and attained the disputed status or rank (Rohner and Rohner 1970:95-105; Rosman and Rubel 1971).

In industrialized countries, we also have various ways of ranking people. Some rankings are based upon **achieved characteristics,** such as accomplishments in the arts and sciences or the position and authority attained within an occupation, while others are based largely on **ascribed characteristics,** such as sex, race, and age. Other than the biological ones, the primary way we have for ranking large groupings of people is social class membership. Social class membership in industrialized societies appears to be generally based on three major dimensions: occupational prestige, amount of education, and amount of income. In determining social class membership in industrialized societies, amount of income appears to be the most important of these dimensions (Huber and Form, 1973).

Inequalities of some sort characterize every human group. But for inequality to be based on the possession of wealth requires an economic surplus and the private ownership of economic resources (Bottomore 1966:15). When the technology of a society becomes developed to the point that an economic surplus is created and the economic resources do not belong to the group as a whole but to individuals within the group, the basis for ranking by wealth is created. In human groups that depend for their subsistence upon foraging from nature, little or nothing is left over after the physical needs of the group's members have been met. In such hunting and gathering societies few differences in rank exist, although everyone in the group is not precisely equal.

Major characteristics of industrialized societies include the production of surplus material goods and the private ownership of property. Material goods and services are not equally distributed to the members of technologically advanced societies, and some receive much more or much less than do others. Those who receive more are considered to be members of a higher social class than those who receive less. People who share basically the same position in the system of allocating goods and services are considered to be members of the same **social class** (Dobriner 1969:216). Members of a family share the same class position, and, as did the parents of Bob Smith and Bill Robertson, they pass the family's class circumstances on to their children. In industrialized societies people have developed a social hierarchy "based directly upon the possession of wealth" (Bottomore 1966:4).

Sociologists typically divide Americans into three major social classes: the upper, the middle, and the lower. Each of these three major divisions is often further subdivided into an upper and a lower. Thus, sociologists tend to speak of an upper-upper class, a lower-upper class, an upper-middle class, a lower-middle class, an upper-lower class, and a lower-lower class. These class divisions commonly used by sociologists are not necessarily the same as the way most Americans think of divisions among people in our society. Many Americans tend, rather, to think of the United States as a classless society. They do, however, regularly make both gross and fine distinctions regarding the amount of wealth people have, the styles of life people lead, and the types of people who live in their society. The model by which most Americans appear to picture society is that of the **continuum,** that is, they tend to think of people as ranked from more to less income or by patterns of material consumption, with only fine gradations separating them. (See Figure 2.1.)

The scarcity of common thinking in the United States in terms of social class appears unlike common conceptions by Europeans who demonstrate much greater class consciousness. The tendency of Americans to think in terms of a classless society could be partially due to the expanded middle income grouping of people in the United States which blurs distinctions between the extreme income groups. This picture or model of society is also lent support by people knowing others who have bettered their positions in life, those who have attained *upward* **social mobility.** Not thinking in terms of social class may also be partially due to deep-rooted feelings against social class differences brought to the United States by European immigrants. These im-

Figure 2.1 The Continuum *

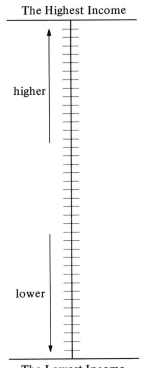

The Highest Income

higher

lower

The Lowest Income

* The continuum is a model for representing aspects of social life. In the continuum, whatever is being ranked is simply placed from highest to lowest. Figure 2.1 represents a common conception of social divisions, the ranking of people by income with only small gradations separating them.

migrants had bitterly experienced hardened class lines in Europe, and a common motivation of their trek to the New World was an attempt to free themselves from the constrictions of social class lines in which they had been forcibly enmeshed. Also contributing to the model of the continuum is the publicized mythology of the equality of American citizens, regularly taught in our public schools and just as regularly emphatically proclaimed by our public officials. The continuum may also be a carry-over from a conceptual model that apparently was once more applicable to American life than it now is, a model based on greater equality between people due to the leveling effects of the western frontier. The frontier represented not only challenge and hardship but also a place where one could escape many of the restrictions imposed by the surrounding society. It was a new, developing region where people ranked others not primarily by family connections but by their individual attributes, especially by their personal skills and the relationships they developed with neighbors and townspeople. As a person made his way in life, he began from an economic base which set him apart but little from those around him. Opportunities for cheaply acquiring land and for putting it to productive and profitable use appeared unlimited to the restless settlers of our ever westward-moving frontier. (Cf. Bottomore 1966:50–55; Ferris 1963; Wyman and Kroeber 1957.)

The United States, however, has always been far from being a society composed solely of equals. From its beginnings not only was its population characterized by inequalities of various sorts, but settlers from Europe also brought with them ingrained ideas of class distinctions since they had grown up in a society in which by both law and custom people had lived within a system in which firm lines separated large groupings of people from one another. Although class lines in the Colonies were more fluid than those in Europe because of greater social mobility due to easier access to ownership of land and greater intermingling of groups, especially in the North compared with the South, there were basically five classes, or strata, in our early history. These were: (1) an upper class consisting of large landowners, the more influential religious and political leaders, wealthy merchants, and the successful professionals, primarily lawyers and doctors; (2) a large middle class made up of skilled workers, the less wealthy merchants, professionals, and landowners; (3) a lower class consisting primarily of tenant farmers and unskilled workers; (4) white indentured servants; and (5) by 1700, the greatest cleavage between groups in the population, a separate class ranked beneath the others consisting of slaves. Although class lines were generally less fluid in the South, they became even more rigid as greater reliance for economic success was placed on the ownership of slaves. (Cf. Adams 1971, Main 1965, and Nettles 1963.)

But the frontier did serve as a leveler between many people, mitigating many of the cleavages that developed in our early history. When the frontier became an established region in the 1880s and 1890s, however, new factors were introduced which were destined to exert far-reaching effects on American stratification: Industry rapidly developed, efficient communications expanded at a quick pace, and industrial and financial trusts emerged that led to increased inequalities in wealth. In the absence of the mitigating effects of the frontier, these continued separations of people on the basis of wealth led to broad cleavages along class lines which came to closely resemble those in Europe. An upper class possessed of a heightened consciousness of similarity with one another and of significant differences from others continued to develop. Their consciousness of identity became even more highly pronounced over time, as signalled by the development of the *Social Register,* the founding of exclusive boarding schools and country clubs, and the transmission of wealth and social position through family connections (Bottomore 1966:49).

Consequently, the continuum is not the model commonly used in sociology. As the lines are not firmly drawn between most social classes in the United States, however, and we have no laws that govern according to class membership the wearing of clothing, the use of speech, access to higher education, and so on, as some societies have had, sociologists differ regarding the criteria for social class membership in American society. This has led to some dispute among sociologists regarding the number of people who belong to each social class and, in some cases, even to disagreement regarding the number of social classes the United States has. Social class membership is roughly figured, however, as consisting of an upper class of approximately 1 percent of the population of the United States, an upper-middle class of 10 percent, a lower-middle class of 32 percent, an upper-lower or working class of 39 percent, and a lower-lower class of 18 percent (Coleman and Neugarten 1971:273). The social class model commonly used by sociologists can be illustrated by the graph shown in Figure 2.2.

As we analyze this model, which is an overview of the national system of stratification in the United States, we should note that it is primarily based on an analysis of urban America. It does not adequately cover our rural areas, where, for example, small towns have their own systems of stratification, in which people appear to place greater emphasis on personal reputations in their rankings of one another. We should also note that this model is only one of a number of ways of identifying major strata in our population; that instead of six strata or classes it could just as well be based on four, ten, or whatever. But as it is the major model of stratification used by sociologists, we shall examine it in some detail.

Class lines are the most rigid between the upper class and the other social classes. The **upper class** is also the most clearly identifiable, con-

Figure 2.2 Social Class Divisions in the United States *

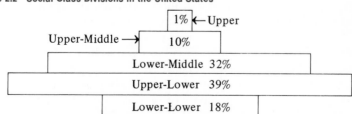

* Sociologists do not think of the distribution of wealth in the United States in terms of a continuum. This figure more accurately portrays the sociological model, the grouping of large numbers of people who have similar life chances.

tains the smallest number of people, and is the most difficult to enter. Many names from the upper class are familiar not only to the general American public and to the aristocracy of Europe, but in some cases they are also familiar to people in even remote parts of the world. The Rockefellers, Mellons, Morgans, Fords, Chryslers, Harrimans, Carnegies, Roosevelts, Morgenthaus, duPonts, Kennedys, and the Vanderbilts are names from the upper class.

The **nouveaux riches,** persons who have only recently come into their wealth, are looked down upon by members of the upper class because they do not possess the "proper" family background. Consequently, sociologists sometimes divide the upper class into those who have possessed their wealth for long periods of time, the upper-upper class, and those who only more recently have become wealthy, the lower-upper class. To be a member of the upper-upper class, one (or one's family) must not only possess great wealth, generally in the millions, but ordinarily one must also be a member of an "old" family. High emphasis is placed on descent from a family or families in which wealth has been possessed for generations.

Members of the **upper-upper class** are educated at exclusive private schools and elite universities. Listing in the *Social Register* or *Blue Book* is taken as a sure sign of membership in this class. A name dropped from the *Social Register* is a sign of disgrace and loss of standing within this social class, while a name added to the *Social Register* is a certain indicator of achieved entrance into this elite group. Listing in the *Social Register,* especially in the case of men, is also a major indicator of the possession of power in American society. Intermarriage is the rule, with people in the upper-upper class almost always marrying others who possess a similar background of wealth, power, and the requisite social standing (Domhoff 1971:76). The upper-upper class is a closed group of people who have a highly developed consciousness of membership in an exclusive social class. This feeling of cohesion is developed through interacting with one another, as evidenced by the limited number of schools they attend and the summer and winter resorts they frequent, their common practice of intermarriage, and even by the fact that the same bands play at their parties and debutante balls (Domhoff 1971:76–99).

Members of the **lower-upper class** have generally not been educated at schools as elite as the ones persons from the upper-upper class attend. Their money is "new" or recent, and they are therefore somewhat "suspect" because they have not yet withstood the test of time in demonstrating loyalties, nor have they acquired the "proper breeding." Members of the lower-upper class generally strive for social acceptability by the "older" families, and while most fail to make it into the privileged inner circles, they calculatingly cultivate friendships and

"I may be a philosopher, George, but I say, if we didn't *belong* on top, we wouldn't *be* on top."

The upper-upper class is a closed group of people who possess a highly developed consciousness of membership in an exclusive social class. They pass on to their children opportunities which tend to maintain them in the privileged circumstances into which they are born. (Drawing by Lorenz; © 1960, The New Yorker Magazine, Inc.)

business relationships to make it easier for their children to gain the sought-after standing. They frequently attempt to aid their children's admission into the top class by sending them to elite schools they were themselves unable to attend. Marriage into an "old" family represents admisson into the upper-upper class.

Despite the differences between these two divisions of the upper class, its significance as a social class is that its members garner the top prestige and power positions in the country. They direct the leading corporations, insurance companies, and banks. Moreover, they largely set "policies for research foundations, university corporations, foreign policy associations, economic advisory committees, and departments of labor" (Leggett 1972:11). They are extremely influential in shaping both the basic foreign policy and the social legislation of the United States, thereby both directly and indirectly affecting members of the other social classes and, indeed, of people throughout the contemporary world (Domhoff 1971). This class personifies power and privilege in America.

The **middle class** includes almost half the population of the United States. Unlike the upper class, it is not a clearly defined group of people who have a highly developed consciousness of their position, who know who the others in their social class are, and who develop this consciousness of identity through interacting with one another within a limited number of settings. Gross differences, rather, in life styles and attitudes characterize the amorphous group known as the middle class. This class is also divided into two strata, the upper-middle and the lower-middle.

Upper-middle class persons are primarily our college-educated, managerial level businessmen and successful professionals. In large cities managers and professionals are the major representatives of this class, while in smaller communities the more successful independent businessman is the more typical representative (Coleman and Neugarten 1971:262). The persons who make up this approximately 10 percent of the population highly value career advancement, they are usually willing to move geographically when necessary for business or professional reasons, and they emphasize to their children the importance of delaying gratification of their needs in order to attain future rewards. Like the upper class, the upper-middle class has a much higher membership of WASP's (White Anglo-Saxon Protestants) than one would expect by chance.

The **lower-middle class** has historically been composed of clerks, salesmen, and small businessmen, but today it is more typically represented by white-collar workers who never reach the managerial levels. The lower-middle class also includes the more highly trained blue-collar technicians and the better educated service workers. Core values in this group include a strong family orientation with an emphasis on hard work, honesty, decency, and respectability.

The **lower class** is also divided by sociologists into two strata, an upper-lower and a lower-lower class. The **upper-lower class** shades into the lower-middle class, making it difficult to conceptually distinguish them. Generally, however, members of the upper-lower class are blue-collar workers, persons who primarily work at skilled or semi-skilled manual jobs. Partially for this reason they are also sometimes called the **working class.** Members of this class frequently consider that only when a person is doing something with his hands is he or she doing "real work," that positions at the supervisory and managerial levels involve something other than "real work." Upper-lower class people generally pride themselves on respectability and take the possession of material goods, especially home ownership, as symbolizing success in life. Compared with middle class persons, they belong to fewer clubs and organizations. Non-occupational life mainly centers around watching television and visiting with relatives and friends.

The most underprivileged groups in American society contain a larger number of minority group members than their proportion of the population. Their children inherit discrimination which sharply cuts their opportunity for adequate housing, education, and employment, tending to maintain them in the class circumstances into which they were born. (Courtesy of Wide World Photos)

One of the major differences between the two lower classes centers around regularity of work. Although both have low incomes, members of the upper-lower class pride themselves on respectability derived from working regularly. This, indeed, is one of the major characteristics by which they distinguish themselves from those they consider the "ne'er-do-wells" beneath them (Kahl 1957). Members of the **lower-lower class** are generally considered disreputable by persons from other social classes. They are ordinarily unemployed at least part of the year. They do seasonal work and fill similar jobs requiring a low level of skill, such as migrant farm and domestic work. Their employment is uncertain, their wages low. They tend to live from day to day, carrying a fatalistic attitude about what will happen to them in life. They are generally more alienated from the larger society than are members of the other social classes, more distrustful of the police and the government, and perhaps more cynical about religion. Lower class persons are less likely to belong to a church than persons from other social classes, but, if they do belong, chances are that they are members of a fundamentalist sect such as the Southern Baptists, the Jehovah's Witnesses, or the Pentecostals (Lenski 1963). Both lower social classes contain a disproportionate number of minority group members than one would expect by chance, and, in both, traditional sex roles predominate.

The social class and continuum models are not necessarily incompatible. There is much to say for the common-sense conception of a continuum, and there is also ample evidence to demonstrate the existence of social classes in the United States. If we view social classes as groups of people ranked together on a continuum, who have approximately equal access to what is available in society, people who have similar chances in life, we can then use the model of social stratification shown in Figure 2.3. A major advantage of this model is that while it shows that people are grouped together in similar life circumstances primarily according to income, it also demonstrates that there is much shading of one social class into another. This model more accurately pictures differences between the lower end of one social class and the upper end of the one beneath it as slight, while it still groups large numbers of people together according to income similarities.

I certainly do not want to give the impression that sociologists think that all people within a particular social class are alike. People within the same social class are separated by vast gulfs of many sorts, a fact each person is intimately familiar with regarding his or her own social class. People tend to stratify fellow members of their own broad economic-occupational-educational groupings that sociologists call social classes. Some people within a particular social class are classified by others as being more honest, less intelligent, more outspoken, less

Figure 2.3   The Continuum and Social Class Divisions *

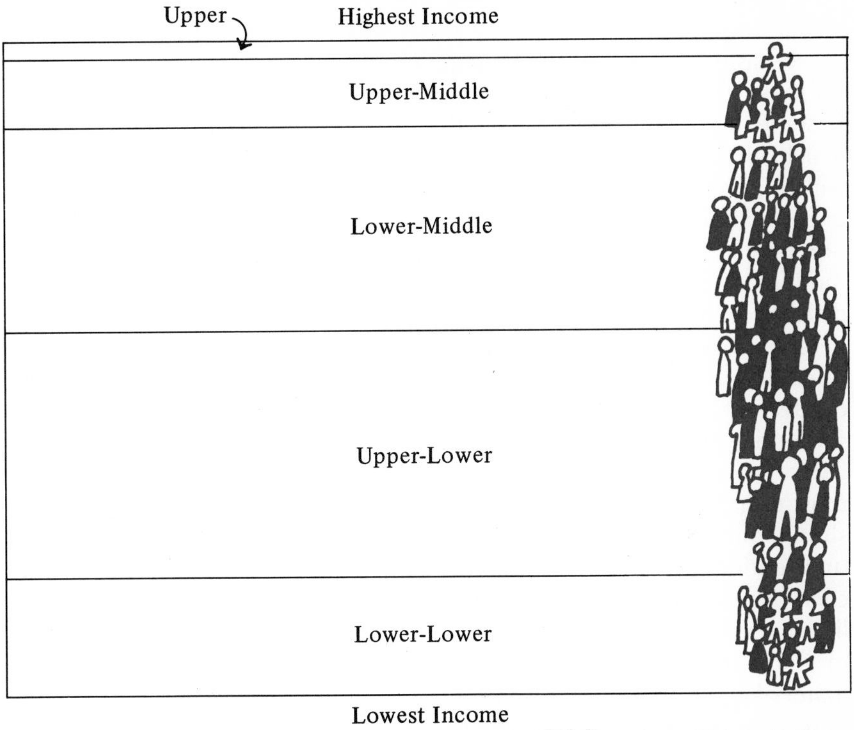

Lowest Income

* This figure combines the continuum and social class models of Figures 2.1 and 2.2. In this figure the social classes are portrayed as being on a continuum, but, as in Figure 2.2, large numbers of people who have similar life chances are grouped together, with the blurring of differences between the top of one social class and the bottom of the next highest social class becoming emphasized.

pleasant, more dependable, and so on. This **within-class stratification** is called **status.** Status is the standing or position someone occupies within his or her social class. Thus a member of the lower-lower class can well be considered hard-working, ambitious, and respectable by persons from other social classes. In the same way, this person can have a similar reputation with other members of his or her own social class. These reputations represent the person's status, that is, how an individual or family is ranked *within* a particular social class. The loss of standing I mentioned earlier caused by being delisted from the *Social Register* is another example of status within a social class. Such a person's social class membership perhaps undergoes no change, but his or her standing or status within that social class certainly does.

   To study social stratification means to study how inequalities are organized in society, that is, how a society's rewards are distributed and its scarcities allocated, and to study the hierarchical arrangement of class positions which results from the distribution of inequalities (Dobriner 1969:214). The study of social stratification is an essential part of exercising the sociological imagination, for where one is born in society makes a considerable difference in what happens to a person in life. If someone with a particular birthmark is born into a primitive group which differentiates its people according to this criterion, that person will be ranked high or low. His resulting ranking will either deny or grant him access to the best which that society has to offer, and his or her total life is thereby affected. So it is with social class ranking in modern societies. Social class membership makes literally a world of difference for what happens to a person in life. Social class membership affects what one becomes—not only the type of work one will do as an adult, but also the way one is likely to view the world, one's attitudes, what one holds dear in life, and, in general, what type of person one is likely to become.

It is no exaggeration to say that social class membership affects almost every aspect of a person's life. It is one thing to live in congested slum housing where several persons share a single bed and where unrelenting daily competition for food between the children and the cockroaches and rats is accepted as a fact of life, and quite another to live in a spacious home where household help and food are to be found in abundance. Although differences in the extremes in the social and material environments are easier to specify than are their effects on perceiving the world and living within that world, we can note that, as with Bob Smith and Bill Robertson, even officials of society react differently to people on the basis of social class. It is extremely unlikely that Bill Robertson would ever be charged with the theft of two quarts of beer from a drug store. First of all, Bill is unlikely to commit such a crime, as money to pay for his needs and desires is no problem. Second, even if he were to do so, in all probability the matter would be hushed up and privately resolved so it would never come before the courts. Additionally, members of Bill Robertson's social class are not shot by the police. The contrary is similarly true: Members of Bob Smith's social class are not paid social visits in their homes by ranking political figures, they do not receive private tutoring or equestrian lessons, nor are their marriages of the slightest interest to newsmen. If they do travel abroad, it is more likely that they will experience the climes of Vietnam, Laos, or Cambodia than those of England, France, or Switzerland.

When I spoke earlier of social class determining one's life chances or the probabilities regarding the fate one may expect in life, the word probabilities was crucial because we are dealing with statistical chances.

Any particular individual, because of a variety of factors, can find himself in a situation that makes his life circumstances different from most persons in his social class. Some people also find themselves in circumstances which lead to a change in their social class membership, moving either upwards or downwards, resulting in corresponding sharp changes in their own circumstances and in the life chances of their children. Most people in our society, however, live out their lives in the same social class in which they were born.

What are those life chances? Keeping in mind that there are individual exceptions, that we are speaking in terms of probabilities, and that the amorphous middle classes especially are characterized by much variety, here are some of them. To take the most obvious, one's chances of working at an agreeable job, of living in the best available housing, of residing in the least deteriorated neighborhoods, and of attending the best schools increase as one goes higher in the social class hierarchy. This is known as a **direct relationship,** that is, the higher the social class the better the chance of being characterized by such favorable circumstances.

Not so well known is that happiness in marriage is also at least partially related to social class. In general, the lower the social class the less the proportion of happy marriages. It appears that happiness in marriage is highly influenced by sharing activities, holding mutual interests, and engaging in open communication. This type of interaction is less likely to characterize lower class marriages than marriages among middle and upper class persons. Marital relations in the lower classes are more likely to be hostile and exploitative, with the husband maintaining a highly authoritarian role in the family and his wife reacting with hostility to her forced and degrading subordination. Even sex in marriage differs qualitatively between social classes, with lower class males being more likely to regard coitus as proof of their manliness rather than as an expression of affection (Weinberg 1970:153). Such factors make marital break-ups more common in the lower classes. Social class not only affects the chances that a child's homelife will be disrupted by marital break-up, but it also influences the type of marital break-up. Because people in the lower classes are not as able to afford the attorney fees and court costs required for divorce, desertions are much more common among them than in the other classes.

Social class membership even plays a considerable role in determining the chances that someone will be born a bastard. The illegitimacy rate is in an **inverse relationship** to income, that is, the higher the family income, the less the proportion of unwed mothers. In Chicago, about 41 of every thousand children whose families have annual incomes above $8400 are given birth to by an unwed mother. This figure takes a sharp increase to one-third of all births, 337 per thousand, when the family's income is between $2,000 and $4,249 (*Public Health Reports, 81,* September 1966). In other words, the chance that a child is born to an unwed mother is eight times greater at this poverty income level than it is in the "more affluent" group.

Similarly, the chance that a son will be physically and psychologically abused by his father is greater in the lower classes. Perhaps because they have such little chance of getting ahead in life, combined with their much greater chances of being personally and economically exploited, lower class fathers are greatly frustrated; out of their frustration and anger they tend to react more violently to their sons than do fathers in the other social classes. This leads to greater tension in their homes, which often breaks into open conflict and results in the son being alienated from his family. This appears to at least partially account for lower class boys' greater acceptance of "street culture" and their tendency towards delinquence and violence (Weinberg 1970:154).

Social class membership also plays a critical role in helping determine whether one will make it through the first critical years of life as infant mortality rates also vary inversely with social class. Of every thousand infants born from mothers living in poverty areas of Chicago, for example, about thirty-eight die before they are a year old. This compares to twenty-two infant deaths for nonpoverty areas and fifteen for families whose income is above $8,400 (*HSMHA Health Reports, 86,* March 1971:237). Over-all in the United States, the infant mortality rate for whites is 16.8; but at 30.2 for nonwhites, infant mortality almost doubles (Friedman 1973:230). What these cold figures hide is the tragic human waste that they represent. With the current inadequacies of our medical delivery system, the white infant mortality rate, although lower, already represents thousands of needlessly lost lives, while the higher nonwhite figure represents that many more infants being annually sacrificed. If the nonwhite infant mortality rate were the same as the rate for whites, about ten thousand fewer nonwhite babies would die each year.

This differential mortality rate by social class which begins in infancy follows people throughout their lives. No matter what one's age, the lower one's social class, the greater one's chance of dying. This holds true for both men and women and for all the three major variables used to define social class: occupation, income, and education (Guralnick 1962, 1963a–c; Spiegelman 1963, 1968). Persons whose annual family income is less than $2,000 have a mortality rate of about sixteen per thousand, but this rate is cut in half for persons whose family income is $10,000 and over (Kitagawa and Hauser 1968, 1971).

Part of the explanation for these differential mortality rates by social class lies in what social class membership means in the United States. Because of one's position in the social class hierarchy, one is either denied or granted access to the goods and services our society has to offer. The higher one's income, the more access one has to the goods and services available in American society. The lower one's income, the less the access. And this includes access to good medical care. The higher an American's income, the more frequently he visits both physicians and dentists (Gleeson and White 1965), while persons with lower incomes simply cannot afford to avail themselves of medical services as frequently. The better the medical services available in a community, the lower the infant mortality rates, and good medical services are much less likely to be available in nonwhite areas (Friedman 1973). Because lower class women do not receive as adequate a diet or as good prenatal care as do women from other social classes, we can say that social class even affects Americans before they are born.

With the pervasive forces of advertising in American culture, especially with the highly influential shaping of desires through the medium of television, most Americans wish to consume material products at a high level. With the ubiquity of television sets in the United States, lower class Americans are no exception to this frantic desire to consume. They possess fewer means to legitimately achieve this goal, however, than do persons from other social classes. This has been suggested as a major reason for members of the lower class showing up so heavily in the crime statistics: They desire what most Americans desire, but because they do not have the same access to the legitimate avenues of achieving their material desires, they more frequently than others turn to illegitimate means (Merton 1968). Although less opportunity to achieve goals legitimately in the face of deep-rooted desires to possess as many things as possible is certainly instrumental in some lower class crime, I do not think it is a good idea to unquestioningly accept official crime statistics for, as with Bob Smith, many other factors are at work to produce greater crime rates for the lower class. In Chapters 12 and 14 we shall examine in detail how the authorities single out lower class persons for special treatment before the law.

Members of the lower class are also much more likely than persons from other social classes to be victimized as consumers. For purchases other than food and clothing (and sometimes these also), they are generally faced with the alternatives of foregoing most purchases or paying for them on credit. Credit always involves some risk for the lender, but with the insecurity of income among lower class persons this risk sharply increases. Accordingly, creditors demand higher interest rates for small loans, with 26 percent for the first $500 borrowed being common. This interest rate sharply drops to 12 or 18 percent after the first

$500 is paid off. Consequently, the poor pay more when they buy on credit, as they are much more likely to be extended credit only for small amounts. When payments have been made regularly, credit companies do their best to get the loan refinanced, as the higher interest is applied to the money first repaid. A refinanced loan means that the higher interest rate is paid once more. When a loan is partially repaid, some of our major credit companies that specialize in loans to poor people then send tantalizing advertisements picturing highly desirable, but expensive, consumer goods in order to lure the debtor into extending his loan. Many lower class families stay in debt for many years in just this way. It is hardly necessary to add that lower class persons are more likely than others to have their goods repossessed and their wages garnisheed and to become involved in related civil suits about which they have little understanding and even less power to combat.

If we want to raise our social class and better our lot in life, our best chance of doing so is by means of education, as higher education usually leads to better-paying employment. (Sociologists call moving up or down the social class ladder *vertical* social mobility.) We find here also, however, that the social class of one's parents is the major key to determining whether one will attain higher education or not—and the access to goods and services to which such education and increased income lead. For example, not only is someone's chance of going to a private rather than a public school greater if his or her parents have a higher income, but so is the chance of taking a college preparatory course and even the likelihood of completing high school. Children from the lower social classes are not only more likely to attend a public school, but they are also more likely to take a commercial or trade course while they are there. They also have a much higher chance of dropping out of high school. This, in turn, keeps them in the lower social classes by denying them access to the better-paying and more prestigious jobs. The lower-paying jobs, when even these are open to them, greatly determine their life style, which, in cyclical fashion, affects the life chances of their own children.

Across the nation, middle and upper class children do much better in our educational system than lower class children. Although commonly done by both teachers and parents, this fact cannot be explained away simply by saying that lower class children are less intelligent. Children who measure superior in intelligence do not by any means have an equal chance of being successful in high school and attending college. On the contrary, a person's chance to take a crack at this main avenue of upward social mobility directly depends on family income (Mulligan 1951). Even though the child's academic ability is high, the less the parent's income, the less his chance of getting to and getting through college (Coleman and Campbell 1966; Sewall and Shah 1967).

Not all lower class children are destined to be school drop-outs, however: Some do succeed in our educational system. Our schools act as a
sieve, recruiting some of the more able, persistent, and conforming
lower class youngsters for upper-middle class positions. Selectively recruiting from the lower class may well stabilize the American political
system by presenting evidence to those who didn't "make it" that they
could have done so, if they had just tried harder. That this homily does
not square with the facts matters little, for it is how reality is defined
that determines "facts" for people, a matter we shall extensively deal
with in coming chapters. The evidence of upward mobility decreases
pressure for social change, which might otherwise mount to revolutionary proportions and overthrow the social system itself (Jencks and
Riesman 1972).

Social class membership exerts even greater effects on people than
the external ones regarding mortality, medical services, educational
achievement, and life styles. By means of social class "society penetrates
the inside of our consciousness" (Berger 1963:82). Growing up within a
particular social class leads us to think about the world in a particular
way. Our participation in a social class, for example, affects the way we
feel people ought to treat each other. Our fundamental ideas about
right and wrong, what is proper and improper, are heavily influenced
by the social class in which we grow up. If we were to have grown up in
the lower-lower class, the chances are that we would feel that a woman's
place *is* in the home taking care of the children, cleaning the house,
doing the washing, and cooking the meals. We would probably feel that
such tasks are "unmanly" and that any "real man" vigorously avoids
doing them. We would also probably feel that it is the husband's responsibility to "go out into the world" and bring home a paycheck.
Whether we are male or female, the chances are that we would feel that
such separation of activities represents the *natural* ordering of relationships between the sexes and that something is wrong with someone
who does not follow them. We would be much less likely, however, to
have this basic orientation regarding what the world of the sexes is like
if we had been raised within a different social class.

Similarly, our chances of possessing a fatalistic attitude towards what
happens in life depend to a large extent on our social class. If, on the
one hand, we were to have been raised in social class circumstances
where our father's job is a precarious thing, where we are not always
certain where our next meal is coming from, where the police are
viewed as dangerous enemies, where our teachers give the impression
that they do not like us, and where we get the idea that we cannot plan
for the future because the future never seems to work out as we
planned it, we are quite likely to feel little control over our lives and to
think of life in terms of fate or luck. If, on the other hand, our father

owned a large factory and it is his decision which determines whether people work or not, if he and our mother regularly give orders to household help who dutifully follow them or lose their job, the police smile at us and are courteously helpful, teachers cooperate with our desires, and future plans regularly unfold, we are likely to think of ourselves as being in control of and mastering our world. Such differing basic orientations to the world, derived from our social class circumstances, penetrate our consciousness. They become a part of our basic orientation to the world, a part of the framework by which we interpret life. They affect the ways in which we view our own person, as well as what is happening to and around us.

To study social class membership is a major way of exercising the sociological imagination, for when we understand what life is like within a particular social class we gain an understanding of what people are like and of why they are that way. We then better understand their fears and hopes, their joys and frustrations, their sorrows and angers. By studying social class circumstances, we learn vital aspects concerning the **structural restraints** on the ways people approach life, on how they view themselves, and how they view the world around them. When we understand the pervasive influences of social structure, we have then gained a much clearer vision of the social forces surrounding people which exert such deep and lasting effects on the type of people they become.

One sociologist put it this way: He said that if one has accurate information on someone's occupation and income one can then estimate quite accurately the part of town in which he lives; the size and style of his home; the interior decor of his home, including what pictures are likely to be hanging on the walls, the books or magazines likely to be found there; the type of music he is likely to listen to, and whether this music originates from concerts, the stereo, or the radio; which voluntary associations he probably belongs to; the way he speaks; his political affiliation, and his views on public issues; the number of children he has; the likelihood of his coming down with various diseases; and even whether he likes to have sex with the lights on or off (Berger 1963:81).

That is indeed a lot to know about someone. And in such ways the study of social stratification is critical to exercising an adequate sociological imagination. Each society around the world has developed some system of ranking its members. When one knows what that system is, its bases, and its significance for the people involved, one has gained a significant understanding of the people in that human group.

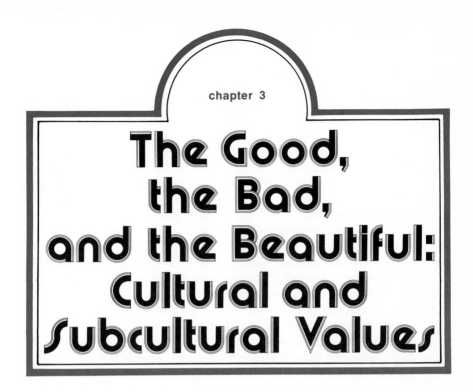

chapter 3

The Good, the Bad, and the Beautiful: Cultural and Subcultural Values

The sociological perspective or imagination views people within the context of their broader cultural or social milieux, and in this chapter we shall examine one of the major elements of the American milieu. We shall look at how values within a society or culture help determine the way people are. We shall focus specifically on the shaping effects of values in American culture.

Culture is the total way of life of a group of people: It includes their artifacts, the structure of their group, their belief system, and their language. Although the group of people who make the artifacts, who are living in some organized fashion, who do the believing, and who communicate with one another is usually referred to as **society** by sociologists, in many ways this is an artificial distinction. There is no compelling reason to analytically separate the concepts of culture and society. In most introductory texts these concepts are differentiated in the first part of the book, but then used interchangeably later in the same book (Arnold 1970:4–5). What sociologists call society goes under the name of culture when the same aspects of human life are studied by anthropologists (Mills 1959b:137). Sociologists are as interested in a people's total way of life as are anthropologists; and like anthropologists they also make the study of values and language a central part of their endeavor, because values and language determine to a great extent what types of persons live in a particular society or culture. After we have focused on values and culture in this chapter, we shall turn in the next to the importance of language in influencing what people are like.

In the last chapter I emphasized that it makes literally a world of difference into which group in society a person is born. As we saw, the world is viewed in sharply contrasting ways by members of the various social classes, with behaviors, attitudes, and beliefs differing according to social class membership. The world is seen in even more radically differing ways by people from different cultures. Chinese and Americans, the Bantu and white South Afrikaners, Russians and English, the French and the Eskimos have constructed worlds that are hardly similar. People in each culture socialize their offspring into a world which has already been constructed before their birth, and in so doing they produce what we might call different varieties of people: people with dissimilar goals and aspirations, contrasting ideas of right and wrong, and varying patterns of behavior. These differences are much more than a matter of external appearances involving readily apparent variations in manners or in clothing style: They affect the total person. A chief determinant of these differences between people is their **values,** ideas people hold about what is worthwhile or desirable in life (Rokeach 1973).

The task of specifying the values generally held by Americans is made difficult because of America's **pluralistic society;** that is, the United States is made up of many contrasting groups, groups which hold values that sharply compete and sometimes conflict with those followed by other groups. Certain overarching or general values, however, characterize life in America. While there is some disagreement among social analysts of American life regarding just what these generally agreed-upon values are, they appear to center around success, materialism, money, work, education, individualism, efficiency, "know-how," progress, equality, democracy, patriotism, religiosity, white superiority, male supremacy, and romantic love, monogamy, heterosexuality, height, and youthfulness. We shall discuss each of these ideas about what is desirable in life.

Americans place such a heavy emphasis on work and success that these values have become a religious force in American society. This central value that work itself is good and that everyone should work hard at some job and tangibly or materially demonstrate his success has been called the **Protestant Ethic** (Weber 1958). The Protestant Ethic (sometimes spelled without capitals) has been one of the major shaping factors in American life, probably leading to the high creativity and production rates characterizing Americans, as well as to their high rates of tension and ulcers.

American society is pluralistic, composed of many groups which hold sharply competing and often conflicting values. (Courtesy of Wide World Photos)

Values strongly held by the members of a society become intimately intertwined with ideas of morality. As values represent what is thought to be good and worthwhile in life, people who demonstrate that they are following major cultural values are thought to be virtuous, while those who do not follow them are thought of as immoral persons. Thus to "not work" when one is physically capable is usually considered immoral, a violation of the protestant ethic, while to "work hard" is viewed as virtuous. People generally feel that there is something wrong with someone who does not follow major values, perhaps that he has a vice of some sort, such as "laziness," which mars his entire being. Consequently, people who are on welfare are not only considered unfortunate, but they are also commonly thought of as immoral. At the basis of the common attribution of immorality to those on welfare is this violation of major values, values thought of as being the essence of American morality.

What is thought of as moral or immoral is not a constant matter, however, and the hold of the protestant ethic has greatly diminished in recent years. It is now generally considered to be not quite as bad to be on welfare as it once was, and many people feel that no one ever knows for certain that he will not need welfare at some time in his life—but to stay on welfare and not make a serious attempt to get off it goes beyond the pale and is considered highly immoral. We shall deal with cultural differences in morality in Chapter 5.

The major values of a culture do not exist in isolation, but they form clusters of related values. In **value clusters,** each value is directly tied into other values: Each value is an integral part of a larger whole. The generally held belief by Americans that success is important, for example, is intimately related to the general expectation that a person should work hard, get a good education, and make as much money as possible. Success is usually measured in terms of material attainments, primarily money. The possession of material objects becomes the major means by which Americans acknowledge one another as successful.

In the value cluster surrounding success in American life, we find hard work, education, money, and material possessions. Also central to this "package" is individualism. Emphasis is placed on the individual becoming successful through his own efforts. If someone does not "make it" or fails to "get ahead" to the degree that others expect, fault is generally found with the individual, not with the social system. It is thought that an individual who "failed" lacked abilities, or that if he had abilities he failed to apply them in the right way. Within this individualistic orientation or framework, "tough luck," "fate," "chance," and "bad breaks" are frequently put forth as justifying explanations for a person's lack of success.

A major part of socializing children, getting them to be what others expect, is teaching them to follow the predominant values of their culture. Teaching values is essential in the **socialization** process, and parents strive to see that their children closely match what they consider desirable in life. As we shall cover in the latter part of this chapter, in a pluralistic society major differences in values exist between the various social groups, resulting in children being socialized into differing sets of values. But parents who accept the generalized notion concerning what success is in American life, and most parents do, ordinarily follow the whole cluster surrounding success: They try to prepare their children to reach this goal by teaching them to work hard, to attain as much education as possible, and to highly desire material objects.

As I discussed in Chapter 2, the major avenue today for changing one's social class and bettering one's lot in life is education. Such a high emphasis has been placed on education in the United States that it, too, has become intertwined with morality. People who have an opportunity for higher education and who do not take it are sometimes considered to be doing the "wrong" thing—not looked upon as simply making a

Parents teach their children their own sets of values. The "corner" of society into which one is socialized as a child lays foundations for how one perceives and reacts to the world. (Courtesy of Wide World Photos)

bad choice but as becoming involved in an immoral act. They are expected to do everything they can to better themselves, to demonstrate success as commonly viewed by Americans, and they have failed to take available steps in that direction—or so goes common reasoning in some quarters of American society. As with most morality, later consequences can change people's evaluations of past acts; and, in this case, if the individual acquires the material acoutrements of success without higher education his prior decision not to go on for more education is re-evaluated in a positive light.

I wish to emphasize again that the United States is a pluralistic society and the degree to which such values are held greatly differs among the various groups in this country. Lower class persons generally place much less value on education, for example, than do middle and upper class members of our society. They also strongly emphasize "getting ahead" in life, however, although their opportunities are much more limited and their chance of success is extremely curtailed. In common with most Americans, lower class persons also place heavy emphasis on attaining material objects as a sign of success (Liebow 1967). When we are dealing with general values in American culture, however, the pluralistic nature of the United States should be kept in mind.

Efficiency is another major value in American life. Americans are expected to accomplish their tasks efficiently, whether they are working in the classroom, in the office, in the factory, or at home. "Efficiency ratings" have long been a regular feature of the business world, but they are now rapidly being expanded to other areas of life. Even in primary and secondary schools, teachers sometimes receive such ratings. Not only do American businessmen pride themselves on the efficiency with which they accomplish their goals with a minimum of effort and cost, but Americans informally rank themselves on this same value. American children are socialized into the value of efficiency early in life, and with much effort they learn not to "waste time" or to do something in an "awkward manner." They learn that many aspects of their life will be judged by its "efficiency," that "lack of efficiency" will bring ridicule, while "awkwardness" can relegate them to the unenviable standing of social outcasts (cf. Dexter 1964). The emphasis on how fast one can accomplish a task is seldom absent in American life. Even when someone is engaged in recreational activities and is supposedly relaxing, it is not uncommon for him to speak of how fast he drove to his destination or how many fish he caught within a particular time. Americans sometimes even boast to their neighbors about how quickly they can mow their lawns. Not to be efficient is taken as a sign of failing to follow a cherished ideal. When values are violated, negative terms are directed against the violator, and in this case such a person might be called lazy, careless, or lackadaisical.

In the same way, progress is held up as a virtue for us to follow. Americans have become accustomed to rapid technological change. They not only expect that their world will continue to change at a rapid rate, but they also anticipate that the direction of change is towards some vague thing called "progress." Americans believe that society

Cultural value systems channel behavior into paths considered appropriate. Major values in American society center around "getting ahead," which almost inevitably is measured in terms of material accumulations.   (Courtesy of Cartoon Features Syndicate. Cartoon by Erikson.)

should continually progress, that we should constantly build "more and better" gadgets for the common man and attain an ever-increasing gross national product. Americans appear to anticipate that we will efficiently "progress" both as a nation and as individuals into infinity.

Our corporations publish annual "progress reports," but they, too, are not limited to the business sector of our society. American students receive "progress reports" at regular intervals in the form of report cards. Training to "progress," to regularly evaluate one's own performance, and to accept the idea that others will evaluate the "progress" one makes, apparently essential features of modern life, are all part of that first report card so simply but ceremoniously presented in our grade schools.

Progress and efficiency are directly tied into the general value of American "know-how." It is generally believed by Americans that our scientific and technological knowledge is superior to that of the rest of the world and that our way of doing things is better than the way they are done by other people around the world. We know how to do things well, we know how to do them fast, and we know how to make them apply to the goal of "progress." This view of the supremacy of the characteristics of one's own group compared with others is known as **ethnocentrism.**

American ethnocentrism met with a hard blow in 1957 when the Russians put up their first Sputnik. Americans at that time generally viewed Russians as a cloddish bunch of peasants who were held in virtual slavery by cruel and blood-thirsty communist masters, an image elaborately contrived and continuously reinforced by our politicians via the American press. Americans had been systematically taught to view the Russians as ill-clothed, ill-housed, ill-fed, and ill-bred. Their ignorance was an essential part of this concocted image of "the enemy." We were flabbergasted when they sent up their Sputnik, and stunned when they began testing the survival of animals in space. We were suddenly confronted with the alarming possibility that *their* science and aspects of *their* school system might be superior to ours. With alarm and in protective reaction we embarked on a crash program of bolstering our science and mathematics courses in our high schools, colleges, and universities. We immediately upgraded our development and application of space technology, which culminated in a fabulously expensive, fast-paced international race to the moon. We were finally able to point our ethnocentric finger with pride when in 1969 it was Neil Armstrong, *an American,* who took the first step on the moon, that unforgettable "one small step for man, one giant leap for mankind."

American "know-how" had indeed been vindicated. Ours had proved mightier than theirs. But the image of "the enemy" was never again to be the same. We had been incontrovertably confronted with stark and dramatic evidence that others could pass us by in our strongest areas of accomplishment. This is a hard lesson for any people.

Just as the first six values that we discussed are part of a larger whole, forming a cluster around the value of success, so the values of efficiency, progress, and "know-how" are interrelated. It is a general American orientation that as long as we efficiently apply our knowledge or technical skills we will progress as a nation and continue to maintain our supremacy in world leadership. Part of this orientation dictates that although we might be challenged from time to time, as with the Sputnik, German cars, and Japanese transistors, such challenges will only serve to spur us on to greater creative effort and better application of our knowledge, but they will not stop our progress unless we begin to let up on our efficiency.

Equality, democracy, and patriotism also form a value cluster. We hold the general belief that the "all men are created equal" proclamation, as enunciated by the American patriarch Abraham Lincoln, represents reality. If we don't quite believe that this holds true for abilities, in the light of the regularly recurring disconfirming evidence presented by persons who are born with severe physical deformities and mental retardation, we then believe that it *should* be true for physical and mental abilities, and that it *is* true of opportunities facing Americans. This generalized belief that all or at least most Americans have an equal opportunity in life is highly related to the value we place on individualism and to the general view that those who don't "make it" have failed to take advantage of the opportunities this country provides. We have already touched on inequalities of opportunity in Chapter 2, and we shall continue to do so from time to time as it is such a significant and pervasive characteristic of American life.

Closely related to the value we place on equality is our emphasis on the concept of democracy. As though in a chorus, primary teachers faithfully reiterate to our youngsters that "everyone has a chance to grow up and become President of this nation." This belief is certainly an expression of faith in equality and in democracy. Although the American public appears to have become somewhat more sophisticated about the workings of our government in recent years, there is still a generalized belief that by means of the ballot box we are all able to participate equally in deciding who runs our government. This is the "one man, one vote" idea so prevalent in our culture. This view leads to the idea that if we don't get good political leaders it is the fault of an electorate which has not adequately exercised its power at the ballot box. In spite of the Watergate revelations, this belief persists.

Values, and their supporting beliefs, form a picture of reality. They provide an image of what the world is like. When the image they present is strong, as in the case of central cultural values, they are able to block contradictory evidence out of our perspective and even out of our consciousness. In this case they block out of our vision the fact that only two persons have a chance of winning the Presidency and those two are decided through a nomination process which involves only a select few persons, the delegates to the Republican and Democratic national conventions. These delegates are by no means representative of the electorate, but, on the contrary, they are primarily white, male, and middle-aged. Moreover, 40 percent of them have incomes over $20,000 a year (the McGovern Commission 1971). Similarly, the evidence we have in such ample supply that American life is characterized by inequality is in some cases blurred and in others obliterated by the constant public reiteration of the value of equality. Values serve as blinders, directing us to see only part of the world around us and to interpret that part of the world in a way commensurate with the orientation provided by the value. It is not surprising that ethnocentrism and "blindness to the facts" characterize all peoples, for all peoples see the world through the blinders of their cultural values.

It has traditionally been felt in the United States that the purpose of government is to serve its citizens, to carry out the wishes of the electorate, and that though the government sometimes fails in this task it usually serves this purpose. Although this idea suffered a severe blow with the Watergate revelations, the view persists that the government serves its citizens and obediently responds to their will. On this orientation is built the related value of patriotism so widely and fiercely held by Americans. Because the government brings blessings to its people, citizens are expected to be patriotic, that is, to respond with loyalty and obedience to the dictates of our government. In its extreme form, unquestioning allegiance is expected in all cases. The most intense and uncompromising form that the value of patriotism takes is perhaps exemplified by the view that proclaims "our government, right or wrong."

This central value of patriotism, by its very nature, must be ethnocentric, as it calls for placing one's own group above all others. Patriotism so colors perception that many Americans feel that our form of government is the best in the world, bar none. Some even feel that God guided the Pilgrims on their trip to the new land and influenced the Founding Fathers to write the Declaration of Independence. It is not unusual to find people who feel that God desires democracy, that it is *the* form of government which is "God-pleasing." People who express such deep-rooted beliefs in the American form of government also tend to belong to fundamentalistic religious sects. In the world-view subscribed to by such persons religion, democracy, and patriotism blend into one another. Each reinforces and is a part of the other. The world is seen in the stark colors of black and white, and little or nothing falls into a grey area. Not to subscribe to unquestioning patriotism is, for these people, to rebel against God himself.

Religiosity is, indeed, a major American value. It usually does not take such a fundamentalistic turn but is more easy-going, with the general expectation that one will "be religious." This typically follows the path of "belonging to" an organized religion, usually that of Protestantism. A lesser value has traditionally been place on Roman Catholicism and Judaism. The Ku Klux Klan, for example, a group opposed to change in the traditional American way of doing things, opposed not only blacks but also Roman Catholics and Jews. It is not generally felt necessary, however, that one "belong to" a religion to "be religious." Believing in the existence of a Supreme Being and supposedly following some set of divine precepts are usually sufficient to demonstrate conformity to this value. It is expected, however, that true Americans are monotheists.

Perhaps the best example of an American who never joined an organized religion but who publicly affirmed and followed this core American value is Abraham Lincoln. Although Lincoln never joined a religious denomination, his speeches were heavily laced with references to God and to man's place in God's will. It is still traditional for American Presidents to make reference to the deity in their inaugural addresses, although this is frequently done in just their first and last paragraphs. Our coinage and paper money also reflect this central value with the phrase required by law, "In God We Trust." This required phrase on our money also demonstrates the connection between our values of monotheistic religiosity and materialism and success, just as the phrase "One nation under God" in our pledge of allegiance illustrates the intimate interconnection between religiosity and patriotism.

Another major value in American life is white supremacy. As with most of the others that we have discussed, this, too, is not a recent value but is part of the historical fabric of the United States. From the beginning of this country we have placed a high value on whiteness of skin. This is demonstrated most clearly in the historical relationships of white Americans or "Anglos" with those of "a different color"—the Chicanos, the Indians, the Blacks, and the Orientals. Anglos seemed to feel that God had given this "new land" to White Western European people and that it ought to be taken by force from the "Redskins." They also seemed to feel that those with black skins were meant to be "hewers of wood and carriers of water," for the whites of course, and that the "Yellows" were unwanted interlopers in a white society. It is interesting to note that Orientals were highly desired when they first immigrated to the United States. Cheap labor was desperately needed at that time for building railroads in the West, but when the Central Pacific Railroad was completed, the Chinese then became economic threats. The view underwent a dramatic change—from looking at them as "worthy, industrious, sober, law-abiding citizens" to "unassimilable, deceitful, servile opium smokers" (Simpson and Yinger 1965:91). The Chinese became so undesirable that in the Idaho Territory they were even levied a special tax of four dollars a month (Gerassi 1968:132). White reaction to those of different skin colors has been marked by mass slaughter, enslavement, lynching, mob violence, and the "more subtle" forms or patterns of discrimination that still persist in our country, such as those in housing, education, employment, and even our current immigration laws. It is probably impossible for someone other than a white to become President of the United States, and it is still extremely difficult for a nonwhite to be elected to Congress. Relationships between blacks and whites will be dealt with at some length in later chapters.

In the same way that Americans value white supremacy, we also value and practice male supremacy. Males have traditionally been thought to be "superior beings" in a variety of ways—from their physical strength to the comparative working of their minds. There is, accordingly, more of an emphasis in our culture for males to succeed than for females, and women are ordinarily held to subordinate roles in society—either taking care of the children and doing the dishes at home or performing menial secretarial tasks in the office (Coser 1974). There are, to be sure, exceptions, but they are exceptions to the general rule. We shall also focus on major changes occurring in this area of American life in later chapters. In the same way that white is traditionally felt to be superior to black, so male is thought to be superior to female. It at least seems legitimate to make this assumption from the behavior of Americans, especially those in the business world. In a like manner, it is doubtful whether a female will ever ascend to the American Presidency.

The values strongly held in the culture into which an individual is born shape and help determine what the individual becomes. People born into a system of values, as all people are, will generally cherish the goals they represent and attempt to match them in some way in their life. For a person born and raised in our culture the values of education, individualism, efficiency, hard work, and so forth become part and parcel of the way he thinks and of the way he approaches life. They become major "orientational devices" by which he views the world and his place within the world. They shape not only his ideas, but also his goals and aspirations. They form a model of what the world is like, and this model becomes an essential part of the framework by which he interprets the world. By studying the cultural milieu into which an individual is socialized (**enculturation** is the anthropologist's word for the process of socialization), we strive for the contextual understanding of humans called for in the sociological perspective. In this striving, the study of values is essential.

Studying cultural values allows us to examine effects of culture which are usually invisible to those who are members of the culture, even though they are being so pervasively affected by them. Just as the last thing a fish would ever discover would be water, so the last thing a person discovers is his own culture (Linton 1936). Our value in the United States on romantic love is an example of this failure to perceive the effects of that which is closest to us. We feel that people should get married "because they love each other," and in our songs, literature, the mass media, and our common "folk beliefs" there frequently runs the theme that "love conquers all." We feel that it is natural that love should be the basis for marriage, and yet we find that this idea is by no means universal. In many other societies in the world marriage is based on quite different lines, such as family relationships or economic considerations. Just as our cultural values of equality and patriotism blind us to aspects of discrimination and inequality, so our value of romantic love also blinds us to negative effects of basing marriage on love, such as the inherent instability of such marriages, as discussed in Chapter 1.

The emphasis on romantic love in our culture rarely allows Americans to question this cultural premise for marriage. We usually feel that love will somehow or other win out. We assume that marriage is and should be a matter of individuals freely selecting one another. The facts, of course, are quite the contrary, and love appears to be largely dictated by the "social channels" of social class, race, age, and even height. It goes without saying, of course, that related major American values in the cluster of love and marriage are those of heterosexuality and monogamy.

Although values form clusters and blend in with one another to form part of a larger whole, there are also conflicts and contradictions between major American values. The values of equality, democracy, opportunity, religiosity, and success, for example, do not match too well the value we have traditionally placed on white supremacy. Yet these values exist side by side in American culture. They not only coexist in the general culture, but individuals sometimes also simultaneously hold them. Some of our most blatant racists, for example, hold dear the values of religion, equality, patriotism, and democracy, and tears will readily come to their eyes when the Star-Spangled Banner is played. It appears to be an essential part of the human condition, or of human nature, that people are able to hold contradictory values simultaneously.

Contradictions among the general values of a culture can especially characterize a society undergoing rapid **social change** because old values have not yet entirely given way to emergent new values. With rapid social change it is common for contradictory values to simultaneously coexist. In American culture, for example, we have changed from a prevailing theistic orientation to a scientific one, but we have not entirely made the change. We are still in the midst of metamorphosis, and our values reflect this contradictory emphasis. At the same time that we place a general value on a religious orientation to life we interpret life from a scientific framework. In traditional religion the two are by no means compatible, as one negates the other: either God or scientific laws, either the immutability of the principles of science or the intervention of God in human affairs. Yet we value both religiosity and scientific training and orientations. Side by side they exist in the American value system.

Similarly, we value both hard work along the lines laid down in the protestant ethic and the avoidance of work along the lines of the developing concept of leisure as exemplified by *Playboy*. At one and the same time we hold contradictory values regarding sexual restraint, indeed prudism, and gratification of sexual desires to the fullest, including the blatant commercial exploitation of sex. We value both conformity and individualism, mass education and anti-intellectualism. Each value contains or implies its opposite. Rapid social change means an unsettling of orientations to life, the development of competing ideas about what is valuable in life. While social change is in process, the old has not yet given way to the new. Adherents of both are found in the same society, and, indeed, as we have seen, contradictory values can be and are simultaneously held by the same individual.

Values sometimes undergo slow and barely perceptible modification as the effects of generations of experience gradually accumulate. The net result of such **cultural drift** is change over a long period of time, although for any two contiguous generations the differences may be inconsequential and perhaps go unnoticed. At other times values change rapidly in response to developments in technology, as with the coming of the automobile to the American scene and corresponding wholesale changes in our ideas of sexual propriety and courting procedures, as well as our changing patterns of residence and place of work. Values can also change in response to **culture contact,** people of one culture coming into contact with influences from another culture, which may be peaceable, with people willingly adapting their ways to the new, or may involve force and constraint, as in the case of war between nations.

Although people may resist change in their values, in a society undergoing rapid technological and social change people are immersed in change. Such change cannot help but affect the values people hold.

Sometimes such change in values is unpredictable and humorous, as in our currently changing value on height. We are now placing much greater value on height than we did just a short time ago. Not only is height essential for one to become a "basketball bonus baby," but height appears to be of critical importance for pursuits in which stature is irrelevant to the particular task. The beginning salary of University of Pittsburgh graduates, for example, is correlated not with achievement, but with height. Graduates who are six feet one inch tall receive 3 percent higher beginning salaries than those who are under six feet, while graduates who are six feet two receive 12 percent more (Deck 1968). "Tallness" has become so valued in contemporary American culture that short people are discriminated against not only in the more visible area of marital choice but also in political and economic careers (Feldman 1972).

Similarly, we are placing ever greater value on youth. Although the reasons for this changing value are complex, perhaps central to an understanding of our increasing emphasis on youth is change itself. That is, American society is in the midst of social change so rapid that we are continuously embroiled in things new and different. We barely get used to some aspect of life, and there immediately appears something to replace it. Things become obsolescent before they are off the drawing board. We have a hard time catching up with the mad swirl around us, seemingly threatening to engulf us all. But those who are best able to keep pace with frenetic change are the youth. It is they who have not become as accustomed to traditional ways, they who have less of the past to throw off when it is required to adapt to the new. It is they, in fact, who sometimes insist that change is not fast enough. While the old lament the change, the young groan over the slowness of it all. Today's world does seem to belong to youth, for their own newness to the social scene matches well the newness of change in which we are all constantly immersed.

As I have emphasized, a major problem with specifying general American values is that the United States is a pluralistic society. An American does not find himself or herself a member only of "general American culture," but he or she is also born and raised in some specific corner of American life. The specific "corner" of life in which an individual finds himself imparts to him ideas, beliefs, values, and a picture or model of the world which can radically differ from persons who are born into and participate in other groups. If a group has a general set of expectations for its members which differs from other groups in the same culture, it is known as a **subculture.** A subculture is really a world within the larger world of the national culture. *This world within a world* has its own unique and dynamic character, which provides a different orientational framework for its members (Komarovsky and Sargent 1949:143; Gordon 1947). Subcultures have their own symbols for dealing with the world, including their own special language or **argot.** We are all vitally affected by the "mother tongue" we learn, and in the next chapter we shall focus on the significance of language in developing basic orientation to the world.

Each group holds down a particular "corner" in life. Each has its problems with the physical and social environments for which people must work out solutions (Laswell 1965:211). The solutions they arrive at in dealing with their particular problems become part of the **normative expectations** of the group, the way the people in that group are expected to deal with life. Values, standards, beliefs, and general ideas develop about what is right and wrong and about how one should live in and deal with the world. Ideas develop and are passed on concerning what is expected of people if they are to remain in good standing in the group. These normative expectations, the generally accepted way of doing things, become an essential part of the way members of that group view the world. Normative expectations are the essence of the culture of the subculture, that which imparts to its members their unique identity in the larger world. Socialization into a subculture centers around teaching normative expectations to members new to the group, as a newcomer's acceptance in the subculture typically depends on his following the footsteps of those who have previously solved their problems along a certain line.

As we saw in Chapter 2, the essential differences between social classes involve not only money but also, and critically so, major differences in basic orientations to life. For this reason the upper class in the United States can be said to compose a subculture. Similarly, the lower class has its own set of subcultural orientations. These orientations represent major ways people who find themselves in the poverty sector of American life have worked out an adjustment to their limiting life circumstances. The term "culture of poverty" has been coined to refer to these subcultural characteristics, in this case characteristics sometimes including heavy drinking, borrowing, immediate spending of income, dropping out of school, irregular work patterns, frequently changing jobs, fighting, brawling, gambling, trouble with the police, and having more children than one can adequately support. **Culture of poverty** refers to such characteristics, which cyclically perpetuate poverty (Lewis 1961).

An essential part of using the sociological imagination, to grasp the social milieu that surrounds people and is so influential in determining what people become, is understanding subcultures. For example, it is impossible to adequately understand streetcorner groups without knowing the values present in this subculture. Without knowing their values, one can see their behavior only as puzzling or perhaps as psychopathic or even as the product of a group of mental defectives. One such gang, for example, recruits the "most able" teenagers in their community and enforces on them a high set of standards of fitness and personal competence (Miller 1958). Yet, their major activities center around assault and theft, activities they know violate the law. They regularly engage in gang fights, stealing autos, assaulting individuals, shoplifting, and mugging. Though their lawbreaking may at first seem senseless, their activities make sense once we place them in the context of the group's major values: trouble, toughness, smartness, and excitement. Committing these illegal acts matches their values. When they participate in criminal acts, they are demonstrating to one another that they possess masculinity, bravery, daring, skill, the ability to outsmart others, and shrewdness, while they simultaneously experience the added thrill of danger. Placing their criminal activities in this context allows us to see that, though their behaviors may at first appear senseless, they are, on the contrary, a logical outcome of their subcultural value orientations.

In addition to social class, subcultures are also *regional,* as with major differences between the ways people of the South and the North approach life, as well as major orientational and value differences between "country folk" and "city folk"; *religious,* as with the Jehovah's Witnesses and Christian Scientists; *racial,* as with American Indians and blacks; *ethnic,* as with German and Irish immigrants; *religious and racial,* as with the Black Muslims; and *religious and ethnic,* as with the Amish. Subcultures can evolve around almost any *interest, activity,* or *experience,* as with the pool hustler subculture (Polsky 1969), hobos (Anderson 1923), jack rollers (persons who specialize in robbing drunks) (Shaw 1930), homosexuals (Newton 1972), prostitutes (Murtagh and Harris 1957), hippies (Davis 1967), nudists (Hartman, Fithian, and Johnson 1970), mate swappers (Bartell 1971), cabbies (Henslin 1967), prisoners (Kirkham 1971), drugs (Yablonsky 1965), and alcoholics and gamblers (Sagarin 1969). Persons involved in each of these activities hold down a particular corner in life, they develop solutions to the problems they confront, and they pass these ways of life on to others. Thus a subculture arises over what separates people from others, and the subcultural perspective is perpetuated as the basic orientation of that group.

The values of a subcultural group are ordinarily a "variation on the theme" of the general value orientations characterizing the larger society of which it is a part. Although the members of subcultures amplify particular values as they develop their unique ways of relating to one another and looking at the world, they usually are in a fair amount of agreement with the general cultural orientations in which they are ultimately embedded. When, however, the subculture represents a set of values or definitions of reality or ways of viewing the world which "stand against" or are in opposition to the values or orientations of "the dominant culture," the group is known as a **contraculture.** The values of contracultures, and usually also their way of life, sharply conflict with those in the dominant culture. Some values of all subcultures probably conflict in some way with the dominant culture, but in a contraculture this conflict is central (Yinger 1960:630). If the differences are great enough, they can begin to challenge the way of life worked out by the dominant culture. Members of the dominant culture can come to feel that their cherished values are threatened. When this happens, they can become aroused to collectively meet the perceived threat, and the contraculture runs the risk of being snuffed out. Social pressures and in some cases even overt violence will be brought into play in order to eliminate what is perceived by the members of the dominant culture as a "threat" to the way of life they have learned to value.

The Mormons are a well-known example of this happening in the United States. Mormon views of God differ sharply from the theological views acceptable to most Americans, and dominant religious values were once felt to be threatened by the existence of this group. Mor-

The values of a contraculture sharply conflict with those of the dominant culture. When behaviors sufficiently challenge the dominant way of life, the enforcement powers of the State are brought to bear to suppress the challenge and to maintain the established social order. (Courtesy of Wide World Photos)

mons also once practiced **polygyny,** believing that it was quite all right for a man to have more than one wife at the same time. This was perceived by members of the dominant culture as a direct threat to their view that **monogamy,** the marriage of one man to one woman, was the only "right" way of marriage. The Mormons were also "clannish," sticking together and supporting one another, which made others even more suspicious of them. Moreover, the Mormons were hardworking and thrifty, and the lands they settled became successful farms, posing yet another threat to the precarious status of their neighbors. Additionally, politicians felt that Mormons would vote in a block, blindly following whatever their leaders told them, and that if the Mormons became both successful and numerous they would pose a threat to the political order. Consequently, those representing the "right" way of American life persecuted the Mormons in Kirtland, Ohio, burned their homes and crops in Independence, Missouri, and confronted them with further armed conflict in Nauvoo, Illinois. Even after they were forced to emigrate from Illinois to Salt Lake City, Utah, where they had few neighbors to become upset by their contrasting way of life, the national government was still concerned about the polygamy issue and passed its first anti-polygamy law in 1862, further modifying it in 1882 (Berrett 1944; Anderson 1966).

Although our society is still characterized by sporadic violence, and it was only a short decade ago that four little black girls were killed by a bomb hurled into their Sunday-school classroom and a year later that civil-rights workers Chaney, Goodman, and Schwerner were murdered, we appear today to be somewhat more tolerant of subcultures and contracultures in our midst. At least no one is killing Mormons because they are Mormons. Our sprawling, pluralistic society is marked by the juxtaposition within the same national boundaries of many different groups holding extremely varied ideas about the world. Although relationships are not always peaceful, there is now less violence among our subcultural groups than there once was.

Certain forces tend to dissipate subcultures, propelling Americans towards similarities along the lines of a "general American culture" (Gordon 1964). A major force towards such homogeneity is our system of mass production and mass communications. Television is a great "leveler" of people, teaching common speech patterns, disseminating numerous similar ideas to the masses of our people, instilling common goals and values, acquainting people with the latest gadgets available for an "easy" life, and developing in our people the desire to consume more and more and to ultimately resemble "the typical American" as portrayed on this medium.

The term "melting pot" is frequently used to characterize the process of **assimilation** in American life. Although there is a tendency for Americans to become similar and to internalize general American values, the "melting pot" image of the United States is misleading: Different metals are indeed melted, mixed, and hardened into a new product, but it does not work out this way with people, as the continued existence of contrasting subcultures in the United States testifies.

Our metropolitan areas, for example, are still filled with subcultures, and sometimes contracultures, with their contrasting and conflicting patterns of behavior. In many ways, St. Louis, Missouri, is typical of this urban pattern. In St. Louis, what is called the "Okie" area is an area settled by white rural migrants who are primarily from the "boothill" of Missouri. It is marked by cheap housing, high unemployment, much mobility and school truancy, sporadic violence, and many small bars featuring country-western music. St. Louis also has areas with high concentrations of single ethnic groups. Although in earlier years these areas were inhabited almost exclusively by persons from the same ethnic background, there has been much flux in recent years, and they are no longer marked by such high ethnic concentrations as they once were. St. Louis used to have Jewish enclaves, whose inhabitants have now mostly dispersed to the suburbs, sometimes in the wake of the sprawling black ghetto. From at least one building where the cornerstone reads "Synagogue," on Sunday mornings "soul music" is heard. Additionally, St. Louis has an area where primarily "hip" persons live, where the clothing and hair styles sppear strange to a "typical" American. Some areas are inhabited primarily by students, and in another small area gypsies live. There also are, of course, residential areas which follow class lines. Some areas are inhabited primarily by the lower or working class with their small homes, others by the middle class with their somewhat larger homes, and still other areas boast spacious well-groomed lawns with mansions set well back from their private streets, where the more wealthy St. Louisans live. St. Louis also has areas whose population is composed primarily of transients, where many winos and panhandlers are segregated amid missions and liquor stores, and a large area made up primarily of businesses and warehouses that becomes desolate at night since the vast majority of those using this area depart for their bedroom suburbs promptly at five p.m.

The suburbs of St. Louis are similarly diverse. One of its suburban communities is Kinlock, one of the only all-black cities in the United States, with an all-black political administration. It is marked by extreme poverty. Other suburban areas are more typical of the United States with "pockets" of blacks. Most St. Louis suburbs are all white, and some are characterized by extreme wealth, such as Clayton and

Ladue, where it is not uncommon to find homes with fourteen rooms or more where the families employ full-time household help. Other suburban communities, such as Richmond Heights and Maplewood, are inhabited primarily by members of the working class. With these characteristics St. Louis resembles most of the major metropolitan areas in the United States, characterized by areas of functional diversity, ethnic and social class segregation, and a myriad of subcultures marked by variant life styles.

To gain some idea of the significance of subculture socialization in our pluralistic society, consider what a difference it would have made in the type of person you are if you had grown up in an entirely different group. Suppose that you had spent your early years in a hippie family which emphasized self expression and living in the present, rejected the materialistic orientation of American society, de-emphasized patriotism, and believed that early experimentation with drug experiences was desirable. Or what if you had grown up in an Amish family and had learned to reject motor-driven vehicles, believed that farming the land was the God-pleasing way of making a living, formal education was suspect, and new-fangled gadgets were viewed as temptations of the Devil, designed to lead you down the road to perdition? Or what if your parents had been Black Muslims who believed that blacks are the superior racial group and that whites and their white institutions are allowed to dominate society only as a form of punishment, whose demise is inevitable as Allah unfolds his masterful plan? Or what if you had grown up in a home where your father was the president of a major corporation, with an income of $500,000 per year, and from infancy you took servants, private tutors, and world-wide travel for granted? Or what difference would it have made for who you are today if you had grown up in a family whose parents had just moved from a southern farm where they had barely eked out a subsistence living, to the city where they continued subsistence living, you had trouble adjusting to the large urban schools where the teacher "talks so strange," your classmates called you a hillbilly, and your unrealized dream in life was to sing on Grand Ole Opry?

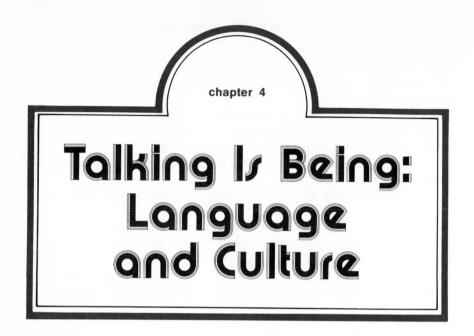

chapter 4

Talking Is Being: Language and Culture

Language may first strike you as a strange topic for sociology. What does language have to do with sociology? If you think about it for a moment, it will become apparent that the study of language is critical to a sociological understanding of people. "You're a nigger!" shouted the man in anger, and the response to his statement was immediate violence which resulted in his quick death. "Sir?" replied the student incredulously as he was unexpectedly called upon in class. "No, Greta, that isn't a flower. It's a weed," the father patiently replied to his daughter. "Wow, was it ever a groovy trip!" the hip girl exclaimed to her boyfriend.

Seldom do we speak words which trigger death, but all of us use language to express emotions, to ask questions, to explain what we mean, and to indicate differences in status appropriate to the situation. By means of words we tell others how we feel, what our problems are, what our point of view is. We use words to exchange insults or compliments and to state what is important to us. It is a common observation that words are powerful, and sociologically they are powerful because, among other things, they greatly determine how others will react to us and we to them. To use the word "sir" or "nigger" is to do more than speak: Such words indicate significant social positions. They categorize both the speaker and the one spoken to. Words may make interaction flow smoothly, as in the case of "sir," or as in the case of "nigger" they may abruptly trigger a violent termination of the interaction.

One cannot understand why people deal with one another as they do without understanding not only the meanings which they give to words but also the rules under which they use those words. Under certain circumstances, for example, the word nigger is considered perfectly proper by both the one using it and the one to whom it is directed. When a black ironically communicates status by calling his black friend a nigger, for example, no offense is meant and none is given. In this context the term evokes an entirely opposite meaning than the one triggering violence. Similarly, the use of the word sir can lead not only to a positive response, but can also be derisively used and result in immediate negative reactions.

There is no doubt that the use of words is important for our life with others, but just how does language fit into the sociological perspective? We must first note that, contrary to the idea many people hold, only human beings have a language. Language, in fact, is one of the major characteristics which separates people from animals. Every human group has a language, while no nonhuman group has a language. It is true that animals have ways of communicating with one another, but these are rudimentary communications, primarily giving warning of danger, indicating the location of food, or communicating a claim to territory and a readiness to defend its boundaries. The worker honeybee is even able to communicate to other bees the location of nectar sources, including the distance and direction of the source from the hive. Wild chimpanzees use both vocalization and body gestures to summon, threaten, and alert one another (Brown 1965:246). The beaver slaps his broad tail sharply against the surface of the water to alert other beavers to the presence of territorial intruders. Some species of birds employ elaborate gestures to communicate mating desires.

Most species of animals have some means of communication. Their communication, however, appears to be biologically built into them and is primarily expressed instinctually, without the necessity of learning. Human beings have something similar to this means of communication, which we call natural signs. **Natural signs** are biologically based communications that impart information concerning biological needs, such as the cry of a baby when he or she is hungry or in pain.

Although animals and infants are able to communicate rudimentary messages, what they do not have is the means of communication we call language. **Language** is a complex of symbols which can communicate an infinite variety of messages. Language is not instinctual, but is learned over a period of years through a complicated process as yet little understood. Although human infants are not born with language, unlike animals they are born with the *capacity* to learn language. This capacity to learn language appears to be related to brain size and to as yet unknown characteristics of organization of the brain (Brown 1965:248–249). From the forty-five basic sounds or **phonemes** in the

Language is the basis of human culture. By symbolic communications human beings pass life experiences from one generation to the next. Without language, human culture would be little advanced beyond that of the lower animals.   (Courtesy of Wide World Photos)

English language, an individual can learn over 100,000 basic units of meaning or **morphemes** (roughly equivalent to words). Although humans can learn to recognize and understand this vast number of morphemes, it is only the rare person who can *produce* more than 10,000 of them (Miller 1951 in Brown 1965:248). Comparable means of communication simply do not exist among animals.

The significance of language for human development can hardly be overestimated. Language lies at the root of culture. Indeed, communicating through language is the basis of culture. Without language, human culture would be but little advanced beyond that of the lower primates. Some animal species are able to transmit a small amount of knowledge across generations, but this is primarily limited to information about the location of waterholes, feeding places, and some habits of enemies. Most of whatever knowledge an aged anthropoid has gained from his experiences perishes with him, however, and each young chimpanzee is forced to begin life from scratch, just as his ancestors have done for millennia (Wynne-Edwards 1962 in Brown 1965:250).

Language changes all this for humans. Language allows human experience to be cumulative. By means of language one generation is able to pass many of its significant experiences on to the next, allowing that next generation to build upon experiences it may not itself undergo. Building upon cumulative experience allows humans to modify their behavior in the light of what previous generations have learned. This is the central sociological significance of language: *Language allows culture to develop by freeing people from being limited to their immediate experiences.*

Without language, people would be limited to communicating by some system of grunts and gestures. These grunts and gestures would greatly shorten the *temporal dimension* of human life. Communication would be limited to a small time zone surrounding the immediate present, to events now taking place, which have just taken place, or which will immediately take place—to a sort of "slightly extended present." One can grunt and gesture concerning a danger through which the group has just passed, but how could one in the absence of language embody experiences much beyond the immediate present? How could one share ideas with others concerning events in the past? There would be little or no way to communicate to others what event one had in mind, much less one's ideas or feelings about that particular past event.

The possession of language, however, entirely changes this for humans. It is language which makes possible our having a past and a future, two vital aspects of our humanity which are a watershed distinguishing us from animals. When humans talk with one another, they are exchanging ideas, that is, they are exchanging perspectives. Their words are the embodiment of experience, distilled and codified into a readily exchangeable form, mutually understandable for members of the same linguistic group.

Language provides a social past. In the absence of language, an individual would have memories of experiences and events, although these would be extremely limited since we pinpoint experiences by words and bring them more under our control of recollection by associating experiences with words. What memories exist in the absence of language would be highly individuated because they could be but rarely communicated to others, much less discussed and agreed upon. But with language, events can be codified, that is, they can be attached to linguistic symbols and then brought back to the present by means of those verbal symbols. Human beings are able to talk about past experiences and, while talking about them, to communicate with one another their ideas about those past experiences. They can exchange ideas on what has happened and in so doing develop perspectives on past events. Through their linguistic communications they are able to arrive at shared ways of viewing the past. Thus language extends the temporal dimension of human experience and provides a *social*, or shared, past.

Language also extends the temporal dimension of human experience forward by *providing a social future*. When people communicate about past events, they are able to come to an understanding of how they will act in similar circumstances. By sharing perspectives through language, people can modify their own behavior. They can agree to change what they are going to do because they have communicated to one another their viewpoints and desires. Arriving at shared ideas through the exchange of words, people can decide to pursue certain courses of action. Language, then, extends communication to a present not yet arrived. People are able to plan activities with one another. Language enables people to agree with one another concerning times, dates, and places. Language also allows them to come to some sort of agreement concerning purposes of planned behavior, the reasons for which they will get together.

Without language, how could people ever plan future events? How could they possibly communicate goals, purposes, times, and plans? Whatever planning could exist in the absence of language would be limited to extremely rudimentary communications, perhaps to an agreement to meet at a certain place when the sun is in a certain position. But think of the limitations in telling someone of just a slight change in this simple arrangement, such as that one "can't make it tomorrow."

Getting together for agreed-upon purposes is the essence of *goal-directed* behavior, so essential to human life. Such planning, or deciding now concerning future activities, allows collective or group action to unfold beyond the immediate present. Collective action is obviously basic to human life as we know it, but not usually so obvious is its *linguistic basis*. Collective or group action means that different individuals are joining their activities into some intended sequence. An individual is able to perform a small part of a larger activity, knowing that others are performing related parts and that the sum of their segregated activities will blend together into some larger whole. Although the individual may himself directly deal with but a small part of the whole and by direct experience be limited to knowledge only about his part, communicating through language provides him with knowledge of the larger whole.

Because language allows future-oriented, cooperative, goal-directed activity to exist, human activity is able to become incorporated into **systems.** That is, what would otherwise be but the isolated activities of individuals become incorporated into larger, integrating wholes. Language allows human beings to greatly extend their interconnections with others beyond immediate, face-to-face groups. Linguistic communications permit our biological needs to be translated into extended networks or interrelated patterns of social behavior. Thus people are able to involve themselves in joint activities which fantastically extend their connections with others. These linguistically based social interconnections allow human beings to develop beyond being foraging, nomadic groups. Because people can communicate with others their goals, ideas, and willingness to participate in cooperative action, they are able to develop extended networks of production and distribution of goods. Although language does not by any means *guarantee* cooperation among people, it is an *essential* condition for such cooperation; that is, without language cooperative human endeavors over time could not exist (cf. Malinowski 1945; Hertzler 1965; Blumer 1966).

Because human beings possess language, they are able to share ideas with one another. *Shared ideas are the essence of culture.* It is language which allows shared ideas to exist. When people talk with one another, they are doing much more than "merely talking": They are sharing perspectives about the world. Through their linguistic communications with one another, people develop ideas about the way the world is and about how people should act in the world. Without language, there could be no shared ideas and, consequently, no culture as we know it.

Through language, **collective sentiment** develops among people. This collective sentiment, centering around ideas and understandings about social life, becomes a unifying characteristic of people living together in groups; that is, by their linguistic communications members of a group arrive at shared understandings of the world and of their place in the world. These shared understandings are verbal representations of collective experience. As I shall discuss in greater detail, meanings are not inherent in the world itself but are produced by people through communicating linguistically. Language, thus, is the basis for creating **reality.** It is the creative tool by which people define their worlds of human experience.

When a child is born, that child is entering a group which already possesses networks of social behavior and shared ideas on how to view reality. Through direct physical contact, some quite gentle as with mothers nursing their infants and some not quite so gentle as with swats across the rear, the newcomer to the group learns something about the ways his group views the world. By direct physical contact he learns a limited amount about what others expect of him, something about his social boundaries and the physical limitations to his movements. But learning by physical contact is highly limited, and parents usually can hardly wait until they can *tell* their children what they expect of them. As soon as they are able, and indeed a good while prior to the child's understanding of verbal symbols, parents talk to their children. In addition to loving monologues with their infants, parents also vocalize commands and desires of which the child has no understanding. When the child is able to understand words, parents attempt to bring his behavior under the control of their words as much as possible, that is, they expect him to obey when they *say* something. The use of words, or communicating through language, is critical in the socialization process.

As a child learns his group's language, however, he is learning much more than how to respond to parental commands and desires and how to utter sounds similar to those spoken by the people around him. Language is not merely a means of expression but a kind of mold which shapes the minds of the children who learn it as a first language.

As any group of people go through life and confront the various problems of living that face them, they incorporate these experiences into their language. They give names to events and objects in their environment that they find significant. By naming aspects of their experience, they retain that experience. When something is given a name it does not simply pass away, but becomes verbally embodied and remains a shared part of the group. This process is called giving **cognitive form** to experiences in life (Hertzler 1965:27).

The group the child joins has already crystallized its collective experience into words. These words embody and perpetuate a particular way of looking at the world. Speakers of a language are literally partners to an agreeement to see and think of the world in a certain way—not the only possible way. The world can be structured in many ways, and the language we learn as children channels our thinking into a particular structure. Language is not a cloak following the contours of thought, but language is a mold into which infant minds are poured (Whorf 1950 in Roger Brown 1970:237).

The words that result from linguistically crystallizing human experience are **concepts.** Concepts are "mental images" or "convenient capsules of thought" (Hertzler 1965:27). They are the ways by which human experience is verbally identified. Concepts are not isolated, but related to one another. When people speak about their experiences in life, they are picking certain things out of their vast stream of experience. As they speak about them, they are relating one experience or idea with another. The framework into which they fit their experiences is called a **conceptual scheme** or **conceptual system.** The conceptual scheme, the interrelated system of concepts that people apply to their experiences, provides a context which interprets or gives meaning to those experiences. People who possess the same conceptual scheme possess the same framework for interpreting what happens to them. They consequently share understandings and meaning.

To illustrate conceptual schemes, let us take an extreme case. Suppose that a person has become tired of living, but he lacks the courage to commit suicide. Suppose also that this person goes to a priest with his problem and the priest agrees to grant his wish to kill him. Now this is certainly a bizarre situation, extremely unlikely to occur. But suppose that it has taken place and is now front-page news. What would your reaction be? For most of us it would be that of shock. But why? What conceptual system would we be applying to the situation that leads to this reaction? It would center around two major, interrelated Occidental ideas: the infinite value of life and the traditional role of the priest to sanctify or protect life. These ideas or concepts are interrelated, that is, they are part of the same conceptual scheme or conceptual system.

By placing an event within a conceptual scheme, we receive an interpretation of the event, that is, events take on meaning when we apply concepts to them. This is sometimes called the **conceptual penetration of reality.** Through metaphysical, supernatural, or other-worldly teachings we have learned to view life as valuable, and to view or to conceptualize priests as upholders of "ultimate values," including this one. These are things taught to us from the beginning of our childhood socialization into American culture. Even the concept "man of God" is part of this conceptual scheme. So is every movie in which a priest will sacrifice everything in order not to reveal what was told him in confession. Bing Crosby and "The Bells of St. Mary's" can well become part of the formation of these concepts, as does every war movie in which a soldier who died for his buddies is hailed as giving the supreme or ultimate sacrifice. And on and on. Our socialization into these values has been thoroughly extensive, continuously buttressed by parents, friends, teachers, preachers, and the mass media. The concepts have this social origin, and we have learned well how to apply them in such a way as to interpret events as do others around us, that is, according to our culture's standards.

But what is reality here? A priest kills. An individual has requested a priest to kill him, and the priest has complied with that desire and request. Those are the "objective" facts. But "objective" facts do not provide meaning. To have meaning, "objective" facts must be interpreted. They have to become part of the person, or subject, who is seeking meaning. When this occurs, we can say that they are becoming "subjective." They become part of the person, by being placed within the conceptual scheme or system of interrelated concepts held by the individual.

Note that this is a *social* process. Although it is indeed an individual who applies the concepts and derives meaning, the person does so by applying concepts he has learned from others, that is, the concepts are not his own creation. They originate external to any particular individual. They are concepts one learns from others in society. Hence, they are social in their origin, and this process is called the **social construction of reality.**

Language itself is an interrelationship of concepts and is thus a symbolic framework for interpreting human experience. Words name things in our environment. As things are named, they are being categorized or put into a system of classification. The things can then be separated from each other as well as related to each other. In this way they can be both comprehended and utilized.

At an early point in his life, the child learns that the objects in his world have names and that the sounds used by his parents and others refer to those objects. This is a tremendous discovery for the child because he is then both able to communicate his needs to others through using the correct sound or word and to respond to the desires of others by means of verbal communication.

Language works much like a sieve: The words or concepts of our language let in certain parts of our experiences and prevent others from entering our consciousness. What is let in and what is kept out largely depend on the language we learn. When children learn the words of their community, they are also learning the culture of their community. Their language imparts to them a particular model of the world. In acquiring a language they are learning what the world is like from the perspective of their group, the point of view that will soon be their own (Brown 1965:339; Hertzler 1965:41–42).

Because using language means that one can communicate about things not physically present, people are able to learn about things they have not directly experienced. People can, for example, learn racial prejudice even before they have met anyone from another race. If the parents of a white child talk about "niggers" being dirty or lazy or if the parents of a black child talk about "honkies" being untrustworthy or immoral, racial prejudice can become a part of the child's social inheritance. He can become negatively disposed to persons representing another race and intensely dislike them even before he has seen such a person.

This is the power of language in constructing the human social world. Racial prejudice, to continue this example, is frequently taught in an overt manner by juxtaposing in the same context linguistic terms such as "nigger" and "dirty," "honky" and "bigot," and so on. But racial prejudice is also taught through language in much more subtle ways. Think of the American nursery rhyme common in the white community which begins, "Eenie, Meenie, Miney, Moe—Catch a nigger by the toe." Many parents who recite these lines as they play with their child's toes do so without a thought regarding the content of what they are saying. But, upon reflection, we can see that it does, indeed, teach content. Whites are dominant (they are "the catchers"), blacks are subordinate or the objects of action by whites (they are "the caught"), and along with this whites gain from blacks in one way or another ("make him pay, fifty dollars every day").

If a child in America does not learn racial attitudes through nursery rhymes as this, he certainly learns at an early age by means of language that his world is divided into two major groups—blacks and whites. Through language, and sometimes by such a simple teaching device as a nursery rhyme, the child learns his culture's racial categories at a tender age. Dominant attitudes towards races and ethnic groups are further taught through continued linguistic communication with members of one's own ethnic group.

When a child learns language, then, he is not simply learning neutral sounds. The sounds may in and of themselves be neutral, but when these sounds are incorporated into a linguistic system they are filled with meaning. Among other things, language teaches **norms,** the accepted rules, customs, or standards for behavior. Language plays a significant role in teaching the morality we shall discuss in the next chapter. By means of language, group members pass on their ideas of right and wrong regarding the particular categories into which they divide the world. Words are taught within a context of meaning, and this meaning context exerts a great influence over behavior. When a child learns the word "sex," for example, he learns a vast array of expectations concerning his own and other's behavior. If the word "sex" is spoken in hushed tones, is connected with words which a child learns have negative meaning such as "dirty," or is not to be discussed at home because "nice people don't talk about it," he is learning much more than just a word which refers to some aspect of his environment. He is also learning associated behaviors and related attitudes toward that to which the word refers.

From the example above of the priest and killing, note the complexity by which we learn the basic concepts with which we approach the world and by which we evaluate what happens in life. Our basic concepts, such as those concerning the value of life, go so far back into childhood that it is extremely difficult to even recall learning them. They become something not external or superficial to us. They become, rather, part of our very being, part of the basic, generally unreflexive ways by which we approach the world. They form the usually unquestionable basis for interpreting reality. They are part of the basic orientational framework which we share with almost all Americans, part of the general Occidental and American culture which gives us our identity in the world, which separates us from people in cultures which have differing conceptual systems and, resultingly, different interpretations of reality.

By learning language, the child comes to grasp the viewpoints and to understand the feelings and sentiments of others in his social group toward their physical and social environments. Language prepares him for and inducts him into the **roles** the group has for him, the parts he is to play in life. By doing this, language also imparts an identity to the newcomer. Through learning his name he learns that there is a word which distinguishes him from others in his group, that he is an individual, and that he is related to others in certain ways. Language teaches him not only that there is a person called daddy or father, for example, but by learning such concepts he also learns paired terms which place him in relationship to others in his group. Not only is there someone called "father," but he is himself a "son," and when he learns the concept "son," he learns that this is a relationship which has specific expectations attached to it. By means of language the newcomer learns the perspectives of his groups, which then fundamentally and significantly shape his entire personality (Lindesmith and Strauss 1968:233–234).

The importance of learning language for shaping personality and for "becoming human" is illustrated by the study of an isolated child (Davis 1947). Isabelle was an illegitimate child who was kept in a semi-darkened room with her deaf-mute mother until she was six and one-half years old. At this age she was discovered and removed from her limited and limiting environment. At this time her behavior was described as being "like that of a wild animal." She acted as though she was "afraid and hostile and she made only a strange groping sound instead of speech." She behaved like an infant. She was so unresponsive to sound that people first thought she was deaf like her mother. After it was established that she could hear, she was thought to be feeble-minded. She then underwent systematic training, and in just a week she made her first attempt at vocalization. In two months she was able to put sentences together. She was able to write and recognize words and sentences on the printed page before a year was up. Several months later she had a vocabulary of between 1500 and 2000 words. In two years she went through the stages of learning which usually require six, and by the time she was fourteen years old she had completed the sixth grade in public school. Her behavior was similar to that of other children her age. With the acquisition of language and contact with persons who spoke to her and to whom she was able to speak, her personality underwent an amazing metamorphosis.

Because it is primarily through language that one learns the expectations of one's group, failure to learn a language prevents adequate socialization. Helen Keller is another example of a person who acquired language later than most people. She was both blind and deaf. When she was seven years old, she began to receive instruction in communication. She learned how to spell, with her hands, words naming the objects in her environment. With considerable difficulty she found that the objects in her environment had names. She reports that with this discovery the world seemed to open up to her, that words made the world blossom for her. By knowing that objects had names, she was able to picture her world: This knowledge allowed her to "see" objects and to conceptualize relationships between those objects. Not only did learning language give her words for objects so that she could more adequately deal with the world, but acquiring language also changed her attitudes toward the things in her world, toward people, and even toward herself. Learning language fundamentally altered her own person and her relationship to others (Keller 1917).

Helen Keller "hears" Anne Sullivan by feeling the vibrations on her lips. Learning language fundamentally altered Helen Keller's perceptions of herself and her world, dramatically transforming her self concept, her personality, and her social relationships. (Courtesy of Wide World Photos)

For how we picture the world, for how we view ourselves, and for how we look at our relationships to others, all of us depend upon the acquisition of language. The concepts which our language provides give us a ready-built way of viewing the world. Our concepts or categories order or structure "reality." These resulting definitions of reality are part of the cultural heritage provided by the group for its newcomers. For example, each group of people develops concepts or categories pertaining to "food" and "nonfood", but each group develops its own particular categories. Consequently, Americans "do not see grasshoppers as belonging to the same category as pork chops, orange juice, and cereal; other peoples do."

" 'The facts' simply never stare us in the face. We see them always through a glass, and the glass consists of the interests, preconceptions, stereotypes and values we bring to the situation. The glass is our frame of reference" (Cohen 1955:52–53). The primary shaper of this frame of reference through which we view the world is language. The categories our language provides greatly determine how we see the world. In the English language, to use another example, nouns are static, while verbs are dynamic or demonstrate action. When we apply nouns such as "peace" or "happiness" to conditions, we tend not to see action, while if our language provided different categories of thought for these same conditions we would perceive them as containing greater activity (Whorf 1956). We would then tend to see them as ongoing processes, not as static conditions.

To illustrate how objects and events in life do not contain built-in meaning but receive their meaning by being placed within a linguistic or conceptual framework provided by our culture, we can use the example of skin eruptions. Eruptions on the skin are something which probably everyone experiences at some time or other in his life. But what does it mean for someone when he has a skin eruption? The meaning is dependent on how the person classifies the skin eruption, on the conceptual framework within which he places it. The conceptual scheme of a culture may provide for classifying "small-red-close-together-slightly-raised-bumps" in one way and "black-bumps-with-white-centers" in an entirely different way. The location on which the eruptions appear on the body may also partially determine the meaning given it. In one case the individual may be kept away from other people and be administered certain medicines, while in the other he might be allowed to continue his everyday routines. Similarly, a skin eruption might be classified differently, and receive entirely different meaning, depending upon whether it came on suddenly or developed slowly. The meaning of a skin eruption is not a part of the skin eruption: Meaning is determined by placing it within a conceptual framework. Similar eruptions will be classified quite differently from one culture to another, with sharply differing meanings being given the eruptions (cf. Frake 1961). But when we place a skin eruption into the conceptual scheme provided by our culture, we then "know" what that skin eruption means.

Death is also universally experienced. It is a truism to say that everyone must die at some time, but because death is characteristic of human beings and because they have developed language, people *know in advance* that they will die. It is perhaps possible, but extremely doubtful, that people would have this knowledge if they did not possess language by which they learn that there is a history of death which has preceded them and to which they shall fall heir. As they do with their other significant experiences, people categorize death. The concepts they apply to this aspect of humanity give meaning to death, something which we assume animals do not have because they lack language by which to conceptualize and categorize.

As with other human events, the meaning given death is culturally rooted and linguistically based (Henslin 1970; 1972a). Some cultures provide categories which specify that death is brought about by witchcraft. In one such culture, the Azande, survivors must then consult a

Death is an event around which each culture develops strongly-held expectations or customs. These channel perceptions and behaviors into ways deemed culturally appropriate. (Courtesy of Wide World Photos)

poison oracle, choose an avenger, employ a magician, and perform certain rites in order to bring about the death of the witch who caused the death in the first place (Evans-Pritchard 1937:540–544). When a member of the Kaingáng tribe of Brazil dies, however, those remaining must pack up their camp and move because the category into which Kaingáng people learn to place death indicates that ghost-souls are threatening the security of the group (Henry 1964:67). Among the Navaho, in contrast, death is taken to mean that someone has failed to observe the proper rituals of daily life. The eternal forces of Nature have become imbalanced, and one is well advised to perform religious ceremonies in order to counteract the bad influences and re-establish the necessary equilibrium between people and Nature (Hoijer 1954:100). In another culture, one with which you are more intimately familiar, death sometimes means a sign of God's activity. Death traditionally signifies that God has stepped in and taken someone's life, perhaps in judgment or perhaps in mercy.

In this culture death is usually avoided as a topic of conversation as it is considered too indelicate, or perhaps too threatening. In any event, when people feel that a certain aspect of life is highly indelicate, they tend to develop less offensive words,   **euphemisms,** to refer to the matter (Hertzler 1965:276). American English provides abundant examples of euphemisms for death: It is referred to by such terms as the end, asleep in Jesus, gone to Glory, called beyond, dissolution, kicked the bucket, departure, and release. Dying is called expiring, giving up the ghost, passing away, breathing one's last, and leaving this vale of tears. Similarly, corpse preparers are called morticians, and they don't talk about corpses. They speak of bodies or even of patients. The "patient" is "prepared" in a "preparation-room," then "dressed" in a "slumber-shirt," placed in a "casket," and after being stored in the "reposing-room" of the "funeral home" the "patient" is "laid to rest" in a "memorial-park," his "final reposing place" (Mencken 1945:287–288 in Hertzler 1965:277). The social significance of euphemisms is that they indicate topics about which there is some form of cultural taboo. Studying the euphemisms of a language may be one way of studying major cultural values.

When a language provides words to designate a certain part of the environment, people are provided a conceptual tool for perceiving that part of their world. As with death and skin eruptions, people see the world differently according to the way their language divides up the world of experience. So it is with the word *war*. This word communicates the idea of armed confrontation. It is usually fairly easy to see whether a particular interaction between nations is war, that is, people generally agree whether or not the term war should be applied to a situation. When, however, modern international relations at a recent historical point came to be highly pitched in hostility, but always fell short of armed confrontation, a new term was coined to conceptualize this state of affairs. The term "Cold War" communicates to us that we can actually be at war without being in armed conflict. The particular "war" is "cold," not "hot." A person growing up in a society in which the term "Cold War" is used perceives international relations in a manner quite differently from a person growing up in a society where there is no such word or its equivalent. The term "Cold War" collects various experiences under this one label, organizes them so the individual perceives relationships between them which he would otherwise not see. The words of a language serve as a means of alerting people to particular aspects of their social and material environments.

Language not only helps determine what we perceive and the meaning we give to the world around us, but language also *indicates action*. The way language divides the world indicates how we should act towards the world. When, for example, someone receives meaning about his skin eruption by placing it into a cultural category, that person is also being given direction for "proper" action. Depending upon the meaning received from classifying the eruption, the person may stay home and take medicine or continue his ordinary routines. Similarly, how people classify death indicates whether they should think of God, perform religious ceremonies, hire a magician, or pack up their belongings and move the camp lock, stock, and barrel. The concept of Cold War also indicates action: Any move whatsoever on the part of "the other side" is to be viewed with suspicion and distrust. If the other makes an overture of peace, we should view it as a trick, while if they show hostility we are to then know that they are merely showing their true colors. So it is with the concepts in all languages: They define reality for us by influencing both perception and action.

Yet the process of the conceptual ordering of reality is not automatic. We share basic concepts, and we share basic ideas of how and when to correctly apply those concepts, that is, we share ideas concerning the appropriateness of what concepts apply to what situation. Consequently, we derive meaning in common with others around us. But more is involved. This is a creative process. We have not all learned to apply all concepts in identical ways. There are differences in our experiences of living in society which lead to a somewhat different content of the concepts and to somewhat differing ideas about how to apply them to what situations. Moreover, alternative concepts are available for the same situation. Which is chosen largely depends upon individual background experiences. But the choosing is real. The individual has alternatives available to him. He selects from those alternatives. He applies the concepts. He interprets **objective reality.** He derives meaning. He thus creates his interpretation of reality, like an artist who selects and applies the colors available to him and creatively produces a picture of reality.

The fact that language is not the same around the world helps maintain different orientations in different cultures. But neither is language the same for all the various groups making up a pluralistic society. These differences also affect perception and action. Just as there are general cultural influences and varying subcultural influences in a pluralistic society, as we discussed in the last chapter, so in our pluralistic society different groups of people have different languages. Special languages (*argots*) characterize different racial and ethnic groups, occupations, geographical areas, age groups, and perhaps even the two sexes. Because of their unique positions, people in each of these groups experience life differently from others. By the various concepts that they develop, they mark out these experiences and their corresponding perspectives. Learning these languages, in turn, leads to differing perceptions of reality.

To demonstrate how special languages divide up the world, marking out what is important to members of the group, and how argot leads to different perceptions and to corresponding action, we can use an example from an occupational subculture. Cab drivers have their own peculiar problems, and in their conversations they mark out what is significant to them through an argot we might call "cabby-ese." The following terms from this special language are everyday words cabbies use to communicate with one another: (1) "ace man," the cabbie eligible for the first order when several drivers are parked at the same cab stand, (2) "bucket load," a passenger who doesn't pay his fare, (3) "flag load," a person who "flags down" a cab, (4) "liner," a person who wants the cab driver to put him in contact with a prostitute, (5) "no go," a location to which the cab driver was dispatched but at which no passenger was waiting when he arrived, (6) "stiff," a passenger who does not tip, and (7) "weekender," a part-time cabbie (cf. Henslin 1967).

Becoming proficient in the argot of "cabby-ese" is an important part of learning to be a cab driver, for this special language marks out what is important for the cab driver and facilitates communication between drivers. After one learns "cabby-ese," one begins to think of the world in line with the ways this particular language divides it. Each term has its own particular effect in influencing the novice cabby to perceive the world as cabbies perceive it. Each influences the cabby to think of people in a particular manner and to act in an "appropriate" way towards them. When one learns these terms (not simply as a definition, but as a regular part of one's communications), the social world takes

The special languages developed by subgroups in a pluralistic society mark out the members' unique experiences and affect both their perceptions and behaviors. (Photo by Jeffrey Schamberry)

on a different perspective. Some of the effects of these terms on the cabbie's perception and action are indicated in Table 4.1.

This example from "cabby-ese" demonstrates that when one learns a language, even a highly specialized language within one's own general culture, one is being taught both perceptions of the world and expected actions toward the world. To further illustrate the importance of language in determining perception and behavior, think what it

Table 4.1 Cabby-ese and the Social World

Term	Some Effects on How Cabbies Perceive the World	Indication of Appropriate Action
1. Ace man	a. Some cabbies are legitimately eligible to make money on the next order, while others must wait. b. The world is highly structured into persons who have rights or access to something and others who do not have rights or access to it. c. People must take their turns in this highly structured world.	a. Try to "ace out" fellow cabbies by getting to "cab stands" before they do.[1] b. As orders are given according to "ace position," be on the alert for other "empty cabs" as you are returning to a "cab stand." c. Stay near the radio if you are in "ace position" so you don't miss out on your order. d. Wait your turn if you've been "aced out." e. If there are too many cabs at a "stand," go to another "stand" or "cruise" for passengers.
2. Bucket load	a. Most passengers pay willingly. b. Some passengers try to skip out on their "fare" if they get the chance.	a. Be suspicious of a passenger's intentions. b. Always guard against giving a passenger the opportunity to leave your sight before paying.
3. Flag load	a. Some people who want a cab haven't telephoned for one. b. Flag loads are, in general, to be less trusted than are "dispatched orders." [2]	a. Constantly be on the look-out for flag loads ("cruise"). b. Drive near the curb so you can quickly pull over if someone "flags you down." c. Be suspicious of persons who try to "flag you down," especially if it is a man at night or in a "bad neighborhood."
4. Liner	a. Some men who desire prostitutes don't know where to find them. b. Liners have ready money to spend.	a. Find out where prostitutes work. b. Help a liner out in order to make extra money. c. Charge a liner his "fare" plus whatever else you can get out of him for giving him this service. d. Work out *in advance* your financial arrangement with a liner. e. Be careful of the "cab squad" if you work with liners.

Table 4.1 Cabby-ese and the Social World (*continued*)

Term	Some Effects on How Cabbies Perceive the World	Indication of Appropriate Action
5. No go	a. Some people who "call in" for a cab will not be at their location when you arrive. b. Others will have changed their minds about taking a cab by the time you get there. c. You never know if you have an order for sure until a passenger actually gets into your cab.	a. Rush to your order before the caller changes his mind about wanting a cab. b. Don't be overconfident. c. If you get a no go, radio the dispatcher so you can be given "ace position."
6. Stiff	a. Some passengers never tip. b. Passengers can be "sized up" as to whether they are stiffs or not. c. You can be wrong in "sizing someone up." d. If a passenger is a stiff, what you do won't affect your tip. e. If you didn't get a tip, it probably had nothing to do with your services. f. If you don't treat passengers right, you can make stiffs out of them	a. Figure out whether your passenger is a stiff or not. b. If he is a stiff, do nothing extra for him: Don't even be polite if you don't feel like it. c. If he isn't a stiff, be your usual self, or even do extra things in order to increase the size of the tip. d. As you can't tell for sure until after the trip, err on the side of giving the passenger the doubt.
7. Weekender	a. Cabbies who own their cabs ("company men") are committed to cabdriving, while those who do not own theirs ("weekenders") have only a peripheral interest in the job and company. b. "Company men" have higher status than weekenders. c. "Company men" make more money than weekenders.	a. If you want to succeed in the world of cabdriving, buy your own cab.

[1] Quotation marks indicate additional terms in the cabbies' argot.
[2] For an analysis of trust and cabbies, see Henslin 1972b.

would be like if our language had no words for "husband," "wife," "son," or "daughter." If we did not have these words or their equivalents, we would literally be living in a different world. Such concepts divide social reality into a particular form: They are categories both into which we place people and by which we determine our behavior towards others once we "properly" categorize them. Such words as these, as well as "rich" and "poor," "nigger" and "honkie," and so on, structure our world into particular relationships. They define certain behaviors as "appropriate" and other behaviors as "inappropriate."

Words are never just words. Words represent reality as experienced and structured by one's group, and they impart reality and structure to one so that he also sees the world from the framework of his group. Language points out what is "real," indicates what is significant, dictates how one should see, helps determine what one sees, and indicates action. In such ways language exerts a remarkable degree of influence over human behavior.

Because language is so very influential in human affairs, it is apparent that whoever controls language controls people. It is for this reason that dictators ordinarily "dictate" what their people shall hear on the radio, read in newspapers, books, and magazines, and see on television and in the movies. Attempts at such "dictation" are not by any means limited to dictators, however. Most leaders of governments appear to desire to control what their people read, see, and hear. Language has such a remarkable effect on what people perceive, think, and how they act, that if a leader is able to control what is communicated to his people he is able largely to control both their thoughts and their behavior. To have such power is the ultimate in **social control,** restraining others by channeling or regulating their behaviors and beliefs and, ultimately, their thoughts and feelings.

Although few have such control, governmental leaders around the world, whether theirs be a dictatorship or monarchy or an elected government, attempt to manipulate the key linguistic symbols of their culture in order to control their people's behavior. They speak of "the enemy" (whoever it may happen to be at any particular time for any particular country) and of the glorious goals of their leadership, all the while attempting to control thought and action through manipulating key terms such as democracy, communism, capitalism, socialism, loyalty, obedience, patriotism, citizenship, freedom, liberty, independence, and individualism. Governmental leaders who are able to control the outflow of words in mass communication are that much more able to infuse their own leadership with authority and to hold their people *from within* by selecting the thought materials at their disposal. They can shape their people's convictions, and they can ultimately, even,

By carefully manipulating major cultural symbols, political leaders around the world attempt to infuse their own leadership with authority and shape their people's convictions and emotions. In control of these, they can the more easily sway large groups of people. (Courtesy of Wide World Photos)

exert a great deal of control over their people's emotions (Hertzler 1965:287–289).

Language itself is a form of social control. No matter what political system we happen to live under we all acquire a mother tongue. This native language contains a basic structure which directs our thought and action. Thus we all come under the control of persons long since dead, the countless people who originated and modified our language long before we were born. The heavy hand of the past lies on us all, for none of us can assign arbitrary meanings to terms and be understood. Linguistic meaning is a collective creation which is antecedently given, symbols by which our thought is manipulated by those who have lived before us (Mills 1967b:434).

Although all of us, through language, come under the control of ancestors and politicians, by the use of language we also bring others under our control. Even greetings control behavior. In saying "Good morning," we establish an entirely different context for behavior than by saying, "Ugh! I have to look at you again!" In many ways such simple verbal rituals as greetings not only permit but also compel reciprocal reaction from the other. In countless similar ways all of us as a daily part of our lives influence and even manipulate others by the use of words, while we ourselves are similarly influenced and manipulated. We praise, we flatter, we gossip, we call other names, we are satirical and threatening, cajoling and sincere, open and reticent—and in so doing we influence others and are ourselves influenced. Such is the power of words (cf., Hertzler 1965).

Though we all influence others through words, most of us influence only a few others. Most of our linguistic influence is limited to the few members of our **primary groups** (the intimate, expressive relationships which are extended over time: our family and friends) and to a few people in our **secondary groups** (the more formal groups to which we belong, such as those at work or in clubs). It is one thing to influence others by how we greet them in the morning, but quite another to control the basic concepts from which people view the world. To thus linguistically **structure reality** for people is power. One measure of the amount of power a person possesses is the number of people whose basic concepts he controls. This is the basic reason that each repressive government wishes to control the press, showing why, if we wish to maintain at least some degree of freedom in structuring our own realities, such attempts must be vigorously rejected.

In spite of the fascinating significance of language in determining what we perceive, how we evaluate what we perceive, and what our personalities will be like, most of us are unaware of the critical part language plays in everything we do. We are born into a language, and from the moment of our birth to our last breath at death "we are literally bathed in a sea of words." We live not only within a world of physical objects, as do animals, but also within a world of ideas, a system of interpreting the world. This world of ideas, or **ideational framework,** by which humans give meaning to their experiences in life is rooted in language. Though without language we would have no future and no past, we would participate in little cooperative action, our creative potentialities would be almost completely undeveloped, our personalities would be startlingly different, and we would not even think as we do, we are generally unconscious of the central role of language in our lives. Language, like light and air, is an aspect of human life we seldom question or analyze (Hertzler 1965:19–20; 42; 69); yet it is central for the sociological understanding of why people are the way they are.

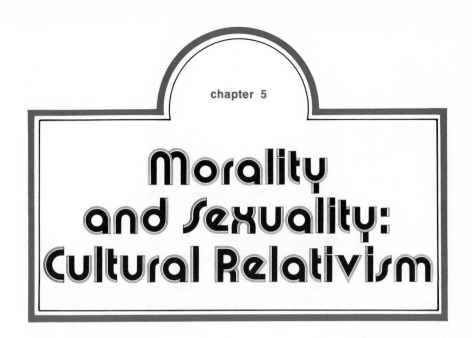

chapter 5

Morality and Sexuality: Cultural Relativism

By virtue of their birth children gain membership in a group which has its particular history and its unique way of doing things. Entrance into a culture, as we have discussed in Chapters 2, 3, and 4, means entrance into a world already constructed. Essential to this process of becoming part of this world is learning the group's ideas of what is proper and improper. The **morality** a person possesses, his judgment of the rightness and wrongness of behavior, is a consequence of his group membership. Different groups, different ideas of right and wrong. Different groups, different morality.

Morality is of utmost concern to sociologists since people's ideas of right and wrong so heavily influence their behavior. Human sexual behavior is particularly surrounded by ideas of right and wrong. Wherever you go around the world, each human group has specific ideas about what constitutes sexual propriety. We shall focus on this basic human activity as we sketch a sociological understanding of morality.

Although the human sex drive is universal, how that drive is expressed is far from universal. This basic part of our biological heritage, which ordinarily seems so personal and intimate, is regulated by society. No society in the world regards sex as purely a personal matter. In each society rules about sexuality are firmly laid down, examples of good and bad are held up to the members of the group, and by both example and precept newcomers to the group are socialized into the group's framework of sexual morality.

Perhaps the basic reason that societies around the world attempt to regulate how their members express their sex drive is because human sexuality is intimately tied up with the institutions of society. **Marriage,** for example, is the way the group defines proper, extended sexual relationships. More than group control over private sexual relationships is involved in marriage, however. Through establishing marriage practices, the group also exerts control over the formation of new family units, the birth and socialization of children, the granting of status, the division of labor, and the acquisition and inheritance of property. Because the larger group usually has a significant stake in seeing that marriage is carried out in the way it considers proper, though marriage is both intimate and personal it is far from being merely an individual matter.

Marriage is a central part of the traditional ideas and customs of a society regarding proper relations between the sexes. All societies have basic, traditional ideas concerning how people are expected to interact. Some people are expected to act one way, others another; certain persons are granted privileges denied others in the group, and so on. In whatever way a society is structured, these fundamental ideas concerning basic relationships between people are part of the established and accepted social order. They provide the core of the basic expectations within which people live out their lives, the framework of expectations by which they measure or evaluate one another.

The human sex drive, however, is imperious. It can propel individuals into acts and relationships which the group might merely consider ill-advised, into behavior looked upon as improper, or even into activities which the group defines as criminal. Such activities and relationships present in some way a threat to the status quo, to the established social order, to the acceptable or customary way of doing things.

Because of the imperious nature of the human sex drive, and because of the close connection between the sex drive and the basic order of a society, such as its forms of marriage, property, division of labor, and the socialization of children, all societies attempt to control the ways their people express their sex drives. The ideas, expectations, and norms (rules) concerning human sexuality become an essential part of the group's culture. They become major mechanisms for controlling human behavior, ways by which behavior is channeled and shaped into a form the group considers proper or right.

The child needs his group in order to survive. Unlike most animals, the child's dependency period is a long one. It takes many years after birth for a child to be able to get along without his parents or some other adults who take their place. Each of us, however, even after we become adults, is always dependent on others for our well-being. Truly none of us is an island unto himself. We always need other people. We depend upon others not only for our physical needs but also for our ideas about the world. But the first few years are especially critical in this shaping process. We are born without ideas about the world, and our basic or primary group fills this void by teaching us what the world is like from its perspective. In order to remain in good standing in that group so essential for our survival, we must follow the expectations of others concerning what is "correct and proper" in life, including their expectations concerning the expression of our sex drive.

One of the first things a youth learns about expectations of sexual behavior is that he is not permitted sexual relations with his parents or his **siblings,** his brothers and sisters. This prohibition against sexual intercourse and marriage among certain relatives is known as the **incest taboo.** Although the incest taboo is found throughout the world, the form that it takes varies widely. Some cultures primarily prohibit sexual relations between parents and their children and between brothers and their sisters, but in other cultures marriage between first cousins is also prohibited, as in twenty-one of the states in this country (Caprio 1955:190). In some cultures first cousins on the mother's side call each other brother and sister and regard marriage and sex with one another with horror. Yet in these same cultures marriage between first cousins on the father's side may be desirable, and in some cases, even mandatory. Other peoples do not necessarily consider blood relationships in the same way we do (Herskovits 1972:19).

In some cultures the incest taboo is greatly extended, and sexual relations are prohibited among persons for whom we readily permit marriage. The Mundugumor of New Guinea, for example, have a greatly extended incest taboo. Because of the complex way they reckon blood relationships, for a Mundugumor man not only are his sisters and mother ineligible sex partners, but so are 75 percent of all the women in the society. Seven of eight women are also ineligible marriage partners for Mundugumor men because of their greatly extended incest taboo. The Mundugumors are so incest-conscious that they also feel that if a man marries a woman young enough to be his daughter, no matter what their physical or social relationship, it is close to incest. The Mundugumors become upset because they feel that if a woman can even be classified in the same generation as a man's daughter it is too close for comfort (Mead 1950:157–58).

Not only do cross-cultural studies demonstrate that some groups greatly extend the incest taboo beyond the **nuclear family,** the group consisting of parents and their children, but these studies also show that some groups permit sexual relationships among persons for whom sex is almost unthinkable in American culture. For example, the Thonga of East Africa permit a hunter to have sexual intercourse with his daughter before he goes on a lion hunt, and the Azande of Central Africa permit male members of their high nobility to marry their own daughters (La Barre 1954:123). Some sexual relationships which are definitely incest for Americans are even required in other places in the world. Probably the best examples of this are ancient Egypt, the Incas of Peru, and the old kingdom of Hawaii. In these cultures brother-sister marriages were required for members of the high nobility (Beals and Hoijer 1965:515).

Although what is defined as incest varies from group to group around the world, no human social group permits its general populace to practice sexual relations between siblings or between parents and their children. Groups that do permit sexual relations between members of the nuclear family, other than between the parents, do so only for particular classes of their people, such as the nobility, or for special situations, such as the Thonga lion hunters the night before a big hunt. A situation uniquely handled by the Burundi of tropical Africa permits mother–son sexual relations. If a new husband is found to be impotent, the young Burundi bride gets up the morning after the wedding, walks to the center of the compound, and announces to the village in a loud, clear voice: "I did not come here to go to bed with another girl." The Burundi believe that a son's impotence is the fault of the mother, that she must have inadvertently allowed the dried umbilical cord to fall on the male organ of her newborn son. Just as the impotence is the mother's fault, so the cure is also up to her. The parents get their son drunk on beer, the father leaves the house, and the mother then has intercourse with her son. It is reported that the Burundi place much confidence in the success of this remedy and that it allows the young couple to be reunited in order to face the "other risks" of married life (Albert 1963:49).

From cross-cultural studies, then, we find that sexual practices regarding the incest taboo differ markedly among different peoples. Some cultures not only tolerate but also approve and in some cases even prescribe father-daughter, brother-sister, and mother-son sexual relations, something Americans find extremely abhorrent. To persons in such cultures, however, these behaviors are not shocking, abhorrent, or revolting. On the contrary, they are defined by people in these groups as natural forms of behavior. *Group membership determines what people consider to be moral or immoral behavior,* what they look at as right or wrong, proper or improper, acceptable or unacceptable in life. *This principle applies* not only to sexual behavior but *to the evaluation of all human behavior.* A person growing up within a particular culture or social group learns to view the world from the perspective of that group. There is no "natural" morality, but morality is dependent on the ideas one acquires from one's culture. Morality is part of what may be called our **social or cultural inheritance.**

Incest itself is not only relative (no pun intended), as we have seen, but it is also probable that all of us experience sexual desires toward members of our nuclear family as a regular part of our growing up. It is not likely that people have a natural abhorrence to incest. On the contrary, because people who grow up in the same family usually have similar attitudes, values, needs, and background factors, mate selection *within* the nuclear family would probably be a very frequent choice if it weren't for the existence of the incest taboo (Lindzey 1967). In other words, it is probably a social rule prohibiting incest which keeps us from having sex with our close relatives.

If this strikes you as an idea so extreme that it couldn't possibly be true, it is probably due to your being so thoroughly socialized into our form of the incest taboo from such an early age. We find, for example, that incest is actually not as uncommon in the United States as most of us think. The incidence of incest in the United States is approximately five cases for each thousand persons, but most cases of incest go unreported because of fear of retaliation or because of embarrassment (Karpman 1954; Oliver 1967:77; Lindzey 1967). We have this rate in spite of our severe informal prohibitions and even in the face of formal penalties threatening lengthy imprisonment.

The idea that it is *normal* for daughters to want to go to bed with their fathers and brothers and for sons to want to go to bed with their mothers and sisters is certainly a strange idea for most of us. But the naturalness of incestuous desires has even been made a cornerstone of psychoanalytic theory. Freud theorized that for adequate socialization it is essential for a child to overcome his sexual desires toward the parent of the opposite sex and transfer these desires onto someone whom the social group defines as proper, a person of the opposite sex who is not a member of his family. Freud also theorized that men who fail to adequately transfer their sexual desires from their mothers suffer from an **Oedipus Complex,** while women who fail to overcome their sexual attraction for their fathers are marked by an **Electra Complex.** Such persons are thought to make an unsatisfactory adjustment to members of the opposite sex. I don't want to give the impression that sociologists emphasize what Freud taught or theorized, because most don't, but I'm mentioning Freud because his ideas have had such great influence on Western thought. They also lend further support to the idea that incest, or at least incestuous desires, are a normal part of life. But, as with other sexual desires, it is the group's influence through social norms which largely determines how such desires shall be translated.

With such exceptions as the Thonga, Azande, and Burundi, and the ancient Egyptians, Incas, and Hawaiians, the incest taboo prohibiting sexual relations between close family members exists throughout the world. The sociological explanation for this general prevalence of the incest taboo centers around socialization. Through the family the new generation is given its fundamental introduction to life. Parents provide their children their basic orientation to the customary behaviors and belief patterns of the society they are joining. It is theorized that incestuous relations would complicate and disrupt this essential process of socializing the new generation into society.

For example, in a culture which has a nuclear form of the family, such as ours, if the father were to have intercourse with his daughter, could his role still be that of disciplinarian? Or must his role change to that of lover, which is quite a different matter? In this case, should the father console his daughter as a husband when his wife disciplines her, or should he reinforce the discipline as a father? Paternal incest would also lead to conflict between the wife and daughter. Should the wife treat her daughter as a rival or as a subservient second wife, or should she interact with her in the ways we ordinarily associate with the roles of mother and daughter? Husband-wife relationships would also become more complicated. Would, for example, the wife become the husband's main wife, or would she be a wife relegated into a secondary position? Or would she even be "the mother of the other wife?" Father-daughter incest would thus disrupt relations between the father and daughter, mother and daughter, and husband and wife. Similar disruptions would occur with maternal incest.

Such disruptions are called **role conflict.** Role conflict means that what is expected of a person in one relationship or role is incompatible with what is expected of him in another relationship. Each person occupies certain positions in life, or plays certain roles, such as those of daughter, mother, student, employee, and so on. In role conflict, if a person meets the expectations or obligations attached to one role, his behavior conflicts with the obligations belonging to another role. It is felt that the role conflict resulting from incest within the family would lead to insurmountable problems which would greatly interfere with socializing children into becoming the type of adults the larger group desires. Accordingly, we find, with certain patterned exceptions as we have already noted, that the incest taboo in the nuclear family is common throughout the world (Malinowski 1930:630; 1955:210–217).

This emphasis on varying cross-cultural attitudes and behaviors regarding the incest taboo is meant to underline the point that the group in which one grows up determines the morality one will have and to demonstrate the diversity of morality to which socialization in different groups leads. If someone grows up in a culture in which lion hunters cohabit with their daughters before a big lion hunt, he will consider this to be the right way of handling things. If he grows up in a society where impotent males solve their problem by having sex with their mothers, he will consider this to be the proper way of taking care of that problem. *These actions are moral* within the framework of the expectations established by the particular culture.

In our society, however, such activities are quite different matters entirely. We don't have many lion hunters in our midst, but we do have impotent males. If impotent males in the United States were to try this "cure," they would not be likely to receive laudations for their efforts. They would be more likely to be arrested because they have violated the law. Or they might well be incarcerated in a mental hospital because "normal" people would not think of doing such a thing. Perhaps if the matter were handled more informally, such an individual might simply be "ridden out of town" and told never to show his face again. A few years back, tar and feathering might have done the job, but in one way or another such known offenders will be quickly and not so gently removed from our midst as a "threat to morality." They would be thought of not only as mentally deranged, but also as threatening the very structure and well-being of society. Yet, in the culture of the Burundi, this same behavior is approved, and a mother who refused to cooperate with this expectation would be viewed as failing in her maternal duty.

In order to gain a better understanding of the sociological perspective of morality and to place American behavior patterns within a broader cultural perspective, we shall look at other examples in the areas of sex and marriage. We find, for example, that societies differ drastically regarding their views about premarital pregnancy. At least one society, the Mentawei of Indonesia, requires that a woman give birth to a child *before* she is allowed to marry. By giving birth to a child she demonstrates her fertility to potential husbands and her consequent desirability as a wife. Additionally, among the Banaro of New Guinea a girl is required to become pregnant and bear a child before her husband is ever allowed to have sexual relations with her. Banaro wives must bear a child fathered by a specified friend of the groom before the groom is allowed to have sex with his young wife (Murdock 1949:5).

Although this particular requirement for marital sexual relations probably sounds strange to those of us who have been socialized into the values of American culture, upon reflection it appears that perhaps our own customs regarding premarital pregnancy are also rather strange. For example, not only have we given up chaperonage in our culture, but we also permit and even encourage situations in which our youth are able to participate in premarital sexual relations, such as using automobiles for dating, attending drive-in theatres, and going to house parties where the parents are absent. Yet, although we have developed dating patterns which greatly contribute to premarital sexual intimacies, we soundly and righteously condemn the product of those intimacies, premarital pregnancy. Wouldn't this conflicting pattern appear strange to persons who weren't so thoroughly accustomed to it that they took it for granted as the normal way of doing things?

Although contemporary Americans allow divorce and remarriage, thus tolerating having more than one spouse as long as it is only one spouse at any given time, we otherwise practice strict **monogamy.** Monogamy appears to us to be the "normal" way of marriage, and as long as we are exposed only to a society that allows one mate at a time per member, we continue to think of it as normal. It might come as something of a surprise, however, to find that of 238 societies which were studied, only 43 practice monogamy while 195 follow a form of marriage in which an individual is able to have more than one spouse at the same time (Murdock 1949:24). As **marriage** is simply the way a group legitimizes the more or less permanent sexual relationships common within the group, it is not surprising that the form of marriage varies around the world.

Some societies practice **polyandry,** in which a woman is allowed to have more than one husband at the same time; some practice **polygyny,** in which a man may have more than one wife at the same time; and others are thought to have practiced **group marriage,** in which there are two or more husbands and two or more wives at the same time. One of the strangest forms of marriage, at least from the perspective that Americans view "strangeness," is the custom of the Nayars of Malabar (La Barre 1954:112–113; Gough 1959). Prior to puberty Nayar sisters are married at the same time to the same husband. Their groom, however, is not allowed to have sexual intercourse with any of his wives, and three days after the marriage all the girls are divorced from their common husband. The divorced husband disappears forever from their lives after receiving gifts from the family. The Nayar women are allowed lovers, but their lovers can never be their divorced husband. They bear children fathered by their lovers, but their lovers have no economic responsibilities to the children and never receive the status of husband, as Hindu Law says that a woman may have only one legal marriage in her lifetime. The male who exercises authority over the children is the woman's eldest brother, not the father or the lover. No doubt this form of marriage strikes you as very strange, but our marriage form, with either the expectation of spending approximately fifty years with the same spouse or of having a series of legal spouses

Each society develops customs to maintain social order by channeling relationships among its people. Marriage is a means of legitimizing the more or less permanent sexual relationships which have become common within a society. Shown here is a wedding ceremony in the Philippines. (Courtesy of The American Museum of Natural History)

during one's lifetime, would probably also strike the Nayars as being rather strange.

Although the custom of mate swapping appears to be growing in contemporary United States (Bartell 1971), this practice is ordinarily considered to be immoral by Americans. In one particular group, however, not only is mate swapping not considered immoral, but morality expectations are just the opposite of ours: For a woman not to have sex with someone to whom her husband sends her is considered wrong. The Eskimos practice wife-lending, and an Eskimo husband will beat his wife if she refuses to bestow her sexual favors on the man to whom he lends her. In the severe climate in which Eskimos live, a man who is going on a trip needs to take someone with him in order to prepare his food, to help prepare the game that he kills, and to chew his boots to keep them soft. It is necessary for survival for two to go on such a trip (Freuchen 1961:85), and the Eskimos feel strongly that this should be a heterosexual couple. If a man's wife is ill or indisposed, his neighbor will obligingly lend him his, and it is expected that he will return the loan if his neighbor finds himself in similar circumstances. If any Eskimo wife were to refuse to cooperate, she would be defined as unfaithful because she did not perform her wifely duties.

We might also note that the influence of our social group also extends to the sense of smell, and this has created problems for anthropologists doing field work among the Eskimos. To be a good host usually means to share good things with your guests, and this is as true for Eskimos as it is for Americans. Unlike Americans, however, a good Eskimo host shares his wife with an overnight guest, and both the husband and wife become extremely offended if a guest should be so rude as to turn down the offer. The expectation of accepting such generosity has created a dilemma for anthropologists. For some this dilemma has probably been moral, but apart from that, a major source of the difficulty is that Eskimos also believe that a woman makes herself erotic to a male by rubbing her face with blubber and perfuming herself by pouring urine over her hair (Ruesch 1959:65).

Expected age differences between marital partners are also culturally based. Although we have no formal rules concerning age differences between marriage partners in our country, we generally expect that husbands and wives will be somewhat similar in their ages, with the male typically being just slightly older than his wife. If there is a large disparity between their ages, we tend to think something is wrong, especially if the bride is much older than her husband. In extreme cases, such as if the bride is eighty and her groom sixteen, we might also tend to think that there is something "immoral" about the matter. We find that in some other societies, however, it is not unusual for there to be great dissimilarity in the ages between marriage partners. In some groups adults are even married to infants. The Chukchee of Siberia, for example, allow mature girls of about twenty to wed baby-husbands who are only two or three years old. The bride nurses her little husband and cares for him until he is old enough to fulfill his conjugal duties. The Chukchee feel that the parental care which the wife bestows on her baby-husband later creates a lasting emotional bond between them as husband and wife (Levi-Strauss 1956:273). The Tiwi of Northern Australia practice an even earlier marriage age. They marry off babies as soon as they are born. In some cases they marry them even before they are born. If it turns out that they made a mistake in guessing the sex of the child, upon birth the child is simply married to someone else (Hart and Pilling 1960:14).

Expectations concerning homosexual behavior also vary around the world. Some cultures, such as ours, demand that their members be exclusively heterosexual, but in forty-nine of seventy-six primitive societies studied (64 percent) some form of homosexual activity is considered both normal and acceptable. The Kerski of New Guinea require anal intercourse between males before they are allowed to have sexual relations with women (Ford and Beach 1952). The ancient Greeks placed a higher value on homosexual relations than they did on heterosexual ones (Licht 1952). One might think, because of the biological make-up of people, however, that heterosexuality in marriage would be required throughout the world. But in several parts of Africa women of nobility are allowed to marry other women. In these marriages an unacknowledged lover fathers the children. The mother then follows the prevailing rights of fathers and gives the child her name, status, and property (Levi-Strauss 1956:273; Querlin 1965:113).

Americans have come through a different history than have other peoples. They have faced unique problems, and they have, accordingly, developed their own ideas of what is right and wrong. Some of our cultural history traces back to the ancient Hebrews, where lineage was reckoned through the father, and we still give our children the last name of their father, dropping the mother's name entirely. Our cultural history also goes back to the early Christians, and we have from them a heritage which emphasizes the virginity of the bride, although this expectation is becoming increasingly honored only in the breach. From the early English we received an emphasis on romantic love which is still with us. From them we also received the practice of the double standard in which the female is expected to remain pure but the sowing of wild oats by the male, although not formally approved, is winked at. The double standard has become somewhat subdued in recent years, but it is still partially with us. From the American colonies we received the idea that sex is sinful, an activity of which God doesn't quite approve but which is necessary for propagation. Denigrating sexual relations, however, has greatly diminished in our current history, especially among our contemporary adolescents. From the American colonies we also received the idea that bachelorhood is a self-indulgent luxury. We retain carry-overs of this idea, and a great variety of pressure is put upon men to select a bride (Frumkin 1961). Those who fail to do so pay for their nonconformance on April 15 of each year.

In order to understand our ideas of morality, it is essential to understand our history. Current cultural beliefs and practices have not suddenly appeared in a historical void, and knowing whence we have come helps us to understand why we have our particular cultural traits. Knowing our past also helps us to understand the changes taking place in our current morality, the phenomenon known as the "sexual revolution." To understand change, we must understand where we have been, where we are, and the forces within our social milieu which are exerting pressures toward change.

The sociological perspective on morality, then, is that the basic values and behavioral patterns of any individual anywhere in this world are due to the group or groups into which he has been socialized. The values that you hold are as determined by your cultural, societal, and social location as are those of anyone and everyone else. The general culture into which you were born (e.g., Western culture), the society into which you were born (e.g., the United States), and your particular social location (i.e., your subgroup membership in society such as your sex, family, social class, and religion) are what form, shape, and determine your basic values, attitudes, goals, beliefs, and behaviors. This is true not only for you, but for every individual in the world. If you had been born into a different social location or had been socialized into a different culture or society, you would now possess an entirely different set of behaviors and values. What you believe about sex, love, marriage, heterosexuality-homosexuality, incest, proper ages for marital partners, and so on are but an accident of your birth and upbringing.

Behavior which in one culture is frowned upon, considered improper, and in some cases even makes an individual subject to a prison sentence may be approved in another culture. In some cases the proscribed behavior of one culture is even the requirement of another culture. Morality is dependent on the expectations contained in the culture into which one is socialized. Although we ordinarily think the contrary, there is nothing in an act itself which makes it bad or good. Bad and good are value judgments passed on acts according to standards which are relative to the culture.

"Now don't go joining any sex revolutions or anything."

We learn our values and behaviors through our membership in social groups. When change in our group membership means exposure to different ideas, it is often accompanied by changes in our values and behaviors. (Courtesy of Cartoon Features Syndicate. Cartoon by Weaver.)

Groups of people around the world develop over time ways of dealing with their particular problems. They try out various solutions. They find some of them successful, and they incorporate the ones they are satisfied with into their general expectations of what people should do in particular situations. These "tried and true" ways of handling problems, of getting along in the world, become the "expected way" of living—for them. The members of the group come to feel that theirs are the "right" behaviors, and they come to consider that behaviors which differ from theirs are inferior or even "immoral."

Each human group has not confronted the same problems in the same way. Nor has each group developed the same solutions even when they have dealt with the same problems. Any number of solutions exist to problems, and groups of people around the world happen on to a number of the possible ones as they work out their own realities. None is "more right" than another.

This is a **culturally relative perspective** of human behavior. In this perspective the patterns and characteristics of behavior of any group, including one's own, are viewed as being but one of a great number of possible patterns. In **cultural relativism** no pattern of behavior is looked upon as inherently superior, whether it is ours or not.

But cultural relativism is not the ordinary way people look at the characteristics of other groups. Most people do not view morality as relative, but they think of the behaviors they have learned as possessing an intrinsic quality which makes them right. We have a gut feeling against cultural relativism, a feeling that our morality is *not* "just one of a possible number of ways of behaving" but that it *is* the right way. This gut feeling is called **cultural** (or **phenomenal**) **absolutism,** and it is not peculiar to us. People around the world have it. People from every culture have a deep-rooted feeling that *their* way is the *right* way. All people tend to be ethnocentric because for all of us our basic morality, our fundamental ideas of right and wrong, is laid down at a tender age. During those first critical formative years, our parents, who appeared to us to be the very incarnation of authority and rightness, told us in no uncertain terms what was right and what was not right. We were punished in some way for doing that which was "not right," and rewarded for doing that which was "right." We learned that right and wrong were as different from each other as night and day, and it is no wonder that we retain a gut feeling for intrinsic rightness. We, consequently, are caught up in an emotional reaction whenever our basic ideas of right and wrong are challenged (Herskovits 1972).

Challenge is precisely what cultural relativism does. It views your behaviors as merely one of a number of behaviors you could have learned. It just so happened that you were born into one particular culture instead of another. If it had been another, not only would your behaviors be different from what they now are, but so would your ideas of right and wrong.

One of the major proponents of cultural relativism once came face to face with ethnocentrism, but the obverse of the way we usually experience it. Melville J. Herskovits, an anthropologist, arrived in Dutch Guiana to do field work among the Bush people. He brought with him much equipment for his survival and for his work. He also brought gifts for the people he was going to study. The Bush people consequently thought that he must be an important person, and they asked him how many wives he had. When he told them that he had but one wife, some thought that he was lying to them. Others, who believed him, thought that he was a very foolish man indeed to have just one wife when he could afford several. Still others thought that he should now begin behaving like a proper man, and they gave him the unexpected opportunity to acquire more wives (Herskovits 1972:102–103). Herskovits reports that he did not take anyone up on the offer.

In order to understand people, it is essential to try to view the world from their perspective. Only when we grasp how others define situations, how they have worked out reality, are we able to see what things mean to them. We then can work from within their framework of interpretation and make sense of the same things in the same way. Without this approach, all sorts of misunderstandings can arise, as when British radio broadcasts to Arab countries during World War II began with the crowing of a cock. Little did the British realize that the crowing of a cock was an obscene symbol to the Arabs (Herskovits 1972:86).

It isn't too difficult for Americans to understand the culture of Western Europe. Customs of various sorts differ from one Western European country to another, but the basic orientation regarding fundamental expectations of behavior is usually similar to ours, or at least the differences are ordinarily slight enough for us to adjust with but little difficulty. This is because we are closely related culturally to Western Europeans because of our immigrant past. We are sometimes, in fact, called Euro-Americans. But it is another matter entirely when it comes to understanding people from a non-European background, where the fundamental expectations of life laid down in childhood differ radically from ours. Then we literally move into different worlds. For example, an Arab is systematically trained as a child to use his left hand after urination and defecation, and his right hand for eating. Through harsh punishment and scandalizing rejection, absent-minded substitution of the wrong hand is entirely eliminated. Consider his plight when he sees an American put food in his mouth with his left hand. This sight is as revolting and disgusting to him as it would be for us to see someone wipe his mouth with dirty toilet paper (Campbell 1972:xviii).

Just as the Dutch Guianans and Arabs evaluate others according to their own standards, so we, too, are ethnocentric. Fortunately, we are less ethnocentric than we once were. Prior to World War II, most Americans were absolutists in their orientation to other cultures. They felt that there was only one proper approach to life, and that was the American way. Although we still have much of this attitude among us, it was previously much more extreme. Cultures were then thought of in terms of cultural evolution. People developed according to laws of social evolution, with societies moving along a fixed path. Each society had to go through fixed stages. We, of course, were at the top of this evolutionary scheme, and others were destined to go through the stages through which we had already passed. It even became a "scientific" theory that primitive peoples did not think in the same way we "more advanced" people do. Their thinking was thought to be less logical than ours, taking more the form of a sort of "prelogical mentality" (Herskovits 1972:6–7, 27).

Although we are all ethnocentric in our orientation to life, which aids us in adapting to our own culture by leading us to seldom question the norms in which we are immersed, ethnocentrism can greatly impede our understanding of others. Misunderstandings between cultures today are more serious than ever before, as they could touch off the final conflagration that would engulf us all.

The world is shrinking. Not the physical world, but the cultural world. At one time we were greatly isolated from other cultures, and they from us. But no more. With recent technological advances, indeed breakthroughs, in communication and transportation, we are only separated by seconds from communicating with others anywhere on this planet, and just a few hours separate us from direct physical contact. The need for understanding other peoples is critical in our current era. With modern weapons systems, we cannot afford to be complacent in our understandings. We cannot afford the luxury of allowing misunderstandings to go uncorrected. To gain the perspective of the other is essential in this critical process of understanding other cultures. This is where cultural relativism can play an important role in overcoming our in-built ethnocentric biases by helping us to accept other cultures *on their own terms.*

3

Living Within Society

chapter 6

Life as Symbol: The Symbolic Interaction Perspective

Human beings live within a meaningful world, that is, what they see, what they hear, or what they otherwise experience has meaning for them. Meaning, however, as we studied in Chapter 4, is not contained in the world itself but is abstracted from human experience. **Meaning** is an agreed-upon way of interpreting reality. When people agree on an interpretation of an object, event, or relationship, they are then able to use the object or event or a representation of it as a symbol to communicate that meaning to others. Events, objects, and relationships, as well as their representations, become part of the **symbolic world,** the common world of meaning which people share with one another.

To be human is to live within a world of symbols. To be socialized is to be able to correctly use the symbols of one's group. The concepts of language, for example, are symbols: They are sounds which *represent* something other than the sounds themselves. The concepts of language are sounds to which have been assigned arbitrary or agreed-upon meanings. The concepts of a language do not automatically convey meaning, but people must learn what the sounds represent. This, in short, is what **symbols** are: They represent something beyond the immediate situation, and they are capable of conveying meaning to someone who has learned what they represent. A symbol can be anything. It is any object, event, relationship, situation, or any other thing to which people attach meaning and by which they communicate meaning with one another.

Studying how people use symbols and the role symbols play in the construction of reality as people interact with one another is what the

symbolic interaction perspective in sociology is all about. Length of hair, for example, is symbolic. That is, length of hair is not just hair of a certain length, but represents something other than the hair itself. Hair length is a symbol which communicates information to others. When the Beatles burst upon the social scene in 1963, their hair length created an amazing furor around the Western world. Adults picked up a message they felt was "encoded" and "transmitted" in the Beatle's hair style. And, for the most part, they didn't like the symbol. They found the message extremely disagreeable.

Length of hair, however, as with the rest of the world, has no inherent meaning. Whatever meaning length of hair has for anyone is meaning which humans have arbitrarily attached to it. Human beings make hair symbolic, for hair, by itself, is simply hair. But people *give meaning* to length of hair, and hair then becomes a symbol. As with all symbols, it then represents whatever particular meaning people have given it.

The major symbolical aspect of hair centers around the division of the sexes. As I mentioned in Chapters 2 and 3, the divisions between the sexes are the strongest in the lower classes. It is here in American society where the most traditional ideas of sexual divisions are maintained. Men are strongly felt to be one way, women quite another. And in the symbolic sense, never the twain shall meet. Some things are felt to apply only to men, others only to women. A "real man" looks and acts differently than a woman. Men communicate to others that they are "real men" by surrounding and immersing themselves in a symbolic world which represents their idealized form of manliness. By using symbols, they communicate to others that they are rugged and tough, the essence of masculinity as defined by their group.

As with the values we discussed in Chapter 3, symbols also come in clusters. These interrelated symbols combine to communicate an integrated message about the person. By means of clothing, tatoos, fingernail length, hair length, ways of speaking, and ways of walking, men *symbolically separate* themselves from women. They symbolically stake a claim to a unique sexual identity. The walk that is meant to distinguish men from women in its exaggerated form can be described as a sort of swagger. Their speech may be liberally sprinkled with "cuss words," which are thought appropriate for men but not for women because "men are like that." Similarly, they tell jokes centering around sexual exploits, which are often thought inappropriate for "ladies."

As values often become intimately interconnected with morality, so do symbols. As we covered in previous chapters, at a tender age people receive their basic orientational framework regarding what the world is like and what their place is in that world. One major aspect of the socialization process is that males and females learn how they *ought* to

Although by today's standards they appear conservative, the Beatles' violations of the basic symbol of hair length touched off controversy throughout the Western world, ushering in not only stylistic changes but also radically transforming the meaning of this symbol. (Courtesy of Wide World Photos)

be. These expectations of sexuality provide an essential *identity* for the individual. This is an internalized identity which people externally symbolize.

To violate these fundamental expectations of the way people *are* becomes a moral issue. People can violate these expectations by doing something which does not meet the standards attached to their sex. In such cases, the behavior itself becomes symbolic of inappropriateness. But to violate expectations, it is not necessary that people *do* something. They can simply *look* wrong, that is, they can use the wrong symbols.

This is the basic reason there was such a furor over the Beatles: Through their hair length the Beatles symbolized a violation of the traditional division between the sexes. Long hair represented femininity: The Beatles weren't females, yet they wore long hair. Something was fundamentally, morally wrong. Basic aspects of sexual identification were being directly challenged by means of this simple, but complex, symbol. It does not matter whether or not the Beatles knew they were involved in so basic a challenge or whether their startling appearance was merely for publicity or group identification or whatever. Original motivation aside, as the Beatles ushered in this challenge, they brought a symbolic revolution along with it.

A basic characteristic of symbols is that they are subject to change. As the meaning of any symbol is not inherent in the symbol, but symbols simply possess whatever meaning people give them, people are well able to change the meaning attached to a symbol. So it is with hair. If one looks at a picture of the early Beatles, it is difficult to see what people found upsetting, for the Beatles had fairly short hair compared with many of the current hair styles for men. But that is because hair as a symbol has undergone a major change in meaning. Long hair no longer simply represents femininity, or a few occupations not in the symbolic mainstream such as scientist and musician. The meaning has

Because the meanings of symbols are arbitrary, they are subject to wide variation and change. Hair is one of the better recent examples of a symbol undergoing drastic change in content. (Courtesy of Wide World Photos)

changed, and today long hair can represent anything from "being hip" to hippies, from radical nonconformity to rigid conformity with changing styles.

In a pluralistic society, symbols can and do vary with the groups making up the society. Members of different social classes, for example, symbolically separate themselves from other social classes. By using symbols, they stake a claim to a unique identity. Items of clothing, ways of speaking, and "general bearing" are major symbols in this process of claiming and maintaining a separate identity. Though it is difficult to specify exactly what they mean, people speak of "more refined" gestures being used as one goes up the social class ladder and "coarser manners" becoming more common as one descends the social class ladder. Whether these particular descriptions are apt or not, they do indicate a common recognition of social class differences, pinpointing behavioral symbols separating the social classes.

Because the meaning of a symbol depends upon the meaning people give it, different groups in a pluralistic society can give the same symbol different meaning. Hair, to continue our example, no longer has the same meaning in the middle and upper classes as it does in the lower class. There are still some lower class bars, for example, which a "longhair" is well-advised to avoid. If he enters these bars, he will be at least harassed, if not physically assaulted. It is doubtful that the same is true for bars habituated by members of the middle and upper classes.

The reason members of the lower class have been less amenable to hair change is probably their financially unpredictable working situation, as mentioned in Chapters 2 and 3. They enjoy considerably less security and well-being in our society than do members of the other social classes. This may well lead to their making other parts of their lives more secure, that is, they can increase the predictability of at least part of their lives by emphasizing the firm nature of the symbolic ordering of social relationships. Members of all social classes symbolically order social relationships, such as between the sexes, which underlies the resistance hair style changes initially met in all the social classes. But in the lower class world, filled with such greater uncertainty and insecurity, these symbolic differences between the sexes may well take on greater significance. With a world so uncertain, so subject to change in spite of one's best intentions and efforts, at least one should be able to count on women being women and men being men. Because the sexes are viewed as being essentially different, it is felt to be only right that they also look different. But if this, too, changes, the world becomes just that much less predictable and orderly.

Though resistance to this change has perhaps been greater in the lower class, it does not mean that the change will not come about. Sports figures are highly admired among working class males, and what happens especially in baseball and football is ardently followed in lower class bars and homes. As sports heroes wear longer hair, it should become increasingly difficult for working class males to look up to them and not see that their long hair has nothing to do with their degree of masculinity.

A central sociological significance of symbols is that they establish boundaries. They provide identity by differentiating between members and nonmembers, just as hair length has traditionally served as a boundary-maintaining mechanism in the Western world. Each group in society adopts symbols it feels are appropriate and fuses those symbols with particularized meaning. The symbol then sets off those who belong from those who do not belong, as with the "secret" handshakes of lodges, fraternities, and even Boy Scouts. Similarly, groups adopt particular clothing or uniforms, insignia, rings, and so on, some of which we shall treat more fully in the following chapter. Christians and Jews claim identity from non-Christians, non-Jews, and from each other through the symbols of the Cross and Star of David. Specific groups within these larger divisions also symbolically establish a claim to their unique subidentities, such as the Jehovah's Witnesses use of a unique translation of the Bible.

Symbols are especially significant in establishing subcultural identification. The religious-ethnic subculture of the Amish is characterized, among other things, by black clothing, horse-driven carriages, restrictions against electricity and telephones, and distinctive farm implements, furniture, and books (Hostetler 1970:9). The lower class black male subculture utilizes hats, a particular walk (one of its extremes is called the "pimp's walk") (Suttles 1968), and smooth, rhythmic gestures. Though the particular symbols adopted by members of each subculture vary, each symbol is infused with meaning which the members use to communicate with one another, through which they subscribe to some common fate or identity, and by which they separate themselves from nonmembers.

Symbols operate similarly on the international scene. Nations adopt symbols which represent their unique identity among the nations of the world and through which they impart a national identity to their citizens. Central in these national symbols, of course, is the flag. But language is at least as important a symbol. Language is not only composed of symbols, but language itself also serves as a symbol of national identity, as in the phrase, "the English-speaking nations." The importance of language for national identity was driven home to me during a stay in Belgium. As an **outsider,** that is, one who does not sympathetically

By means of symbols nations also stake a claim to unique identity. By infusing objects with meaning, the members of a nation subscribe to a common fate or identity which separates them from nonmembers. (Courtesy of The United Nations)

understand the symbols of a group from the perspective of the group's members, I thought of the tiny country of Belgium as a single unit. I was informed in no uncertain terms that there was no such thing as a "Belgish" people, as indicated by there being no "Belgish" language. There were the Flemish, who had their own culture with its own language, its own artists, its own symbols with which members identified, and there were "the French" who merely lived in a part of Belgium. *They* did not have their own culture, but even spoke French as their native tongue. My, need I add, Flemish informant also stated that the Flemish desired to secede and form their own country, with its own national symbols, including Flemish currency in place of the current Belgian *francs.*

Primarily by amplifying the example of hair, I have analyzed several aspects of the symbolic interactionist perspective. In summary, symbols are a representation of something other than the symbol itself; they provide a major means by which people agree upon the meaning of the world and thus make their lives more predictable and orderly; they are vitally connected with morality; they are subject to change since their existence and use is dependent upon the meaning which people give them; the same symbol can have different meaning for different groups; and symbols establish boundaries and provide a unique identity for members of various groups, subcultures, and nations. We shall now turn to another major aspect of the symbolic interactionist perspective: the symbolic nature of the rise, maintenance, and change of the self.

Symbols are instrumental in the development of the self. By **self** is meant that a human being can be an object of his own action, that is, "he can recognize himself, for instance, as being a man, young in age, a student, in debt, trying to become a doctor, coming from an undistinguished family and so forth" (Blumer 1969:12). The term "self" means that an individual is able to act toward his own person and guide his actions toward others on the basis of this type of awareness of his unique identity, that is, he is able to guide his actions on the basis of who he perceives himself to be.

Essential to the symbolic interactionist perspective is the view that people are neither born with a self nor is the self something which automatically and mysteriously unfolds from within the individual. The self is a gift from society, not inborn in people. The self emerges or develops through social interaction. The self develops because we are members of social groups. The **primary group,** which as we noted in Chapter 4 is composed of persons who meet on an extended, expressive, intimate, and face-to-face basis, is especially significant in the development of the self. The primary group is the first group an individual joins. He is first a member of a family and later a member of a play group. These, as well as later primary groups in life, are the most significant groups in the development of the self (Cooley 1962). It has been said that the primary group is something like a social midwife to the biological individual, nursing it into the self and ultimately into a practicing member of society (Anderson 1971:18).

It is through **role taking** that the self develops, that is, the ability to put oneself in the shoes of someone else. The child first goes through a **play stage** in which he takes the role of particular individuals, one at a time. He attempts to play the role of his father or mother, or a policeman, priest, cowboy, and so on. By taking the role of an individual in the play stage, the child begins to obtain a view of himself from the outside, so to speak, and the self begins to be organized. He then passes through the **game stage** about the time he enters school. During this stage he begins simultaneously to take on the roles of several people. To participate in a baseball game, for example, he must be able to anticipate what the pitcher will do, the catcher, the basemen, and the outfielders. By mentally picturing their roles, or anticipating their actions toward him, he begins to see himself in relationship to others.

At this point he is developing the ability to think about his own person in the same way that he is able to think about any object in his

Taking the role of other persons is essential to the development of the self. By anticipating the actions of others toward oneself, one sees the self in relationship to others. Team games are one means by which this ability develops.   (Courtesy of Wide World Photos)

world. This is called **becoming an object to oneself.** Essential to one's becoming an object to himself is this capacity to take the role of others, to be able to think about what others expect of him, and to evaluate what he thinks their ideas of his performance are. He learns to put himself in their shoes and to think of himself from their perspective. In the game stage, he learns to mentally react to his own person as others would, and in this way he anticipates their roles in cooperative effort and their ideas of his role.

From the play stage, in which he took the role of but a single individual at a time, and the game stage, in which he simultaneously took the roles of more than one individual, he comes finally to the point that he is able to take the role of an abstract community. This abstract community is called the **generalized other.** This means that the individual has the capacity to think of what some larger group in society thinks about him or is expecting of him. The generalized other for a priest, for example, might be what he thinks priests in general or the laity in general think of him.

Note that the self arises, develops, and becomes organized through interaction with others. The individual internalizes what he thinks are the reactions of others to him. Essential in this process are **orientational others,** the significant persons who are around him during this formative period. They give specific form to the self. From them he learns his ideals, values, norms, morality. It is they who provide him his native language, which, as we saw in Chapter 4, has such a profound influence on his perception and on his being. From his orientational others he gains not only a perspective on the world but also a perspective on his own person. He learns who he is by the reactions of others to him. He internalizes his perceptions of these reactions, and these internalizations form the basis of his self—of who, how, and what he thinks he is (Kuhn 1964).

The self of the child undergoes much sharper fluctuations than does that of the adult. The child does not at first have much of a core on which to fall back upon, and sharp changes in the way others react to him (e.g., "You are a naughty, nasty boy!") are thought to result in related changes in the self. As the individual matures, he internalizes a wide range of experiences, which leads to greater stability in the way that he thinks of himself. Then when he is subjected to changes in his social environment which might otherwise lead to changes in his self concept, he has this solid core of previous experiences which he can fall back upon and by which he is able to interpret any particular interaction.

As the individual's circle of interaction widens, his conception of his self is modified. He incorporates and integrates his ideas of how others are reacting to him into his idea of who he is. In a pluralistic society, the individual is a member of many groups and enters into many contrasting relationships. Groups and relationships significant to him become important in this ongoing shaping process surrounding the self. Orientational others, significant in shaping the self, change during the life cycle of the individual. Where once parents were the most significant, later the peer group takes over, especially during adolescence. Later orientational others include one's spouse, close friends, and perhaps employees and employers in close working associations (Kuhn 1964). It is not as though the self, once arisen, is in the form it will always be. Just as the self arises in interaction (hence the phrase, "a gift from society"), so the self is modified by further interaction.

Systematic reactions by others tend to have a systematic effect on how an individual thinks about himself. For example, if only one person says that you are stupid, it is usually easy enough to throw this off and disregard it, knowing that a great number of other people think differently of you. But if several persons begin to react toward you in a somewhat consistent manner which you interpret as meaning that they think you are stupid, it is not as easy to handle. The tendency is to think of the self in a way somewhat consistent with the reactions of others.

In this example, the significance of orientational others can be emphasized. Suppose that the single individual who said that you were stupid was an orientational other, someone whom you respected and trusted. Suppose, moreover, that this person was dead serious in his evaluation and furthermore that you knew he had your best interests at heart. It would then not be so easy to throw off his evaluation, as orientational others are critical in giving shape to the self.

To say that we can "throw off" certain negative information given by others means that we can and do play an active role in maintaining our self-concept. We are not simply passive acceptors of the reactions of others. When negative imputations are made against the self, for example, the individual may well move into a protective reaction. Depending on who made the charge of stupidity in the above example, a number of courses of defensive action and self-evaluation would be open to the individual. If the reaction were from most of his teachers, he might quit school, syaing that higher education is not what he wants and that he has always wanted to become a plumber; if it were made by a particular teacher, he might drop quantum physics, let's say, and take other classes which he finds easier; if it were said by some of his buddies, and they were serious, he might give up his old friends; if it were his girlfriend, he might well soon be seen hand-in-hand with someone new; if it were his parents, he might move out of their home and take an apartment, join the armed services, or move to San Francisco and become a hippie. In one way or another the individual will take steps to protect the concept of self which he has so painfully developed through the years. Far from being an automaton, he will attempt to maintain the image that he has acquired of himself by actively protecting the particular object which he has become to himself.

From such an example, we can readily see the importance of how we react to others. Our reactions have a potential effect on the self-concepts of others. This is especially true during a child's early formative years when he does not yet have a solid core of experiences upon which his self is securely moored. For example, no matter how physically attractive a girl might be according to prevailing cultural standards, if she is consistently told by others, especially by those within her primary group, that she is ugly, she will tend to think of herself as ugly. She will incorporate or internalize this reaction by others into her self. To overcome such a negative view of the self would take consistent reactions by others in which they in one way or another communicate that she is not ugly, but beautiful or attractive or pleasing to look at. This is one of the most unfortunate aspects about poor teachers in grade schools. They can do such devastating harm to a child's partially developed self-concept. The child may well look up to his teacher as a sort of superior being, and if disparagement or even discouragement come from the teacher, it can work severe damage and have far-reaching consequences on the development of the self (cf. Dexter 1964).

To develop a good self-concept in children, it appears essential to consistently tell them when they are young that they match prevailing cultural values. For Americans this means telling them that they are "pretty," "smart," "good," and so forth. In some other culture it might mean being told that they are brave or generous or strong or psychic. We see ourselves through the eyes of others: What we think that others think of us becomes the way we think of ourselves. We see ourselves as reflected in others' reactions toward us. Thus the term **looking-glass self** is used to describe the anchorings of the self in our evaluations of the reactions of others to us (Cooley 1956).

Having a self allows a human being to act toward himself as he might act toward others. In symbolic interactionism the self is considered to be the central mechanism with which the human faces and deals with his world. He guides his actions through his consciousness of himself as an object. He is able to take note of the things in his environment, to think about them, and to act accordingly. He is able to evaluate others' ideas about him, reflect on them, and make changes in his behavior. In the symbolic interactionist perspective, human beings are not simply biological organisms which passively give off behavior in response to external stimuli. Rather, they confront the world. By actively involving themselves in the world, people are instrumental in making their own world (Blumer 1962:181).

An individual incorporates into his self-image new information from his interaction with others. As he internalizes this new information, his self-concept undergoes change. Changes in the self are usually so gradual that the individual has no difficulty seeing continuity between his behavior and his self. Sometimes changes in the self are so gradual, though cumulatively effective over longer periods of time, that the individual hardly notices that he has changed. When, however, he is brought face to face with an attitude or idea he once held but has now discarded, he can find the change in himself startling. At other times, change in the self is due to disjunctive experiences, that is, experiences incompatible with the self, and the self undergoes rapid change as the individual attempts to survive the trauma. This is frequently the case when an individual is jailed for the first time in his life: The experience is incompatible with his ideas about his self, and something must give. Similar situations pertain to boot camp, divorces, and incarceration in prisons and hospitals. A friend of someone who has undergone such experiences but who has not seen him for some time is likely to notice the contrast, rather than the continuity. He will notice differences between the former self and the current self and probably ask, "What happened to you? You're so different. You're not the same person I knew."

Not only does the individual become an object to himself, but so do particular aspects of his biography. Thus what one has experienced in the past can become a symbolic object. The individual remembers certain aspects of his past and interprets them in a particular way by fitting them into a conceptual framework. By interpreting past events, they take on meaning for the individual's present, with significant events of the past becoming symbolic rootings for the self. A girl who has lost her virginity in the back seat of a car, for example, has undergone an event significant for shaping the self. That event certainly has meaning for her. What that meaning is, however, is not built into the act itself, but like other symbols it depends upon the framework within which she interprets the event. She might look on the loss of her virginity rather matter-of-factly, as simply part of an inevitable metamorphosis from childhood to adulthood. She may fondly remember the event with pleasure, or it may symbolize the brutishness of men, or her own rebellion, or her "animal nature," or her weakness, or her key to finding the meaning to life through the love she shared. It could symbolize any of these and more.

But whatever this event symbolizes, its meaning can be turned around. Like all symbols the past is also not safe from reinterpretation. It, too, can be placed within a new framework and given new meaning. Suppose the girl is now converted to a fundamentalist sect. She learns about sin, and instead of sin being a vague, abstract concept she now directly and seriously applies it to her own life. Her past then takes on different meaning. The loss of her virginity now represents the work of the devil, the sin of the flesh, a sign of her former lost state. It now means ignorance, stupidity, and immorality (Berger 1963). The meaning of the symbol has been radically altered because the self has undergone significant change; and the past, a symbol intimately connected with the self, changes also.

In the preceding section of this book I placed heavy emphasis on the role of the cultural milieu in influencing people, in structuring what people become. In the first chapter, however, I briefly mentioned that not only are people being shaped by the events of history but they also play a role in shaping history. At this point I wish to emphasize that people are not simply passive agents in life. Humans actively confront their social and cultural worlds. Though the basic structure of culture and society determine much of what humans become, especially, as we discussed in the last three chapters through giving them a language and socializing them into a system of values and morality, people are far from automatons. People are active in creating their own worlds. They note what is in their world, evaluate these things, give them meaning, and act on the basis of that meaning. People are not merely subsumed under the forces that surround them, but they actively make decisions on how they will be and how they will act within their world.

Basic to their decision-making is a conscious process involving the self. People align their own actions to the actions of others by ascertaining through the interpretation of symbols the intentions of others. They determine for themselves the meaning of the acts of others. Essential to this process is "taking the role" of the others around them. By taking account of others and by evaluating their actions or potential actions towards them, they actively confront their world, interpret it, and act on that world. In this way, people actively participate in the construction of their world and purposely forge their conduct upon these interpretations. In order to understand people, then, it is essential to understand how people define their world (Blumer 1969:15–16).

This point touches directly and deeply into the heart of the symbolic interactionist view of human nature. According to the symbolic interactionist perspective, people are not only acted upon, but they also act; they are not only controlled, but they also control; they are not only influenced by symbols, but they also use symbols to influence others. Not only does language and other symbols set limits and determine orientations for people, but people also utilize linguistic and non-linguistic symbols to establish definitions and to effect changes in both their natural and social environments. People are, in other words, not only products of their environment but also actively involved in shaping that environment, and, ultimately, in shaping their own selves. From this sociological perspective, human beings are not viewed as being merely passively socialized into an already-made world which determines what they become. The focus in this perspective is on people as active agents in influencing the world that, in turn, has so much influence on them.

As I have especially emphasized in preceding chapters, in this process of self-involvement in defining reality, membership in groups is of the utmost importance. The self is an integration of experiences with others, and by the choices they make people have a hand in the development of their own selves. When someone chooses one job instead of another, one marital partner instead of another, one school instead of another, that individual is making choices between alternatives which have far-reaching effects on the development of his self. Whenever a person chooses a significant experience, he is not only choosing to involve himself in an activity which affects his self, but he is also choosing to forego another experience which would have affected the self differently. Whenever an individual gives primacy to one significant group or activity, the individual is actively involved in the development of his self (Kuhn and McPartland 1954).

Another type of group, one in which the individual is not necessarily a member, is also highly significant for people as they confront the world. People think about these groups when they are considering doing something or when they are evaluating something they have already done. These groups are called **reference groups.** Reference groups are groups to which an individual may or may not belong but to which he refers when he evaluates his situation in life or when he thinks about a particular course of action which is open to him. People frequently consider the consequences of their acts in terms of what others will think about them if they do or do not perform a certain action. They often make decisions to act or not to act according to their evaluation of the potential reactions of others. The groups people refer to at such times are their reference groups.

When deciding a course of action, people also consider the likely reactions of specific persons who are important to them, persons we might call **reference individuals.** For example, a male lawyer might have an attractive woman as his client in a divorce suit. During his conversations with her, he might find that she is not only attractive to him but also attracted to him. He might very well be tempted to initiate an affair with her, but in contemplating the consequences of such interaction (if he pauses to contemplate, that is), he may think of the reaction of his reference group ("What will the local bar association think of me if they find out about this?"), or he might consider how particular reference individuals might react ("What would my wife do if she found out?").

Reference individuals do not have to be physically near an individual for them to be important in this symbolic process. They can be spatially separated, as with a fiancé in the army. They do not even have to be alive. They can be both spatially and temporally separated, as with a deceased spouse; and it is not uncommon to find widows and widowers acting in a certain manner because the one to whom they were so close but who is now dead "would have preferred it that way." Reference individuals need not have ever lived. They can be entirely fictive, as with fictional and imaginary characters. Though the practice is more common with children, some adults reflect on how a fictional hero would think of their actions, and change them accordingly.

Parts of the symbolic interaction we learn are learned so early in life and are so consistently reinforced by others in our continuing interaction that it is difficult for us to even remember that we learned them, much less that they are arbitrary symbols used for communicating messages. We learn, for example, how to walk in the "right" way. We learn what it means to "walk like a man" or to "walk like a woman." Because we learn "how to walk" at a very tender age and because we do so much of it in the "right" way, our walk becomes so "natural" to us that we seldom think "how to walk": Our walk becomes "second nature" to us. A man with the "wrong walk," however, will almost immediately be thought of as effeminate, and a woman as masculine. It is also likely that others will suspect that such an individual is a homosexual or that he or she at least has homosexual inclinations.

Our way of walking is so ingrained into us that it is difficult for us to think of it as a form of learned behavior, but a cross-cultural perspective allows us to overcome our ethnocentric view of how men and women "naturally" walk. Men and women in the Tchambuli tribe of New Guinea, for example, have just the opposite "sexual walks" from ours. In this group the woman struts and swaggers, while her husband, with his "delicately arranged curls" and his "handsome pubic covering of a flying fox skin highly ornamented with shells," exhibits the greater hip undulation. Tchambuli expectations of behavior by sex are so contrary to ours, moreover, that it is the man who does the shopping, performs the household duties, and is the less responsible, emotionally dependent person. The Tchambuli woman, in contrast, is the more dominant, impersonal marital partner who does the fishing and trading and controls the family property (Mead 1950:172–190).

Our speech patterns are another example of symbols that are often not recognized as symbols by their users. Our basic speech patterns are taken-for-granted aspects of our selves. Though much of their symbolic aspects lie beyond our consciousness, speech patterns act as symbols as we interact with others. By our speech, others classify us as "being of that sort." Others then assumes that they "know" something about us because they have so classified us, that is, meaning of who or what we are comes about by fitting this symbolic aspect of our presentation of self into a conceptual scheme.

The symbolic nature of aspects of the self which are ordinarily below our awareness become much more apparent if we find ourselves in an unfamiliar environment or if they are otherwise called into question. In a radically different environment, such as in a remote part of a foreign country where tourists seldom venture, an American immediately recognizes his native countrymen. Even though one may be from Mississippi and the other from Massachusetts, suddenly the symbols of which we are ordinarily unaware but which we possess in common come into play, and each realizes that through them he "knows" significant things about the other.

Because people live in a world of symbols, by manipulating symbols we are able both to create and to maintain a particular view of the situation or definition of reality. Genital exposure, for example, is a form of behavior whose symbolic meaning makes it very disturbing for most Americans. We are socialized at a very early age into society's dictates concerning the situations and circumstances of allowable and unallowable genital exposure. Although infants appear to be unconcerned about who sees their genitals, parents do not seem to share this view, and at an early age they tell their daughters to "keep your dress down," "don't let your underwear show," and so on. When an American woman undergoes her first vaginal examination, it is frequently a traumatic experience. She must overcome her early socialization and learn to tolerate an unrelated man's examination of her "privates," which no longer remain private. To help overcome this problem, the medical profession manipulates various symbols in order to define a vaginal examination as asexual interaction. The doctor typically leaves the room to allow his patient to undress, although he will be present after she is undressed. The nurse remains in the room while the doctor examines the patient, playing the role of chaperone. A drape sheet is placed over the patient's breasts and legs in such a manner that it conceals her pubic region *from herself* but exposes it to the doctor. After the examination, the doctor again leaves the room so the woman won't be dressing in front of a man. Through such manipulations of symbols, the total interaction becomes defined as asexual. Yet it is a man who is digitally probing the vaginal area of a woman (Henslin and Biggs 1971). Through the manipulation or use of symbols, we all define our worlds of reality. In this particular case, without symbols the meaning of asexuality could not be maintained. Indeed, it is the complex manipulation of symbols which allows such interaction to exist.

This example illustrates collective action by individuals. By jointly manipulating symbols, people sustain a definition of reality which serves them all: It allows the physician to perform his work with a minimum of disruption and the woman to feel secure and "not violated." Whenever people work together in groups, they work within a definition of the situation which is maintained by means of the manipulation of symbols. This is true whether the group is as small as the doctor, nurse, and patient in a vaginal examination or whether it is as large as a modern army engaging in a campaign, a corporation seeking to expand its operation internationally, or a nation trying to correct an unfavorable balance of trade. A definition must be developed on the basis of symbols. By symbolically constructing and maintaining meaning, people are able to interpret reality in common with others. They are able to agree on the meaning of what is happening, and to act accordingly. The "meanings" of symbols are formed, sustained, weakened, strengthened, or transformed, as the case may be, through interaction (Blumer 1969:16, 20).

Understanding the symbols in the social world not only helps us to understand the behaviors of individuals, but it also leads to an understanding of larger subcultural groups interacting within society, and even of societies interacting with or reacting to one another. The understandings we gain through symbolic interactionism are an important part of the sociological imagination, for they enable us "to link the private and the public, the innermost acts of the individual with the widest kinds of social-historical phenomena" (Gerth and Mills 1964:xvi).

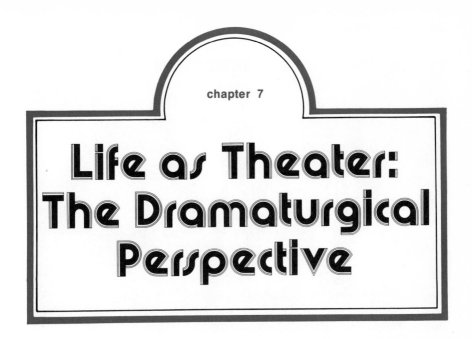

chapter 7

Life as Theater: The Dramaturgical Perspective

As we have just discussed, in the socialization process the newcomer to society learns the major symbols of his culture and the subgroups to which he belongs. Another way of saying that someone is a socialized member of society is to say that he is able to apply the symbols of his groups in an acceptable manner, that is, he knows the cultural meanings of objects, events, and interactions and is able to adequately manipulate these meanings in his everyday life with others.

Because humans are so adept at establishing meaning through manipulating symbols, sociologists frequently refer to people as actors. The name given the orientation in sociology which has acting and roles at its central focus is **dramaturgy.** In the **dramaturgical perspective** human life is viewed as being similar to the theater, with the analysis of behavior focused on the various masks people wear as they try to get their point across in their dealings with others. From this perspective the social world is looked at as being made up of actors and audiences, scripts and scenes, parts and performers, images and masks, costuming and make-up, directors and stars, stagehands and understudies, and presentations of roles and deliveries of lines on various stages.

Basic to the **dramaturgical analysis** is the idea that in all situations, from the most esoteric to the most mundane, people use symbols to communicate to others ideas about themselves. As we analyzed in the last chapter, each individual internalizes a self based upon his interactions with significant others. This internalized self is critical for the individual as he interacts with others, for people attempt to project the self to others through the use of symbols. A good part of everyday life

Basic to the dramaturgical perspective in sociology, based on the analogy of the theater, is the view that each person learns to play roles as an essential part of his or her socialization. Our everyday lives center around the performances we present to others, and they to us. (Courtesy of Wide World Photos)

centers around **impression management,** that is, as a regular feature of their lives, people constantly attempt to control or manage the impressions which others form of them. To analyze the means or techniques by which people in everyday life communicate ideas about themselves to others is what the dramaturgical perspective is all about.

To manage or control the impressions that others receive from and about us, we manipulate **sign-vehicles,** the ways we communicate information to others. Three major types of sign-vehicles are our appearance, our manner, and the social setting in which we interact. The **social setting** is the place the action unfolds. This is where the curtain goes up on our personal performances and we find ourselves onstage playing parts and delivering lines. The setting might be a classroom, an office, a bar, or a home. It is wherever we interact with others and includes whatever **scenery** is present, the furnishings used to decorate the setting such as desks or bar stools. We utilize settings to manage the impressions others receive about ourselves when we, for example, allow ourselves to be seen in certain places, but not in others.

Settings, with all their scenery, sometimes become so intimately associated with the actors who regularly perform in the setting that we often take the setting for granted. Like language, settings become so familiar to us that we ordinarily think little about them. Yet, settings are extremely important for determining what sort of interaction takes place. For example, the physician takes meticulous care to surround himself with scenery which communicates an elaborately contrived message about himself, usually that he is a person who reflects "good taste," that he is qualified by an excellent education, and that he is proficient at his work. Even the decor of his office is carefully selected to augment this message. By surrounding himself with scrupulously chosen items of scenery, not the least of which are the diplomas that hang conspicuously on the walls of his office, he attempts to manage an over-all impression of medical competence. The setting creates the desired effect: It reflects "good breeding," radiates confidence, and communicates trust, making people feel comfortable about the sort of doctor who is treating them. From the setting alone, even people who have never met him "know" that he is a doctor, and a good one.

The second major sign-vehicle which we use to control impressions is **appearance.** Appearance refers to how people look when they play their roles, including the props people use to manage impressions about themselves. **Props** are like scenery, but they decorate the person rather than the setting. The professor with his pipe, the student with his pencils and notebook, the executive with his suit and briefcase, and the factory worker with his lunch bucket and more casual clothes are all examples of people using props to communicate messages about their

"Afford it? Look—if everybody could afford this car, who would you impress?"

As a regular part of our everyday lives, all of us use props to communicate messages about ourselves. (Courtesy of Cartoon Features Syndicate. Cartoon by Bernhardt.)

roles in life. The use of make-up and one's hair style are also essential features in communicating self-messages through appearance. Props and other aspects of appearance serve as a sort of grease for everyday interaction: They aid people in their interactions by letting them know what to expect *from* others and how they should react *to* others.

As an ordinary feature of our everyday lives, all of us regularly use appearance to communicate messages about ourselves. By means of props we communicate to others that we belong to a certain sex, that we have attained a particular status in life, and even that we are some specific type of person. By clothing, for example the delinquent demonstrates that he is rough and ready, the executive and professor that they are respectable, the prostitute that she is available for a price, the judge that he is honorable, and the minister, priest, and rabbi that they are "men of God." By refusing to wear or insisting on wearing a beard and long hair, by driving a certain make of automobile, and even by smoking a particular brand of cigarettes we manage impressions about our social statuses. Unfiltered Luckies or Camels, for example, currently represent masculinity, but the contrary is communicated through smoking Eves, Virginia Slims, or Embras.

Similarly, we utilize the third major sign-vehicle, **manner,** to supplement our management of these desired impressions about ourselves. Manner is how we go about playing our roles. Through manner we especially communicate to others information about our feelings and moods. By our manner, for example, we inform others that we are angry or happy or indifferent. This indicates to others what they can expect of us as we play our roles. The fact that we have particular roles to play doesn't mean that we always play our roles in exactly the same way, and by our manner we control information by giving out cues, sometimes warnings, regarding how we are going to play our particular part in the ensuing interaction.

According to the dramaturgical perspective, then, we are all actors attempting to manage the impressions others receive of us. Students sitting in a classroom, for example, are all playing the role of student, at least to the point of being present in class. All are interacting in the same setting, but the types of information they communicate to others come in fascinating varieties. At least six major styles of playing this single role mark contemporary college students. The casual student communicates through his manner of indifference that he is aloof from the subject. He demonstrates that he is not "caught up" in what is occurring in the classroom, but at the same time he shows that he is willing to play the academic game at least to the point of minimum note-taking. The disdainful student communicates his general skepticism by sitting way back in his chair, as though he is daring the professor to say something worthwhile. He frequently wears a half sneer throughout the lecture to complete the impression that he is above it all. The person playing the role of the industrious, serious student takes down almost every word that is said, occasionally even rubbing his eyes with one hand while exhaustingly continuing to write with the other. The scholar, on the other hand, is noticeably selective in his note-taking, thus giving the impression that he already knows much of what is being said but is taking down an important point or two merely to refresh his memory. By carefully worded questions directed to the professor, but with his classmates also very much in the forefront of his mind, he communicates that he is fairly bristling with intelligence and information appropriate to the situation. The hippie says by his clothing that even though he is present in the classroom, no one is to mistake his alienation from society. The IBM type, in contrast, communicates through his appearance and manner that he is an up-and-coming member of the executive world and others should be aware that the classroom is but a temporary step in his long but sure climb up the ladder of executive success.

Impression management centers around two major types of expressions, expressions given and expressions given off. **Expressions given** are those aspects of the presentation of self which are thought to be under the control of the actor. They include such things as the actor's speech and his appearance, including his use of props and any other symbols by which an actor knowingly communicates information to others. **Expressions given off** are also sign-vehicles which communicate information about an actor to an audience, but they are thought to be less under the actor's control. Expressions given off include such things as nervousness, sweating, blinking, drooling, stumbling, spilling food, slips of the tongue, stuttering, rumblings of the stomach, flatulation, blushing, and signs of being startled.

Because we know that people are attempting to manage the impressions we receive of them, we try to pick up signs which might give us knowledge of the "underlying" meaning of their performance. We look for cues which might indicate what a person "really" means by what he is saying or doing: We attempt to find ways by which we can evaluate his performance and discover his intentions and motivations. We want to know what is going on in his mind, for this will help us interpret what he is saying and doing.

A major means of testing performances is to check whether the expressions a person gives off match the expressions he gives. If someone delivering a public speech, for example, is attempting to convince us that he really knows what he is talking about and that we should likewise be confident with the position he is presenting, if he is nervously clutching his hands, no matter how smooth his verbal delivery, we gain unintended information by which to evaluate him. As people know that others evaluate communications in this way, however, they attempt to bring the expressions they give off under their control. A speaker, for example, will attempt to hide signs of nervousness, doubt, and embarrassment. In other cases, a speaker will feign such signs if he thinks his audience expects them and they match the impression he wants them to have.

Just as role presentations in the theater take place on a stage, so people utilize stages in the presentations of the self in everyday life. Two stages are involved, a front stage and a back stage. The **front stage** is where performances take place. Here people present their acts to audiences. In the **back stage,** on the other hand, people relax from their performances. Here they "let their hair down" and prepare for future performances. On the back stage they check their costuming (clothing) and their masks (make-up and hairdos).

When guests are formally invited to middle-class American homes, such as when the boss comes to dinner, the front stage ordinarily consists of the living and dining rooms, while the bedroom, bathroom, and kitchen serve as the back stage. For dinner guests, the preparation for the performance begins in the bedroom and bathroom prior to the guests' arrival. Common terminology picks up the dramaturgical flavor of such activities, for people speak of making themselves and their homes "presentable" when they are getting ready for guests. This is exactly what they are doing in their "preparation rituals," making the self presentable for others. By carefully preparing the setting and their own appearance, the host and hostess attempt to communicate desired self-messages through controlling the scenery and their grooming. The guests have also engaged in similar preparation rituals in the back-stage privacy of their own bedrooms and bathrooms. Those who are hosting the performance, however, are primarily responsible for its success. They go through not only the additional preparation ritual of making the front stages of the living and dining rooms presentable for their expected audience, but they also become involved in tasks in the back stage area of the kitchen, as the food is prepared and various behind-the-scenes activities are undertaken in anticipation of the coming main performance.

When the guests arrive, they are properly greeted. In the *"greeting ritual,"* the performers are careful to demonstrate anticipated and required deference and warmth. The guests' wraps are also put away during the greeting ritual, and the audience is then seated. The performance has actually begun with the greetings, for they are an essential part of this communication process, but greetings are a sort of pro-

O'BRIAN

"Now, don't get panicky. I'll have you looking ten years younger in no time."

Areas of our homes and public places are set off as back stages, places in which we can relax from performances and prepare for the self-presentations we give to others. (Drawing by O'Brian; © 1961, The New Yorker Magazine, Inc.

logue to what we might call the "performance proper." The living room is usually the setting in which Act One of the performance proper unfolds. Before-dinner drinks and perhaps hors d'oeuvres are served, accompanied by preliminary "small talk."

After the proper time has elapsed, the performers are ready for Act Two. Just as the change in setting from foyer or hallway to the living room signalled the change from the prologue to Act One, so a setting change from living to dining room signals the transition from Act One to Act Two. Additionally, the hostess may well verbally announce this transition by stating that "dinner is ready." The guests are then ceremoniously ushered into the dining room for the meal. If the actors are playing traditional parts, the guests will comment on the quality of the meal during this second act. The husband will respond by beaming, but he must be careful not to overdo it, while the hostess will shyly smile and say something to the effect that it isn't quite as good as she wished. This will probably be accompanied by loud protestations to the contrary on the part of the assembled guests. The termination of Act Two is sometimes signalled by a "shall we go back to the living room" statement.

In Act Three, the guests are again seated in the living room, perhaps with after-dinner drinks in their hands, for further reciprocal symbolic presentations of the self in gesture and conversation. If the visit has any particular underlying purpose, such as requests for a raise or the announcement of a promotion, it is probable that it will be carefully brought out during this third act. What we can call the postlogue consists of *"departure rituals"* in which the guests typically say how much they have enjoyed the evening and how good the meal was, the host and hostess express their pleasure that their guests could have been with them, and both parties state that they must soon get together again.

If during the performance anyone has had to leave the front stage for a visit to the back stage, such as the hostess to the kitchen or the guests to the bathroom, it is usually announced by prefacing the departure with *"excuse rituals."* Excuse rituals usually involve some form of, "Please excuse me for a moment; I've got to check on the roast," or "Excuse me, but where is the bathroom?" Excuse rituals are not requests for permission to leave, for no one would ever think of saying no to the speaker. They are, rather, announcements of intention to leave the main interaction in order to take care of side involvements or personal matters. The audience is being ceremoniously informed that the departure is not to be taken as a sign that the one who is leaving is demonstrating lack of interest in the interaction.

It is considered in somewhat bad form to engage in excuse rituals during the focus of the performance, the meal, and pains are taken to insure that personal needs are disposed of prior to the meal. The host or hostess will frequently provide bathroom opportunities immediately prior to the meal by saying, "If you want to wash up, the bathroom is just down the hall." That not simply "washing up" is intended is indicated by the frequency with which the invitation is met with demurs to the effect of, "No, that's okay."

Front and back stages are mobile, not fixed. A front stage, for example, can later serve as a back stage. Thus, after the guests have departed, the husband and wife frequently relax in the living room and discuss the evening's performance, both theirs and their guests'. The husband and wife are likely to sit around and discuss how things went, comparing notes on their perceptions of how their performance was received. In this way they play the role of dramaturgical critics, commenting on both good and bad points of the performance. In the back stage at this time they might even practice their roles for future performances. If they do so, they serve as directors for each other by saying such things as, "Look, next time we have guests would you please not take your shoes off?" "Would you please make sure dinner is on time so we don't have to sit and wait?" or perhaps, "Next time will you keep the kids from bawling and interrupting us in the middle of the football game?" In such ways self-presentations are developed and further refined for future performances.

No particular dinner with guests is going to go exactly according to the script I have just outlined, of course. Differences centering around personalities, pressing problems, previous amount and type of interaction with the guests, and so on, will characterize any actual dinner. But that we can analyze a "typical" middle-class dinner in such a way that people recognize it as being similar to numerous ones they have attended or given indicates that a general cultural script, though with individual variations in each performance, is being followed. Standardized lines and roles, parts and scenes, are part of each interaction which is at all routinized or occurs with any frequency. In the dramaturgical perspective, such aspects of everyday life are abstracted and subjected to analysis, resulting in a different, and perhaps novel, way of viewing our lives.

Impression management centers around presentations of the self. By means of the sign-vehicles we utilize, we make **identity claims** to others. The sign-vehicles which we choose to communicate information about the self say, in effect, that we are a certain type of person. The inherent message of the setting we use and the appearance and manner we present is that we are the type of person who has the *right* to use those sign-vehicles; that is, by using a particular set of sign-vehicles, rather than others, we are attempting to lay claim to a particular identity. For example, by being present in a certain setting, such as a school or hospital, and by presenting some specific appearance while we are there, perhaps aided by the props of a notebook or white uniform, we are claiming a distinct identity, in these cases perhaps those of student or nurse or orderly. Even the way we act, our manner, is a claim to an identity. Professors act differently than students, nurses than patients, and so on; and when we act in a particular manner, we are making a claim to the social identity which goes along with it.

Whenever we make a claim for the self, our claim is open to evaluation by others. When our claim is honored by others, we enjoy **consen-**

sual validation of the self; that is, others are agreeing that we are the self we are presenting. Having our identity claims honored is the case for most of us most of the time. Whenever we make a claim for the self, however, we run the risk of a discredited self, that is, we may be claiming more for ourselves than others are willing to grant. A **discredited self** means that others have refused to acknowledge as legitimate the self someone has presented. In such cases, the identity a person has claimed has been rejected by others, making it extremely difficult for him to continue to present that self to that audience. With a claimed self discredited, an individual is faced with the choice of withdrawing from the interaction, perhaps going to another group where his claim will be accepted, as with a child who is rejected by his peers but finds satisfaction being the leader of a younger group, or remaining in the group and either negotiating a different consensus on the self or adamantly insisting on the claimed identity in spite of the negative reactions of others.

Two ways the self can be discredited are by **performance illegitimacy** and **performance failure.** By our performances we not only stake a claim to being a person who has the *right* to make the performance, but also we are communicating to others that we are *capable* of properly carrying out the performance. Our identity claim can be invalidated on either account.

If in the first case, regarding **performance legitimacy** or the right to play a particular role, it turns out, for example, that we have fake credentials, our self will be discredited and our audience will no longer accept our performance. Such is the case that crops up in the news of the nation every few years with persons who have never attended medical school but who have been practicing medicine. It typically turns out that such a person has assumed the identity of a physician in another part of the country or of a deceased individual and has been "operating" under his credentials. No matter how good his performance has been, no matter how satisfied his patients are, he will not be allowed to continue the physician role, for according to prevailing standards it was illegitimate for him to perform that role in the first place. He leaves the role with a discredited self, with others concluding that he was not that type of person all along.

In the second type of self-discreditation, that of performance failure, it is not the legitimacy of the person's performance which is being challenged, but the adequacy of his performance. This type of discredited self is sometimes due to an incongruity between the claimed self and the performance. At one university where I taught, for example, students would never take a particular speech professor seriously. The reason was that he stuttered. A stuttering speech professor is certainly something of an anomaly, but it does not necessarily mean that he does not know or is incapable of teaching the academic discipline of speech. Yet, because his performance was judged as inadequate by his audience, the content of what he said mattered little to his students.

Even though a person may have legitimate claim to the performance he is giving and may also be giving an adequate performance, the performance may still be rejected. This may occur because of an incongruity between the appearance of the performer and expectations of what he should look like. This is the case, for example, with a public speaker who is both an acknowledged expert on his subject and delivers his lines convincingly, but who midway through his lecture finds that his fly is gaping wide open.

The dramaturgical perspective on social life sometimes strikes students as being a bit far-fetched. Most of us do not typically think of ourselves as actors. Except for unusual situations, we tend to think of our behavior as expressing "the real me." We frequently feel that if the "real me" is not being expressed in our interaction there is something very basically wrong with the situation. We tend to feel that there is something fake or fraudulent about any such interaction.

Part of the resistance to the dramaturgical perspective which some students experience is based on the idea that if we are acting then we are not sincere. According to the view of dramaturgy, however, *we are sincere if we mean the part we are playing*. **Sincerity** is delivering our lines and playing our parts and meaning them. **Insincerity** is not believing our lines or parts but delivering them anyway. This dramaturgical idea of sincerity and insincerity matches well the definition in general use, where hypocrisy, for example, is commonly viewed as doing or saying one thing but believing another. When we are insincere, we may convince others but we aren't convincing ourselves, and we know that we are a fraud and that what we are doing is a sham. According to the dramaturgical view, then, acting does not necessarily mean insincerity, and when someone means what he says and does (that is, he believes his lines and part), that *is* the "real me."

Still, it is difficult to shake the idea that there is something insincere about playing roles in everyday life. Yet, we obviously do play roles, and we do so as a regular part of our lives. We believe our parts so well that we ordinarily fail to see their acting aspect. This point can be better demonstrated by the following conversation, which, although fabricated, is a composite of various student reactions to the dramaturgical perspective:

"Wow!" said Joe Believer. "That's a mind-blower. I just had a class where the teacher said we're all actors. Not just like actors, but real actors."

"What do you mean?" asked Susan Sincere.

"We're all putting on performances for others. All the time. Not just when you're doing something you don't believe, like when you gotta apologize and you're not sorry. But all of us all the time. Like whenever we're talkin' to somebody, we're puttin' on an act for them," replied Joe.

"You don't believe that stuff, do you?" asked Susan.

"Yeah. It makes sense. We're all playing parts, like in a big stage performance. Real life is a big stage, see, and we're the actors. Regular people. You and me. All of us," continued Joe.

"You can believe that if you want to, but I just don't see how you can be so stupid to swallow it. I'm not acting for you. Or for anybody. I'm just myself. Just me. Just Susan Sincere. I don't put on performances for anybody!" exclaimed Susan, scornfully shaking her head.

"O.K., let's get going," said Joe, giving up. "They're all over at Bill's, and we're running late."

"Oh, no! I forgot all about the party, Joe. It'll take me about an hour."

"What for?"

"You don't think I'm going like this, do you?" replied Susan indignantly. "I've got to take a shower, change my dress—I wore this one last time—take care of my hair, get my fingernails ready, put on my make-up, and, you know, make myself presentable."

"Oh," replied Joe.

How do we square our feelings of "just being ourselves" with the dramaturgical view that we are acting roles in life? Are all of us, indeed, continually putting on performances for others? The key to the answer is two-fold: It involves (1) our socialization process and (2) the repetitive nature of most of our interactions.

According to the dramaturgical perspective, we are taught early in life to be actors, and to be the best actors that we can possibly be. We become such good actors, in fact, that most of the acting nature of our interaction disappears from our own awareness. From our earliest years we are coached by accomplished actors, our parents, to give acceptably correct performances. Most of us learn to give such good performances that even we come to believe them. It works this way: In our early childhood years we are systematically taught the collusive nature of presentations of self, as when our parents tell us not to say or do certain things "when Uncle Charley is here" or "when the preacher visits."

Children are especially cautioned not to speak about certain family skeletons such as the breadwinner being arrested for drunken driving, Frank flunking out of college, or Mary being pregnant but not yet married. In other words, at a very early age children are taught not to speak to some people about certain things, to speak in a particular way for other people ("Be polite when Aunt Sandy comes."), and to change behaviors to fit different audiences ("Don't shout or tear up the house when she arrives."). In such ways, children learn at an early age *to adapt their presentations of self to match the expectations and requirements of different audiences,* and parents breathe a sigh of relief when their children have mastered this lesson and they no longer have to worry about what they'll say in front of visitors.

An essential aspect of socializing children, then, is teaching them to be actors and to be effective ones, because a good deal of what will happen to them in life depends on their adaptability in presenting the self. Because we learn this lesson so early in life, however, and because it becomes such a regular part of the way we go about our lives, the acting aspect of presenting the self largely drops out of sight.

The second reason most of our acting lies below the level of our perception is that most of our interaction is repetitive. Most of what we do during the course of a day, for example, consists of things we have done many times before. We have gone through similar interactions many times previously, and we have become very familiar with how others expect us to present the self: We have learned our parts, that is, what to do, and even our lines, that is, what to say. We have learned both what the expectations are of people around us and how to meet those expectations. If we don't meet them, we know standard ways of accounting for our failure. We know what to do because we are well socialized into handling recurrent situations, in getting through our daily lives, which usually consist of dealing with one set of fairly standardized expectations after another.

Repetition in interaction tends to lead to comfortability: We know what is expected of us, and we know how to go about meeting those expectations. Being comfortable in what we do helps to conceal from our view that to meet the expectations of others means to say and do things which the other person has in mind, that is, to follow a sort of script which we may have had no hand in writing but which we are called on to play. Because we ordinarily interact in such routine ways, we generally present the self in a largely automatic fashion, seldom having to question how to play the roles expected of us. We give repeat performances, so to speak, making slight adaptations as the occasion warrants.

We begin learning some of these expectations or roles so early in life, and they are so repetitive in a myriad of situations, that they literally become "second nature" to us, not only becoming largely imperceptible to us but also seldom even requiring thought as we perform them. Our sex role is a good example of this.

Sex role conditioning in American society begins immediately upon birth. The infant is given a "boy's" or "girl's" name, and he or she is then wrapped in pink or blue. Parents are quick to proclaim to the world (to relevant groups, really) by means of announcements, cigars, and word of mouth to which sex their baby belongs: "It's a boy!" "It's a girl!" This distinction is important to them, and they easily become upset and are quick to correct the error when people mistake the sex of their child.

From the time of our entrance onto the stage of life until our demise, we are taught that our sex places us into a general category of persons, that our sex makes us essentially similar to about half the population and essentially different from the other half. In our culture a complex set of symbols and devices are utilized in order to separate us into the proper groups. Besides colors and names, certain toys are deemed appropriate or inappropriate solely on the basis of the child's sexual membership, such as trucks versus dolls and flame throwers versus miniature sewing machines. We learn that certain styles of clothing are made for us but not for "them"; certain childhood games and activities are "right" or "wrong" (hopscotch and jacks versus tree climbing); certain manners are appropriate for one but not the other (it is okay for boys to be rough, but girls must be gentle); the same with language (coarser words are allowed for boys); adolescent games are also divided along sex lines (football versus cheerleading); certain occupations are deemed more appropriate for the one sex than the other (political office as opposed to secretarial work).

As we are separated by this major watershed, we painstakingly learn the behaviors deemed appropriate for our group. These are by no means "natural" or learned overnight. They are acquired over such a long period of time and are so consistently reinforced, however, that by the time we become young adults we take our sex role behavior for granted. That is, in most situations we unthinkingly act as a male or female is "supposed" to act in that particular situation. We become so familiar with the expected performances that we can deliver our appropriate lines down to the exact nuance. The role becomes such a part of us that we usually do not have to give even a second thought to what is expected of us. We come to think of our behavior in terms of the "real me," and it is only if we stop to think about how long it took us to thoroughly learn our sex roles that we begin to see how the "real me" was developed externally, how the "real me" is not a natural unfolding from within but is the end result of long, exacting, and intricate social processes.

Our sex role becomes an essential part of the self. We continuously play the role of male or female, giving the performances thought appropriate to our biological sex. Others react to us on the basis of how we perform in our sex role, and we in turn incorporate these reactions into our self concept. As we covered in the material on symbolic interaction in the preceding chapter, we tend to perceive ourselves as we think others perceive us. As we play the role of male or female, we react to the reactions of others. We eventually internalize our perceptions of these reactions, and girls and boys come to think of themselves in different terms. Girls are more apt to apply to themselves such adjectives as gentle, cute, pretty, and cuddly, while boys are likely to think of themselves in such terms as rough, handsome, strong, athletic, and muscular.

Having achieved identity through internalizing the reactions of others, we then desire to present ourselves to others in ways which are compatible with our own self-concepts. As we go about our daily lives, we desire and attempt to project to others what we think about ourselves. As we learn to do this, we become experts at impression management, even though, interestingly enough, much of what we do remains below the threshold of our own awareness.

A major part of the sign-vehicle of appearance by which we regularly communicate ideas of the self to others is clothing. Presumably because clothing either has a good or poor match with our self-concept, we all feel comfortable in some clothing and uncomfortable in others. "Comfortability" in this case means that we feel that there is a really good match between the particular items of clothing and what we think of ourselves. Accordingly, we wear certain items or styles of clothing because we feel that they adequately match what we wish to communicate to others about our self. As our self-concept is ordinarily routinely validated in interaction, it is fairly secure, and we know what clothing we like. Except for the choice or price of specific items, clothing is usually not problematic for us.

For someone whose self-concept is undergoing change or is being challenged in some way, however, as is frequently the case with adolescents, the choice of clothing is not such a simple matter. This is also the case with some occupational changes. The priesthood, for example, is an occupation which enundates the self: Priest and self become thoroughly intertwined. The idea that one is a "man of God" becomes incorporated into the self-concept. As with other roles in life, as one performs this role one tends to become the role. With this high dependence of the self-concept on the role of priest, then, when someone decides to leave the priesthood it is ordinarily a jolting experience to the self: The individual is removing himself from the roots on which a major part of his self is based. As a priest, he knows what kind of person he is. But as a nonpriest, what kind of "self" does he have? A 41-year-old former priest described this disturbing process. After leaving the priesthood in England, he said that he didn't know what kind of person he was in "civilian life." A major problem he confronted was the kind of clothing to choose, and as he said, "Was I a pin-stripe man or a sports jacket man? I didn't know because I had been too long in black" (*News of the World,* June 27, 1971, p. 3).

Although we do not ordinarily recognize it as such, even intimate interaction is a role. Here also the expectations of others govern our behavior. The girl lets out peals of laughter (high-pitched, of course) when her boyfriend tells a joke, to let everyone know what a wise and humorous man she has and that she appreciates him. Part of playing the intimate role, especially for the female in our male-dominated society, means to fulfill an obligation to build the ego of the other, a lesson many formerly married couples have only painfully learned.

Much of the intimacy of couples "going together" is impression management. When such persons are in the company of others, role playing occurs for the benefit of others, as when the couple feels that they must demonstrate by their actions that they are very much in love; they then project this image through public hand-holding and the like. Even when by themselves, however, role playing continues; only the audience has narrowed. For example, suppose a girl is with her boyfriend but her thoughts are taken up by a pressing problem, such as the sociology test she is going to have tomorrow, or perhaps her shoes are hurting her feet, and her boyfriend turns to her and purses his lips. What will she do? One cannot speak for all girls, of course, but typically she will kiss him. Why? Because he expects it. And to *play a role* means to fulfill, or attempt to fulfill, the expectations attached to a position.

Role playing in intimate situations can be further demonstrated by noting that girls who wear make-up on dates generally do not stop wearing make-up even after they are engaged or married. Saying, "I'm putting on my face," to refer to putting on make-up is not simply an idle phrase when viewed from this theoretical perspective. It demonstrates, rather, a deep-rooted common-sensical view which picks up the dramaturgical aspect of everyday life.

With some roles, however, we are extremely conscious of the acting part of our interaction. Heightened awareness of role playing occurs when: (1) our socialization experiences have not adequately prepared us for some required interaction, and, (2) the interaction is not as repetitive as most. Being interviewed for a new job is an example of such heightened awareness of the presentation of self. During the interview we are excruciatingly aware that someone is critically evaluating our performance, and we consciously attempt to manipulate communicative devices in order to "give as good an impression as possible." We know that our prospective employer is a member of our symbolic community and that he will take certain aspects of our appearance and manner as representing something about our person. We know that he is especially searching for predictors of our future behavior. Accordingly, we purposely prepare ourselves for the role of interviewee by checking the mirror to make certain that our hair is neatly combed, that we have no soup stains on our shirt or blouse, and that our shoes are shined. We also take pains to make certain that we are prompt for the appointment.

It is entirely possible that before the interview we have even mentally rehearsed our lines, thinking in advance what we ought to answer if certain questions are asked. Thus prepared, we go on stage. We know that we have to convince the boss or personnel manager, the "drama critic" in this case, that we are the "right" person for the job. Much is riding on projecting the right image, and when the questions come, we know what to reply. If we want the job badly enough, our answers will go something like, "Do I mind coming in at six in the morning? Not at all. I'm an early riser." "Do I mind working overtime on Saturdays? Of course not. I have nothing to do but to devote myself exclusively to you, sir."

It is easier to recognize that we are acting in such situations than during the regular part of our everyday lives because (1) our self-consciousness is heightened, (2) the interaction is highly structured, (3) it occurs in a formal setting, and (4) because of our inexperience (the nonrepetitive nature of the interaction) the lines do not feel natural to us. If we played this part as often as we do our more common roles, however, even being interviewed for a job would come to appear a "normal" part of life and would eventually seem a part of us.

Heightened self-consciousness frequently accompanies entrance into new roles, whether they are formal or informal. When someone first begins teaching, for example, it can be a rather uncomfortable experience. One is likely to think, "What am I doing on this side of the desk? All those years I've sat there taking notes, and now here I am lecturing in front of all those eyes staring back at me." This is perhaps a major reason that we have student teaching, to help the transition of the neophyte from student to teacher by allowing him to act *as though* he were the teacher while he is still a student.

Heightened self-consciousness and awareness of acting also occur with new informal and even new intimate roles. For example, even though a girl has had extensive dating experience, after she has broken off a long-term relationship she may feel uncomfortable as she begins dating again. She may not know exactly what her dates expect, and she can easily find herself giving "standard replies" to some of their questions. As she continues dating, she sometimes realizes that she has given the same answers and recounted the same experiences many times before. She may then encounter the uneasy feeling that her answers, and perhaps his questions and his answers, are merely lines recited because the occasion warrants it. If she comes to this realization, one might say that she is developing a sociological consciousness, at least the dramaturgical brand.

After one has played a role for a while, however, this heightened self-consciousness recedes, taking with it a great deal of the awareness of the acting aspect of the role. One becomes highly familiar with the routines of the part. After a situation is repeated over time, one comes to know what the expectations are. One learns that one can meet the expectations and that one can manage the required responsibilities. One has then learned to successfully present the self in the expected manner. If this presentation is satisfying, it eventually comes to be thought of in terms of the "real me."

One tends to incorporate a role one plays for a long time into the self-concept; that is, one comes to think of the self in terms of the role, as for example, "I *am* a wife, a mother, a daughter, a teacher," and so on. What a person feels he or she actually *is* is intimately interconnected with the major roles the person plays. This further leads to comfortability: The self and the role begin to match each other. The self blends into the role and the role into the self, for identity is achieved through role performance: Successful performance in roles validates the identity claims an individual makes. When the self is thus consensually validated in routine roles and is no longer challenged, self-consciousness markedly decreases.

The dramaturgical perspective on everyday life has even been incorporated into our common speech, as in the phrase, "Don't make a scene." The use of this phrase represents a great deal of sensitivity to the dramaturgical nature of human interaction, for when people tell others not to make a scene, they have in mind a picture of what they want the coming interaction to look like. Through their mutual presentations of self, they wish to create some desired image, and they are warning or requesting others not to interfere with this intended message.

Before a visit to the grandparents or to a good restaurant on Mother's Day, for example, parents often warn their children not to make a scene. The parents desire to successfully carry off a particular presentation of self, one that requires team work, and they don't want their children giving a conflicting performance. They want the grandparents to think that they are doing a good job of raising the grandchildren and the waitresses and other customers to think of them as "a nice family" with polite, respectful, well-mannered children. The children's cooperation is essential for this team presentation of self, for if the children throw either a tantrum or food on the floor, the image being so carefully constructed is irreparably shattered.

Most of us recognize that in some roles rather elaborate theatrical

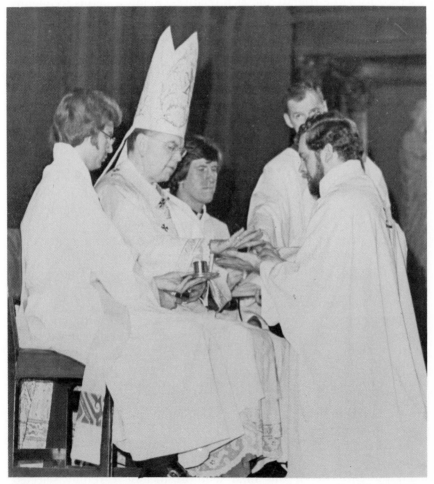

At highly formalized and ritualized events, the dramaturgical devices employed for impression management became readily apparent. The symbols are carefully chosen for the messages they convey. (Photo by Laima Turnley)

devices are employed to manage impressions. At highly formalized and ritualistic events such as baptisms, bar mitzvahs, parades, confirmations, ordinations, inaugurations, and impeachements, dramaturgical aspects of social life are quite readily apparent. We shall briefly examine two such events.

In weddings, the lines spoken by the participants and even their movements are formally prescribed. Highly stylized costumes are worn, traditionally a white "wedding dress" for the major female lead and a dark suit or tuxedo for her male counterpart. In the preliminaries, the audience is seated according to their social roles, with close-up seating reserved for close friends and rich relatives. Being seated is frequently accompanied by music, which is appropriately called a "prelude." After the guests are seated, the leading actors take their assigned places, and the "performance proper" is ready to begin. The bride makes her dramatic entrance at precisely the right moment, walking in a manner which she has practiced well beforehand (perhaps the traditional "hesitation step"), accompanied by her father who proudly escorts her down the aisle in order to officially and publicly "give her away." Highly ritualized statements are solemnly made ("In the presence of God and this company . . ."), questions rhetorically asked ("Do you take . . . ?"), and replies formally given ("I do."). These statements, questions, and replies, with their correct accompanying gestures and intonations, have, of course, all been rehearsed well in advance of the ceremony to ensure the unruffled unfolding of the presentation. The practice sessions are even known as wedding rehearsals.

By examining its parts in this way, it is fairly easy to see that a wedding ceremony is actually a play. It has all the elements of theater, but it is a one-night performance only—except for those who enjoyed it so much the first time that they decide to repeat it. But the cast of characters in repeat performances undergoes sharp change.

Our playing roles in major scenes does not end even with our death. At the time of our death, there is still one final performance to be given. It might be called the Great American Funeral. This last scene is completely under the control of others. The one who has died merely provides the major prop around which the performance centers. The setting for this final act is one of two places, the church or the funeral parlor. The church is the traditional setting in the United States, with its steeple communicating direction to the Great Beyond. The survivors of the corpse find such symbols comforting as they "pay their respects" to the "mortal remains." Major props used to communicate messages about the purpose of this final send-off include carefully selected music, flowers, and appropriate religious symbols.

The second choice of setting for Americans is the funeral parlor.

Contemporary funeral directors like to make up their lack of official connection with the deity by erecting imposing buildings. Neo-funerary architecture is characterized by a circular drive in front of a large brick building which boasts huge white pillars and a massive door. None of this is accidental; all is part of carefully contrived over-all impression management. White pillars communicate solidity and demonstrate continuity with the past, a past going back to the ancient Greeks and Romans and continuing into Early Americana. This symbolic connection with the past is designed to make the bereaved feel that they and their departed loved one are all part of an unbroken succession of humanity, a succession whose origin is lost in antiquity and which will continue infinitely into the future, thus strongly hinting at immortality. The massive door signifies the eternal portals which the deceased has now entered. Additionally, the interior decor is tastefully done up in warm colors and lush carpeting, and this last scene is carried out with the aid of soft organ music and flowers. Where appropriate, the funeral director also tastefully displays the Cross and Bible, or the Star of David and the Torah.

Whichever setting is used, similar expressions are worn by those attending the funeral. Highly stylized expressions are designed to show sympathetic solidarity with the close relatives and friends of the deceased. As befitting Occidental cultural expectations, those closest to the departed demonstrate more emotion, and those farther from him less. It is considered unseemly for persons who were not very close in relationship to show much grief, or for those who were close to the deceased to not show much grief. Similarly, when the deceased was a husband, it is considered unseemly for a mistress to appear at the funeral, for no matter how deep her love or how great her grief, this final presentation is carefully constructed to conceal many aspects of the deceased's former life. Correct attire is, of course, called for in all cases because it signifies respect for the deceased and sympathy for those who must adjust to his departure.

The deceased himself has been carefully prepared for his final presentation. His blood has been drained and replaced with a fluid designed to keep him presentable even after he has been buried, his internal organs may have been removed and replaced with synthetic stuffing, his eyes have been sewn shut so he won't look awry, and a specialist known as a mortician's beautician has attempted to restore lifelike qualities to his facial features. The corpse is also symbolically attired for the final scene he plays: Typically, a female child is dressed in white, and a boy or male adult in a dark suit, while a female adult is usually attired in a simple dress, not in hot pants.

According to the dramaturgical perspective, not only are highly formalized ceremonies such as weddings and funerals to be seen as plays, but so are the informal encounters people routinely experience in their everyday lives. To see the play underlying our everyday lives, one has but to pick out the parts, the lines, the cast of characters, and the various dramaturgical devices utilized to highlight the presentations of self. The dramaturgical perspective thus becomes a conceptual framework for viewing human interaction, providing a startlingly different way to understand life in society.

chapter 8

Life as a Game: The Gaming Perspective on Interpersonal Relations

Not only are we all actors, but we all are game players. Our interaction can be profitably conceptualized in terms of games as well as dramaturgy. The idea that in their everyday lives people are games-players has passed into popular imagery by the best seller, *Games People Play* (Berne 1964), and by many other titles picking up this idea, such as *Games Husbands and Wives Play* (Drakeford 1971), *Games Alcoholics Play: The Analysis of Life Scripts* (Steiner 1971), *Play On* (Schall 1971), *Academic Gamesmanship: How to Make a Ph.D. Pay* (Van Den Berghe 1970), and *The Sex Game* (Bernard 1972).

That gamesmanship applies to the ways in which people deal with one another is a common perception in our society, although it is usually acknowledged in the negative, as in the pejorative statement, "Don't play games with me." People make this statement when they feel that others are somehow not treating them right: these others are baiting them, are insincere in what they are doing and saying, or are attempting to elicit a reaction from them by a means they feel is unwarranted.

People react in this negative way because such gaming is felt to undermine the basic seriousness of intent that, unless agreed to the contrary, is assumed to be one of the fundamentals underlying our social interaction. As we interact with others, we assume that they are serious about what they are doing and saying. If we feel that they are playing games, we take this as a sign of insincerity. Their gaming represents behavior inappropriate to the situation. We then feel that the person does not deserve to be taken seriously, as is reflected in the statement likely to be used at this time, "Don't pay any attention to him. He's only playing games with you."

The social science perspective that places human behavior within the context of game playing, however, deemphasizes this negative evaluation. Rather than viewing games as a violation of people's expectations of seriousness or sincerity, this perspective views all interaction in terms of a **game,** that is, interaction is analyzed within the framework of boundaries, expectations or rules, strategies, tactics, moves and countermoves people use to pursue goals. As they make their way toward their goals, they act (or make their moves) within a set of expectations, as do those with whom they are interacting. People utilize the expectations of others in order to bring themselves closer to their desired goals. From this perspective in the social sciences, games are taken to be part of the ordinary way people present the self in everyday life. Most of life is viewed as a sort of game, with the self-presentations we studied in the last chapter being, in effect, games people play with one another.

As I emphasized in the material on symbolic interaction, the play activities called games are an important means by which children learn about life in society. From the symbolic interactionist perspective, children's games are not frivolous activities, but vital for the development of the self. Through playing games with other children, a child learns to take others' roles, an ability essential for getting along with other members of society. The better someone can take the role of others, the better he is able to anticipate the actions of others toward him and to respond appropriately to the people around him.

When they play their games, children develop more than role-taking abilities. *They also gain particularized understandings of what life in society is like.* They learn, for example, that in games people deal with one another under a set of rules. They learn that these rules are meant to apply to everybody who is playing the game but that the set of rules is subject to change. Sometimes the rules are amicably changed by the mutual consent of the players, while at other times rules change through the use of force or pressure, as when the owner of the baseball bat and ball won't allow his equipment to be used unless he is allowed to be the pitcher and is given special batting preference. By means of their games children are further introduced to the idea that just as there are different roles or positions on a team, so there are various

The highly competitive games we learn to play socialize us into core ideas of American culture, especially the importance of striving for success over others. (Courtesy of Wide World Photos)

roles in life. They learn, moreover, that a person is expected to do his best in the role that he is assigned. Through the highly competitive games American children play, they are also introduced to a core idea of American society: Winning is important, and success, as measured by accomplishments over others, is the goal of their striving. They learn that they must ordinarily compete with one another in order to win, but they also learn that in other situations winning requires cooperation. Team games especially introduce children to the idea that they must cooperate with one another if they are to achieve a common goal. In learning this, they also learn that it is worthwhile to work for a goal larger than the individual self, a goal in which one has a mutual interest with others (Coleman 1966:3). In such ways, then, the formal games children play are intimately interconnected with learning about social life.

The social science **gaming perspective** on human behavior, however, ranges far beyond children's games and includes much more than formal games, whether played by children or adults. Human interaction itself is conceptualized in terms of boundaries, rules, strategies, tactics, moves, and responses. In the formal games people play, the participants play their parts within bounded settings in order to obtain whatever rewards are available. So it is with activities in daily life. We all play games as we deal with others in our family, in school, on the job, and especially in informal interaction with the opposite sex.

School is one of the major areas of modern life in which games dominate relationships. When a person becomes a student, as we all must the way society is set up today, he quickly learns that his well-being in the educational institution centers around the "grade game." Students find that they must regurgitate materials assigned them or about which they have been lectured. Whether they believe or assent to the materials is deemed irrelevant in most of our testing procedures: Students are simply held accountable for familiarity with certain facts. If they reproduce those facts, they receive a good grade. If they do not, they receive a low grade or fail. Because the game is played by professors and students alike, the question that is seldom asked is whether the students' regurgitating of lectured or assigned materials has any bearing whatsoever on their learning. In many cases the teacher does not want to give exams any more than students want to take them, but the educational administration requires the assigning of grades, and examinations turn out to be a handy way of separating the sheep from the goats.

In some forms of the grade game students utilize the impression management we discussed in Chapter 7 as a central gaming strategy, demonstrating that they have indeed become adroit game players. Students are sometimes able to control the expressions they give off, making them match the expressions they give, in order to create a unified picture of reality. In this way they are able to manage a desired impression while moving toward valued goals. For example, if a girl does not have her term paper ready she might decide to tell her professor that she has not been feeling well, or, even, that she has some particular illness. ("Walking pneumonia" or "the bug" appear to be good vague illnesses to choose.) If she comes bustling into the professor's office with a cherubic grin on her face, as well as all dressed up in bright spring colors, he is little inclined to believe her. She might actually happen to be feeling very good at the time that she is talking to him, even though she had been sick prior to her visit. But she probably has a better chance of success by dressing correctly for her role, especially by underplaying her make-up and wearing drabber colors for her presentation.

While clothing and make-up are part of her expressions given, in this case they come close to being expressions given off because they will seem *not* to be as much under her control. In this instance downplaying the make-up will give the impression that she has been feeling badly. An even subtler touch is to apply her make-up to make it look *as though*

Many aspects of the educational system can be conceptualized in the gamesmanship terms presented in this chapter. Some, as the one illustrated, can have far-reaching consequences on future chances in life. (Photo by Laima Turnley)

she is trying to cover the effects of her illness. If she also adds a certain lowness to her voice, and perhaps a little quaver at the right point, these will be taken as expressions given off and will further validate her story.

One of the major educational games is the "degree game." In this game a college degree is pursued for its own sake, without regard for learning: The degree simply represents a marketable product and is valued for what it brings in terms of status and money. Sometimes students become so caught up in this game and become such good game players that one degree leads to another without any specific purpose. I have known students, for example, who initially attended college because their fathers expected it. After graduation, they entered graduate school because of vocational uncertainties or because of a desire to avoid the draft. By the time they received their master's degrees, they had done so well the faculty encouraged them to continue their studies. They did so, but by the time they received the highest degree possible, the Ph.D., they did not know why they had the degree. They had indeed played the degree game excellently, and if the game could have continued until the end of their lives, they might have been content to continue playing it. But once they reached "home," as it were, they were at a loss regarding what to do. They did not particularly want to do research, and they certainly did not want to teach.

Many educational games reach their apex with the M.A. and Ph.D. examinations. Seekers after these degrees ordinarily play the educational game to the hilt, especially when it comes time for them to be examined on their thesis or dissertation. At this point they are given either a pass or a fail grade, which determines whether they receive the degree or not—whether their years of preparation culminate in a goose egg or in the highly coveted degree. For months in advance the student attempts to anticipate the questions he might be asked, and he seeks out coaching by others who have already successfully gone through their defense. More than substantive answers to questions, he learns strategy: If he does not know the answer to a question, he must not admit his ignorance but, rather, find some way to "talk around it." For example, he might not know the specifics called for by a question, but the question might at least touch on a general area he knows. He may then be able to elaborately construct a knowledgeable reply based on a subpart of the question, making it appear as though that were the essence of what he had been asked. If he handles himself well, his examiners may intentionally overlook his answering a question no one asked.

In a major sense the oral examination on the dissertation is in its very essence a put-on game. Frequently, for example, the examiners already know prior to the examination just what the student knows and what he doesn't know. Since they have already directed his thesis and read its various drafts, they would just as soon say, "Your thesis is acceptable. Here's your degree." But most universities require that the candidate for the degree be examined, and both faculty and students are, accordingly, required to play the game. Since faculty members are also forced to play their parts in this gaming ritual, they frequently become caught up in the game and make it sound as though their gaming is serious. By making the candidate sweat it out, they meet his and their own expectations that this culmination of years of academic preparation is a difficult hurdle. At the same time, however, they ordinarily gear their questioning to the student's level of preparation, lest the questions be too difficult and the student not be able to adequately perform. Not only would the student be embarrassed, but so would his teachers whose responsibility it was to prepare him for this day. Accordingly, when the student encounters difficulty in answering, they sometimes provide subtle cues to guide the candidate along the correct path.

In one Ph.D. examination the initial questions were surprisingly simple and straightforward. The candidate began to relax, feeling that he had exaggerated the rigors of the examination. After twenty minutes or so, however, one of the examiners began to unexpectedly attack the thesis. He began a ruthless attack, questioning the competency of what the candidate had submitted. The candidate had never been in a situation like this before, and he was at a complete loss to respond. He first began to tentatively agree with his attacker, giving a "You might be right" type of reply. The other examiners looked questioningly at him, making the student aware that he was not pursuing the right strategy, but he was still unsure how to handle the attack. A second examiner then guided him to a more "professionally appropriate" response by saying, "You don't really believe that, do you?" The candidate picked up this broad cue and at last began to actively defend what he had written, even attacking in return—but more mildly, as befit a mere doctoral candidate in the presence of his judges. He was being taught through this ploy that a Ph.D. sociologist is someone who vociferously defends his work when it is under attack and that a major measure of a candidate's worth to the title of doctor is his display of competence in defending what he has written.

Not only do examiners play games with candidates, but they are at the same time playing *side games* with each other. When an examiner asks a question, he is doing so in the presence of his colleagues. His question reflects on his own self-presentation. Accordingly, the examiner must always make certain that his questions are intellectually phrased, professionally sophisticated, and relevant to the topic. He must also make certain that he is both able to evaluate adequately the answer to any question he asks and that he can appropriately follow it up with relevant probes. In other words, not only is the candidate being examined, but the self the examiner presents is also being critically reviewed by his audience of colleagues. After such examinations, it is not uncommon for committee members to privately comment on the appropriateness or inappropriateness of questions that their colleagues asked.

The final plot in the examination game comes when the examiners in a somber voice ask the candidate to please leave the room. The candidate goes into the hallway, nervously drinks a lot of water for his by now parched throat, smokes cigarette after cigarette, and bites his fingernails—sometimes practically simultaneously. His future professional life hangs in the balance of their deliberations, and he is imagining that they are deliberating whether they should or should not grant him the degree. In some borderline cases, they are indeed doing so. But in most cases, they are probably merely waiting for the appropriate length of time to elapse and engaging in "shop talk," such as someone's latest job offer or publication. Finally someone might say, "I think we've let him wait out there long enough. It's about time to leave." They then slowly file out, wearing very solemn looks, almost as though they were part of a funeral procession. They somberly approach the candidate, and one of the examiners suddenly thrusts out his hand, clasps the hand of the startled candidate, and smiling broadly says, "Congratulations, Doctor."

When a student has finished his formal education, he is by no means finished with games. They only change. He has completed this part of his apprenticeship in gamesmanship, so to speak, and he is now faced with following the rules of employment games. In order for an employee to move up the occupational ladder, he must please his superiors. Although this requirement faces all workers to some degree, it is especially stringent for executives who are expected to achieve success through rigid conformity. Executives must learn well the rules of what we might call the "correctness game," for their future depends on how they are felt to "belong" to the corporation. They are expected to begin their slow but steady climb in the occupational hierarchy with the "correct" degree, to wear "correct" clothing at all times, to exhibit "correct" demeanor with both subordinates and superordinates, to demonstrate "correct" manners at company parties, and even to obtain a "correct" address. The corporation requires strict regimentation in those chosen to "belong" to the corporation. In return for meeting the central expectation of what they call teamwork, including the full-hearted support of corporate decisions with which the executive personally disagrees, the corporation exchanges security in the form of retirement, savings and hospitalization plans, recreational facilities, and bonuses and stock options. Chairmen of the Board make no bones about their central belief that "what's good for the company is the best for the employee" ("CBS Reports: The Corporation," December 6, 1973).

The requirements of this executive game are so far-reaching that they inundate most aspects of the employee's life. American executives are even expected to marry the "correct" wife, a wife whom the corporation feels will best present the image the company is trying to cultivate. To this end, they question those whom they are recruiting for executive positions about their wives, especially about their involvement in community activities. They are especially looking for men with wives who will "help create the executive's image" and who will accept the demands the corporation will make on his time. It is not uncommon for them to aid their executives' conformity by conducting classes for wives in which the benefits and expectations of "belonging to" the corporation can be firmly impressed upon them. The ideal executive's wife has been described as: gregarious, sociable, a "mixer," highly adaptable, a leader, constructive, college educated, a good conversationalist, a good dresser, and, of course, healthy (Whyte 1968).

The executive's choice of wife can be critical for his progress in climbing the ladder of corporate success. When it comes time for promotion, not only is the executive's performance carefully evaluated, but some of the characteristics of his wife are also painstakingly scrutinized. His employer may well evaluate whether the wife dresses well or not, her attitude toward parenthood, and even what sort of housekeeper she is. The decision whether or not to promote a man to a high position in a company has been noted to depend upon whether the candidate's wife drank two or three martinis at the company party or whether she was so foolish as to have the fourth (Whyte 1968:184).

Some of the most highly formalized employment games are played by officers in our armed services. Elaborate rules are built around separating enlisted men from officers. Air Force officers are not only formally told that they should develop close associations only with other officers, but they are also informed that the enlisted man "has no real desire to associate closely with officers; he prefers to relax with his own group" (*Initial Active Duty* 1970:60). Much of the officer's behavior is circumscribed by formal rules, such as those concerning behavior in receiving lines. For example:

> At large official functions a receiving line is customary. The way the receiving line is formed depends upon the position of the senior host or visiting dignitary. The senior host (or visiting dignitary, if there is one) is accorded the position of honor and is the first with whom you should shake hands. Usually he is second in line, preceded by an aide who introduces guests to him. Next in line after the honored person is his wife, if present. Following are other members of the receiving party in order of seniority, each gentleman with his wife immediately after him (*Initial Active Duty* 1970:61).

Not only are formal matters such as receiving lines covered by such rigid expectations, but much of the informal interaction between officers in our armed services is also bounded by formal rules. One set of rules governs entrance into automobiles and small boats, for example, while another applies to aircraft—all based on seniority, of course.

> When accompanying a senior, a junior walks or rides on his left. Military persons enter automobiles and small boats in inverse order of rank; that is, the senior enters an automobile or small boat last and leaves first. Juniors, although entering the automobile first, take their

appropriate seat in the car. The senior is always on the right. In the case of aircraft, the senior usually boards first and departs first. Officers sit in the back seat of passenger cars driven by airmen unless the car is full (*The Air Officer's Guide* 1963:259).

Not only can interaction in formal settings such as school and employment be conceptualized in terms of games, but this perspective can also be applied to more informal aspects of daily life. Interaction in the family, for example, can be analyzed in terms of making moves within a set of expectations in order to attain goals. A teenaged daughter sometimes plays what we might call the "subservient role" game. Her parents hold certain ideas of what their daughter is like, and she manipulates these expectations in order to secure freedoms and privileges from her parents. She knows, for example, that by being "extra nice" in her daughter role, such as volunteering to vacuum the rugs and do the dishes or to babysit with her younger brother she is more likely to receive her parent's consent to stay out later or to date a particular boy about whom her parents are not too happy.

Excuse games are also regularly played by teenagers when they are requested to give an account of their activities. When their parents ask where they have been, they frequently say that they have been one place when they were at another, especially when the place they actually were is a place that their parents do not approve. The same is true when they are requested to tell whom they were with and what they were doing. By no means are teenagers inherently more dishonest than anyone else—it is simply that teenagers early learn during this critical period in which they are striving for independence that in order to get along with their parents they are frequently forced to present a self that they well know does not match reality.

Another game which teenagers frequently play with their parents might be called the "getting the car" game. In this common game the teenager is forced to play an extremely subservient role in order that he might attain the prized goal, the car keys. He is likely first of all to put on a front which is extremely pleasing, perhaps with much smiling. But he must at the same time show that he is worried that he may not receive the car keys that evening. It is a dangerous move to display over-confidence, although it is sometimes strategic to take his parents off guard with such a presentation. He is frequently forced into playing a charade of questions and answers, neither of which are perhaps based on reality, but which must be played to the end. For example:

"Now you're sure you're just going to drive over to Johnson's?"

"Yes."

"Then why do you need the car if you are just going to Johnson's?"

"I told you. I have to pick up Dave and take him with me."

"I don't like that Dave."

"Aw, Mom, Dave is okay."

"You won't be driving fast?"

"No."

"You won't go over 50."

"No."

"You won't be picking up any of that rough bunch?"

"No."

"You won't be doing any drinking?"

"No."

"Well, if you ever do, that's the last time you get the car. Mark my words."

"Yes, Dad."

"And you had better get that through your head. Why, when I was your age my dad didn't give me the car that easy. I had to work in his store on Saturdays in order to get it, and I was 18 before I got it the first time."

"I know, Dad."

"Things are just too easy for you kids nowadays. I don't know what's happening to this younger generation."

"Yes, Dad."

It may very well be that the son in this example is planning on picking up five of his friends, attending a booze party at the lake, and seeing how fast his dad's car will go this time, since it didn't quite break 120 the last time he had it. It can also be that his parents have a good idea of what is "really" happening. But the son must still give the correct responses to the established cues at each point in this game or the final reward will be withheld.

This is an essential expectation of interpersonal games: giving the correct responses to appropriate cues and then making one's own responses serve as cues to elicit desired responses from others. Because we begin learning our culture's symbolic system while we are still infants, and because we gain constant practice at manipulating these symbols, most of us become good game players. We learn the basic rules of the groups under which we must live, what people expect of us, and how to adequately meet those expectations.

The groups around us are constantly threatening to come down our very throats and force us to conform to expectations which are not always our own. It appears that much of gaming is a technique which people develop in order to maintain a semblance of independent action in the face of the smothering and crushing expectations of others in which we are all immersed. Gaming allows us to remain somewhat aloof from what is happening, giving us the chance to chart our own course of action to at least a minimal extent, while superficially meeting the expectations of others. Gaming can then serve as a sort of buffer between zones of contrary expectations. By preventing direct confrontations, gaming is a mechanism which facilitates social interaction.

A good part of dating and courtship behavior is also gamesmanship. People frequently date others for *expressive* or *affective* purposes, that is, because the other has intrinsic qualities which the person feels he or she will enjoy. At other times, dates serve *instrumental* purposes, that is, someone dates another for what he or she can "get out of" the situation. Dates, are, for example, frequently used as props, such as when someone dates a certain person or even a particular type of person in order to elicit desired reactions from others. Dates can be used to be seen in the "right" place at the "right" time with the "right" person. In some extreme cases, members of fraternities and sororities are 'expected to be seen with the "right" girl or guy in order to bolster the image of the fraternity or sorority. Frat men might be expected to date only girls who dress in a certain manner, who hold leadership positions in the school, or whose father is known to be wealthy and influential. Similarly, sorority girls might be expected to date only boys who have achieved standing in campus sports or whose family occupies a high social position in the community. In such cases, the date serves as a prop since the dater is not interested in the person *per se* but in the reaction he or she elicits from others when he or she is seen with this particular person.

A person's date is symbolic of much in life. A date especially reflects on who a person is and what corner in life he or she represents. Accordingly, these game partners are not randomly selected, but a great deal of social control is exerted over who plays the dating game with whom. Certain types of people are not acceptable role or game partners simply because of the "type" that they represent. As I mentioned in Chapters 2 and 3, dates typically follow certain predictable lines, especially those of social class, race, age, height, and, of course, sex. I shall have more to say about the expectation of heterosexuality in dating in Chapter 10.

A corollary of the "quality" game in dating is the "quantity of sex" version of this game. Although girls are not immune from actively entering this game, in our culture it is probably more frequently played by males for a male audience. The goal of this game is to have sexual

TON SMITS

Relationships between the sexes can also be viewed in terms of gamesmanship, as graphically captured in this cartoon. (Drawing by Ton Smits; © 1956, The New Yorker Magazine, Inc.)

relations with as many partners as possible. Unlike the dating game, little attention is paid to who the partners are since prestige is based not on quality but on quantity. The greater the number the male can accumulate, the greater his prestige in his peer group. Extra "points" are usually awarded for girls whom the group finds especially attractive, for virgins, and for girls whom no one else in the group has been able to make.

Variations of this game are perhaps played by most American males at one time or another, but this contest system is especially prevalent among young black ghetto males. In the contest system common in the black lower-class subculture, the participants rely on subtle persuasion and various elaborately contrived schemes to outwit females. The more women a male can claim as having bedded, the higher the status granted him by his peer group. Although females in this urban subculture serve as sex objects, this is not their primary value. They are especially highly valued because they supply males with money and prestige and not, as might be thought, primarily because of sexual gratification. A black researcher who spent much time in this "world within a world" reported that open war is actually declared on all available women (Hammond 1965:9).

A major part of our more usual cultural dating games centers around communication. Dating partners commonly feel that they cannot tell their dates exactly what is on their mind. They feel that they must show that they are interested in the other, after dating a while that they are enamored with the other, and especially that they must withhold negative sentiments from the relationship. Expressing negative ideas that one has about the other would tend to disrupt the relationship, so dating partners ordinarily play it safe in order to maximize gains (Mayer 1957).

Highly related to the withholding of emotions is the self-subjugating role which many American females still feel they must play. In this aspect of the dating game, the female feels that in many ways she must subordinate her desires to those her boyfriend has, that it is better for her if she does not fully express her own person. It is especially of utmost importance that she flatter the male's ego in the area of intelligence. In some extremes, for example, if she knows that her boyfriend received a B in a college course, she must be certain to state that she received nothing higher than a B, and preferably a C—even though she might have received the highest grade in the class. It is probable with the changes being ushered in by the women's liberation movement that such traditional female self-effacement soon will undergo extreme modification, but at least for the present it remains a part of the dating game.

Learning sex roles begins early in life. Before we have even gone on our first date we have had years of training in meeting the expectations attached to this major role. Not only our activities, but also many of the sentiments we experience, become essential corollaries of role-playing. (Photo by Laima Turnley)

Highly elaborated rules, though informal, specifying the conditions under which one can move toward intimacy typically mark the dating game. Current rules seem to specify, for example, that the male will not at all be "out of line" if he attempts to kiss his partner on the first date. It is up to the girl whether she will allow the kiss, but she will not ordinarily be offended if he does attempt to kiss her on the first date, and she frequently will be offended if he does not. If he has not kissed her by the fourth or fifth date, she is likely to think there is something drastically wrong. Either he is not interested in her (but then why is he dating her?) or there is something wrong with him. In any event, lack of kissing is an infringement of rules and leads to questioning of motives and orientations.

Rules, or general expectations, also cover greater intimacy in dating. The move from non-intimacy toward intimacy follows a fairly regular procession from first date "getting to know each other," to kissing, to "light" petting, to "heavy" petting, and on to sexual relations. It is understood by the game partners, though they may express regrets and wishes to the contrary, that at any point the relationship may break up. Sometimes the break-up results from one game player (usually the male) wanting to proceed toward the goal faster than the other game player (usually the female) is willing to allow. If the game relationship continues, it appears to be generally understood that the players are heading toward sexual intimacy.

Although the rules regarding sexual intimacy follow certain general lines, they vary markedly from individual to individual, and a good part of early dating activities centers around discovering what rules one's partner is operating under. Establishing ground (or bed) rules to which both persons assent takes place early in the dating relationship. Much gaming in dating centers around manipulations on the part of one or the other to change these expectations.

As with other aspects of self presentation, clothing is also extremely important in dating games and in sex seduction games. In American society we are expected to wear clothing which both reveals and at the same time conceals our sexual capacities. The female is expected to wear a skirt of a certain length and a blouse of a certain cut in order that she can be identified as sexually attractive, as one who has sexual capacities. At the same time her clothing must conceal what we consider to be the "private" parts of her body. Although American women are permitted to wear clothing which suggests seduction, the amount of allowable decolletage is strictly circumscribed. American women must walk a sort of tightrope between the degree of tolerable expression of seductivity and expectations concerning sexual propriety. Frequently American women find themselves in a bind because of these two mutually incompatible expectations. They must show themselves as sexually respectable and at the same time as sexually available, at least for a potential spouse. If a woman goes too far in one direction she runs the risk of being labeled prudish, but if she goes too far in the other direction she risks the danger of being labeled "easy."

Games between the sexes by no means cease with marriage, of course. Husbands and wives usually play all sorts of games with each other as they attempt to conceal from the other certain information about themselves while revealing only information which they feel is conducive to good relations. They also sometimes attempt to manipulate their marital game partners into an exploitable position. One married friend of my acquaintance, for example, has a "bowling-night" every Thursday. Each Thursday he dutifully leaves home at a scheduled time with his bowling bag in hand, but he never goes near a bowling alley. Instead he spends the night bar-hopping, and when he arrives home he has a built-in explanation for both the early morning hour and the alcohol on his breath, since he "went out for a drink with the boys" after bowling. Married women sometimes use bridge, golf, and "coffee klatches" for similar purposes.

The term "fun and games," which directly picks up the gaming aspect of intersexual behavior, has even entered our common vocabulary. This phrase refers to contacts between the sexes in which there is no intention to commit the self. What happens at the moment is what counts. When someone is entering a "fun and games" relationship, he or she fully expects that it represents but a temporary liaison. He or she is seeking diversion, as on a vacation, or the infamous convention which is anything but "conventional." A "night out" from the marital partner is sought, perhaps attained, and then the individual returns to his regular routines, which he describes by anything but the phrase "fun and games."

A good number of marital games revolve around gaining or maintaining control over the family finances. By means of varying tactics one marital partner will sometimes attempt to control the checkbook. The husband might say, "You just haven't had enough experience in these matters. I'll take care of them." If that doesn't work, he might even more chauvinistically say, "I bring home the paycheck, and I'll write the checks." A wife might attempt to control the checkbook by pointing out to her husband that under his management they are always running short of money and that more control must be exerted on their spending or they will face even greater financial difficulties. Once she has gained control over the checkbook, she will sometimes then attempt to put her husband on a strict allowance, and by being the one who writes the checks, she also then exerts much control over the areas in which they spend their income.

Jealousy within marriage and dating relationships is sometimes not an emotion which is experienced but a gaming role that is played. A husband or boyfriend, for example, may be ready to leave his wife or girlfriend and be looking for any number of excuses to do so. At some point she becomes involved in a flirtation or a man makes a pass at her, and he would prefer to allow the situation to continue to develop since it might provide a legitimating basis for his breaking off the relationship. While he is purposely, hopefully overlooking the event, his friends draw it to his attention, expecting that he will show jealousy and that he will remove her from that situation. Although it is contrary to his actual desires, he feels that he must play the expected role. He then shows protective and justifiable anger and forcibly removes her from the situation in which he would have preferred to leave her.

Breaking up marriages, or steady dating arrangements, are situations in which gamesmanship is frequently exhibited. The "jealous" husband or boyfriend above, for example, feels that he cannot simply desert his partner because he wants to do so but must have some legitimating reason for breaking up. Whatever excuse he finds, he needs one which will serve as a justifying explanation to others around him. He wants to continue ongoing relationships with his friends, and if he callously and coldly leaves his wife or girlfriend simply because he no longer desires to be with her, he may jeopardize their friendship. The wives of his friends, and perhaps also his male friends, might say, "What kind of person would do that?" and might reevaluate their relationship with him. If he, however, has a "good reason" for leaving her, that is, a reason acceptable to others, he is in much better shape. Accordingly, he will sometimes attempt to manipulate the circumstances in such a way that she provides him with that reason. He might provoke an argument, perhaps by failing to meet expectations he knows she has and thus make it appear that she is the one being unreasonable. He can then escalate the argument into a major disagreement and break off the relationship. If he is extremely successful, not only will his friends feel that he was justified, but his wife or girlfriend will also feel that she was the one who actually broke it off.

Games are means by which people communicate desired messages about the self and ways by which they exert control over others. People sometimes, however, play games with only themselves as the game partner. When a student has a difficult term paper to write, for example, he will sometimes promise himself things he finds desirable, such as a beer, reading *Playboy,* sleep, or a movie, after and only after he has finished writing the paper. He knows very well that at any time he can leave for a movie, go to sleep, or lie down with a beer and read *Playboy.* But he makes a bargain with himself that he will not do any of these things until he has completed the term paper. He then pretends to himself that he cannot do them until the paper is completed. He knows this technique is not reality but a means of controlling reality, directing energies towards completing an onerous task in order to attain desired goals.

Such self-games are possible only because, as we discussed in Chapter 6, humans have the remarkable capacity to make the self an object. Because people are able to think of and treat the self as an object, they are able to promise themselves future rewards for present activities, much as they do with another person. A second person is already "objectified," that is, another person is external to the self and is embodied in a distinctly separate physical entity. In *self-games,* such as this one, the self is made into an object which can similarly be promised rewards for responding to wishes. By a creative act, the self is made similar to a second person. The marvelously unique human capacity is that it is the same self which does the promising, cooperates with the desired course of action, and is promised the reward.

Gaming can also provide a welcome relief from harsh reality. We can hide behind various symbols and prevent others from "seeing within." By gaming, we can even provide a cover which hides reality from the self, as with a woman who sleeps with a man from whom she receives regular cash gifts to "help out" with the rent. She might well discontinue sleeping with him if the gifts were discontinued, but the gift must be "freely given" and, even among themselves, never be referred to as payment of any kind. In a similar manner, we all symbolize our world to create the reality we desire. The symbols we develop in our gaming relationships are critical in our construction of reality.

One way of looking at or conceptualizing much human behavior, then, is provided by the framework of games analysis. In this analysis the sociologist is interested in determining such things as what symbols people manipulate in order to gain their ends; who plays what games with whom; what rules they follow; how the rules originate, are maintained, or change; what sorts of games are played in one culture or society compared with another culture or society; how the games differ between sub-units of a society, such as between the varying social classes, the racial, ethnic, age, or sex groups; and how the rules differ when the same game is played within the same society depending upon the sex, race, age, and social class membership of the game players. Unfortunately, very little analysis along the lines that I have just indicated has been done by social scientists, but it remains a promising field for research.

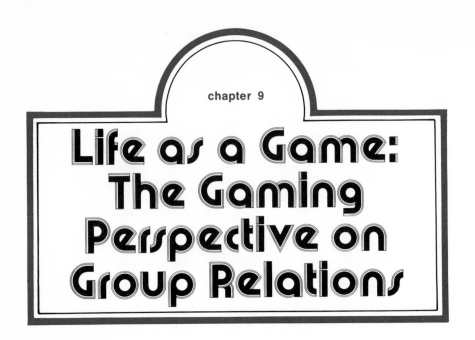

chapter 9

Life as a Game: The Gaming Perspective on Group Relations

Central to the perspective of looking at human behavior in terms of games is control or power. Games are a means of obtaining or maintaining control over a situation, of obtaining power over others, or of demonstrating that one has power over others. This theme has been central in the interpersonal games we have just discussed. By controlling or attempting to control a situation, one attempts to gain desired rewards. For example, in family games teenagers attempt to manipulate their parents into granting desired freedoms, while parents attempt to enforce compliance with their expectations; in occupational games employees attempt to manipulate supervisors into giving them time off, extra pay, or increased status, while employers attempt to increase the work production of their employees; the same is true of educational games, sex and courtship games, and any other interpersonal situations in which individuals wish to achieve goals. **Games** are situations in which persons whose fates are intertwined attempt to achieve goals (Shubik 1964:8).

As we discussed in the preceding chapter, **interpersonal behavior,** that is, behavior between individuals, can be understood in terms of the gaming perspective. By using this gaming perspective, however, we can also gain a different understanding of the relations between groups of people in our society and even of national and international relations. Conceptualizing **intergroup relations** in terms of games yields useful insight both into much of the behavior we regularly see going on around us and into the items that frequently make the evening headlines.

In the pluralistic society in which we live, not only do the various subgroups represent contrasting ways of looking at the world, as we have discussed, but these subcultures, with their varying definitions of reality, also come into conflict with one another. It is not as though these groups peacefully coexist within the same national boundaries, with each having laid claim to a particular area in society that does not impinge on the others. Such a model of life simply does not match the violent realities of American society. A more appropriate model for viewing the groups in our pluralistic society is to see them as conflictual, as continually impinging on one another, as coexisting only by means of very thin homeostatic threads, and as ever ready to erupt in conflict or even to disrupt in violence.

In this **conflict model,** the various groups of society are seen as continuously challenging one another for positions of power and as vigorously competing for scarce resources—whether those resources are material, as with credit, jobs, or housing, or whether they are nonmaterial, as the ability to make power decisions or the protection of prestige and image. As each group jockeys for a better position or attempts to maintain its present position, there prevails only a very unquiet peace or perhaps a tenuous truce between basically conflicting groups. If it weren't for the self-defeating nature of violence, primarily because violence once unleashed threatens to engulf all and also because complete victory appears elusive, intergroup gaming relations would probably be marked by much greater violence than they currently are. As it is, violence is not uncommon, though it is sporadic. Considering the intensity of the competition for scarce resources, violence is only comparatively rarely resorted to, although it is an option open to each group.

A power play or game strategy much more common than the use of violence is manipulating symbols. As we shall focus on in this chapter, by manipulating relevant symbols groups disclose and conceal information about themselves in order to attempt to better their position *vis-à-vis* other groups. This is done in much the same way as people do in the formal or organized games they play during their leisure hours. The games between the conflicting groups of our pluralistic society, however, are infinitely more serious than games between individuals: In the outcome of group games is precariously balanced the welfare of millions of people.

Within the conceptual framework of games and gamesmanship, we shall briefly examine relations between selected major groups within our society: games between the races, with the police, between labor and management, between corporations, and in advertising, politics, religion, protest, education, and international relations.

Relations between blacks and whites in the United States are especially marked by gamesmanship. Some of the presentations of self,
and some of the strategies and tactics in the gaming between racial
groups, are well known. For example, when blacks make complaints
about the way they are treated by the police in some sectors of American society, a common answer which they are given is, "We'll investigate the matter." Once this statement is made, that is frequently as far
as the matter goes since typically the police investigate the police,
making the outcome fairly predictable. No one hears any more about it,
and as time passes even the one who complained tends to forget it, or
as is more likely, he gives up either in despair or fear.

All sorts of gaming devices are used to cool down race relations. One
of these is tokenism. When demands by blacks for access to various
aspects of society to which they have been historically denied admission
become so widespread, insistent, or threatening that they can no longer
be safely ignored, one strategy is to permit access to blacks, but only on
a token basis. Although only a superficial change is made and the underlying discriminatory structure remains untouched, the tokenism
ploy allows whites to say that blacks are not prevented from participation. For example:

> In 1967 I was interviewed for a job in a southern university, which
> for obvious reasons shall remain nameless. Before my visit I was as-
> sured by the administration of this university that its ten thousand
> students had been peacefully integrated following the Supreme
> Court decision of 1954. After I had been on their campus for a few
> hours, however, I had not seen a single black, and I asked my host if
> they actually were integrated. He replied that they were indeed, and
> he then began to talk about faculty welfare benefits. I pursued the
> issue, however, and asked him how many blacks there actually were
> on campus. He said that he did not know for certain, but when I
> asked if he could approximate the number, he abruptly replied,
> "There are seventeen."

Another gaming strategy frequently employed by the white establishment to handle potentially explosive racial situations is to deal only with
peripheral matters. This "strategy of periphery" entirely avoids the
necessity of making changes in the basic relations between our racial
groups. When the "long hot summer" threatens, for example, one
move is to open the fire hydrants in black neighborhoods so the children can play in the gushing water. Pictures of black children gleefully
splashing away are then prominently displayed in the daily newspapers,
usually sans watermelon in today's somewhat more sophisticated age.
This tactic certainly serves a double "cooling-off" purpose, but it does

"Strategy of periphery" is a gaming technique which means to skirt causes and to deal only superficially with pressing social problems. This picture illustrates the "cooling down" of potential trouble, but it is an action which does nothing about the underlying causes of poverty and discrimination. (Courtesy of Wide World Photos)

nothing about poverty, inadequate housing, jobs, education, technical training, or any other aspect of discriminatory social relationships that have led up to the "long hot summers" in the first place.

Co-optation is another strategy frequently used by the Anglo controllers for dealing with troublesome race relations. In **co-optation,** tential or actual rivals, troublemakers, or enemies are recruited to one's own side and used for one's own purposes. This strategy in race relations usually means that black leaders who pose a threat to white dominance of the social order are bought off. Federal funds, for example, are poured into a potentially explosive area and black militants are given official job titles and put on the government payroll. As social change is seldom forthcoming, the underlying purpose of this move appears to be to cool down the situation by providing greater leverage for social control. Providing militants with a regular income gains the establishment greater control over some by instilling loyalty to the employing organization, over others by being able to threaten to cut off paychecks, while from all it drains off energies that tend to disrupt the system. For their part in this game, blacks who know that the white establishment is willing to put up such bribery money sometimes wear "militancy for sale" signs; that is, without actual intent to disrupt the social system they "posture" militancy in order to maneuver the establishment into hiring them.

Another ploy to meet black demands is the racial use of law. When blacks or other minority groups threaten the status quo, whites sometimes respond by using already existing laws to enforce white supremacy. One weapon used by Mississippi blacks in their seemingly endless struggle to secure equality has been the boycott. In Clarksdale, Mississippi, blacks attempting to obtain downtown employment began a boycott directed against businesses that refused to hire blacks. The leaders of the boycott were promptly placed under arrest and levied fines because they had led a boycott. At the same time that "this incident was in progress, the Mississippi legislature was passing a resolution urging good Mississippians to boycott the city of Memphis, because Memphis was failing to hold the line for segregation" (Smith 1967:267).

The boycott is a gaming technique which has effectively been used to force social change. Shown are Rev. Ralph D. Abernathy and Dr. Martin Luther King, Jr., as they were being arrested for leading a boycott in Birmingham, Alabama. They wore old clothes to dramatize their store boycott during the Easter season.   (Courtesy of Wide World Photos)

When existing laws prove inadequate, new laws can sometimes be passed in order to hold blacks down. Historically we have regularly had laws explicitly directed against blacks, such as poll taxes, laws prohibiting racial intermarriage, laws governing "separate but equal" public services such as schools, and even laws stating where persons of particular races must sit in public conveyances or which drinking fountain or toilet they can use. A more recent racially motivated law was passed in 1967 after militant blacks appeared on Oakland streets dramatically displaying carbines and bandoliers. Whites felt both extremely intimidated and incensed, and the California Legislature quickly passed a law prohibiting the carrying of loaded weapons within incorporated areas. Since today's laws cannot overtly discriminate racially, this law applies to both blacks and whites.

The Black Panther Party was just in its infancy at this time, but the impending bill provided the opportunity to dramatically publicize the tiny group. The organization had only about four or five members when Bobby Seale recruited black men off the street, armed them, and with about twenty-eight others ostentatiously carried arms into the Sacramento capital while the bill was being debated. This dramaturgical move cinched the bill's passage, but it also forcefully thrust the Black Panther Party into public prominence, paving the way for their organizing nationally (*Playboy, 20,* May 1973; 73–74).

These techniques by no means exhaust the moves, countermoves, strategies, or tactics employed by whites and blacks in their interracial games. Violence, for example, sometimes marks these racial games, as with ghetto rioting and police brutality. Styles of violence have undergone change, however; lynching, for example, appears to be a thing of the past. The number of lynchings of blacks has steadily decreased each decade since 1890, as shown by Table 9.1. In contrast to past eras,

Table 9.1 Lynchings of Blacks in the United States, 1890–1951

Year	Number Lynched
1890–1899	1,111
1900–1909	791
1910–1919	568
1920–1929	281
1930–1939	119
1940–1949	31
1950–1951	2

Source: Based on data contained in Guzman 1969:58–59; 1951 is the most recent year for which lynching information is reported.

Following the Civil War, blacks posed a political threat to white dominance in the South, and lynching became one of the more forceful means of maintaining the status quo. During this past generation this form of retaliatory social control has practically disappeared from the American racial scene. (Courtesy of Wide World Photos)

today's racial games are more likely to be played according to rules where the interaction between the groups stops short of overt violence.

Games between blacks and whites are nothing new, of course. Alexis de Tocqueville, a visitor from France, observed the American scene in the 1830's and reported on an interracial game of that time:

> He asked why Pennsylvania, a state known for its racial toleration, did not allow blacks to vote. He was told that no law prevented their voting, and when he asked why he did not notice a single black voting, he was told that they "voluntarily abstain from making their appearance." Upon pursuing the matter further, he was told that this was not because blacks wanted to refrain from voting but that if they were to show up at the polling booths the magistrates would not be able to protect them from violence (de Tocqueville 1957:269–272).

Police–citizen encounters can also be conceptualized within a games framework, although we may not ordinarily think of this interaction in terms of games. Sometimes, however, the gamesmanship in such situations is explicitly recognized. For example, the following dramaturgical game has been suggested for someone stopped by a policeman:

> When you pull over, turn off your motor. That way, you're telling the cop you know how serious the predicament is. . . . Look contrite, miserable, and desperate. Call the cop "officer," out of respect, and try to get your voice to break. If your wife is in the car, or some other woman is, have her do all the talking (*Moneysworth, 1,* June 28, 1971, p. 1).

Deference, as illustrated by this quotation, is an essential element for pleasant interaction with the police. Policemen are generally extremely touchy about respect, so much so that they feel they are even more justified to use violence when they are shown disrespect than when they are trying to make an arrest, or trying to obtain information critical to the solving of a crime, than when they are dealing with hardened criminals, or even when they are in situations where they feel it is impossible to avoid using violence (Westley 1953). Accordingly, it is both a truism and an understatement to say that deference pays. To ignore this basic rule of the game is to literally risk life and limb.

Law enforcers and lawbreakers also play games with one another. Policemen and criminals may be enemies, but in at least one sense they are benevolent enemies. Certain rules or expectations govern their interaction, comprising a sort of "cops and robbers" game. This is especially true concerning **moral crimes,** activities that are against the law but that are carried on with the consent of the people involved. In moral crimes, because the acts are consensual one's person or property is not violated. Moral crimes are primarily expectations of correct behavior which have been written into law, such as activities involving gambling, underage drinking, prostitution, homosexuality, and, until recently, abortion.

Equilibrium tends to develop between the police and violators of moral laws. Policemen in our major cities are typically paid off in order to overlook moral crimes on their beats, and, in turn, those engaging in these activities are expected to keep them fairly quiet. As long as no public outcry arises, this equilibrium can continue for years. In the city of St. Louis, for example, a well-known abortion mill was operated by the same people for over twenty-five years.

Sometimes the rules of this game become highly formalized. One researcher reported to me that in a major Eastern Seaboard city bars catering to homosexual clientele must pay the police department five cents for each bottle of beer they sell. Invoices from beer distributors are even subject to police check to make certain that bar owners are not holding out. In another major city, police pay-off in the numbers racket is even more highly organized. These pay-offs are not made on volume, but the police demand and receive fixed amounts of cash on a regular basis, extending up the chain of command from the beat, to the patrol cars, to the precinct, to the division, and up to the borough. Beat policemen receive $624 a year from each location or "spot," while police manning a patrol car are paid $100 per month from each location. This might run up to forty-five locations, but in such cases four officers split the monthly take of $4500 since there are two shifts of two men each. Detectives are paid a higher fixed amount, as befits their higher rank—as are sergeants, lieutenants, and the gambling squad (Pulliam 1970).

From time to time the police are required to arrest numbers operators in order to satisfy the public that they are doing their job. This requires further detailed cooperation. The police contact telephones the operators of a spot and gives the details of the coming raid, while for their part in fulfilling this rule of the game, gamblers "take turns" in being arrested. When the police tip them off that they are going to raid some particular location, the operators decide in advance who will be present when the police arrive, usually selecting those with the cleanest record. When small-fry are sentenced to prison, which is not typical, the controllers of the numbers operation continue paying them their regular salary during their confinement. Their old job is also awaiting them upon their release.

Prostitution, like gambling, is a moral crime whose roots go back to antiquity. The police know that there are always some men who want to buy what some women offer for sale. They also commonly feel that prostitution is not a legal violation serious enough to merit their attention in the first place, and that whatever steps they take will eventually be circumvented. Consequently, the police tend to ignore prostitution unless it becomes too blatant, unless there is a public outcry, or unless some other form of pressure is put on them to curtail hustling activities. An informal "working" understanding tends to develop between prostitutes and police: The police will largely ignore prostitutory activities as long as the prostitutes are quiet as they make their sales. Fines for prostitution sometimes even serve as a way of informally licensing prostitutes. It has been reported, for example, that when prostitutes are regularly arrested and routinely given a low fine they feel they have a license to operate for a period of time (cf. Winick and Kinsie, 1971:218).

In this "cops and robbers" game the basic rule is that no violence will be directed against the police. Killing a policeman is a major violation of the basic expectations in the game, and at this point "all hell breaks loose" as the police mobilize their forces in a concerted manhunt for the perpetrator of the crime. This is also true in other countries, of course, such as England where it is expected that no violence will ever be directed against bobbies. In fact, an informal agreement appears to operate: Criminals in England will not use guns, and only policemen who have passed special tests will do so, and then only under the direct orders of their supervisors.

Although applying games analysis to police-criminal relations can profitably lead to a different understanding of their interaction, the gaming aspects of their relations are seldom readily visible. In labor-management relations, however, the game is much more apparent. Shortly before a contract is up, labor typically begins its gaming moves by demanding higher wages and greater fringe benefits. Labor usually begins with demands so high that it knows management will not meet them, while management, on its part, responds with a counteroffer so low it knows it is unacceptable to labor. Labor then lowers its demands somewhat, and management responds with a corresponding increase in its offer, with this negotiation process ordinarily continuing until an agreement is ironed out. Labor sometimes strategically includes items in its initial demands simply for the purpose of trading for things they do want. For example, labor might demand more vacation for all employees, knowing that this is unattainable, and later "trade" this demand for an item which management is willing to offer. A major part of this game centers around revealing and concealing information: Management attempts to figure out what items the union is serious about and what items are merely negotiable, while labor, for its part, attempts to conceal this information while surreptitiously determining how much management is willing to go above its last offer.

Negotiations ordinarily follow this general gaming format, but at times the game breaks down. Labor sometimes overplays its hand and adamantly insists on demands which management is entirely unwilling to meet, or management may stubbornly refuse to make any offer to labor. Knowing that breakdowns are a possibility, prior to negotiations management is likely to stockpile its products so that it can better weather a strike, while for the same purpose labor attempts to bolster its strike fund. Each side prepares for the worst and hopes for the best.

When negotiations do break down, the game threatens to come to a complete halt. A referee in the form of a labor arbitrator is then brought into play, an individual or group acceptable to both parties whose role it is to impartially reconcile their differences. During this stalemate period, both labor and management make regular self-presentations to the public via the mass media. Although the details vary, each makes statements to the same effect: "We represent a reasonable position. Our offer (demand) is sound, but they are refusing to

bargain with us in good faith." These self-presentations turn into a ritual litany when big unions and big business publicly play this bargaining game.

Corporations not only play games with labor; but they also play
games with one another. This game comes complete with corporate
spies, individuals hired to seek out information on moves being
planned by the opponent, such as new product designs, research results, or marketing plans. Corporations attempt to make "turncoats" of
their competitors' best players by luring them to their side with higher
rewards. Corporations not uncommonly decide to play the game of
monopoly rather than competition, finding it more strategic to buy out
a rival than to compete with him. They then merge their former rival
into their own corporation or maintain it as a separate subsidiary, in either case strengthening their position *vis-à-vis* other competitors. The
federal government sometimes feels that this consolidation move provides an unfair advantage to one team and that it works against the interests of the more passive, captive players, the public. The government has accordingly developed highly complex rules concerning
corporate acquisitions and monopolies.

In order to maintain competitive standing, corporations price their
own products in line with their competitor's. Legitimate tactics in controlling prices include lowering production costs by quality control and
automation, while more under-the-table moves include price fixing,
which guarantees that one's product will not be undersold, and
planned obsolescence, which builds "repeat customers" in the sense
that people are forced to repurchase the same product. Following another extreme tactic, a company will close its doors in the North, where
the price of labor is higher, and move the factory lock, stock, and barrel to the South, where unions are weaker and labor is cheaper.

If, on the one hand, competition threatens to become too keen and it
looks as though major teams might get hurt, there is always the referee
waiting on the side lines to step in and slow down the action by cur-
tailing competition, as did the Federal Trade Commission when it
ruled that Busch Brewery could not lower the price of Budweiser.
Unlike many other games, Busch was able to successfully appeal the
referee's decision (*Commerce Clearing House,* April 21, 1959:75229; June
20, 1960:76878; *Anheuser-Busch, Inc., vs. F.T.C. 289 Federal Second:*835).
If, on the other hand, the game lags in action too greatly, this same referee steps in to get things moving, as when the Federal Trade Commission successfully brought charges against General Electric and Wes-
tinghouse officials for fixing prices on electric light bulbs.

Corporations also play games with one another by means of their advertising. Until recently, a company could neither mention a rival by

name nor directly attack the products of its competitors. A company was allowed only to emphasize the outstanding features of its own products, without referring to the competition. This arrangement has undergone gradual, but extensive, modification in recent years. First appeared oblique references to rival products, such as "the other leading brand," and the famous "We're only number two" advertising campaign waged by Avis against Hertz. Companies were then gradually allowed to mention competitors by name as they extolled the supposedly superior virtues of their own products, and by 1974 the rules had changed to such an extent that in television advertising the imputed inferior qualities of rival products could be pictorially demonstrated in filmed tests.

Each company, however, is acutely aware that too direct a strike at its competition may invite a retaliatory blow against one's own products, resulting in loss greater than the gains one made by the initial attack. In the interest of self preservation, then, companies carefully avoid open warfare as they compete with one another. As with price fixing, much of corporate competition is carried out in clandestine behind-the-scenes maneuvers that prevent intercorporate warfare. This practice also practically guarantees the peaceful perpetuation of the larger corporations. If a major corporation should happen to fall on evil days, however, it is now possible, as in the case of Lockheed Aircraft, for the Congress of the United States to become actively involved. Bail can be paid, the penalty avoided, and the player can continue to participate in the game.

The major role players in the advertising game appear to be the corporate advertising world pitted against the American public, with the Federal Communications Commission cast in the role of referee. Ralph Nader has joined the game as champion of the underdog, charging that American corporations are not so much competitors as they are partners in a joint endeavor to fleece the American public at any cost. He is frustratedly attempting to clarify and change some of the game's basic ground rules.

Although it might seem that the American public would by now be too sophisticated for transparent and simplistic approaches in advertising and product presentation, this appears not yet to be the case. We are regularly bombarded with symbolic manipulations, such as red, white, and blue packaging or containers that appear to hold a great deal more than they do. We are also continually faced with a meaningless array of terms, such as family size, economy size, super economy size, large size, extra large size, jumbo size, giant size, and so on *ad infinitum*. That even the United States government becomes a cooperative ally of advertisers in the production of purposely confusing terms

"A quart is a quart, damn it! How can it be a *big, jumbo* quart?"

One of the most common games in Western culture is advertising designed to increase consumption. Though many approaches are transparent, we are regularly bombarded with a
seemingly never-ending array of symbol manipulations which are designed to distort reality.   (Drawing by P. Barlow; © 1957, The New Yorker Magazine, Inc.)

becomes apparent when we note that the official U.S. grades of olives,
in ascending order, are large, extra large, mammoth, giant, jumbo,
colossal, and super colossal ("The Great American Dream Machine,"
August 10, 1974). Try to figure out the differences among these categories in this terminological morass—even a dictionary is of little help.

A regular part of the advertising game is the exaggerated claim,
sometimes involving "secret ingredient X," a magical formula, or "un-
conditional guarantees" which are *un*conditional in the sense that they
guarantee *no* conditions whatever. For example, one "guarantee" reads:

> The company guarantees to replace any malfunctioning parts due to
> errors in manufacture, provided the malfunction occurs within one

year of the purchase date and provided the purchaser pays all packaging and postage costs as well as all labor charges involved (*St. Louis Post-Dispatch,* Nov. 15, 1971).

This guarantee, for an inexpensive clock, might just as well have read: "This is a guarantee. It doesn't really guarantee anything, but it is designed to make you feel better."

Just as by their interactions individuals attempt to control the impressions others receive of them, so corporations carefully curry images that they constantly parade before the public. As we covered in the last chapter, even the type of wife an executive marries is connected with corporate images. What is hidden behind the corporate facade, however, is frequently a reality too harsh for public presentation. For example, a common strategy in the game of peddling products is to claim that a company exists in order to satisfy customers, when there is only one reason for the being of that company and that is the pursuit of profit—pure, naked, financial profit. Corporations cannot make a bald statement like this, however, for fear of alienating customers. Instead, they cajole the public with such statements as: "We are in business to make you happy," "We may be the only phone company in town, but we try not to act like it," or "We have been at this location for thirty years, and we are here to serve you." This is much more palatable than to say, "The reason we are here is to make money," or, "The reason we are the only phone company in town is that we've either bought out or destroyed our competition, and we're the only one you can do business with whether you like it or not. Pay your telephone bill on time—or else."

The common phrase, "the political game," gives explicit recognition that a good part of this intergroup activity centers around gamesmanship. Perhaps people tend to recognize gaming aspects more readily in politics than in other parts of life because politicians are so transparent in many of their self-presentations, such as kissing babies, running for office wearing a hard hat, or eating ethnic food when campaigning ("I love Jewish rye bread smothered in chitlins!"). Perhaps it is also because people regularly hear so many grandiose promises during a campaign but see no action on the issues in the nonelection years that they frequently realize that a politician's promises are generally not serious but, rather, part of a dramaturgical display in a national game.

But underlying such transparent manipulating of symbols in this national game even more traditional than baseball are symbol manipulations which are not so easy to recognize. For example, politicians will frequently use the patriotism ploy to explain their actions, perhaps saying the reason they voted for or against a particular bill is because it is

Projecting the "right image" is essential to winning political office. Because politicians are frequently so transparent in their self-presentations, people tend to recognize gaming aspects of politics more readily than in many other aspects of social life. (Courtesy of Wide World Photos)

"good for the country" or "best for the state or district." When such statements are made the American flag is sometimes unfurled in the breeze while the national anthem plays, but such statements are ordinarily not presented with such dramatic flair. Instead, the symbols of patriotism and "best interest" are a routine part of the political presentation of self. They are used as explanatory devices to camouflage underlying reasons for voting, whether that reason be vested interest in personal financial investments or the squeeze caused by highly intricate maneuvering between legislators and pressure groups, lobbyists and coalitions. Most of these latter players in the political game are invisible to the public, but it is part of the legislative routine to play the various pressure groups off against one another in order to marshal alliance for future support on bills in which the legislator and his constituents have more at stake. A legislator may even find himself supporting a measure which he personally opposes in order to prevent his constituency from learning his real sentiments and turning him out of office (Smith 1967:132, 137, 139). Legislators must also frequently engage in some fancy horse-trading, exchanging their votes for support on bills that more directly affect their own district. They do not present these trades to the public as the reason for their voting, however, for such an explanation fails to match the impressions they want to manage.

Because personal and group stakes in running for political office are so high, the game sometimes gets out of hand. New campaign financing and spending rules have recently evolved in order to exert greater control over political contenders. In spite of these restrictions and the ever-watchful eyes of the proliferating governmental and citizens groups, campaigners have been known to go to rather elaborate lengths in order to secure their place in the American power scene. The Watergate revelations were certainly ample testimony to behind-the-scenes maneuvers in direct conflict with the freedoms the perpetrators publicly professed to be defending. What someone doesn't know may or may not hurt him, but when its seamy aspects are paraded in full view of the public, political presentations can certainly be irreparably punctured.

Leaders of religious denominations also play games with one another and with their constituents. As in business, their competitive moves are circumscribed by a rigid set of rules. For example, all of our denominations attempt to win converts (or customers), but these converting activities take place under a set of rules designed to protect the special areas

Religious groups have developed elaborate techniques for recruiting new members. Shown here is a gaming strategy not commonly followed by the more established denominations. (Courtesy of Wide World Photos)

of interest staked out by each denomination. This means that although conversions are desirable, it is ordinarily considered hitting below the belt to convert members of other denominations. An ecclesiastical foul has occurred when this rule is violated, and a negative symbol is brought into play: One has "proselytized" a member of another church. This rule against proselytism becomes increasingly lax, however, as one moves away from the heartland of mainstream Protestantism. For example, Lutherans do not ordinarily consider Episcopalians to be "fair game," but that is exactly how they view Mormons and Christian Scientists. The proselytism rule blends into nonexistence when it comes to non-Christian religions, such as the Hare Krishna.

Religious leaders of American denominations are probably as socialized into American values as are any group of Americans. Even though they claim spiritual values as their area of expertise, they end up utilizing material standards to measure spiritual progress. For example, in their annual reports religious leaders point with pride to the total contributions given to their church body, the amount of contributions per member, the number of new buildings begun during the last *fiscal* year, the number of persons attending church on a given Sunday, the number who took Holy Communion, the number baptized, the number confirmed, and the denomination's total membership as measured by number of people or "souls."

As relations between the competing groups in our pluralistic society are tenuous and ever subject to change as groups maneuver or jockey for better competitive position, and as some groups feel that they are being unjustly held down or exploited, various protest games have developed. In these games, whether the major game players protesting against the established order are students, hippies, welfare mothers, women, blacks, or Chicanos, symbols are inevitably liberally used. The peace sign, the raised clenched fist, the clenched fist attached to the biological sign for female, the black beret, grapes, and so on are used to evoke solidarity among followers and to develop a shared perception of the need for changing the system.

Ordinarily people involved in protest activities do not look at their activities as games. Their involvement prevents them from being dispassionate and from taking a look from the outside, as it were. (I, for example, don't personally care one bit for this games analysis when it is applied to my own protest activities, and I emotionally resist such a view. Mine, after all, are moral endeavors.) But games they are, and most serious games indeed, with the potential of erupting into violence and destruction at any time. Occasionally, however, gaming aspects of protest activities become clear-cut, such as when hippies give flowers to the police, or when the police are restrained from using violence on demonstrators and frustratedly "give the finger" instead. In a protest demonstration I witnessed in Heidelberg, Germany, gamesmanship was overt:

The city administration increased its streetcar and bus fares by 50 percent, from eighty Pfennig to one Mark twenty Pfennig—from about twenty-four cents to thirty-six cents. They strategically announced this increase when the Heidelberg University students were on vacation in order to create a *fait accompli* by the time the students returned. It did not work out this way, however, and the students who were still in the city organized a strike.

The students decided on the strategy of disrupting the public transportation system, and they would stand in front of the streetcars and block their passage. As part of their strategy, they would also disperse immediately when the riot police arrived on the scene, thus avoiding direct confrontation with the police. They would then regroup a few blocks away and a short time later disrupt the operation of another streetcar. Over a thousand riot policemen were called in from nearby cities, but they, as well as the local police, would laugh as they approached the demonstrators, and the demonstrators would laughingly retreat. The general feeling of goodwill expressed between the police and demonstrators was probably because the police were largely in sympathy with the cause of holding down the fares of public transportation as they were also from the working class. Some of the riot policemen even accepted the protester's red dot symbol and placed it on the dashboards of their police cars and army trucks. After five days of this mutually enjoyable gamesmanship, however, orders came from above, and the police began to vigorously crack down. They began to arrest demonstrators, quickly breaking the back of the student strike. In the face of this naked show of power, the game lost its fun aspects, and the city bureaucracy easily won a hands-down victory.

Naked power is never far from protest games. The Establishment ultimately controls the forces of power and can call them into play whenever desired in order to change the score. In the concluding chapter of this book we shall examine the bases for social power.

After the generalized riots and disruptions on American campuses in the spring of 1970, state legislatures throughout the nation slashed or attempted to cut state funding to higher education. I take this to be a form of discipline directed against the university for not exerting greater control over their students. This in itself is another game. That is, legislatures have a finite or limited amount of money to disperse among many causes, and being unhappy with what took place on the campuses, they made a deliberate move designed to sanction higher education in order to bring about conformance.

I don't feel that it is overstating the case to say that this situation is similar to a parent cutting off the allowance of a teenage child because the child has violated some rule or parental expectation. Like the child with his parents, universities must attempt to stay in the good graces of those who control their financial allowance. And like the teenager, it is usually necessary to present a certain image in order to communicate a message which says: "Look. I am what you expect." Whereas the teenager might change his image by modifying his hairstyle or dress, whereas he might cut down on his abusive language or begin to do his homework or come home at the expected hour, universities resort to similar tactics. One university, for example, broadcast to the public that because their budget had been cut they were "reducing inefficiencies and promoting economies wherever possible as part of this continuing effort." They then announced that they had eliminated 107 courses from their curriculum following "an intensive review of all course offerings" (source available upon request). People who had access to "behind the scenes information" knew better, however. In actuality, the university had merely publicized a bookkeeping device. Prior to the budget cuts they had already gathered from its various faculties the names of courses which were officially listed but were no longer being taught. They were already planning to drop these courses to bring their list of course offerings closer to their actual curriculum. Their strategic announcement of their already planned cuts, however, was indeed tactically wise in the game of funding of higher education.

International relations can also be viewed within the framework of games and self-presentations. This is indeed a most serious game, however, as its consequences frequently are life or death for vast numbers of people. Much of international relations also centers around the strategy of information control. As nations deal with nations, their leaders anticipate the moves which leaders of other nations will make. As the leaders attempt to gain their desired goals, each side presents an image or manages an impression for the other side. This became especially apparent, almost transparent one might say, immediately after China was admitted to the United Nations. When Peking's delegation arrived in New York on November 11, 1971, the United States prepared what was officially publicized as "a cool but correct reception." Only low-level American officials were present to guide the Chinese delegation through customs, and as they did so, they were extremely careful not to say "hello" to them. As the spokesman for the U.S. mission reported, "We are not meeting them. It may sound silly, but that's the way it is" (*St. Louis Post-Dispatch,* November 11, 1971).

The manipulation of a nation's image is a constant preoccupation with national leaders. Even persons responsible for a junta's takeover of a nation are vitally concerned about the image they present to interested foreign powers. Witness, for example, the common phenomenon of the palace revolutionaries shortly after their takeover making public statements for world consumption to the effect that "We seized power in order to protect democracy" and that "We will hold an election by X date"—a date which appears to be infinitely movable into the future.

When we examine the arms race between the United States and Russia, gaming aspects of international relations become especially pronounced. If either of the two belligerents makes a move to increase its relative position in the arms race, the other follows with a countermove calculated to outbalance the first. If one nation appropriates funds to deploy or develop ICBM's, for example, then the other, in its turn, does the same. This apparently endless race for destruction can be peacefully concluded only when both sides realize that if we discontinue weapons development and stockpiling we will still maintain our relative power—which now appears to be the capacity for each of us to utterly destroy the world. As it now is, each move threatens our relative positions (meaning, I suppose, that one nation might gain the capacity to destroy the world with a bigger bang than the other), and any move by either is met by an appropriate countermove on the part of the other.

The show of military power, used to communicate confidence to citizens and fear and caution to rival nations, is essential to international gaming strategies. If the symbol is successful, the status quo is preserved; if extremely successful, a nation gains negotiating power at the conference table. (Courtesy of Wide World Photos)

From time to time the destructive capabilities of each superpower threaten to erupt in violent conflagration. These periods mark critical junctures in international power games. In the Cuban missile crisis of September 1962, for example, gaming aspects were especially noticeable as Kennedy and Khrushchev squared off against one other, each tensely anticipating the moves of the other, with an audience literally of the world nervously awaiting the outcome—and its own fate. What appeared to be almost a replay occurred about a decade later. During the Israeli-Arab war of October 1973, when things were going badly for the Arabs, Russia threatened to send troops in their support. The United States countermoved with a national alert of its armed forces. Fortunately for our welfare, and the world's, responses were correctly anticipated by both sides and Armageddon was once more avoided—or at least postponed for a while longer.

In the 1973 confrontation, other more subtle gaming aspects of international relations became evident. If Russia, for example, had actually intended to send troops in support of the Arabs, she would have done so. But by publicly announcing this possibility, Russia provided an official games cue for the United States, giving us time to put our troops on alert. When we did so, it then became foolhardy for Russia to proceed with troop movements that could too easily have resulted in hot war. I suspect, however, that Russia had already anticipated our countermove. Our making it then removed the necessity of Russia following through. Russia's announcement of intent accomplished its designed purposes, however, since the Arabs received strong verbal support during their crisis and the United States was put on warning that Russia took the crisis seriously and was willing to use force to protect her vested interests.

The rulers of a nation are also highly concerned about the self-presentations they make to the members of their own nation, and by means of elaborately contrived statements they continually justify their activities. One country, for example, might invade a weaker country, with the leaders giving a "We-must-protect-the-inhabitants-of-that-country-from-communist-conspiracy" type of explanation or a "We-are-protecting-the-freedom-of-those-people" rationale, when the motivation for the act might be something entirely different, such as the protection of resources and markets. Political leaders regularly use **ideology** in dealing with their people, that is, they present reasons acceptable to their populace in order to construct for them a desired definition of reality. For example, in the initial stages of the war in Vietnam President Johnson talked about the responsibility of the United States "to protect a free people." By the late 1960's this explanation had disappeared from public pronouncements because the American public had by that time become both disillusioned with and cynical about our policy in Vietnam, forcing our leaders to provide different explanations to account for our activities there.

Justifying reasons, or ideology, are an important part of the political game. Political leaders use ideology as they attempt to create and maintain their desired definition of a particular situation. Essential to the process of controlling definitions of reality, as we covered in Chapter 4, is manipulating symbols significant to a people. It does not matter what the cultural symbols are. They could be the swastika, the hammer and sickle, or the Stars and Stripes; words carrying strongly negative and sometimes frightening connotations such as huns, fascists, bolsheviks, and communists; or more positive words such as peace and freedom, motherhood and the flag, apple pie and baseball. A central part of the political game involves clothing the self and one's program in positive cultural symbols while decking out one's opponent, whether an individual or another nation, in symbols to which people attach negative sentiments.

If human beings are viewed as goal-seeking, as beings who seek goals available only in limited quantities in opposition to others who desire those same goals, then conflict in social life is natural. Conflict is then an inevitable part of human relations. If we view groups within a pluralistic society as attempting to maximize their interests at the expense of others, then conflict is endemic to relations between human groups. If it is limited resources, of whatever sort, to which nations aspire, then conflict is also endemic to relations between nations.

The question to ask is perhaps not: "Why conflict?," "Why violence?," or "Why war?" It is perhaps more appropriate to ask: "What mechanisms in human relations curtail conflict, impede violence, and ultimately avoid a war of all against all?" It is entirely possible that the answer revolves around that basic ability which separates human beings from the lower animals, the use of symbols. As we covered in Chapter 4, it is our ability to use symbols that allows culture to exist. Our ability to formulate words or concepts allows us to live group life as we know it. By communicating through the concepts we develop, people are able to both conceptualize and plan for a future. Symbols allow people to join their activities to mutually desirable ends. Without symbols, people would be unable to communicate their ideas about life, their desires for the future, or to come to any mutual understanding regarding what life is all about.

The ability to use symbols allows people to formulate rules for the games basic to social life. By manipulating symbols people develop definitions of reality which they then communicate to others. Symbolic communication lays down basic expectations within which group life is lived. The rules under which activities are permitted or not permitted, and for whom, when, how, and where, are communicated through the use of symbols. Particularized ways of looking at and reacting to the world become symbolically maintained. When newcomers are socialized into society, as we shall analyze in depth in the concluding chapter of this book, an essential part of their socialization is learning the basic symbolic structure of their culture. Learning the basic "rules of the game" provides the fundamental expectations regarding presentations of the self, the expectations within which we interact with others. It is perhaps symbolic communication, underlying the games only people play, which allows the social order to exist.

o

chapter 10

Life as Playing the Wrong Game: Homosexuality

Homosexuality. A word which brings panic to the hearts of parents for fear their child might become one. A term which represents derision for most members of American society. A designation which not only brings laughter and scorn but also arouses shock, fear, and shame. An activity which is illegal in most of our states.

Some people are, and some people aren't—or so it is commonly thought. How do they get that way? Are people born homosexuals? Why are they like that? Just "why" are they anyway? We shall deal in this chapter with these and many other questions which are tied up with the emotionally laden symbol of homosexuality.

By way of general introduction, I wish to point out that the sociological view of homosexuality differs radically from the ideas most people have. What you learn in this chapter will, in all probability, not square up with what you have previously learned about the subject. According to sociological theory, homosexuality is not a condition of humans in the sense that it is something one does or does not have. Nor is it a physical abnormality, whether temporary like a cold, or permanent like faulty genetic structure. Homosexuality is, rather, thought to be a social role. Like any other social role, homosexuality is learned behavior. Like other social roles, it also has its typical recruitment patterns, its characteristic behaviors, and its unique problems.

Before going into these, I have to present a background idea which, though not difficult, is startlingly different from what most people think. In fact, it goes directly against common sense, and most people whom you tell it to will probably tell you that you are somewhat imbalanced (although they probably won't put it in such polite terms). But here goes. It is probable that, though humans are born sexual, they are by nature neither *heterosexual* nor *homosexual*. Note that I said probable, for this is a theoretical area in which we have to develop ideas which best meet the facts as we see them. We cannot adequately separate biological nature from social learning in the area of sexual behavior, and no one is about to volunteer their sons or daughters for some Machiavellian experiment to determine exactly what the facts are. Even if they would, the experiment would be banned, so we are left with probabilities and speculations about what is natural about the nature of human sexual behavior.

Neither heterosexual nor homosexual by nature? What is left? A lot, as we shall see. Human sexual behavior may be like human speaking behavior. Though people are born with the capacity to learn language, what language they eventually speak depends on the particular language to which they are introduced. It is possible that human sexual behavior is like this: Though people are born with a sex drive, the capacity to engage eventually in sexual relations, the type of sexual behavior they engage in depends on the particular sexual behavior to which they are introduced. People, in other words, though they have a biologically built-in sex drive, have no corresponding built-in object attached to their drive. Just as people given the right learning experience can learn to speak any language, so those given the right learning experience can learn to respond erotically in a number of ways. People can learn to direct their sex drives toward members of the same sex, as well as toward members of the opposite sex. That toward which the sex drive is directed does not even have to be human, and some people learn to respond erotically to animals and even to inanimate objects.

As we covered in Chapter 5, though sex can be an intimate expression of emotion, how people express their sex drive is not simply a private, personal matter. In each culture techniques are developed for channeling this powerful human drive into the ways thought appropriate within that culture (Murdock 1949:260; Henslin 1971:1–4). Newcomers to each society are thoroughly instructed, if only by example, in the prevailing beliefs and practices regarding the "correct" satisfactions of their sex drive. As we covered in Chapter 6, dramaturgical instruction in "being sexual" is so extensive that it even includes systematic socialization, according to cultural standards, into walking in the manner customarily associated with one's sex.

In each culture, then, people are encouraged and directed to express their sex drive according to the ways developed and thought of as right or proper within that particular culture. In American culture, exclusive heterosexuality is thought to be the only "right" way of being sexual. Homosexuality is viewed as a degrading and shameful condition which

American society is geared to teaching and enforcing heterosexuality. As with other strongly-held values, when it is violated negative sanctions are brought to bear upon the violators, as these two students in Palo Alto, California, discovered when they participated in a class experiment. (Courtesy of Wide World Photos)

afflicts some people, a sinful activity in which some people disgustingly participate, and an abhorrent perversion to be avoided at all costs. Accordingly, American society is geared to teaching, and enforcing, heterosexuality. **Heterosexual** activities and ideas are approved and regularly rewarded, while proclivities toward **homosexual** involvements are met with horror and are severely punished.

It is not uncommon for American fathers to become upset if their sons show interest in playing with dolls instead of trucks and guns. Erotic ideas in jokes, novels, magazines, movies, plays, and most forms of the mass media continuously bombard the American public, but the erotic content of this bombardment is almost exclusively heterosexual. Males are continually taught that it is the feminine form they should desire, and females the masculine. Moreover, at a very early age we are socialized into prevailing dating and marriage games. We learn from personal examples surrounding us and by means of our mass media what is expected of us in terms of asking someone of the opposite sex for a date, premarital sexual activities, going steady, becoming engaged, getting married, having a family, and on and on. Always these ideas which demonstrate what is expected of members of American society are heterosexual in their orientation. The opposite is almost unthinkable for Americans, and homosexual models are nowhere the general standard held up for children to follow.

Yet, in spite of such intensive and extensive socialization, there is in the United States a high incidence of homosexual desires and experiences. The sexual desire for someone of the same sex is by no means limited to a few people who are labeled "queer." On the contrary, approximately 20 to 25 percent of all American males involve themselves in at least one sexual act with another male to the point of orgasm. About 4 percent of American males are exclusively homosexual throughout their lives. Although the comparable figures for American females are somewhat lower, we can safely conclude that homosexual desires and experiences are not rare among Americans (cf. Kinsey *et al.*, 1948:650; 1965:487; Hunt 1973:194).

If it is true that the erotic objects of human sexuality are not inborn but are learned through interaction, in view of the continued exposure to heterosexual ideas and ideals with which people are inundated from childhood it is easy to understand how they learn to become heterosexual. But homosexuality, is it a learned response? Considering the feelings of revulsion which so often accompany the thought of what homosexuals do in private, isn't homosexuality, rather, a perversion of natural feelings? Or perhaps even some persons are born one way, while others, unfortunately, are born the other way? To clarify how "culturally appropriate" sexual objects are learned, let's look at a contemporary example.

American males associate slenderness in females with high sexual desirability. They ravish slender females in their dreams and wait longingly for the next issue of *Playboy* so they can stare at an undressed slender female for a change, one who looks just like the previous play-mates and is but another forerunner of the ones to come. American women are well aware of the American male's passion for slenderness in females, of course, and most try their best to match the ideal desire of their mate or sexual partner, or their potential mates and sexual partners. They drink their Carnation and cans of Sego—and like it. They scrutinize the scales as though their lives depended on it. And a good part of at least their sex life does appear to hang in the balance—because the opposite image immediately turns most American males off.

Are, then, *slender* females the natural erotic object of the inborn sex drive of males? This might certainly appear to be the case at first glance. But that this is not true becomes apparent when we note that some American males have a sexual preference for heavier females: It is the obese who turn them on, while the slender leave them cold. Are these males, then, perverts because they differ in their preferences from prevailing cultural standards? Or is it not, rather, that they have undergone different learning experiences? Can we not account for the differences in their sexual preference by means of their particular biographies, the experiences to which they have been exposed?

That this is probably the direction to follow in seeking an answer to the "why" of the American passion for slenderness becomes apparent when we note that Western males in the past, and males today in some other contemporary cultures, desired their females to be considerably heavier than we now do. To see what used to turn Western males on, look at the women whom Rembrandt painted. Or Raphael. Or Michelangelo. Or Rubens. The Renaissance man, if we can judge ideal sexual desirability from paintings, was passionate about women who looked strikingly different from our contemporary ideal form. And in Arab countries today the male considers female fatness an attribute. This point was brought forcefully to my attention when a Moroccan male, obviously strongly attracted to a particular woman, explained his desire for her by saying that she was so nice and plump. This cultural difference in standards of beauty creates a fascinating complementary and appositional orientation to ours: In Moroccan society fat women can relax, while the skinny ones must continually stuff themselves and worry about *their* weight problem. (Or should we call it an unweight problem?)

As I have previously emphasized, all people tend to be ethnocentric in the way they view the world, looking at their own cultural character-istics as superior and, in many cases, also as natural. People become so established in the dominant traits of their own culture that they take them for granted. They tend to think of them as being characteristics of the natural human state, and not as learned ways of living, perceiving, and of evaluating the world. We are no exception to this. Nor are the Morrocans. Each tends to view his cultural ideal form as natural and is quite surprised to find that people in other cultures hold contrary ideals and desires.

Our brief references to historical and cross-cultural views on obesity make it rather obvious that American preferences for body form are not natural but learned. We can probably readily see that this preference, for both men and women, is the result of our being incessantly surrounded with images of slender people as sexually desirable objects—especially with our so very influential mass media presentations of slenderness in models, cover girls, actors and actresses, and so on. Consequently, we learn to experience greater sexual desire toward a particular body type rather than toward another.

Although it is not as obvious as the point that our culture guides us into looking at certain body types as desirable, the same appears to be true concerning the sex of those toward whom we experience sexual desires. But if this view is correct, with heterosexuality being continuously held out to us as *the way* to be sexual, how does someone ever learn to become a homosexual? Note that this is the same as asking, "How does an American male learn to desire a fat woman?" And we would turn to an examination of learning experiences to answer either.

A person's first homosexual experience or activity usually occurs during adolescence. It is ordinarily the result of chance, not design or overwhelming sexual desire for a member of the same sex. The first experience can be due to a variety of factors, such as seduction by an older, more experienced same-sexed person. But, more commonly, the first homosexual experience is due to sexual experimenting. Adolescents possess, and are sometimes possessed by, a very strong sex drive following puberty. It is not at all uncommon for adolescents, especially males, to experiment sexually in a variety of ways. This experimentation frequently includes trying out various sexual objects.

If someone experiments sexually with a same-sexed partner, and the initial experience is pleasurable, the probability increases that the individual will engage in further homosexual experiences. If, on the one hand, to take the negative case, an individual is caught in the act and is embarrassed or punished or ridiculed or harmed in some way, the chances decrease that he will continue. On the other hand, the following conditions make the likelihood greater that one will continue homosexual activities: (1) the more pleasurable he finds the experiences, (2) the earlier he begins them, (3) the more frequently he has them, and, (4) the better the emotional relationship existing between him and his sexual partner(s) (Steele and Parker 1969). Each homosexual act makes further homosexual experiences more probable, while each homosexual act lessens the positive effects of subsequent heterosexual experiences which the person might have. At some point, the individual may come to prefer homosexual experiences to heterosexual ones.

Although this learning process usually begins early in life, such as in adolescence or even in childhood, it may begin at any point in an individual's life. It is rare, but some people have entered this learning process as late as their fifties and sixties (Dank 1971). When sexual experiences are satisfactory, whether they are heterosexual or homosexual, it is unlikely that a person will begin participating in the opposite pattern. If, however, at any time sexual experiences become dissatisfying for an individual, the possibility of developing the opposite sexual pattern is always present. The longer a person has experienced satisfactory sexual experiences, however, whether they are heterosexual or homosexual, the less the likelihood that he will begin the contrary pattern.

In addition to the pattern of experiencing sexual relations with only either the same sex or the opposite sex, we find that some individuals never establish a sexual pattern with just one sex. Some people fluctuate in their choice of erotic objects, finding both males and females sexually and emotionally satisfying. Men and women with this sexual pattern are called **ambisexuals** or **bisexuals.**

As I have previously emphasized, especially in Chapter 4, the objects in the world, the events of history, and the behavior of individuals do not come with built-in meanings. People "mentally collect" the objects and events they experience. They group together some which they feel are similar, putting them into a sort of "bundle" or "pile." They give that "collection" a certain name, and they think of things which have similar characteristics as belonging to that "collection." People live within a symbolic world of their own creation, and their symbols guide or help determine what they see in the world. People "code" the objects, events, and activities they experience by placing them into conceptual categories. Following the guidelines adhering to their concepts, they then see certain things as belonging or not belonging together.

Sexuality is one of these concepts. Although sexual relations between members of the same sex are nothing new, it appears that it was not until the end of the seventeenth century in England that the idea arose in the Western world that a person is exclusively a heterosexual or a homosexual and that homosexuality is a "condition" which characterizes some individuals but not others (McIntosh 1968:188–189). When this idea became firmly established in Western culture, it became a major determinant of how Occidentals classify sexual behavior.

Classifying humans as either heterosexual or homosexual appears to depart somewhat from what we know about human sexual behavior.

With the various types of sexual behavior and erotic attraction which characterize human sexuality, it appears to be more accurate to view humans as being "more or less" homosexual or "more or less" heterosexual. That is, homosexuality is not a "condition" which affects human beings, but it is a form of behavior or a sexual role which humans learn. The same is true regarding heterosexuality. People learn their erotic attachments, regardless of whether most people in their society regard those erotic attachments as "correct" or "incorrect." When they learn these attachments, they also learn what behavior is expected of them towards those for whom they have sexual desires—just as they learn any role in social life.

We can better understand our own ideas and attitudes toward homosexuality from a cross-cultural and historical perspective. Taking a brief historical glance, we find, first of all, that not all societies have been like ours in their view of homosexual relations. In some past cultures, for example, homosexuality was not disapproved. In fact, homosexuality has even been associated with religious participation. In the ancient Middle East male prostitutes were once employed in some of the temples (McIntosh 1968:186, 187). In Classical Greece, as I mentioned in Chapter 5, not only was homosexual behavior not looked down upon, but it was viewed as being on a higher level than heterosexual relations. The ancient Greeks considered men superior to women, and they correspondingly figured that sexual relations between a man and a woman was an act between a superior being and an inferior being. This was all right, but when two superior beings had sexual relations, this was obviously the superior act. Older Greek men who could afford it would hire a young boy to serve as their sexual object, while maintaining other sexual relations, such as with a wife.

Because homosexual relations were viewed in Classical Greece as both normal and desirable, persons engaging in sexual relations with members of their own sex were not thought of as having a "condition" which led them into a despicable and shameful activity. They were open about their homosexual activities, and a person was not classified as being either a heterosexual or a homosexual. One engaged in sexual relations according to who was available and who one preferred. No stigma was attached to choosing a same-sexed partner, nor was there stigma for choosing a sexual partner from the opposite sex.

Taking a brief cross-cultural view helps us place our own ideas, attitudes, and practices regarding homosexuality-heterosexuality into perspective. In a survey of primitive societies, 64 percent of the societies (49 of 76) about which anthropological information is available consider some form of homosexual activity to be normal and acceptable (Ford and Beach 1952:17). Some societies, such as the Siwans of North

Africa, even expect *all* their men and boys to engage in homosexual sodomy. The Siwanese, in fact, think a man is peculiar (one might say "queer") if he does *not* have sexual relations with both males and females (McIntosh 1968:187). The Kerski of New Guinea also practice universal male homosexuality. Before a Kerski male is granted full social status and before he is allowed to have sexual relations with women, he is first required to go through a passive stage of sexual relations with older males and later to engage in active sexual relations with younger males (Benedict 1939:17). Arunta males of Australia commonly take an older bachelor as a wife. The younger male lives with the older male for several years, until the elder partner breaks away after selecting a female wife for himself (West 1967:17–18).

These sexual orientations are certainly different from ours, but what I wish to especially emphasize is that, in direct contrast to American culture, in some societies homosexuality is viewed as a *normal* activity. In some it is even required. People engaging in homosexual relations in these societies are not looked upon as perverse, or sick, or sinners. Nor are they viewed as exclusively heterosexual or homosexual. They are, rather, sexual, and they participate in whatever sexual experiences are available to them as regular members of that society.

A major factor which leads some Americans into exclusive homosexual preference and others into exclusive heterosexual perference seems to be the concept we have that homosexuality is a "condition" of abnormality. Since it is a threatening thought for most members of our society to either admit to or to experience an erotic attraction for someone of the same sex, they are unlikely to be open to such feelings or even to admit it if they do experience them. If an American who views himself as a heterosexual experiences such feelings, he is likely to quickly put them out of his mind, or to immediately classify them as something else, placing them in a category which is not threatening to the sexuality in which he has been so carefully instructed and around which so much of his identity centers. This is probably also true for persons who look upon themselves as confirmed homosexuals: Admitting to or recognizing an erotic attraction to members of the opposite sex can be as equally disturbing for a homosexual as it is for a person with a heterosexual orientation to admit sexual attraction to a member of his own sex.

Learning this dichotomous categorization of heterosexuality-homosexuality affects both our perceptions and our behavior. If we did not have this "either-or" classification of human sexuality, it appears that people would be much more open to a greater variety of sexual experiences. As it is, however, homosexuality is an emotion-laden symbol which directs our interpretation of behavior into predetermined avenues. This dichotomous category guides us into narrowly classifying both what we see occurring with others and that which we ourselves experience. The category closes off, and even makes unthinkable, certain types of experiences which might, in the absence of the category, very well seem "natural."

Concepts, labels, or categories which sharply divide the world of people into one of two things—either one "is" or one "isn't"—sometimes also lock people into behaviors. For example, if someone is discovered in a sex act with a member of the opposite sex, all sorts of negative consequences may ensue, depending upon such things as the ages of the persons involved, their prior relationship, and the situation under which they were discovered. But even though their discovery may result in negative reactions such as shame, embarrassment, scandal, or even arrest, these persons at least have the satisfaction of knowing that their sexual partner was of the "right" sex. Their choice may have been ill-advised regarding place or time or some such thing, but no one will label them "queer."

Someone caught with his pants down with a member of the same sex, however, faces an entirely different situation. In American culture, everything about such a situation is viewed as being wrong. Such a person will receive a pejorative label, that of "queer," which in some cases can mark him in his community for the rest of his life. He can become stigmatized. He can become suspect in almost any activity in which he engages, even if it is merely telling a joke. ("Why did he tell *that* joke with *those* gestures?") He is also likely to become the butt of jokes in his community. After discovery, he may have little chance of successfully learning to play the more acceptable heterosexual role. He can become isolated from many choices in behavior which otherwise would have guided him into heterosexual involvements. Mothers, for example, will not approve their daughters dating him, while the daughters will probably not want to risk their reputations by being seen with him. Since he still has a strong sex drive, if heterosexual activities are largely cut off from him he will be more likely than ever to further turn to homosexual involvements. When the stigma of homosexuality closes off heterosexual relations, it opens homosexual ones, and it is they which are likely to provide an individual with the satisfactions around which he will build his sexual identity. Thus, giving a negative label to someone, as in such an extreme case, can lead to the very behavior which the label is meant to prevent.

When someone first engages in acts considered deviant by his society, he is said to be involved in **primary deviance.** At this point he still thinks of himself as a conforming member of society, although he is commiting acts which are viewed as wrong by members of his society, and perhaps also by himself as he, too, has been socialized into the same culture. ("I shoplifted the sweater, but I'm not a thief.") If he continues with his deviance, however, he is likely at some time to come to the point where he looks on the deviance as a part of himself, that is, he will think of himself in terms of the deviance and begin to organize his self-concept in one way or another around the deviant role. ("I am a thief.") When this happens, he has entered **secondary deviance** (Lemert 1951:75–76.)

To move from primary to secondary deviance (that is, when someone comes to the point where he incorporates ideas about the deviant role into his self-concept and views various aspects of life from that perspective) usually requires dealing in some way with the label society places on the disapproved behavior. He may perhaps reconceptualize the label, giving the behavior new meaning. It is particularly difficult for someone to satisfactorily adjust to a label like homosexuality, which carries with it the idea that one is queer, perverted, abnormal, sick, or depraved. No one wants to think of himself as being that kind of person. How, then, does someone come to think of himself as a homosexual?

In order to make a satisfactory adjustment to his behavior, the homosexual must successfully neutralize the negative content or connotations in the label which we typically apply to homosexuality in our culture. One of the major factors which appears to aid this *neutralization* process is positive experience with other persons who also prefer sexual relations with members of their own sex. A newcomer to homosexuality learns that people who think of themselves as homosexuals are about the same as anybody else in society—with the marked exception of their sexual preference. They hold down jobs, vote for public officials, own their homes or rent apartments, drive cars, go bowling, and so on. They are similar to most people in society—except their preference of sexual objects differs sharply from that which is acceptable in our society.

The individual then undergoes **resocialization.** He unlearns many of the stereotypes of homosexuality into which he had previously been socialized as a member of American society. The newcomer learns that: Some homosexuals do have psychological problems, while others do not; some homosexuals do well in their jobs, while others do not; some homosexuals are creative, while others appear to have no creative ability whatsoever. The newcomer to the male homosexual subculture learns that: One cannot tell who a homosexual is by looking at him— some homosexuals do "swish" around and act effeminately, while others do not; some persons who are very effeminate-looking have an exclusive heterosexual orientation, while others who are extremely masculine in appearance are oriented exclusively towards sexual relations with members of their own sex; very few male homosexuals ever wear female clothing; some homosexuals are indeed hairdressers, interior decorators, and male nurses, while others are lumberjacks, policemen, and boxers, but the vast majority hold down run-of-the-mill types of jobs in all walks of life.

The novice to the homosexual subculture learns that no stereotype adequately characterizes homosexuals. He learns that whatever characteristics some stereotype emphasizes, there are homosexuals who epitomize the opposite traits. The novice to male homosexuality learns, for example, that there are indeed homosexuals who are both effeminate in their appearance and in their desires; that is, some homosexuals not only enjoy raising the pitch to their voice while using such terms as "my dear" and gesturing outlandishly in a feminine manner, but they also desire to play a passive sexual role—for example, to be approached by others instead of doing the approaching, to be seductive instead of seducing, to have someone buy their drinks or open doors for them, and to "reluctantly" give in when sexual overtures are made. He also learns, however, that this characterization of homosexuals as effeminate by no means does justice to males who have a sexual preference for members of their own sex. While there are homosexuals who are effeminate, there are at the same time homosexuals who despise effeminacy in every way. In one extreme, for example, they love to noisily roar around on Harley-Davidson "hogs," to wear thick boots and black leather jackets with silver studding, to guzzle beer, and walk with a swagger. Those in this "leather set" are also ready to fight at the drop of a hat. They feel that "swishy" types give homosexuals a bad name, and they consequently enjoy beating them up when they cross their path (private communication to the author). The vast majority of homosexuals, however, appear at neither extreme but look at both the "swishy" and "leather" types as representing fringe areas of homosexuality.

When the neophyte learns such things, the content of his category of homosexual undergoes a sharp metamorphosis. He learns that, though he might be a homosexual, this does not mean that he is perverted, abnormal, sinful, filthy, shameful, or mentally ill. When the category of homosexual takes on a meaning of self-esteem and self-worth, he is then able to be comfortable in applying the term to himself. Learning a concept which satisfactorily describes to himself what he is, and how he is, helps him to adjust to his sexual preferences. If, however, he does not successfully neutralize the negative content of the category of homosexuality as it is typically perceived by "straight" members of American society, he is unlikely to make a satisfactory adjustment to homosexual life. He will probably then experience both psychological and behavioral difficulties.

As we saw in Chapter 3, groups of people who experience their own corner in life develop a characteristic life style built around their unique experiences. They develop their own ways of viewing the world, their own ways of conceptualizing their experiences, and their own patterns and styles of communication. Homosexuals, like cab drivers and teenagers, Mormons and the Amish, have also developed their own subculture built upon the unique identity which they are staking in the world. Just as being heterosexual is much more than having sex with members of the opposite sex, so being homosexual is much more than having sex with members of the same sex. There are all sorts of expectations homosexuals have which someone who wishes to be accepted in this subculture must meet. Sociologists call these expectations the *homosexual role*.

The homosexual subculture is extremely important in this process of resocializing the neophyte into the ways of homosexuality as they are practiced in American culture. The homosexual subculture is especially of great help in neutralizing the negative aspects of the category of homosexual, which, as we have seen, is necessary for satisfactory personal adjustment to the role. From the homosexual community, the novice learns new linguistic categories by which he can view and evaluate himself. Learning these symbols helps him in the process of adjusting to the homosexual role.

Within this subcultural community, he finds acceptance and support for his sexual preferences. He experiences social support vital for the formation of an adequate self-concept. With relief, he learns that there are other persons who not only accept, but also share, his feelings and preferences. He finds that he is no longer surrounded by people who would react with disgust and loathing if they were to become aware of his sexual preference. He is finally able to drop the mask of heterosexuality which he has so uncomfortably worn. He also learns how to make sexual contacts with persons who share his sexual preference, and as a new member of the homosexual community he typically becomes an object of admiration, of envy and desire (Gagnon and Simon 1967:182–183; Leznoff and Westley 1956).

"Coming out" in the **gay world,** that is, when someone first begins to publicly acknowledge a homosexual identity, is ordinarily an intensively troublesome time for the individual. "Coming out" marks a crisis period because at this point the novice to homosexuality is taking a step which means leaving behind much of the solid grounding on which he has previously based his sexual identity. It is a transition period in his resocialization during which he accepts the label of homosexuality and during which the male must learn new concepts of masculinity, the female of femininity. The individual learns new ways of playing his sexual role. During this crisis of "coming out," many male homosexuals engage in "camping" behavior, that is behavior designed to be outrageous, such as using exaggerated feminine gestures, and, though more rare, wearing feminine clothing (Gagnon and Simon 1967:182) After he has "come out," the individual ordinarily becomes more comfortable with his homosexual role, establishes a more solid sexual identity, and drops most of his camping behavior.

Individuals have been known to "come out" as late as the age of 65, but the average age is closer to 19. Approximately 50 percent of males who "come out" experience their first sexual arousal toward another male before their thirteenth birthday, 30 percent before they turn eleven. It takes approximately six more years on the average for them to apply the label of homosexuality to themselves, however, such that they are able to publicly identify themselves as a homosexual to a homosexual subculture (Dank 1971:183; personal correspondence with Martin S. Weinberg).

After coming to terms with his sexual orientation, reestablishing his sexual identity, and finding some niche in the homosexual subculture, the homosexual's major problem is that of evasion. Until 1961 sexual relations between members of the same sex were illegal in all of our states. Illinois was the first state to thoroughly revamp its laws regarding sexual behavior. In 1961 Illinois removed the illegality of private homosexual acts between consenting adults. The following year the American Law Institute adopted a model penal code recommending the removal of penalties for private sex acts between consenting adults. Connecticut, Colorado, Oregon, Ohio, North Dakota, Delaware, and Hawaii have followed suit by removing their penalties against both heterosexual and homosexual private consensual sodomy (Hunt 1973:197).

These acts remain illegal, however, in the majority of our states, confronting most homosexuals with a legal problem as they follow their way of life. Although enforcement of the law is ordinarily sporadic in most places, nonexistent in others, with homosexual behaviors being tolerated on a regular payoff basis to the police in still others, the possibility of arrest is always present. In Texas, for example, committal to the State Prison for sodomy offenses is not unusual (Schatzki 1971:2). In some states conviction for homosexual acts can actually carry up to life imprisonment, as in Nevada and New Mexico. And this is for an act taking place with the consent of another person over eighteen years of age (Schur 1965:78; *Civil Liberties, 302,* May 1974). Contrast this with the eight states in which for the same act a person cannot be sentenced to even a single day.

Even in the states in which private homosexual acts between consenting adults are legal, the homosexual still runs legal risks. In these states the police simply work around the law by arresting homosexuals on misdemeanor charges of soliciting, disorderly conduct, lewd and lascivious behavior, and vagrancy. These are actually the charges brought against homosexuals in most states, with the felony statutes rarely being invoked (personal correspondence with Martin S. Weinberg).

In addition to danger from the law, the homosexual risks ostracism from persons who are important to him, such as his family and heterosexual friends, and ridicule, gossip, or even physical violence from still others. In many occupations he also runs the risk of losing his job or his clientele. This risk appears to be especially high in the professions. Schools, for example, do not like to have homosexuals on their staff, and patients, clientele, and parishioners do not ordinarily care for their doctor, lawyer, or minister to be a homosexual. Consequently, evading discovery and social control is frequently a major aspect of the homosexual role in American society.

Accordingly, many homosexuals enter "safe" occupations, that is, occupations which already have a homosexual linkage, such as those of the artist, the interior decorator, the dress designer, and the hairdresser. In occupations in which there is greater toleration of homosexuals, individuals are able to be more open about their homosexuality, both on the job and in their social life. In these occupations the homosexual need not be as anxious nor as secretive about his sexual orientation, for the consequences of discovery are greatly lessened. A socialite for example, does not ordinarily care if the interior decorator she hires is a homosexual, and she sometimes considers his homosexuality to be a bonus because of the common myth that homosexuals are more creative than heterosexuals. The reason for this myth of creativity is probably because of the greater toleration for homosexuals in certain creative occupations such as interior decorating, painting, creative literature, designing dresses, and dressing hair. Since greater toleration for homosexuals exists in these occupations, a larger number of homosexuals enter them than one would expect by chance. Homosexuals in these occupations then become more visible to the public because they are able to be more open about their sexual orientation, and the creativity of the occupation becomes associated with homosexuality.

Homosexuals in low status occupations also tend to be less secretive regarding their sexual orientation. This is probably because the risk of discovery does not carry with it such great financial loss as do the professions since similar jobs are ordinarily readily obtainable (Leznoff and Westley 1956). It is quite another matter, however, with persons who work in our higher status occupations. There the risks of financial loss and loss of prestige are much greater, and persons in higher status occupations, such as the professions, tend to be more secretive about their homosexuality. They tend to be **covert homosexuals,** or as they are known in the gay world, "closet queens." Homosexuals in these occupations tend to present a heterosexual front to ther business or professional associates, and frequently to their wives and children since marriage is expected of them, while they but furtively engage in homosexual behavior. They tend not to be active in gay bars, as do **overt homosexuals,** those who have come out in the gay world and publicly acknowledged a homosexual identity. Since covert homosexuals are frequently unable to risk revealing their sexual orientation, they sometimes resort to purchasing anonymous sex. They sometimes cruise places where they know homosexuals gather, covertly picking up male prostitutes and paying them for fleeting and depersonalized sex, as well as patronizing male houses of prostitution and utilizing the specialized services of call boys (cf. Humphreys 1970a, 1970b, and 1971; Pitman 1971).

Many homosexuals, however, walk a path somewhere between the extremes of these overt and covert types. It is frequently the case that homosexuals living in larger urban areas pass as heterosexuals as they work at their jobs or businesses during the day, but at night and during the weekends and holidays they openly lead homosexual lives. With the anonymity afforded by vast numbers of people, such as in New York City where it is unlikely that one's leisure hours' path will cross those of one's work associates, they are able to actively participate in the homosexual subculture and perhaps identify themselves as homosexuals to their neighbors and yet maintain a heterosexual image at work. Their personal and economic lives become schizophrenically distinct from one another. Five times a week they carefully put on the uncomfortable mask which gains them acceptance and respectability with the majority, dutifully labor at their tasks while presenting to the world an image they are only too fully aware does not match reality, while impatiently waiting for five o'clock when they can again present a self which they feel is truer to their personal orientations.

Homosexuals, along with heterosexuals, are also intensively, extensively, and continuously affected by the culture and society in which they live. The connection between occupations and styles of homosexuality illustrates ways in which American heterosexual culture gives shape to the roles within the homosexual subculture. Based largely upon their status, occupations contain a built-in differential reaction to homosexuality and entail different consequences if someone's homosexual preferences are revealed or discovered. These factors greatly determine the style of homosexual role that one will follow. The dominant heterosexual culture, primarily by means of occupational status and size of population in which the individual lives, even affects ways in which homosexuals make sexual contacts. These factors greatly determine the amount of openness or furtiveness involved in sexual encounters. Although homosexuality goes directly contrary to the dictates of American society, even in such intimate ways the life styles of homosexuals are affected by their dominant culture.

Because of typical reactions to homosexuality in American society, there are not many places in which those who have learned to prefer members of their own sex can safely relax and openly let their sexual preference be known. At the same time, there is a large number of homosexuals in our culture, and since they also desire places of recreation where they can meet others who feel as they, the "gay bar" has developed. The **gay bar** is a bar which caters almost exclusively to homosexuals. Gay bars are located in all our major metropolitan areas. They exist with the cooperation of the police, and as mentioned, they frequently operate on a direct pay-off system. In the gay bar homosexual behaviors not tolerated in other public places are accepted and sometimes encouraged. Depending on what is permitted in the particular community, here persons of the same sex hold hands, dance with one another, cuddle, and kiss. In gay bars flirtations take place, dates are made, and sexual liaisons are kept or broken. Gay bars especially serve as centers of communication: It is here that persons who overtly define themselves as homosexuals can keep up with what is happening to others in the homosexual subculture.

The sociologist, thus, looks at homosexuality as a role which is learned like any other role. He does not view homosexuality as being caused by inborn or genetically determined characteristics. *No* such characteristics, whether chemical, biological, or psychological, have ever been isolated which distinguish the homosexual from the heterosexual. The distinction between heterosexuals and homosexuals appears to lie solely in the object of sexual preference. What someone prefers for sexual satisfaction is certainly not exclusively a part of human nature. Whatever the particular choices of an individual, they appear to be learned choices. Individuated learning experiences within a cultural context appear to account for homosexuality—and for heterosexuality. One learns to be homosexual in the same way that one learns to be heterosexual. The process is the same, although the content differs.

If a behavior or service is barred by law or custom but is highly desired by many, subterranean institutions are likely to emerge. The bar catering to homosexuals is one such example, providing a bounded, quasi-sanctioned area for homosexual social activities. (Courtesy of Wide World Photos)

Where animal behavior is greatly under the control of instincts, human behavior is not. The lack of instinctual control over human behavior has allowed people to develop fascinatingly diverse cultures and subcultures. That human behavior is primarily, if not exclusively, learned behavior makes the human infant exceptionally malleable for adjusting to any culture. Perhaps the lack of an in-built or instinctual sex object attached to the human sex drive is a part of this plasticity, that aspect of human nature which has allowed *homo sapiens* to take over the planet Earth and, while doing so, to create their fascinating array of unique life styles.

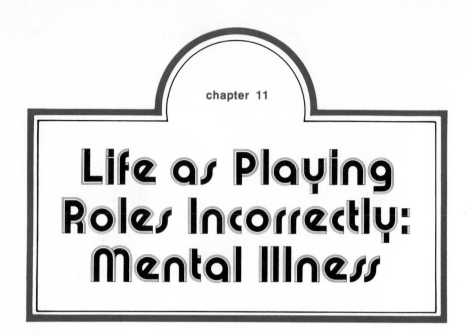

chapter 11

Life as Playing Roles Incorrectly: Mental Illness

Mental illness does not exist. It is not an illness, a "thing" with which one is afflicted, as are pneumonia, cancer, lung disease, heart attack, pellagra, or syphilis. Illness is a biological (physiochemical) abnormality of the body or its functioning, but mental illness is not this. If it were, we could simply call it illness, and we would have no need for the qualifying adjective "mental" (Szasz 1969:55).

Not only is mental illness not an illness, but it is also not mental. It is not a "thing" inside someone's head or in someone's mind. The concept of mental illness is measured not by the mind, but by behavior. Mental illness is a concept which refers to human behavior—to things we can readily observe when we look at people. It is a linguistic category by which we interpret behavior, judging whether that behavior is "normal" or "abnormal." Rather than referring to the mind, mental illness refers to certain types of disapproved behavior, especially behavior which fails to meet the fundamental expectations we have of normal members of society. Certain types of disapproved behavior are taken as a "sign" of "mental" illness. We shall develop these points in some detail.

As I have previously emphasized and reemphasized, we people live in a symbolic world of our own making. We constantly interpret what is happening by us, to us, and around us, placing events into conceptual categories which our culture provides for "things-that-are-like-that." When we classify events into categories, they take on meaning for us since they are then seen as being "similar to" other events with which we have had previous experience. In this way conceptual categories

Because bizarre behavior is upsetting to interaction, frequently persons who demonstrate unusual behavior are locked in "mental hospitals," where they are either resocialized or simply put out of sight. (Courtesy of Wide World Photos)

provide "meaning" for what would otherwise be essentially meaningless events.

In this symbolic world in which we live, behavior is also symbolic. As we discussed in Chapter 7, through their behavior people symbolically communicate meaning to others. By utilizing settings, appearances, and manner, people in everyday life present a self to audiences. A vital part of the self they present is a symbolization of social statuses: The presented self communicates to others, for example, whether one is male or female, wealthy or poor, youth or aged. By the self they present people also communicate information concerning their moods and feelings. Another vital aspect of the impressions people manage is that they are also commonly interpreted as an important indicator of whether people are normal or abnormal. It is this symbolic aspect of human behavior on which we shall focus in this chapter.

Our behavior is circumscribed by all sorts of **norms** or expectations, and during even the simplest encounters people regularly check the match between behavior and norms. Behavior is taken as a symbol of who people are and what they are like. The norms or expectations governing interpersonal behavior are not only applied to specific acts ("a normal member of society will not steal") but also to a fascinating variety of understandings which we only implicitly hold concerning how people should comport themselves in any given **encounter** or face-to-face interaction. These **implicit understandings** of everyday interaction involve such things as posture, facial expressions, gestures, the content of our speech (what we say), and the form of our speech (how we say it).

We learn these implicit understandings so intensively, beginning at such a young age, and so extensively, as they are regularly reinforced by most people with whom we come into contact, that they become part of the **background expectancies** of our everyday or routine interactions. They form the "taken-for-granted-assumptions-of-what-normal-people-in-society-are-like." We grow so familiar with these implicit understandings that they become a part of our background for living, the basic assumptions within which we present the self to others and by which we evaluate the presentation of self made by others. Because they are *background* expectancies, however, we are ordinarily not conscious of them—unless they are in some way called into question. Yet, like language, though they are ordinarily below the level of our awareness, these background expectancies are a critical influence on our behavior.

The amazing extent to which background expectancies govern our interaction can be demonstrated by the following simple experiment. Suppose that in your next conversation you were to insert your little finger up your nostril and maintain it in that position throughout the encounter—while keeping everything else normal, such as the tone of your voice, your facial expressions, your posture, and other gestures. Persons interacting with you would tend to find this behavior extremely upsetting. Yet there is no *specific* rule which says that it is wrong to keep a finger inserted up a nostril while engaged in face-to-face interaction. It is simply a part of the *implicit* understandings with which we enter and continue encounters: It is implicitly understood that no one will do this—at least not someone who is a "normal" member of society.

Fundamental background expectancies also involve posture, and it would be similarly upsetting to others if during a conversation someone held one foot in the air or if he were to continuously jump up and down. Likewise regarding eye contact: if, instead of meeting the other's eyes, one were to stare in the area of his navel, at his crotch, at his feet, or even at the top of his head, one would quickly disrupt the interaction. The person doing this would not be violating any specific rule, however. We have no specific rule which states that for a specified minimum length of time we should look at the eyes of the persons with whom we are speaking. Although unstated, the rule or background expectancy is there nevertheless. We all, as members socialized into the ordinary expectations of face-to-face interaction in our culture, know what sort of eye contact is expected of us. And we unthinkingly meet these expectations "as a matter of course." We also, as normal members of our society, assume that there is something wrong with someone who fails to meet these expectations.

When someone violates expectations concerning specific acts such as "don't steal," we apply a specific label to him such as "thief." We do this for most behaviors which are violations of specific expectations such as those concerning sobriety, killing, sexual propriety, truthfulness, and honesty. Our culture provides specific corresponding labels for these violators: namely, drunkard, murderer, whore, liar, and cheater. Thus, when explicit rules or expectations are violated, explicit labels are attached to the violator.

It is quite a different matter, however, when it comes to the **residual rules,** those background expectancies of behavior which are assumed to hold for everyone in society and which are rarely explicitly examined. Our culture does not provide particularized labels for violators of the taken-for-granted aspects of interaction. Yet, violations of background expectancies are disruptive to interaction and are disturbing to us. Since we are not provided an explicit vocabulary for dealing with residual rule violations, we tend to categorize violations of implicit understandings into a general, catch-all category. The primary concept which Western culture provides for categorizing this type of violative behavior is mental illness (Scheff 1966, 1970).

Because most of us in the Western world have been socialized into a psychiatric model concerning residual rule violations, most of us make the assumption that there is "something wrong inside someone's head" which leads to such unheard-of behavior. We usually assume that a person who violates these fundamental expectations of what "normal" people are like is suffering from some sort of underlying mental illness which causes him to behave so strangely. The term mental illness assumes that an illness of some sort affects someone's mind which, in turn, affects his behavior. No particular germ, virus, chemical, or disease, however, has been localized as the basis for our various classifications of mental illness, such as manic depression, schizophrenia, or paranoia.

A contrasting way of looking at mental illness is to concentrate on that which is visible to us—the behavior of people. Instead of trying to look inside someone's mind in order to understand his rule-violating behavior, we can, rather, look at his behavior. We can examine how he might have learned that particular behavior, and how and why others react to him the way they do.

We might first ask why some people violate the taken-for-granted background expectancies of the way normal people in a society present the self. The question of causation of human behavior, however, is an extremely difficult one to deal with adequately. We must first note that any behavior can originate or arise from many sources. Human behavior is ordinarily not due to any one particular cause, but is, rather, associated with many underlying factors. This also applies to the violation of residual rules.

Some residual rule-breaking behavior, for example, has an organic basis, that is, such behavior can be due to genetic, biochemical, or physiological conditions. Persons with a certain genetic structure, for example, are not able to focus their eyes during an encounter in the way which is ordinarily expected in our culture. Nor for the same reason can some people maintain the expected coordination in their speech or in their movements. Residual rule violations can also be due to ataxia, which is caused by damage to the spinal cord or brain (Rosen and Gregory 1965:434). Toxic reactions can also lead to such violations.

When we know that there is an organic base to such violations of background expectancies, however, we do not classify these violators as mentally ill. We attribute their bizarre behavior to physical illness. It is only when we cannot locate an organic cause for such behavior that we turn to mental illness as our explanation. For example, we once placed persons sick with pellagra in mental hospitals, involuntarily hospitalizing them because of their failure to adequately maintain interaction rules. When it was later found that their pellagra, with its aberrant behavior, was due to vitamin deficiency, these persons were declassified from mental illness to physical illness and were then treated in the fashion which our doctors ordinarily treat persons who have physical medical problems (Szasz 1969:55).

When LSD first began to be used in the 1960's, newspaper accounts appeared throughout the nation headlining how LSD was causing mental illness. Day after day readers were treated to the sordid details of one case after another of persons who had ingested LSD, had consequently "lost their minds," and had then been committed by family and psychiatrist to mental hospitals, where it was speculated, they might have to spend the rest of their lives as mindless idiots. There was shortly hardly a person around who did not know with certainty that LSD caused mental illness. It turned out, however, that the reason LSD was leading to such difficulties was that it was an unfamiliar hallucinatory experience. People taking LSD did not at all know what to expect. When they suddenly experienced extraordinary perceptions they were startled, disturbed, and became emotionally upset. They panicked. They thought their perceptual changes might be permanent. Psychiatrists were equally inexperienced with the effects of LSD at this time. When people were brought to them who were incoherently attempting to describe such things as their existential unity with plants or the personality of colors it was not surprising, with their socialization into Western background expectancies, their psychiatric orientation, and their lack of experience with the effects of LSD, that psychiatrists immediately proclaimed these people mentally ill and ordered them locked up. Because the "experts" in mental illness had made their examinations and officially proclaimed their results, the public was further reinforced in their connecting LSD with mental illness.

After more people had experimented with LSD, however, a drug subculture developed in which LSD ingestion became a normal part of life. Within this subculture people learned what to expect from LSD, and they began to experiment with the drug while experienced users were with them. These "trip guides" were able to assure the novice that what he was experiencing was to be expected, that it was temporary, and that he should relax and enjoy the novel experience. Consequently, newspaper accounts connecting LSD with mental illness disappeared, even though the use of LSD increased thousands of times over (cf. Becker 1967). In metropolitan areas where physicians have become experienced with the effects of LSD, persons experiencing bad trips are now treated in standard medical facilities rather than in "mental" hospitals.

When no organic basis for residual rule violations can be discovered, however, what are their possible causes?

As we detailed especially in Chapter 5, cultures vary widely in their expectations of proper and improper behavior: Behavior considered appropriate by the members of one culture may well be considered inappropriate by members of another culture. Cultural relativity in what is considered normal behavior goes much deeper than expectations concerning specific acts. As with the concepts provided by language, the guiding principles that underlie behavior also vary from culture to culture. The background expectancies by which we evaluatively approach life, including the basic ways of acting towards others which we learn in childhood, are also relative to the culture in which we are raised.

Because these implicit understandings of the normal way of doing things vary so widely, a person who has learned the set of background expectancies appropriate to his culture sometimes experiences **culture shock** when he is exposed to another culture. He becomes disoriented regarding how to respond to others. His basic orientation to life undergoes severe challenge because the other culture contains sharply contrary expectations of fundamental behavior. People there live in literally a different world of background assumptions. For example, when speaking to men, Arab women frequently avoid eye contact by averting their eyes. To do otherwise would likely be taken as a sign of immodesty. Arab men, in contrast, maintain tremendously greater eye contact than Americans accept as normal, so much so that Americans report that they feel when speaking to an Arab male that they are continually being scrutinized.

Eye contact is one thing, and an American in an Arab country is likely to be merely amused at these differences. But basic expectations of direct physical contact also differ radically, and at this an American is likely to be more than amused. He is likely to become confused about how to interact with others, for when Arab men interact with other men they utilize much closer physical distance than Americans. They frequently touch the persons with whom they are interacting. They touch the other's arms, hands, back, and so on, with the consequence that a Westerner feels that his "personal space" is constantly being violated. Unlike American culture, it is also not unusual for Arab men to hold hands with male friends. To observe this is one thing, and the American observer may well find it humorous; but for an American male who has been so thoroughly socialized into studiously avoiding direct physical contact with other men, apart from "contact sports," it can well be upsetting to his fundamental expectancies concerning the way men should interact with one another. The same behavior obviously has different meanings in each culture (cf. Hall 1969:154–164).

If an Arab male who has been socialized into such markedly differing background expectancies visits the United States, he will tend to constantly violate what Americans feel is the way "normal" people behave. If we do not know that he comes from such a different cultural background, we are likely to think that there is something drastically wrong with him. We might think that he is a homosexual, or perhaps classify him as mentally ill. If we do know the difference in his cultural background, however, we are not as likely to so classify him. As we still find his behavior disturbing, however, we are likely to continue to think of him as being somewhat odd, especially if he continues to touch people during conversations or insists on holding hands with his male friends. Cultural differences, then, can in some cases account for violations of residual rules.

Similarly, subcultural differences in socialization can also underlie residual rule violations. In a study of Chicago ethnic subcultures, for example, it was found that Italians learn to look more directly at the person to whom they are speaking than do blacks (Suttles 1968). Blacks then feel that Italians are staring at them and consequently tend to distrust them. Black females, on the other hand, learn to sit differently than Italian females, and persons from an Italian background tend to think that black females are "on the make." These differences sometimes lead to humorous situations, while at other times they can result in serious incidents. When differences such as these vary highly from the "general expectations" within the larger culture, they easily lead to others thinking that such persons are odd. Without knowing the factors which underlie their behaviors, others can well feel that there is something fundamentally wrong with these persons. In extreme cases, they may perhaps even feel that persons with such different characteristics are suffering from a mental illness of some sort.

An individual can also undergo particularized or idiosyncratic learning experiences that lead to his violating residual rules. For example, an individual may have been punished, or rewarded, for certain forms of touching, looking, speaking, body posturing, and so on, which differ from general cultural expectations. The particular ways he has learned to interact in face-to-face situations can then conflict with the expectations most people have. Individuated learning experiences within our culture can then lead some people to violate the background expectancies which the majority of us take for granted as being normal.

In addition to organic or structural bases, cultural and subcultural socialization, and individuated learning experiences, stress can also lead to behaviors thought inappropriate (Scheff 1966). An individual facing a severely problematic situation, a situation in which he is undergoing much stress and traumatic pressure, can easily begin to violate taken-for-granted interaction assumptions. Such violations can arise through deprivation of food or sleep or the hardship of combat, or they can be due to the fear of failing in a situation in which the individual has much at stake and where he is motivated by a strong desire to win or succeed. Residual rule violations, for example, sometimes occur during times of final examinations at a university, or when someone is laboring under a demanding work situation with a tough boss, when bill collectors are hounding him, during a difficult pending divorce, after quarrels with a loved one, and so on. In such cases of stress people sometimes "don't feel up to" putting out the energy to meet background expectancies concerning politeness, modulated voice, proper dress, promptness, high work production, cleanliness, or our highly segmented hours for sleep, work, play, and so on.

In a similar manner, residual rule violations can also be due to anger or to pain experienced in interaction. An individual may become extremely frustrated with certain aspects of his life in which he has much emotional investment, such as when his relationship with a loved one is

"Be reasonable, Harry. You just *can't* stay in bed until they get rid of air pollution, traffic congestion, stickups, strong-arming, and all that!"

Violations of basic assumptions of interaction can occur for many reasons, two of which are fear and stress. (Courtesy of *Saturday Review*. Cartoon by Al Ross.)

ruptured or when he finds it painful to continue his attempts at succeeding in higher education. Out of this frustration, with its resulting anger, he may say, in effect, "The hell with you and the hell with everything in life." He may decide that the game is not worth playing because he is bound to lose and will only continue to be hurt. He may subsequently withdraw from interaction, refusing to be involved. In extreme instances, he may perhaps even refuse to speak to others. Or, instead of withdrawing, he may choose to strike out at those whom he feels have hurt him. In some cases, such lashing out at others will be limited to verbal attacks, but in others it will involve inflicting injury or death on those he defines as his enemies. Persons reacting in these ways to anger or pain are likely to be thought of as abnormally hostile or aggressive, and such labels as depressive or homicidal psychopath are likely to be tagged onto them.

In some cases, a person reacting to extreme pain or anger may simultaneously withdraw and strike out at others. Cases of "revenge suicide" are examples of this type of reaction. In **revenge suicide** an individual withdraws from painful interaction by means of self-inflicted death, but at the same time he intentionally inflicts pain on those persons he feels have hurt him (Douglas 1967:310–319). Instances of "revenge suicide" which I came across in my research on suicide included people leaving suicide notes which blamed others for driving them to their death. A wife, for example, might be directly named in the note left by her husband, being singled out for scathing denunciation. Other cases were more dramatic in their final symbolic presentation of self and involved making certain that the body would be found in startling circumstances. One husband, for example, shot himself while sitting at the kitchen table. His body remained in an upright position, with the wall behind him covered with blood and gore. This man knew at what time his wife would be coming home and that she would first be enter-

When people feel that interaction is too painful to continue, they are confronted by a number of alternative forms of withdrawal, including that demonstrated in the preceding illustration. Shown here is an individual dramatically opting for the most extreme form of withdrawal. (Courtesy of Wide World Photos)

ing the kitchen. And there he was waiting for her. Two other cases involved garage doors with automatic openers controlled from the family car. When the spouse came home and pressed the button which triggered the garage door, it was like the curtain going up on a stage. The body, jarringly dangling from a rafter at the *front* of the garage, greeted the returning spouse. Individuals giving such final dramaturgical presentations of the self are certainly reacting to anger, frustration, and pain in ways which violate fundamental background expectancies of what "normal" people are like. If they are members of Western culture, they will ordinarily be labelled mentally ill because of their actions.

Residual rule violations can also serve as mechanisms for testing boundaries, gaining attention, extending experiences, and teasing and hurting others. Children often test boundaries because they want to discover just "how far they can go" and will violate any number of residual rules in pursuit of this discovery. Adults will also sometimes test the reactions of others by violating residual rules. Under some circumstances, people find the purposeful violation of residual rules an effective way of drawing attention to themselves. Individuals who wish to extend their experiences beyond humdrum daily life will also sometimes purposely violate residual rules in order to "see what it is like" to act differently than others expect. People also sometimes use residual rule violations in order to tease or hurt others through bringing shame, ridicule, or embarrassment upon them. For example, in one case a man was extremely angry with his girlfriend. She was the "prim and proper" type, highly conscious of the reactions of others and a person who greatly conformed to the "social graces." The couple got into a heated argument on the way to a dinner party, and later when they were seated at dinner, the boyfriend studiously picked his nose at the table.

Residual rule violations can also be accidental. Because of a misunderstanding of the requirements of the occasion, for example, someone can appear at a formal dinner attired in inappropriate clothing. Or through a series of fortuitous circumstances, an individual may arrive late at a social occasion, touch someone where he or she shouldn't be touched, misappropriate property, say the inappropriate thing or in some other way act inappropriately to the situation. By misunderstandings, then, or through a series of fortuitous circumstances, an individual can make an incompetent or inappropriate presentation of the self and thereby violate the background expectancies of others.

Humor or joking is a final source of violations of background expectancies. A major element underlying jokes is ludicrousness. People often find it humorous when aspects of people or a situation do not match because something is terribly "out of place." Consequently, many of our jokes refer to inadvertent violations of residual rules. Since we frequently find the ludicrous humorous, people sometimes purposely violate background assumptions in order to create humor, as, for example, the classic wearing-a-lampshade-for-a-hat party behavior.

As an essential part of being human is to give meaning to what is in the world by classifying it, people also classify behavior. We know what behavior means when we place it into the linguistic categories our culture provides. When someone acts "inappropriately" regarding his *setting* (one does not play blackjack during church service), his *appearance* (one does not wear a bathing suit to a formal dance), or his *manner* (a man does not burst into tears because he failed an examination or his car won't start), others categorize his behavior.

When people attach to behavior the various labels available in their culture, violators of residual rules are not always, or immediately, tagged with the label of mental illness. We are all allowed some leeway in not following rules. We all have a certain amount of **deviance toleration** if we have ordinarily been meeting background expectancies. When violations of residual rules occur, reasons for the behavior may be apparent, or may be found, which excuse the violator. His behavior can then be satisfactorily accounted for, and others are able to avoid attributing mental illness to him. "Excusable" violations can occur because of (1) situational factors ("She is under much stress because of the death of her child.") (2) status ("Boys will be boys."), (3) lack of status ("She is only a child—what can you expect?"), (4) intent ("He did it as a joke."), and (5) non-intent ("It was merely an accident that could have happened to anyone."). In cases such as these, the violations carry "built-in" explanations which excuse the violator, that is, the category into which the act is classified is one which contains an acceptable explanation of the violation.

Deviance toleration is not unlimited, however, and the situation had better not recur too frequently, those in a particular status can overdo it, as can those engaged in joking behavior, and similar accidents had best not befall the same individual—or people will tend to look for other explanations of the behavior. When behavior which violates implicit understandings occurs frequently, others are likely to discover a pattern of repetitive or even habitual behavior. They are then likely to take the behavior as being out of the ordinary "excusable" variety and classify it as being "extra-ordinary" in some way. In cases of violations of background expectancies, that category is likely to be mental illness. In our psychoanalytically and psychiatrically oriented culture, when it comes to behavior which bizarrely or repetitively violates background expectancies, the general public is sensitized to think along the broad lines of mental illness. Professionals in the area of "mental health" are inclined to utilize more specific categories, such as paranoia or schizophrenia, when dealing with the same behaviors.

For whatever reasons an individual may violate background expectancies, his behavior can be reinforced; that is, the individual may find them rewarding. For example, he can receive personal satisfactions through the attention he is given because of the unusualness of his behavior, or because of the humor which results, or because he "got his way," and so on. The individual then tends to repeat similar behavior in similar circumstances. The recurrence of the behavior may be further reinforced, and eventually the individual may come to regularly engage in that particular behavior (Tabor, Quay, Mark, and Neeley 1969:354).

If idiosyncratic behavior is reinforced and becomes a pattern with an individual, it is then difficult for others to continue to excuse or to justify his behavior. If his behavior does not seriously disrupt relations with others, the individual can still escape the label of mental illness. In these cases, he is likely to be known as a chronic latecomer, for example, but not as mentally ill. His behavior may be classified as being a rather strange, but harmless, personal habit. When his patterned deviance is severely disruptive to interaction, however, or felt to be harmful to the group's well-being, but the behavior is not against the law and there is no specific cultural vocabulary to account for it, then the conceptual category or label of mental illness is likely to be used to classify the violator.

Once someone is labelled mentally ill, the label itself influences how behavior is perceived. Just as in the case of a person becoming classified as a homosexual, when this label is applied people tend to take a "new look" at the individual. They reconceptualize much of the person's behavior which they had previously accepted as normal or for which they had previously provided excuses. This same behavior now takes on a different interpretation. When this happens, the amount of deviance toleration allowed the individual may go sharply down. No longer will his behavior be accepted as "strange, but normal." It now becomes "strange and abnormal." In some cases, deviance toleration can also increase, as people come to expect that the individual will violate background expectancies. ("What can you expect? After all, you know how he is.") But in either case, after the label of mental illness has been applied the behaviors are thought of as abnormal.

The person who is labelled mentally ill is also affected by the label. He can begin to doubt the meaning of his own behaviors. He can begin to wonder if he is not, in fact, too greatly out of the ordinary. Even if he rejects the label, he may begin to troubledly question his underlying motives for committing certain acts. He may then begin to wonder if he is, in fact, "one of those." If the individual ever comes to the point of accepting the label of mental illness, his self-concept undergoes abrupt change. He reconceptualizes his own self in his own mind and is likely to think of himself as a person who has a sickness in his mind which is leading him to act in strange ways. If this occurs, he has moved from primary to secondary deviance.

Following the **labelling theory** of mental illness, then, we can understand "odd" or "bizarre" behavior without the concept of mental illness, without needing to think of a person's "mind" being in some way "infected." We do not need the concepts of disease or illness to understand patterned or recurrent "strange" behaviors which do not have an organic base. Such a person can be understood within the context of behavior which originally came about for any of the reasons we have just discussed: The behavior was reinforced; once it became patterned, it was no longer excusable; labels were then applied; because of new ways of thinking about the person, perception of behavior then changes on the part of both the one who was labelled and those who did the labelling. To see how this *labelling process* works, we can examine the case of paranoia.

Persons who are classified as paranoids believe, among other things, that people are persecuting them. The traditional psychiatric view of paranoids is that they are suffering from delusions: They are merely imagining that they are undergoing persecution. They are thought to have something pathological within them which leads to their bizarre behavior. Without accepting this psychiatric notion and its related assumptions, persons who had been labelled paranoids were studied (Lemert 1962). Their families were interviewed, as well as their work associates, employers, attorneys, and police; even their court records and psychiatric histories were examined. The conclusion reached was that these persons had undergone actual persecution, that they had not simply imagined it. These persons had typically been threatened with or had undergone a personally disruptive loss of status, such as the death of a relative, demotion at work, failure to be promoted, life changes due to age, or the breakup of their marriage. The individual felt that these status changes or threats were "intolerable," and under the resulting stress they reacted to others in ways which resulted in persistent difficulties. They sometimes became arrogant, insulting, presumed privileges, or struck out aggressively against persons who were close to them. Persons around them, in turn, found these reactions "intolerable," and they then began to react with suspicion and even fear. Communication became increasingly stifled. Relatives and associates began having a difficult time relating to them, beginning to talk among themselves about the "strangeness" of their behavior. The individuals perceived that others were talking about them, and they magnified this situation. They especially noted discrepancies between how they were previously treated and how they were now being reacted to. Further suspicion and mistrust grew between them and others around them, resulting in communication becoming even more stifled and cooperative behavior becoming even more difficult.

The initial loss or threatened loss of status made it difficult for these persons to continue to present a satisfactory self to others. The self they presented became discredited. When discrepancies developed between the self they presented and the self accepted by others, so did suspicion and mistrust. Others become less and less willing to interact with them on the basis of the definition which they were offering of themselves. Eventually a conspiracy developed among those around them to exclude them from participating in group activities and plans. As the individuals became increasingly isolated from their significant others, they became more and more "locked into" their behaviors; that is, their perception of and reaction to this "process of exclusion" created further problems for interaction. These problems further closed the channels of communication, perpetuating the cycle. Their interpersonal difficulties were eventually classified as symptoms of "mental illness," and they were finally pressured or compelled to undergo psychiatric treatment or committed to a mental hospital. When they were finally seen by a psychiatrist, their behavior was classified as delusional, and the specific tag of paranoia was attached to them.

A major problem for any society is social control. For social interaction to smoothly unfold and for society to exist and culture to continue, people must know what others expect of them, what to expect from others, and be able to depend upon those expectations. In order to accomplish social control, various mechanisms are utilized to sanction behavior that is upsetting or disruptive to others. Also basic to the process of establishing and maintaining social order is *making people predictable* by channeling them into social roles. For example, by making parents, milkmen, teachers, secretaries, or janitors of people, we know what behavior to expect from them.

As an aid in social control, categories are provided in each culture for judging the adequacy of **role performance,** the way people play their roles. Persons doing the judging ordinarily place themselves into categories by which they identify themselves as normal, conforming members of society. When they classify as deviants of one sort or another persons whose behavior is unlike theirs, they attain a firmer identity for themselves as solid members of society. The existence and application of these labels gives them greater security by providing an identity which conceptually separates themselves from persons who have contrary traits. Persons who in some way are felt to be threatening to the social order are then classified as outsiders. Use of pejorative labels marks out and classifies the boundaries between acceptable and unacceptable behavior (cf. Erikson 1966).

When people become unpredictable, that is, when they no longer adequately fulfill their roles, the social system threatens to break down. When people do not know what to expect from others, background expectancies become problematic, instead of being a basic part of what people can take for granted. This breakdown in expectations threatens cooperative action in the present, and makes future planning almost impossible.

When people fail to play their roles in the ways they are expected, **sanctions,** devices used either to keep people in line or to bring them back into line, are then put into effect. When someone has violated explicit rules, explicit sanctions in the form of labels and reactions follow. Someone who steals will be called a thief and might be arrested; someone who kills will be called a murderer and might himself be killed; someone who exhibits sexual preference for his own sex will be called a homosexual and might be arrested or ostracized from heterosexual society; while someone who strips for a living may be called a whore and will probably no longer be welcome in polite society.

The specific categories provided by our culture are insufficient to cover all behavior. Labels are especially inadequate when it comes to violations of residual rules. Yet people who break residual rules for which we have no specific label also pose problems for interaction. When people engage in behavior which is unthinkable for a "normal" member of society, they threaten others by creating uncertainty regarding what to expect from them in any given situation. People also feel that such persons are threatening the social system within which interaction takes place since others can no longer count on them to fulfill their part in cooperative endeavors.

A major sanction for residual rule violators is labelling them mentally ill and from then on treating them differently from persons who do not have that label. The mentally ill label contains the idea that one had better keep an eye on such persons because they are untrustworthy, unpredictable, and perhaps personally dangerous or even threats to the social order. Those to whom this label is applied are in many cases even looked upon as abnormals who should be locked up until an expert in the area of "mental illness," a psychiatrist, pronounces them "safe" for "normal" society. The category of mental illness, thus, serves as a major mechanism of social control, maintaining the status quo of the social order in the same way as do the categories we apply to specific norm violations such as prostitution, delinquency, and murder.

In this way the "mental health" profession, with its mental hospitals, psychiatrists, and its essential concept of mental illness, is a major mechanism of social control in contemporary Western culture. We have our police, courts, jails, and wardens for people who violate explicit legal rules, while we have our police, courts, mental hospitals, and psychiatrists for people who violate implicit rules. Thus the concept of mental illness and the related mental health establishment are major means of enforcing compliance with fundamental expectations of everyday interaction and routine role playing.

The underlying fundamental tautology of this psychiatric model of life is seldom recognized. It goes this way: Who are the mentally ill? They are those who rape, who withdraw from interaction, who molest children, or who react in "bizarre" ways when you deal with them. How does one know they are mentally ill? Because they have raped, are withdrawn, have molested, or have acted bizarrely in some way. A "normal" person, that is someone who is not mentally ill, would not have raped, withdrawn, molested, or acted bizarrely. Behavior, in other words, is taken as a sign that there is something fundamentally wrong with the person's mind, perhaps a disease or illness, and we know there is something wrong with his mind or have evidence of the mental disease or illness because of his behavior. The whole system is thus built on a self-fulfilling tautology.

The category of mental illness is so pervasively effective in our culture and its supposed underlying reality so taken for granted that court hearings which decide whether or not a person shall be committed to a mental hospital take but an average of 4.1 minutes (Miller and Schwartz 1966:28). Since we are so thoroughly socialized into the concept of mental illness, it is usually difficult for us to think of it as being a nonexistent entity or to recognize the underlying tautology which supports it. In order to better see its nonexistence and tautological base, it may be profitable for us to briefly examine the relationship between the concepts of mental illness, witches and witchcraft.

At an earlier period in our history, witches were commonly thought of as real beings with extraordinary powers. Upon examining the historical record, however, it appears that the label of witchcraft was applied to residual rule violations. When fundamental cultural expectations were violated, such as someone being disobedient to parents or other authorities, practicing unacceptable sex, or having other than monotheistic or Christian beliefs concerning God, they were sometimes thought to be under the influence of witchcraft or to perhaps be witches themselves. Priests and police were then brought to bear as agents of social control for the Church and State in order to enforce compliance with the right way of behaving and the right way of believing. Torture by flogging, water, and fire was considered to be an acceptable technique to protect God and society.

In the eighteenth and nineteenth centuries many of these behaviors were reclassified from witchcraft and sin to mental illness. They were then given medical terms in place of theological ones, and torture by imprisonment, lobotomy, and electroshock therapy became the "more enlightened" methods used to elicit conformance and protect society. Sanity, according to Benjamin Rush, the Father of American Psychiatry whose portrait still adorns the official seal of today's American Psychiatric Association, became defined as the "aptitude to judge things like other men, and regular habits," while insanity became "a departure from this," and included such things as chagrin, shame, terror, and anger (Szasz 1970:137–141).

With this change from morals to medicine even lying became a disease, as did alcoholism and crime. Alcoholics, criminals, and liars came to be viewed as persons who had a "disease" in the "mind." How did anyone know that a disease was "up there?" Very simple: the mental illness tautology was developed. Persons without the "disease," the "normal" members of society, would not lie, drink to excess, or commit crimes. Therefore, self-evidently, persons who did these things had the disease. This view became so pervasive (and this will sound as though I must certainly be exaggerating the situation, but I'm not) that being black was viewed a disease. Blacks became defined as white persons who were suffering from mild leprosy that led to excessive pigmentation which caused their blackness (Szasz 1970:138–139).

This view certainly strikes the modern ear as the extreme in ludicrousness, but when we take a look at some of our current concepts of mental illness as they are applied to behavior, we might find that our contemporary situation is not much improved. For example, as we covered in Chapter 3, youth is a major value in American culture. Accordingly, its opposite, age, is devalued. One way of dealing with the devalued commodity of age is to associate it with mental illness. Instead of defining it as normal for some people in this age group to have difficulty in caring for themselves, to have their memories dim with time and their concentration shrink as they turn more and more to the past, we tend to conceptualize such characteristics as a sign of an underlying "mental illness." We even give it a specific name, senility (Lowenthal 1964; Miller and Schwartz 1966). This conceptualization allows us to define them as psychiatric patients, making it easier on the younger generation as they commit the older to institutions in which they are locked up until their uneasy death. I assume that if a chemical base for their unacceptable behavior is discovered that they will be redefined as suffering from a physical illness and be treated in a different fashion.

Among the major values in American culture is that of youth. American society does not quite know what to do with those who lose this value, and has developed no similar strong traditions of appreciation for being aged. (Courtesy of Wide World Photos)

If mental illness does exist, when they examine people psychiatrists should be able to tell who has a mental illness and who doesn't. They should certainly be able to tell the sane from the insane. This idea was tested, but psychiatrists did not fare too well. Five men and three women volunteered for an experiment in which they became patients in twelve different mental hospitals in five different states. Each pseudopatient went to the admissions office and complained that he had been hearing voices. Beyond this "symptom" and changes in name and occupation for the sake of anonymity, all other biographical facts were accurately presented. When they were in the hospital, each pseudopatient *acted normally*. Each dropped *all* symptoms of abnormality, engaged in ordinary conversations, and so on. Yet, the biographical information which each pseudopatient had accurately presented was reinterpreted as representing a sign of maladjustment and a symptom of "mental" illness. All but one were classified as schizophrenic. Not a single pseudopatient was discovered to be sane, even though their behavior was normal while they were in the hospital. They were kept in confinement from seven to fifty-two days, with an average stay of nineteen days. When they were released, it was not because they were now judged to be normal but because their schizophrenia was judged to be "in remission" (Rosenhan 1973).

This residual category of mental illness is so broad that it is a tremendously helpful device for persons involved in social control. *Any behavior can be labelled mentally ill.* In 1860, for example, an Illinois woman was incarcerated in the Jacksonville State Insane Asylum because she had a disagreement with her husband, and the Illinois laws explicitly stated that a married woman could be "detained in a hospital at the request of the husband." In the 1820's masturbation was a form of solitary sexual behavior disapproved by our theologically dominated society, and, unbelievably enough, a new concept entered the medical repertoire, that of masturbatory insanity. Forms of this concept clung to our culture for a long time, and even in 1940 an indication of masturbation in a candidate was a legitimate basis for rejecting him for the United States Naval Academy at Annapolis. As recently as 1959 masturbation was described as a symptom of mental illness (Szasz 1970:14–15, 181, 201, 202). The flexible social control term of mental illness has also been and is today, applied to persons who use drugs, to persons who are suicidal, to persons who demonstrate a sexual preference for members of their own sex, and to persons who trade their sexual favors for cash or other goods. Additionally, some "authorities" want to apply the label of mental illness to all criminals, looking on crime itself as a form of mental illness and viewing "all felons as mental cases" (Roche 1958:241). Mental illness is indeed a flexible term well utilizable for any and all social control purposes.

The committal of Mrs. Henrietta Wright to an insane asylum demonstrates further how this concept is inextricably bound up with social control. Was she committed because of a disease in her mind? Well, maybe. Her offense was that she was a black. No illness there. But she attempted to register and vote. Still no illness there. But it was in Mississippi just twenty days after the Voting Rights Act of 1965 was passed. Perhaps she had an illness after all. What black in his or her right mind registered there in 1965? In any event, she was beaten by the arresting officers on two separate occasions, including being kneed and having her head knocked against the concrete floor of her cell. She was then committed to the type of prison we reserve for those who violate our background assumptions. Her husband was informed of the coming "mental" examination, as required by law, but the letter informing him was mailed after the examination had been completed. She later sued the state for damages from both the arresting officers and the doctors who committed her, but was defended unsuccessfully by the American Civil Liberties Union (Garbus 1971:3–77).

When the concept of mental illness is broadly applied, it appears that none of us are safe. One study would lead us to believe that 80 percent of the population has at least one psychiatric symptom (Srole 1962). Once the category of mental illness is applied, it is like quicksand:

When one attempts to extricate oneself, one only becomes further enmeshed in it. The person who accepts the category is looked on as a fortunate individual who has "insight" into his "illness," while the person who denies that he is mentally ill is told by the experts that he is so ill he does not recognize his illness. Neither escapes castigation. As it has been noted, the person who arrives early for an appointment is suffering from anxiety, while the person who arrives late is obviously exhibiting hostility. But even the person who arrives on time is not safe from this point of view, for he can be said to be suffering from compulsive behavior (Szasz 1970:30–35).

Again, by making a cross-cultural comparison we can gain insight into our behaviors and into the ways we classify behavior. This is especially instructive in the case of mental illness because we can see that different conceptual categories *for* behavior lead to different expectations *of* behavior and to different reactions *to* behavior.

Members of every culture must adjust to their environment. Members of all cultures must work out means of adjusting to the reality contingencies which surround them, whether those contingencies are other persons or the elements. In adjusting to these contingencies, people around the world have developed different expectations of behavior. The resulting patterns of behavior which have come to be accepted as normal in some cultures would immediately make anyone in our society who follows them a candidate for a straight jacket. The Dobuans, for example, are an extremely suspicious people. They constantly fear that someone might poison them, and for this reason they never leave their cooking pots untended. They are distinguished by ill will, treachery, hostility, and heavy use of magic, and they are, in general, an extremely antagonistic people (Benedict 1934:130, 251). Similar examples can be multiplied, such as drug use by members of the Native American Church; drinking patterns of the Navahos who drink as fast as they can to get drunk as quickly as they are able (Honigmann 1967:388, 393); and beliefs which we would call delusions, such as those of the Dinka who believe they are blood relatives of the crocodiles and that they can swim the crocodile-infested upper Nile without being harmed (LaBarre 1954:241).

Behaviors which some groups consider normal are behaviors for which they would immediately be subject to arrest in our society. The Flatheads of Idaho, for example, used to bind a flat board against the front part of the heads of their children in order to produce a recessed forehead. Other groups bind the heads of their children with cloth in order to produce elongated heads. The Bagandas of Africa place discs in their children's ear lobes, gradually increasing the size of the disk until as adults they are able to wear 6- to 8-inch discs in their ear lobes.

Similarly, Suia males of Brazil wear large discs in both their lips and ears (Hoebel 1966:279, 285). Although this may not be that much different from our practice of piercing ears, if it occurred in our culture such behavior would certainly be defined as child abuse. Anybody practicing it would most probably be looked on as having some sort of underlying mental illness. After all, what "normal" person would do such a thing?

In the same way that behavior considered normal by others is looked on as abnormal by us, behavior normal to us would be taken as abnormal by members of other groups. For example, the Hopi Indians emphasize loyalty to the group as perhaps their number one virtue. Individuality and competition are thoroughly deemphasized, while a premium is placed on cooperative behavior. Hopi Indian children can be taught to play basketball very well, but they refuse to keep score. They will play for hours without a thought of who is getting ahead. Similarly, a highly skilled Hopi stonecutter is content to receive the same pay as an unskilled day laborer (Lee 1959:20). In contrast, most Americans are systematically taught to be competitive, to constantly try to "succeed," to "get ahead," and to "be better" than others. In our culture, these behaviors are considered "normal." But if a Hopi Indian were to act like this, he would be looked at as bizarre. If the Hopis used the category of mental illness, they would probably apply it to this deviant in their midst.

The conceptual categories which our culture provides greatly determine what behavior means to us. They direct us to develop particular expectations of behavior, they guide us in evaluating that behavior, and they aid us in knowing how to react to that behavior. In the ways we classify behavior, we also decide whether others are normal or abnormal. If we decide that behavior is abnormal, we are likely, in the absence of legitimating excuses to the contrary, to attribute mental illness to the person. But there is no such "thing" as "mental" illness. Mental illness is not a disease of the mind. It is, rather, a conceptual category used in the Western world to negatively evaluate and bring under control certain forms of disapproved behavior—primarily violations of residual rules. The category is so broad and so vague that it can be and has been applied to almost all culturally disapproved behavior. But that is precisely its unique value for those who are interested in controlling the behavior of others. The concept of mental illness is infinitely flexible, and hardly a more ingenious mechanism could be developed for purposes of social control.

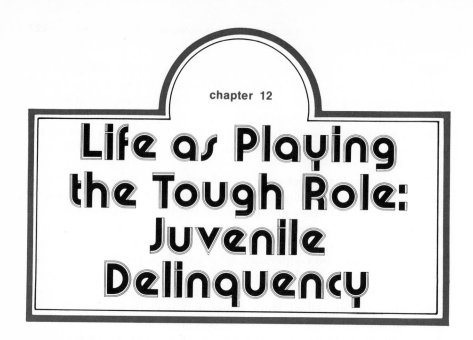

chapter 12

Life as Playing the Tough Role: Juvenile Delinquency

The typical juvenile delinquent is a teenage male from the lower class. Why not females? Why not the middle and upper classes? Why the adolescent years? Why delinquency? We shall examine these questions and present a sociological theory of juvenile delinquency. In doing so, we shall examine relationships among many of the concepts we have previously discussed, especially those of social class, values, subcultures, symbols, meaning, morality, social control, police discretion, neutralization, labelling, conceptual categories, and the presentation of self. As we analyze juvenile delinquency, we shall again be applying the sociological imagination.

There is no single cause of juvenile delinquency. This is a lesson which sociologists have learned well in their various studies: No **monocausal** (single cause) **explanation** suffices to explain social phenomena. Many aspects of life in society must be taken into consideration if we are to explain adequately why people act the way they do. We found in the last chapter that this was the case when we had to examine many possible underlying factors in order to account for the violation of residual rules. We also need to examine many factors to explain even such "simple" aspects of social life as why an individual works at a particular job, or why he works at all, why he purchases what he does, why he shops at a particular store, why he gets married or does not get married, why he does or does not have children, why he goes to school or drops out of school, or even why he wears the clothes he does or why he speaks in a certain way. This lesson of needing to seek many causes (the need of a *multicausal* approach) to understand human behavior also applies to the more esoteric or sensational aspects of human life, such as the problematic one of juvenile delinquency.

In order to understand juvenile delinquency, the first thing we must look at is the larger conditions in which human beings find themselves, the culture which surrounds people and gives shape to the ways in which they live out their lives. In searching for causes of juvenile delinquency, culture is more significant than one would first think. It is characteristic of industrialized societies that people are not allowed to take on adult roles, such as regular work and marriage, until they reach their late teens or early twenties. During this limbo state, they live in a literal "no man's land," possessing a vacuous, uncertain identity known as youth or adolescence. As you are intimately aware from your own experience, adolescents have left the status of child, but they have not yet attained the status of adult. As we shall see, this characteristic of industrialized societies is crucial for understanding juvenile delinquency.

Members of contemporary industrialized societies have learned to take this lack of status of adolescents for granted. Many assume that it is an inherent human condition not to take on adult roles until such a late age. This lack of adult status for persons in their teens, however, is by no means universal. For example, in primitive societies at puberty male youth typically undergo an initiation ceremony which marks them as adults. The initiation ceremony is but one of several **rites de passage,** ceremonies customary in a society such as marriages, confirmations, first communions, and funerals, which publicly mark out major status changes through which individuals pass. This particular *rite de passage* grants adult status to the younger members of the society, literally transforming them from children to adults. Successful completion of the initiation rites grants them legitimate claim to the status, rights, and privileges of adulthood in their group. At the same time, however, since they are now full-fledged members of the adult community, they are also expected to take on adult responsibilities, even though it is recognized that they are less experienced than others and still have much to learn. Whatever learning takes place following the initiation ceremony, however, occurs within this newly bestowed adult status (Benedict 1938).

Lack of adult identity for adolescents has not always been characteristic of the Western world. Surprisingly enough, at one time in the Western world we did not even think of adolescence as a special period of life. In medieval society there were no concepts similar to ours to distinguish the special statuses of childhood, adolescence, and adulthood. Children were not weaned until a much later age than we are accustomed to, in some cases not until they were about seven years old, but at that point they were plunged directly into adult life. They were

primarily considered to be small adults, sort of adults inhabiting minia-
turized bodies. After weaning, boys and girls were separated into sex-
linked activities. Girls learned household tasks, while boys were appren-
ticed into an occupation. If a boy was a member of the elite of society,
he might be sent on to school, but more commonly he also directly entered adult activities. In medieval society, there was no "in-between status" equivalent to that which we accept as normal for those in their teen
years. There were, for example, no games in medieval society that were
exclusively children's games. Adults played the same games children
played, while children mingled freely with adults (Sjoberg 1963:176;
Aries 1962).

Especially relevant to our concern here is the age of legal offenders
and reaction to breaking the law. The law-breaking activities of persons
below the age of eighteen or twenty-one were handled in the same
fashion as the law-breaking activities of people we call adults. If, for example, the law provided for an offender to be put to death by burning
or hanging, then the offender was burned to death or hung—
regardless of his age. Girls as young as thirteen, for example, were
burned to death as punishment for their imputed law violations, while
we have records of eight-and ten-year-old boys being hanged for theirs
(Blackstone 1899:1230).

For a period of time following industrialization in the West, children
continued to be treated as adults. At an early age they entered full-time
remunerative employment in order to contribute to the material support of the family. Children were especially desired as workers because
they could be hired for less than pocket money, driving down labor
costs. Employers recruited armies of children, sometimes threatening
to fire parents if they sent their children to school instead of work
(Kuczynski 1946:24). Children would exhaustingly labor at machines
for up to fourteen grueling hours a day. Sometimes they were even
chained to their beds at night to make certain that they were available
for work the next morning, and then chained to their machines during
the day to make certain they remained at their task. Reform movements spearheaded by the incipient international trade unions ushered
in child labor laws. By 1879 it became illegal in most instances to employ children under the age of ten, while by 1916 the minimum age
had increased to fourteen (Kuczynski 1946:115; Phelps 1939:16–18).
Expectations of lengthened education similarly developed, and *persons
in their teens came to be thought of as a special class of people.*

Reconceptualizing the social reality of age marked a historical watershed in the ways people of this age were thought of and reacted to.
After the conceptual category was developed that separated those in
the age we now know as adolescence into a special status, laws were

changed to fit this newly developed social category: Juveniles became separated from adults before the bar of justice. In 1899, in Illinois, the first juvenile court in the United States was established ushering in a change which was eventually adopted by our other states.

It is important for our discussion to note the significance of this development in legal distinction. Only because we have this special legal category in which people are differentially dealt with according to age do we have juvenile delinquency. Without it, we would simply have crimes committed by people, with little or no distinction made regarding the age of the offender. This may sound like an extremely finely drawn point, and in many ways it is, but it is most significant for providing a historical context for understanding juvenile delinquency. Law violations by people whom we now call juveniles have certainly occurred over the years. The violations are not new. It is the conceptualization of those violations and violators which is new. Because we now have the concept of juvenile, we mark out our world in a manner quite differently from that which people previously did. We apply this concept of a special age status to law violators, and in this way we *conceptually produce* the legal category of juvenile delinquency.

Following the reform movements concerning child labor, the idea continued to develop that increased formal education was necessary for youth. Younger adolescents became mostly unemployable, although there were still agricultural jobs for rural youth and part-time, after-school jobs for urban youth. The "school year" had been patterned after the agricultural season, and rural youth were regularly taken out of school by their parents in the early spring and fall to help the family during the most pressing times of planting and harvesting. Though it has become much less common, in some of our rural areas this practice is still followed.

As the idea of the desirability and necessity of increasing the period of formal education continued to develop, a larger and larger group of our people became increasingly unemployable. Today this group of unemployables includes almost all our adolescents, including the older ones. Now that we have entered a highly automated era, it is commonly thought that our adolescents generally lack the skills necessary for financial independence. Whether this is true or not, and it appears that only minimal training is necessary for many positions, adolescents certainly lack the opportunity to remuneratively employ whatever social or economic skills they have, as well as being denied the chance to learn skills they could market at this age. They are, rather, sent to classrooms for year after year of learning from books.

I have not yet specified a "cause" of juvenile delinquency. What I have done is to indicate the *structural* conditions which allow delinquency to exist. (Cf., Werthman 1967.) To see the critical importance of these economic factors combined with the recently developed social redefinition of a special age group into "adolescents," we can note that most juvenile delinquents leave their law-breaking activities behind when they reach late adolescence or when they enter their early twenties. They are commonly said to "mature out" of their delinquency. What happens is that it is at this point in their lives that they are finally allowed to take on adult roles, specifically the two primary granters of adult status in the Western world: "making a living" in the labor market and getting married.

These cultural factors, rooted in economic conditions, adequately explain the age involved in juvenile delinquency. But how about the social class make-up of the typical delinquent? Why are delinquents in the United States ordinarily recruited from the lower class, and not some other social class? To get at factors which underlie this aspect of delinquency, we must understand some of the differences in the value systems and ways of achieving identity in the social classes.

Achieving an adequate self-concept appears to be a major goal for everyone. For persons classified as adults in our society, major areas in which the self is interactionally claimed and validated are marriage and work relationships. It is especially by our performance in occupations and marriage that our claims to being adult are acknowledged by others. Being denied these major mechanisms by which adult status is typically granted members of Western culture, adolescents seek identity elsewhere.

As we previously discussed, especially in Chapters 3 and 5, humans are problem-solving or goal-oriented beings. Essential to being human is to work out solutions to problems in the attempt to reach desired ends or goals. As we discussed in Chapter 3, when people develop solutions to problems, these solutions become part of the group's culture. They become part of the key expectations governing the behavior of the members of the group. When they become part of the group's basic framework of expectations, they are then essential to the ways members of that group look at the world and evaluate one another. These expectations are critical for members of the group, for members are judged according to how they meet them.

This principle of cultural and subcultural expectations based on solutions to problems applies to the youth in all our social classes. One of the major solutions to the central problem of achieving identity which has been worked out by our middle and upper class youth is success within the educational system. Middle and upper class youth, in general, receive a good part of their self-concept validation through educational attainments. These come largely in the form of attaining good grades and recognition for participating in school sports and various other organized extracurricular activities the school system offers. Identity achievement within the school system is facilitated for our middle and upper class youth because education in the United States is primarily a middle class experience (Friedenberg 1963; Kozol 1967; Jencks and Riesman 1968). Our schools are primarily based on middle class values and skills. They are almost exclusively run by middle class administrators and staffed by middle class teachers. Middle class youth fit well into this system, as do upper class youth who also at an early age are trained in paper and pencil skills which almost guarantee their success in our educational system. We also maintain a system of private schools for the elite where from grade school through college upper class skills and values can be instilled at a price our elite can afford.

Lower class youth, however, do not fit very well into our school system. They first of all do not receive equivalent intensive at-home training in the verbal skills which aid educational success. This greatly detracts from their performance as long as they remain in school. Nor do they as frequently receive the encouragement and rewards for bringing home good grades and teacher reports. Moreover, compared with middle and upper class children, not only does their lack of fluency in middle class vocabulary and grammar hamper them, but their fluency

The public educational system is primarily a middle-class experience. Not matching the experiences and orientations of the middle class, lower-class youth disproportionately drop out of the school system. (Photo by J. Paul Kirouac)

in words considered "bad" by their teachers also works against them, as does their grammatical construction and pronunciation, which is considered "wrong," and their manners and demeanor, which are considered "improper." With the conflicts which result, lower class youth drop out of school at a much higher rate than youth from the other social classes.

Being not only denied adult status through occupations and marriage, but also unlike our other youth, usually not finding identity through participation in the school system, lower class youth socially construct an identity in which the occupational and educational systems largely become irrelevant. Through interaction they validate their own sets of values, their own beliefs, and their particular frames of reference (Cohen 1955:67). As we discussed in Chapter 3, lower class male adolescents develop a subculture in which the norms for granting status center around the major values of trouble, toughness, smartness, excitement, fate, and autonomy (Miller 1958). Lower class boys value trouble because it relieves monotony, providing a welcome source of excitement. During situations involving trouble they are able to exhibit their smartness and toughness, as well as express autonomy or freedom from authority. With their belief in the role of fate in their lives, they feel that some persons who "make trouble" are lucky and don't get caught, while others are unlucky and there is nothing much one can do about it.

It is not enough, however, for an individual to simply make a claim to values such as toughness and smartness. As we discussed in Chapter 7, identity claims must be validated through interaction with others. Accordingly, the individual must demonstrate to his peers that he actually is tough or cool. This need of demonstrating the self within this subcultural value system often leads to involvement in gang activities. Especially valued are situations which involve risk-taking, as participation in risk situations can demonstrate that an individual is what he says he is. Sometimes this form of identity claim involves playing games with the law, such as joy-riding, where one takes the risk of stealing a car and openly being seen riding in it. Stealing also serves as a way of validating claimed identity, especially when peers are able to observe the theft and the boy is able to demonstrate bravado during his escape (Werthman 1967).

Through such activities many lower class youth construct an identity for themselves. They make claims regarding who they are, and by means of their behavior they validate those claims. It is only at a somewhat later age that activities such as stealing lose some of their identity validating aspects and take on more instrumental purposes; that is, stealing is later primarily engaged in for what it can net materially.

When stealing becomes more instrumental, the boys decrease the risk component. Shoplifting, for example, becomes more of an instrument for attaining desired clothing than for interactionally validating the self by demonstrating toughness or smartness. The social construction of the self is still apparent in such an activity, however, since desired clothing enables an individual to wear the correct props and thus present a desired self to others. At a later point, after they have dropped out of or finished high school, the boys cut the risk down even further, and they become increasingly reluctant to even talk about such activities (Werthman 1967).

In this lower class male subculture, honor or reputation becomes all important. Members are continually concerned that their "rep" matches the values held by their peers. Not only is it important for them to establish a "rep" with male friends, but it is also important to gain a "rep" with girls. This, too, can be attained by showing toughness since lower class girls appear to admire toughness in their men. A major way of achieving a desired "rep" with both males and females is through participation in gang fights.

Lower class males are not immune from the more general cultural values which tend to mitigate against or are opposed to delinquency. They also learn these values, and they must deal with them. In order to protect the self-concept from social values which condemn the activities in which they are engaging, they develop their own definitions of reality. They symbolize their activities in a way which helps neutralize appositional values and facilitates committing delinquent acts. Specifically, they deny responsibility for their acts: They pick out an idea which has become increasingly popular in our culture and defensively employ it by saying that society has made them the way they are. They also deny harming anyone, saying that no one was really hurt by what they did. When someone was hurt by their actions, they then deny that the person they hurt was a victim. They are liable to claim that the person they beat up provoked the beating, and he merely got what was coming to him. They sometimes turn the attack on their accusers, saying that the police are corrupt and brutal, and the laws unfair. They also call on higher loyalties to defend their acts. They might say, for example, that they had no choice in participating because they needed to protect fellow gang members from getting hurt in a fight (Sykes and Matza 1957).

By techniques such as these, juvenile delinquents are able to neutralize cultural values which stand in opposition to their activities. For many delinquents, however, such neutralizing of activities is unnecessary because they subscribe to moral codes which support their acts. That is, many delinquents find nothing to neutralize because they believe that their law violations are moral acts (Hindelang 1970:508).

With either neutralization of general norms or a moral code which approves law-breaking activities, set within a value system of identity achievement which greatly encourages and in some instances requires them (which, in turn, impede lower class youth from achieving success in our schools), lower class males become heavily represented in delinquency statistics.

This is not to deny that there are middle class delinquents, just that the *typical* juvenile delinquent is from the lower class. Middle class youth appear to be increasingly becoming hedonistic or pleasure-seeking, to be developing greater status uncertainties, as well as to be developing a culture of leisure characterized by much money and few responsibilities (England 1960). In the upper and middle class youth cultures, criminal acts sometimes also net desired prestige, with members similarly priding themselves on being smart enough to be able to get away with illegal acts (Weiner 1970). For example, the number one crime in the exclusive town of Birmingham, Michigan, is shoplifting by teenagers of affluent parents. When they are caught, some of them are even carrying credit cards for the same store in which they were stealing (CBS-TV, "What Happens if The Dream Comes True?" November 25, 1971).

In one college situation with which I am familiar, eight girls who are now in their senior year shoplift each weekend. They share the same dormitory suite, by choice, so they can the easier maintain both their friendship and shoplifting activities. On each Friday or Saturday they get together in one of their rooms and plan their next shoplifting excursion. They decide where they are going "to shop" and what it is they are looking for. They then go out as a group, splitting up into pairs in the various stores. They have practiced their shoplifting techniques over the past three years so they know how to keep an eye out for store employees while simultaneously engaging in chit-chat and picking up desired items. Most of what they shoplift is clothing and personal items. They can well afford to purchase most of these items, but they obviously find it much cheaper to get hold of them in this way. They also enjoy "putting one over" on the owners and managers of the stores. They express only a low awareness of risk, but they possess a highly developed verbal repertoire regarding justifications for their activities. A major justification points to capitalists who are "ripping off" the public with the girls only rightfully getting some of it back.

Even though many middle and upper class youth are involved in committing delinquent acts, another major factor operates to disproportionately make delinquents of lower class adolescents. To become a juvenile delinquent, as measured by local and state police reports or according to the statistics of the *Uniform Crime Reports* of the Federal

Bureau of Investigation, one must be arrested and charged with a law violation. Those who get the official label of "juvenile delinquent" attached to them are, by definition, juvenile delinquents. Those who commit the same acts but are not arrested are, by the same definition, not juvenile delinquents; that is, although they, too, have committed acts of delinquency they do not show up in the official reporting, and they are, consequently, not classified as delinquents.

In deciding who shows up in these official measuring rods of juvenile delinquency, social class is extremely important. Middle and upper class youth are given much greater protection by their parents against the labelling activities of the police and courts. Middle and upper class parents are, first of all, more likely to directly interfere with the labelling process, and, second, to be effective when they do so. They have greater power to effectively challenge the police definition or version of what happened. They have access to first-rate, experienced lawyers, and they are often able to exert personal, economic, and political pressures to bring about a change in the way their children are handled by

Values common among lower-class males, especially those of toughness, trouble, and fate, frequently result in behaviors which come to the attention of the enforcement agents of society. (Courtesy of Wide World Photos)

official agencies. In such ways they are often able to arrange to have verdicts favorable to their children brought in, and in many cases they are even able to arrange to have the charges dropped entirely. The police are intimately familiar with the greater power of middle and upper class parents in influencing the judicial process. Consequently, they are themselves more likely to merely talk to middle and upper class youth about the same behavior toward which they would act punitively if perpetrated by lower class youth (Cicourel 1968).

An additional factor in bringing middle and upper class youth less frequently before the bar of justice for the same acts committed by youth of the lower class centers around the presentation of self. As I mentioned in Chapter 9, presenting a self which communicates respect is crucial for pleasant interaction with the police. Middle and upper class youth appear to possess greater abilities in presenting such a self. This is partially due to one of the factors which provides them with disproportionate success in our educational system in the first place, their greater fluency with standard English—language which by its very nature connotes respect to members of American society. The self which is presented by lower class youth, in contrast, comes closer to the stereotype which the police hold of delinquents and criminals. This not only includes their language but also such things as the "uniform of the delinquent," which at least in the past has involved black jackets and soiled denims (Piliavin and Briar 1964:210). This presentation is more likely to be made by lower class youth than youth from the upper or middle classes.

The better one's demeanor towards the police, the better the disposition of one's case. Or, to put this in the obverse: the worse the police are treated by a suspect, or the less they like him *for whatever reason,* the greater the likelihood that they will charge him with a more serious offense. During the course of their job, the police routinely make decisions according to their own discretion concerning who, when, and why they arrest someone. When they arrest a suspect, it is usually possible to charge him with any or all of several law violations. It is frequently up to their discretion to determine with which violations an individual will be charged. Suspects who are less respectful towards the police end up with more serious charges lodged against them (Lundman, Fox, Sykes, and Clark 1971). These charges can mean simply a greater or lesser fine, but they can also mean the difference between several months in jail or several years in prison.

The importance of self-presentations when dealing with the police is well illustrated by cases involving suspects who showed "proper respect" and those who did not. For example:

An 18-year-old white male was accused of statutory rape. The girl's father was an important political figure, and he was pressuring the police to take severe action against the youth. The sergeant already felt that this male was an undesirable person because he was a member of a delinquent gang, and he had evidence that the youth had been intimate with the girl over a period of many months. When he interrogated the youth, however, he found him to be polite and cooperative. The youth consistently addressed the officer as "Sir" and answered all questions quietly. He also stated that he wanted to marry the girl, and it turned out that he was not a member of a gang. The sergeant's attitude became increasingly sympathetic, and he decided to try and have the charges against him reduced or dropped (Piliavin and Briar 1964).

Contrast this with the following:

A 17-year-old white male had been caught having sexual relations with a 15-year-old girl. When interrogated, he did not show deference toward the officers, responding slowly and with obvious disregard. The officers became irritated, and finally one officer angrily said that the boy was simply a "stud," interested only in sex, eating, and sleeping. He then added that he supposed that the boy "probably had knocked up half a dozen girls." The boy gave back an impassive stare at these comments, and the officers made out an arrest report and took him to juvenile hall (Piliavin and Briar 1964).

In these examples, both young men had solid evidence against them. Significant political pressure was even being brought to bear on the police to prosecute the older youth. Yet, the politeness and cooperation of the eighteen-year-old decidedly changed the picture leading the police to try to reduce or drop his charges while eagerly pressing charges against the younger offender.

Although these examples deal with differing presentations of self by individuals from the same social class, the youth to whom the police responded positively presented a self which is more commonly found among upper and middle class youth. It is they who are both socialized into greater respect for the police and who are better provided with sign-vehicles which communicate the type of self to which the police react more positively. This advantage minimizes the chances of middle and upper class youth showing up on a police blotter.

Another reason for the greater tendency of lower class youth to become delinquent compared with upper and middle class youth has to do with the socialization and opportunity we previously discussed in

When activities of lower-class youth come to the attention of the police, they are more likely to arrest and prosecute them than when the same legal infractions are committed by middle- and upper-class youth. The label of troublemaker further closes off legitimate avenues of success. (Courtesy of Wide World Photos)

Chapter 2. Members of the lower class are probably socialized into desiring financial or material success to the same extent as our upper and middle class youth. Because their incomes are so much lower, however, they have far fewer means for achieving desired success. They are, accordingly, more likely to turn to illegitimate or disapproved avenues, such as stealing, as a means of achieving the material possessions into which they have been so effectively socialized (Merton 1968).

Related to this is an explanation which refers to *greater* opportunity on the part of the lower class. But this is the opportunity for learning how to commit criminal acts, not opportunity for improving one's access to the legitimate means of success. Compared with the upper and middle classes, the lower class subculture contains greater opportunities to learn how to commit crimes, such as techniques of robbery and burglary, which draw the attention of the police. Accordingly, more lower class persons learn the necessary techniques for these crimes than do middle and upper class persons, and with the more generally acceptable avenues to success blocked off to members of this subculture, they are prone to use them (Cloward and Ohlin 1960).

Such factors as culture conflict in school, an emphasis on toughness and identity achievement outside the educational system, lack of opportunity to participate in adult roles, greater police scrutiny, and less income for attaining material goods help to explain why the lower class is disproportionately involved in arrest statistics. But why, then, are juvenile delinquents primarily males rather than females? Why in 1971, for example, were "only" 363,791 females under the age of 18 arrested compared with 1,265,944 males in the same age group? (*Uniform Crime Reports for the United States, 1971:*126) What accounts for approximately three and a half times as many arrests of adolescent males than females?

To answer this question, we must first note something about the sexuality of adolescents. Adolescents, regardless of the social class from which they come, are highly involved in the intricate and demanding process of developing their sexuality. They are in the midst of discovering for themselves what it means to be female or what it means to be male. As we came to see in Chapter 7, beginning with birth our culture places heavy emphasis on the symbolic separation of the sexes. During adolescence, teenagers enter a disturbing period in which they are developing a self-concept built around performance in a sex role. During this trying period, they are extremely sensitive concerning the ways males and females *properly* act. In their upsetting and sometimes traumatizing pursuit after personal sexual identity, they frequently exaggerate "maleness" and "femaleness." For years adolescents have already been intensively socialized into being males and females according to the dictates of our culture, but they are just now "coming into their own." In whatever activities they become involved during this period, they are highly aware that they are performing them within a framework of sex role expectations.

Second, the expectations of "what is male" compared to "what is female" differ so markedly in our culture that males and females are confronted with contrasting sets of problems. Males develop a different set of goals than females, different means for solving their problems on the way to these goals, and a different "measuring rod" for evaluating the self. American males are generally expected to score highly in achievement, exploitation, aggressiveness, daring, active mastery of their environment, and active pursuit after goals, while a whole set of contrary expectations apply to American females. These traditionally center around security with men and sexual attractiveness. Contrary to the male role, the female role involves such things as beauty and charm (Cohen 1955:139).

The third factor we should note concerning adolescent sexuality goes back to the material we covered on differences between the social classes and traditional sex role expectations. Lower class women are not generally expected to compete and excel in the "world out there," but they are expected to build a small niche within a more parochial and protected world. They are expected to meet the expectations which lower class men have of them in the feminine roles of sweetheart, then wife, and finally mother. Juvenile delinquency and participation in gang activities are inappropriate for the female roles a lower class woman is expected to play, while these same activities demonstrate "manliness" for her male counterpart. Consequently, lower class females are much less likely to become involved in juvenile delinquency (Cohen 1955:46).

More than this is involved, however, in keeping the female delinquency rates low. When females are caught violating the law, interactional factors also come into play which further protect lower class females from becoming officially involved in the adjudicating process. Especially important is the presentation of self. The conceptual category of "criminal" or "delinquent" which policemen hold centers around males, not females. Just as when a woman is stopped by a traffic officer for speeding she is more likely to get by with a warning than a man committing the same offense, so it is with delinquency. Policemen are more likely to deal with females informally than when they deal with males, even though the same offense is involved. If a female is arrested, she is also more likely to be released by the court than is a male.

Along this same line of sex-linked role differences, we should note that just as families exert greater social control over their preadolescents than over their adolescents (which helps to account for the low number of preadolescents being arrested for juvenile delinquency), so families exert greater authority over their daughters than their sons.

These explanations appear to account for the fact that the typical delinquent is an adolescent male from the lower class, but what have sociologists discovered about why one individual in the same social class becomes a delinquent while another does not? The answer to this question is extremely complex. To answer the previous questions we have primarily examined *structural* elements (that is, aspects of the way society is put together) which lead to a particular age, sex, and social class linkage with juvenile delinquency. To answer this question, however, we must look at the situations in which the interaction occurs.

We need to know both about the **objective conditions,** characteristics of the situation, and the **subjective conditions,** characteristics of the person. Regarding objective conditions, we need to know where the act took place, its physical setting and its ecological factors, such as in whose "turf" or territory it occurred. We also need to know whom the person was with at the time the act took place, as well as the individual's relationship with those persons.

For subjective conditions, we need to know much about the individual participating in delinquency. We especially need to know about his previous learning experiences. How he views the values dominant in his culture and his subculture is significant, as are the attitudes he holds toward committing acts of delinquency and becoming involved in gang activities. Particularly important is knowing in what ways delinquent behavior, compared with non-delinquent behavior, has been reinforced with him (Sutherland and Cressey 1960; Burgess and Akers 1966). In determining these subjective conditions, it is important to know what the individual's family is like. Even though they are members of the same general social class, families often differ markedly in their values and goals. The goals and values parents teach their children differ accordingly.

To account for any individual's involvement or noninvolvement in delinquency, we need information about the individuated experiences the particular person has undergone. These will then help us to understand with what *predispositions* to act the individual entered a given situation. Especially important in this respect is knowing the person's definitions. How does he view his self? How did he view his chances of successfully evading apprehension when he committed the delinquent act? What did he feel he would gain by committing the act, such as money or standing in his group by demonstrating his "rep"? What was his view of the morality of the act? What provocations or attractions were bound up in the immediate circumstances; that is, in what ways did the individual view the act as appealing (cf. Gibbons 1971:271)?

When we examine such objective and subjective factors, we should be able to account for not only why some classes of people (males, lower class, adolescents) become more involved in juvenile delinquency than other classes, but we should be able to also explain why particular individuals commit delinquent acts. A theory is being developed in sociology which is designed to more adequately deal with this question of the behavior of specific individuals. We shall examine that theory in the next chapter.

Finally, it is relevant to deal with the question of why people typically stop committing acts for which they are arrested when they reach their late adolescence or early twenties. As we have previously covered, we find that at this age people tend to move into a different status system. Different ways of achieving and bestowing status come to be important for the individual. No longer does a lower class male find it as necessary to "get into trouble" in order to demonstrate to his friends that he isn't a sissy, and during these years he typically takes a job, joins the army, or more rarely, goes on to college. In these "occupations" he is conferred status on a different basis. He is able to achieve identity without "trouble" and "the tough role" being the major mechanisms of bestowing it. We can note, however, that the basis of status achievement for low-ranking enlisted men does not appear to greatly differ from earlier lower class experiences—primarily a "rep" for toughness and "rough maleness" or virility.

To explain why any particular individual does not leave law-breaking behind but goes on to a life of crime, we would need to especially examine the labelling process that has affected him. Specifically, what were the processes of informal labelling by neighbors, school officials, and police by which he became defined as a troublemaker? Additionally, in what ways has he been formally labelled as a delinquent through arrest and exposure to the judicial system? In what ways, then, has this labelling process closed off legitimate avenues to success in life *and* opened up access to an opportunity structure in criminality? In what ways does labelling aid the transition from primary to secondary deviance? It is quite obvious, for example, that not all persons committing delinquent acts are arrested. For those who are, it can make a world of difference for learning behaviors and attitudes which facilitate criminality. Detention in juvenile halls, for example, frequently alienates boys from responses which would otherwise minimize their participation in the criminal system (O'Connor 1970).

Parenthetically, we should note that in this analysis we have not even mentioned race. In the same way that sex and social class make a critical difference for involvement in juvenile delinquency, so the race of a suspected law violator can be the crucial difference. Blacks are more likely than whites to be questioned on the street. If they are questioned, they are more likely than whites to be arrested. If arrested, they are more likely than whites to be sent to court. If they are sent to court, they are more likely than whites to receive a more severe disposition of their case (Piliavin and Briar 1964; Goldman 1963; Axelrod 1952; Ferdinand and Luchterhand 1970). So, if we were to add the question of why black males are overrepresented in delinquency statistics, we would approach the answer in the same way as we did the question of why lower class males are overrepresented.

By asking such questions and looking at these varied aspects of life in society, we are using the sociological imagination. We are examining *structural* aspects of society as we view individuals at the center of social forces which exert great effects on their lives. In this case those social forces revolve around cultural expectations concerning sex and age roles, as well as values which are embedded in both culture and subculture. The sociological imagination also directs us to the symbolic manipulations on the part of the individual as he evaluates himself and his behavior, as he works out his problems of identity and status in the ways open to him, and the ways by which he neutralizes his acts and evaluates himself in the light of those acts. On the *interactional* level we also examine the individual as he plays the all-important game of presenting the self to others in everyday life. We pay attention to the effect on the individual of police discretion and of labelling by social control agencies. Moreover, exercising the sociological imagination leads us to examine interaction within a historical milieu, as we especially become aware of the effects of historical and social forces which have led to the conceptual category of juvenile delinquency in the first place.

chapter 13

Life as Making Bargains: The Social Exchange Perspective

Why do people do what they do? This is perhaps the basic question people throughout society wonder about. Why did John drop out of school and become a delinquent? Why did Joan choose to have an abortion rather than get married? Why did the Joneses have so many children? Why do Bob and Nancy plan on having but one child? Why did Carlos and Maria leave their relatives and emigrate? Why did Bill go to Canada to escape the draft, while his brother volunteered for combat service? Why did Helen change jobs? Why did Hank turn down a job to stay on welfare? Why did Carol and George get divorced only six months after their marriage? Why did Frank commit suicide? These and countless similar questions are constantly being asked. People want to understand other people. They want to know why they do what they do.

This is also the basic question in the social sciences, though it is usually put in a different form. The sociologist, along with the historian, the psychologist, the economist, the political scientist, and the anthropologist, focuses on this central concern: the quest for understanding the "why" of human behavior. I have indicated that the basic sociological approach to unearthing the reasons for human behavior is called the sociological imagination. Throughout this book, I have indicated aspects of life in society which go into the make-up of the sociological imagination: historical events; the structure of society, including membership in social class; socialization into cultural and subcultural values; language; morality; living within a world of symbols; presenting the self to others in everyday life; and playing roles and games.

Besides the sociological imagination, another approach used by sociologists in dealing with the "why" of human behavior is *social exchange theory*. Social exchange theory is not so popular with sociologists, however, because its basic orientation is psychological. Many sociologists object to this theory because it focuses almost exclusively on the individual, paying little attention to the structuring or social context of human behavior. Consequently, most sociologists feel somewhat uncomfortable with social exchange theory, usually preferring to examine the relevant social context or structure to explain behavior.

Where the sociological imagination is frequently felt by students to be rather vague, social exchange theory, in contrast, has the redeeming virtues of being more explicit and yielding a close match with what we feel happens to us in everyday life. Social exchange theory brings the analysis of the "why" of what people do down to the individual level, allowing us to examine basic components involved in interpersonal behavior.

The basic assumption of social exchange theory is that people are rational beings who evaluate their possible courses of action and choose those with the greatest payoff. People avoid doing those things which they find punishing, while they seek those which are rewarding. If a particular course of action costs people much, they expect much in return. Succinctly put, the central view of social exchange theory is that "actions are a function of their payoffs" (Homans 1967:31).

The five basic propositions (Homans 1967:32–41) of social exchange theory—also known as **social exchange perspective**—are:

1. The more often a person's activity is rewarded, the more likely he will perform the activity [the *success* proposition].
2. When a person's activity has been rewarded, it is accompanied by specific stimuli of some sort. The more similar later stimuli are to these earlier ones, the more likely the person will perform a similar activity [the *stimulus* proposition].
3. The more valuable the reward of an activity is to a person, the more likely he is to perform the activity [the *value* proposition].
4. The more often in the recent past a person has received some particular reward, the less valuable any further unit of that reward becomes to him [the *deprivation–satiation* proposition].
5. When a person does not receive the reward he expects or receives punishment he did not expect, he will become angry. When someone is angry, the results of aggressive behavior are rewarding [the *frustration–aggression* proposition].

The **success proposition** implies that a person will eventually stop performing an activity when he is no longer rewarded for it. This is in line with common sense. Another finding, unlike common sense, however, is that a person will perform an activity more often and perform it longer after rewards cease if he has been rewarded on an irregular basis than if he has been rewarded on a regular basis. If, for example, he has been rewarded every third time he performed an activity, he will tend to perform the activity less frequently and quit it more quickly when rewards cease than if his rewards had come at irregular intervals. This is the case even though the irregular rewards might actually have totalled much less, averaging, for example, perhaps one reward in six or ten times. Although this idea is highly contrary to common sense, it is well supported by research (cf. Skinner 1953). The timing of rewards is known as a **reinforcement schedule.** The reinforcement schedule with the greatest irregularity and unpredictability of rewards, the variable-ratio reinforcement schedule, is also the most powerful. In this schedule, both the amount and the timing or frequency of rewards vary. This schedule of rewards can easily "hook" a person into particular behaviors, and is the basis for the "addiction" some people develop for playing slot machines.

The **stimulus proposition** implies generalization; that is, when an individual is in a situation similar to one in which he was previously rewarded, he will tend to act in a way similar to the behavior that accompanied his earlier reward. For example, a fisherman who has caught fish in a shady pool will tend to fish other shady pools (Homans 1967:34), while a widow who enjoyed a successful marriage will tend to look for a spouse who has characteristics similar to those her first husband possessed.

The **value proposition** implies that things which are rewarding to some people may not be rewarding to others. By the same token, something which is highly rewarding to one person may be only mildly rewarding to someone else. The more highly a person values a reward, the more likely he is to perform activities which he feels will lead to that reward, while the less a person values a reward, the less likely he is to perform those activities. In line with common sense, the more punishing an activity is to an individual, the more likely he is *not* to perform it.

Value (or net reward) is measured by the reward of an activity minus the cost of the activity. Performing any activity entails not only rewards but also costs of some sort. Sometimes the cost is directly involved in the activity itself, such as the time and effort required to prepare for a fishing trip. At other times the cost is indirect, such as foregoing some other activity which the individual would also have enjoyed. If he goes on a fishing trip, for example, then he cannot attend his friend's birthday party. Value (or net reward), then, is reward minus cost, including the cost of activities foregone.

The **deprivation–satiation proposition** emphasizes the recent past because there are many rewards with which a person can be only temporarily satiated, such as the biological ones of food and sex or the social ones of approval and recognition. This proposition implies that when a person is deprived of something rewarding to him he will tend to perform an activity which has previously resulted in the reward. Likewise, if recently he has been filled to satisfaction (satiated) with a reward for a particular activity, he is less likely to engage in behavior

When an individual becomes frustrated, the chances of his becoming aggressive increase. Such frustration-aggression is one of the key propositions dealt with in social exchange theory. (Photo by Laima Turnley)

which leads to that reward. To be deprived of a reward tends to result in increased activity, while to be satiated with a reward tends to result in decreased activity. The deprived person has a greater tendency to seek the reward than does the satiated person. Simply put, this means that a person who has just finished a big meal is not as likely to engage in behavior which results in food as is the person who has not eaten in three days.

The **frustration–aggression proposition** deals with an emotional state. When an individual has been rewarded in a particular situation in the past, he expects, in line with the stimulus proposition, to be rewarded in similar situations in the present. If the rewards are not forthcoming, he tends to become frustrated. If he is punished instead of being rewarded, he also tends to become frustrated. His frustration tends to lead to anger. The more often he has been rewarded in the past for the particular activity and the more valuable the reward is to him, the greater will be his frustration and anger. The individual is then likely to become aggressive, taking his anger out on something or somebody which appears to him to be the source of his frustration. The target of his aggression, however, does not have to be the source of his frustration. Frequently he does not know the source, or if he does know it he is often unable to vent his frustration on it. In such cases he is likely to take his anger out on any available object, because during times of frustration the results of aggressive behavior are rewarding.

A concept central to social exchange theory is that of **distributive justice**, basically the feeling or view that the reward someone gets out of something should be proportionate to the cost involved. If someone invests much in an interaction, it is felt that he should get much out of it, while if he invests less, he should receive less. In other words, people tend to feel that rewards should be distributed with justice.

What are rewards? **Rewards** can be almost anything. They are whatever an individual finds rewarding, whatever fulfills his needs (Singlemann 1972:415). Not everyone finds the same things rewarding. Some people, for example, receive intense joy from being present at classical piano concerts, and they will engage in any number of activities in order to attend one. For others, baseball games are rewarding to this same degree, and in order to attend a game they will do any number of things, including camping out all night on the hard, cold sidewalk in order to secure a ticket to the world series. For still others, neither musical concerts nor baseball games are rewarding, and these persons will do all sorts of things in order to *avoid* attending them. An old adage caps this point rather succinctly: "One man's meat is another man's poison."

As I have emphasized in this book, socialization into values, beliefs,

To understand human behavior, we need to know what people find rewarding. Through our experiences in the culture in which we grow up, we learn to highly value certain activities and to react negatively to others. This photo and the following one (see page 252) illustrate children being socialized into traditional sex-linked behaviors which, if reinforced, will become central to the ways they evaluate rewards.   (Photo by Laima Turnley)

and behaviors differs not only between cultures but also between groups in the same culture. We would expect, then, since not everyone has been exposed to the same cultural items in the same way, that people will find differing things rewarding or punishing. As I have just indicated, this is how it is with cultural items such as baseball and musical events.

It is also the same, however, when it comes to most biological items: What is rewarding to one person is not necessarily rewarding to an-

(Photo by Laima Turnley)

other. Everyone, for example, finds food rewarding. But what food? For some it is hamburger, but for others grasshoppers. The person who likes grasshoppers may find hamburgers just as revolting as most Americans find grasshoppers. The same is true when it comes to satisfying the sex drive. As we noted in the startling example in Chapter 5, hair drenched in urine can be erotically pleasing to some people. From an example closer to home, some women prefer men with a muscular, athletic build, but not many men appear to prefer similarly shaped women—at least not many contemporary American men. Some people prefer their ideal sexual partner to be slender, others fat; some tall, others short; some bushy-headed, others bald; some clean-shaven,

others bearded, and so on. Similarly, most people find sexual satisfactions with members of the opposite sex, but some prefer the same
sex. A cultural overlay has been firmly laid down over our biological
needs to such a degree that it is sometimes difficult to separate our biological needs from our culturally derived wants. Even when it comes to
biological needs, in other words, one man's meat may still be another
man's poison.

According to the perspective of social exchange theory, people
engage in behavior for what it nets them in rewards. Basic to this view
is that human interaction centers around people maximizing their rewards while they minimize those things they find punishing. In the
view of human nature on which social exchange theory is based, people
are assumed to be purposeful, rational creatures: People go about their
daily lives making plans, thinking about what they can get out of activities, weighing one possible course of action against another—all the
while deciding which activity will lead to the highest reward.

If it is basic to life in society that people are continuously seeking the
greatest satisfaction for the least effort or cost, in order to understand
people we must know what they find rewarding. We need to understand as much as possible about the cultural context in which people
live because it is their experiences in a culture or subculture which lead
them to place different values on the various alternatives which they
confront.

Social exchange theorists propose that almost all of human life is
marked by social exchange. They say that whenever people interact
with one another an exchange of some sort is made. It is quite apparent that this occurs when people are talking with one another, since
conversation, by definition, involves an exchange of words. Conversation also involves an exchange of nonverbal or gestural symbols in the
form of eye contact, body posturing, and various mannerisms. But
when people speak with one another, social exchange also occurs on a
deeper level. In simple everyday conversations, people are intentionally
and unintentionally exchanging various bits of information about
themselves. They are communicating to others information about such
things as their goals, values, backgrounds, orientations, interests, and
competencies or incompetencies.

To varying degrees, then, the self-concept becomes involved in interpersonal exchanges. This applies not only to conversations but to all
face-to-face interaction. Part of these exchanges are rewarding to the
individual, while other parts are costly. When the rewards gained in an
interaction outbalance the costs, the interaction tends to continue or to
recur. When costs outdistance rewards, however, the interaction tends
to terminate or to recur with less frequency.

We can note the operation of this principle among workers in a law enforcement agency (Blau 1955). In this office it was common for the less adept workers to seek advice from their more expert colleagues. In this interaction the less adept workers obviously received valued advice from the more expert workers. But what did the more expert workers receive in return? They were gratified by the acknowledgement of their superiority in performing the required work. Both types of workers profited in this interaction: The less adept received the help they needed, while the more expert workers received valued ego-enhancement. Costs for each worker were also involved in their interaction: The less adept paid in ego-debasement, while the more expert workers lost part of the time they needed for performing their own work.

As long as the rewards remained greater than the costs, this type of interaction tended to continue. When the costs of the interaction outdistanced the rewards, however, the equation became imbalanced in an undesirable direction. It finally came to the point that the more expert workers were giving so much advice that their own work began to suffer. When this occurred, the more expert workers felt that the costs they were incurring for giving advice were greater than their rewards. Their idea of distributive justice was being violated. Consequently, the expert workers began to raise their price for advice. They did this by demanding a greater show of deference for continuing to help their less expert colleagues. The less adept reluctantly paid the greater deference. Giving greater deference, however, violated the less adept workers' sense of distributive justice. The less adept then raised their price in order to balance their part of the exchange: They began to require even more help since they were now giving greater self-abasement. Eventually the price became too high for both types of workers.

The less adept then turned to their less expert colleagues for advice, as the price the less expert workers "charged" was more in keeping with what they were willing to pay. Although they received less in this exchange, their cost was also less. The less adept workers, however, did not entirely stop seeking help from their more expert colleagues. They continued to make requests, but they did so less frequently, with their interaction with the more capable workers again reaching a point of equilibrium where both felt the exchange was fair.

This is a basic characteristic of voluntary human interaction: Equilibria are eventually reached where the participants feel that what they are getting out of the interaction is roughly proportional to what they are putting into the interaction.

Social interaction which continues over a period of time, in this view, consists of a complex exchange of mutually rewarding activities. If an

According to social exchange theory, human interaction centers around an intricate balancing of rewards and costs. An extended illustration of this principle as it was observed among office workers is given in the text. (Photo by J. Paul Kirouac)

individual wishes to be rewarded by another person, he must, in turn, reward the other. Only by giving rewards to others will others give rewards to him. Interaction, according to social exchange theory, consists of individuals incurring costs in order to receive rewards from other individuals who are themselves incurring costs in order to maximize their own desired payoffs. Social exchange theorists take the anticipations people have of rewards they will receive and their evaluations of probable outcomes as the bases of human interaction.

It is important to emphasize that underlying the anticipations and evaluations which people make is a definitional process. Except perhaps for a few biological items, rewards for human beings are not inherent in things. Rewards are, like meaning, dependent upon how people define their worlds. Just as with baseball games, musical concerts, sexually desirable objects, hamburgers, and grasshoppers, rewards are what the individual finds to be rewarding. Things, including the outcomes of interactions, are rewards only as people assign that meaning to them (Singlemann 1972:417).

It is also important to emphasize that it is exactly at this point that social exchange theory sharply differs from the reinforcement or operant conditioning theory commonly taught in psychology. Psychological reinforcement theory focuses on measurable behavior "emitted" by the "human organism": The individual is viewed as a "black box," that is, during a "behavioral emission" we do not know what occurs within the individual, and whatever does occur within that "black box" is deemed irrelevant for understanding behavior. It is the behavior, and its reinforcers (the things which lead to the behavior being "emitted," or "rewards," in social exchange theory terms) which are important. In operant conditioning or reinforcement theory an individual is only the "emitter" of behaviors, not, as in social exchange theory, a calculating, rational person who purposefully acts upon his environment in order to maximize profits. This is, indeed, a radical differentiation between the two theories: In operant conditioning the individual is looked on as being controlled by his environment, while in social exchange theory the individual is viewed as actively reacting to and manipulating his environment.

It is the conceptual process of human beings which is not taken seriously in operant conditioning theory. As we covered in Chapter 4, animals lack conceptualization. Except for highly limited exceptions, animals are unable to communicate with one another information about the world or about themselves. People, however, can, and they regularly do so as a normal part of their lives. To assume that animals and human beings are the same in this respect is to ignore essential differences between them. It is to ignore the conceptual overlay of human conditioning. To use a somewhat homely illustration of these differences, cats will return and wait outside a door from which fish have been thrown. Just as animals return to a place at which they have been previously rewarded, so do people. People working in an office or factory, for example, tend to regularly return to the pay window. But if the management informs an employee that he will be issued no further paychecks, if the employee believes this conceptual communication he will not return to the pay window. Conceptual communication, along with consequent defining processes upon which people make choices as they actively respond to their environment, are essential differences between animal and human behavior. The social exchange theorists make these differences a central part of their work, while the operant conditioners primarily ignore them.

Social exchange theory, the symbolic interaction perspective, the dramaturgical view, and games analysis, however, mesh at this point. They all contain the central principle that people design their behaviors in order to gain favorable responses from others. In games analysis, people make moves or do those things calculated to gain desired ends. In the symbolic interaction perspective, people manipulate symbols in order to maintain their self-concepts and to socially construct reality. In the dramaturgical view, which is a particular form of symbolic interactionism, people play the roles which they find the most rewarding. In social exchange theory, people continue to do those things, including manipulating symbols and playing roles, from which they reap the greatest rewards while incurring the least costs. When role performances, participation in a particular game, or the manipulation of certain symbols are not found to be rewarding, the individual makes changes in his behavior. He then seeks rewards either by presenting a different self to the same persons or by presenting the same self to other people whom he feels might better appreciate him. Or, we can say that he decides to play the game differently. In all four of these major perspectives on human behavior, people are viewed as goal-seeking actors, as calculating, rational beings who constantly seek increased payoffs by maximizing their rewards and minimizing their costs.

An assumption running through this discussion of social exchange theory is that people are *voluntarily* interacting with one another. Social exchange theory applies primarily to voluntary human relationships, that is, to relationships about which people have at least some choice. It is in voluntary relationships that people freely exchange rewards with one another. If a relationship is voluntary, when the rewards people gain from interaction are less than the costs they are willing to bear, they are able to turn to others to try to satisfy their needs.

Power, according to social exchange theory, is the ability of one person to make another person act in a way which the first person desires. Power is possessed when the second person cannot gain the satisfaction of his needs elsewhere. He is then forced to continue to interact even when the costs are greater than he prefers. He either has no alternative, or he fails to perceive an alternative which may in fact exist. It makes no difference which it is, for in either case the other has power over him. The equation of rewards and costs is imbalanced and were he free to do so, the individual would seek his satisfactions elsewhere. But he has or perceives no choice.

Only rarely, however, do power situations approach an all-or-nothing affair: Only rarely does someone have no power in a relationship. Power is usually more a matter of degree. The prisoner, for example, is able to influence his guards' behaviors by how he reacts to their commands, rewards, and punishments (Simpson 1972:13). Although the power of prisoners may not be nonexistent, and though prisoners even riot from time to time, their power is certainly *considerably* less than the guards'.

Social exchange theory is less equipped to handle coercive human relationships than voluntary ones. A main reason for this is because this model of human life was developed from observations of people interacting in voluntary situations. The theory, however, can still be applied to coercive situations, but with greater difficulty. There are also some situations to which social exchange theory does not apply, such as when people do things out of fear, whether that fear is of other men, of their own consciences, or of God (Blau 1964:89). The quandary in which social exchange theorists find themselves in analyzing fear-motivated behavior is that people are acting out of private, internal motivation and there is little or no exchange taking place. Consequently, there is little for social exchange theorists to analyze. We might parenthetically note that symbolic interaction theorists are better equipped for analyzing such situations because people acting out of fear are dealing with symbols.

But social exchange theory does apply to a fascinating variety of human interaction—from formal, monetary exchanges such as payments on a bank mortgage or the purchase of groceries to informal, social exchanges such as conversations, friendship, dating, love, a kiss, marriage, adultery, gift-giving, and most aspects of everyday life.

Gift-giving is obviously an exchange. One person gives a gift to another, while the one who receives the gift thanks the giver or otherwise shows his appreciation. In our culture he is expected to show overt appreciation upon receiving the gift. To do otherwise would at a minimum be bad manners, and it would probably imply all sorts of negative things about the relationship. Even though the giver of a gift will probably not demand anything in return, the one who has accepted the gift is expected to reciprocate in an appropriate manner. It is, in fact, not unusual for him to reciprocate by giving at a later date a gift of equal or superior value. As Aristotle put it in *The Nichomachean Ethics* (Blau 1964:88):

> The gift or other service is given as to a friend, although the giver expects to receive an equivalent or greater return, as though it had not been a free gift but a loan; and as he ends the relationship in a different spirit from that in which he began it, he will complain. The reason for this is that all men, or most men, wish what is noble but choose what is profitable.

The giving of a gift and the resulting obligations are illustrative of other voluntary social exchange situations in everyday life. Basically, whenever an individual willingly supplies rewarding services to another, he obligates the other. To discharge this obligation, the second person must, in his turn, reciprocate by furnishing benefits of some sort to the first (Blau 1964:89). The benefits returned may perhaps not be equal to that which was initially given, but it is expected that they be similarly valued by the participants in the exchange. If, for example, a newcomer to a work situation requests assistance from a workmate, he is hardly able to turn down a similar request at a later time, even though the request of the other may be greater than his own original request. By accepting the initial assistance, he has obligated himself, and he must reciprocate if he is to maintain a smooth-working social relationship. Similarly, if a person gives a dinner party, he expects his dinner guests to reciprocate. As with other gifts, he cannot and will not bargain with his guests about the kind of party to which they should invite him, although "he expects them not simply to ask him for a quick lunch if he had invited them to a formal dinner" (Blau 1964:93–94).

This process of social exchange centering around expectations of distributive justice is basic to social life. The extending of a favor or the giving of advice and the reciprocating of favors, advice, conviviality, or appreciation develops trust between people, a basic component of voluntary human relationships. As someone reciprocates that which was given him, perhaps out of gratitude or even because he hopes to receive more, he is demonstrating that he is the "right" kind of person. He proves himself trustworthy of receiving further favors. Mutual service is frequently accompanied by the parallel growth of mutual trust. Thus, out of social exchange, which may have originated in pure self-interest, trust is engendered (Blau 1964:94). People come to know that they can or cannot depend on one another to play the roles they expect of the other. They learn what to expect of other people and how to act toward them.

Personal attraction is also elucidated by social exchange theory. A person who is attracted to another will usually try to make himself attractive to the other. Thus a boy who is highly attracted to a girl who is less attracted to him will try to make himself more attractive to her. He will perhaps try to impress her in various ways. He will especially go out of his way to make associating with him a highly rewarding experience for her. He might spend much time thinking of ways to please her, as well as spending a good part of his limited budget on her. He will probably do things on their dates which she especially likes, rather than the things he prefers. It is possible that she will eventually find being with him as rewarding as he finds being with her, and the relationship will then be reciprocal. It is reciprocal rewards which become the basis of mutual attraction (Blau 1964:26–27).

Relationships which become this balanced, that is, where each person approximately equally desires the presence of the other, are probably not typical of social life. Frequently the attraction in intimate relations, including marriage and lasting friendships, as well as more temporary attachments, represents an imbalance of interests, sentiments, and contributions. This makes one party more willing to defer to the other's wishes (Blau 1964:27). The one who is less dependent on the relationship has the greater power over the other because he is more willing to risk rupturing the relationship (Simpson 1972:13). In dating and courtship this is known as *the principle of least interest,* meaning that the partner less eager to preserve the relationship will tend to dominate it (Waller and Hill 1951:190–192). The principle of least interest can also hold true in a marriage in which both husband and wife regard the dissolution of their marriage as a disaster. If one person in the relationship desires less intensity than the other, the one desiring the greater intensity is put at a disadvantage. In such a case, the one with least interest will more likely have the greater power in determining how and when they spend their time together (Simpson 1972:13).

The principles of social exchange theory provide a conceptual apparatus with which we can approach a wide variety of human behavior. Marital adjustment, for example, can also be conceptualized in terms of social exchange theory. Adjusting to marriage is sometimes a form of "reality shock," that is, the marital partners come face to face with what marriage is really like instead of their less realistic anticipations of marriage. Such reality shock can be viewed as a realignment of rewards and costs, typically with alternatives now foregone. The first years of marriage are the riskiest in terms of the likelihood of divorce. These are the years in which the major realignment of rewards and costs takes place. If the realignment is successful, that is, if both marital partners find a balance on the reward side of the equation, they will continue the marriage. If not, a separation or divorce is probably in the offing.

As I mentioned in the preceding chapter, the principles of social exchange theory can also be applied to participation in delinquent acts. For many adolescents, the rewards they receive from participating in delinquent activities are greater than the rewards they receive from not engaging in those activities. As an individual works out his self-concept, he is highly dependent on his peers. If the subculture to which his peers belong and in which he is himself immersed has a delinquent orientation, it is extremely difficult for the individual not to participate in delinquent activities. If he refuses to join his peers, he is reacted to derisively. He may be called a "chicken" or "sissy" or some other pejorative label equally held in disrepute in his subculture. His peers may shun him, make fun of him, and in general make life difficult for him. These are extreme costs to an adolescent who is in the process of developing his self-concept because he is highly dependent on peer approval for evaluating who he is in relationship to others. By participating in delinquent activities, however, he receives highly valued rewards in the form of positive recognition and friendship, gaining a desirable reputation within this subculture. When the rewards for participating in delinquent activities outdistance the rewards for not participating in them, or, alternatively, when the costs of not participating become greater than the costs of participating, he will tend to engage in those activities.

If the individual has alternative sources of satisfactions, however, and receives them for not participating, such as from parental approval, and these rewards are greater than those he receives from his delinquent peers, he will probably not show up in the delinquency statistics. This is especially the case if the rewards from the alternative sources will be removed if he participates in delinquent activities. In this event, the rewards for not engaging in delinquent activities outbalance the rewards he receives from participating in them, and he will tend not to become involved.

A major attraction of social exchange theory is that it matches our subjective realities, that is, it parallels what we feel happens to us in life. Contrary to many theoretical formulations which seem so far removed from our experiences, social exchange theory places in readily understandable theoretical terms our own awareness of what we undergo in everyday life. In common with symbolic interaction, games analysis, and dramaturgy, people are viewed in social exchange theory as expressive individuals who evaluatively react to both their physical and social environments. In common with the symbolic interaction perspective which we covered in Chapter 6, in social exchange theory the self is an active agent manipulating the environment on its own behalf.

People come off as people in this theory. Basic to social exchange theory is the concept of people evaluating possible courses of action, weighing these against alternative activities, deciding according to their own evaluations and within their own social constraints which activities they would prefer to engage in, and then doing so. People in everyday life *are* aware that certain alternatives are open to them, while they feel that others are not worth considering because they appear impossibly closed. People *do* have aspirations and expectations. We *are aware of our own drives toward goals. We do* experience the effects of our own goals upon our own behavior. What we desire in life, or desire at the moment for whatever reason, does make a world of difference for what we do. From our own experiences we also know that we tend to avoid punishments while seeking to maximize our gains.

Using the sociological imagination, we can examine the social structural framework which provides the opportunities for and sets the constraints on social bargaining. By adding social exchange theory to the sociological imagination, we possess better tools for explaining why people do what they do as they live their lives in society. Using these tools, we are able to examine both the social milieu within which social bargaining takes place and the personal dynamics of social bargaining.

To illustrate these, I wish to briefly analyze major factors which led to the break-up of a marriage.

Sally was born in 1950, a period of abundance and prosperity in the United States. This was also an era of heightening international tensions due to the cold war, with frequent confrontations between the new superpower of the United States and a fast rising rival in the form of the U.S.S.R. These political events were not insignificant for Sally, although they were less influential in forming her thought-world than they were in shaping her husband's approach to life.

Bill was born in 1941. His parents had lived through the depression of the '30's. While his parents had not gone hungry, they had lost their savings and Bill's father had been forced to take a more poorly paid and much less prestigious job. His family never seemed to get over the depression, but carried it around with them in the form of talk about what it had been like. When he was a child, Bill's parents frequently reminded Bill of the hardships they had gone through. Bill also heard much about the war. Although his father was never in the armed services, friends of his father had been to places such as Okinawa, Pearl Harbor, and Iwo Jima. One of his father's friends had even brought back a sword he said he had taken from a Japanese officer he killed in a cave on some South Pacific island. The fear of depression and the threat of armed conflict were extremely significant in shaping the way Bill looked at the world and in determining how he approached life.

For Sally, the depression was only something she had but briefly read about in her high school history books. She had neither personal acquaintance with the depression nor the threat-producing experience of her parents talking about it. Sally grew up in an age of extensive installment buying and liberal use of credit cards, of easing tension between the world's superpowers, of easier access to higher education. She also grew up in an era of changing roles for women in marriage, for when she was growing up it was quite acceptable and frequently enviable for a wife and mother to have a career outside the home. The women's liberation movement hit the American scene during her late teens, which was also to have far-reaching ramifications for her life. Bill, however, received his major ideas about the proper roles of men and women before women's liberation came along. He learned that it was the husband's duty to support his wife, and the wife's duty to take care of the home. If a wife worked, fine, but it was to be done only with the permission of her husband, and she was still expected to carry the same responsibilities in the home.

These are some of the major factors which went into shaping Bill's and Sally's varying approaches to life. They are part of the sociological imagination, the establishing of the major sociohistorical forces which helped determine the kinds of people they were, the variables which nurtured their world view or **Weltanschauung.** Although Sally and Bill were only nine years apart in age, and although they had grown up in the same area of the same country, they might as well have been separated by a generation or more—for they were a cultural generation apart. The world had changed so rapidly and to such a degree that they had grown up in what for many purposes were two separate worlds.

Eventually Sally and Bill met. Uniting their two cultural worlds was the overarching ideology of romantic love. Both expected that they would some day meet the right person, fall in love, get married, and raise a family. Part of this ideological expectation included living happily ever after. Although Sally and Bill both knew happiness did not automatically flow from love and both were aware that love had many pitfalls, they each held some vague notion of love bringing happiness, because they had both been raised on the idea that love was the essential ingredient to a successful marriage.

In 1970 Sally and Bill were united in holy wedlock, or as they jokingly put it, "The preacher said the words to make it legal." Part of the sexual revolution they had both experienced was the growing acceptability of premarital sex. Sally felt premarital sex was fine, as long as a girl didn't overdo it. Bill had always liked the idea, even before the sexual revolution came about. Their sexual adjustment, in fact, both before and after marriage, was quite satisfying to both of them.

Even with a good sexual adjustment, and even though at twenty-nine Bill was settled down, had finished college, and had a good job, and even though Sally was quite mature at twenty, they were divorced just two years after their marriage. They had decided to wait three or four years before having children, which made the divorce easier for them. Sally remarried three months after their divorce, and Bill is again enjoying the life of a bachelor—but he is still looking for the "right" one.

What happened? They had more going for them than many couples. The sociological imagination focuses on the broad historical forces which shape people, but to see how these work out in everyday life we need something else. Here is the value of social exchange theory.

The goals of Sally and Bill were quite similar. They both wanted to be independent of their parents and to be financially ahead of the game, they both wanted happiness, and they both desired children. But the internal dynamics of their family life was something else. Conflicts began almost immediately after their marriage. Bill expected Sally to take care of the house in the same way she would if she were not working outside the home. He figured his day's work was finished when he left the office, except for keeping a neat yard and a polished car. Sally did not see the matter this way at all. She expected that since she was working at a full-time job they should share the housework. They quarreled about the matter for some time, and Bill reluctantly agreed to take over the heavier work such as washing and waxing the floors. This was less than Sally expected, but more than Bill expected. In this way they negotiated an agreement which was fairly satisfactory to both. Each incurred costs, but the balance remained on the reward side of the equation.

The second major area of difficulty centered around money. Bill wanted to put a large proportion of their incomes into savings and investments. In fact, he desired to put away most of what Sally earned in anticipation of "a rainy day." He also wanted to pay cash for everything except large expenditures such as their house and cars. Sally did not at all agree. She wanted to spend what both of them earned and to also purchase luxury items, clothing, vacations, and household appliances on the installment plan. After many stormy battles over these differences, they agreed to buy less than she desired and more than he preferred. This negotiated agreement was never satisfactory to either. Sally was recurringly bothered because they did not purchase items which she wanted to have, and Bill was similarly disturbed about the interest they were paying on their installment loans. Bill would frequently make comments about the economy, saying "what goes up must come down," while Sally would complain that her friends had more than she. At this point, the rewards each received from their marriage were still greater than the costs they incurred. But each was growing increasingly aware of the costs involved in keeping the marriage going, and fundamental dissatisfactions were rapidly settling in.

The third major area of difficulty centered along a different line entirely. The war in Vietnam was at this point at the height of its controversy. Sally had for a long time vaguely felt there was something wrong about the war, and she now attended a Vietnam teach-in at which she was introduced to the idea that the United States was conducting an imperialistic venture to crush an indigenous liberation movement. She became increasingly convinced that the involvement of the United States was immoral, and as she watched the ten o'clock news she was further revolted at the killings she witnessed. A short time after the teach-in, Sally switched from political indifference to political activism. Bill was, to put it mildly, disconcerted at Sally's change, for his reaction to the political scene was in sharp contrast to hers. Bill was convinced the war was part of a global Communist conspiracy, an outgrowth of the cold war. Although his views became modified somewhat due to Sally's influence and due to changing ideas about the war on the part of the men at work, their differences in view constantly grated at them both. The culmination of this disagreement erupted when Sally held in their home a planning session for a peace demonstration. Bill stormed out of the house and refused to speak to her for several days. It took several weeks more before things got back on a fairly even keel. They agreed not to discuss the war either between themselves or when they were together with friends, and Sally promised not to hold further antiwar meetings at their house. This negotiated peace in their home helped avoid open quarreling, but what she looked at as unfair curtailment of her freedom led to seething resentment on Sally's part. On a couple of occasions Sally tried to explain her feelings, but Bill cut her short, sharply reminding her of their agreement not to discuss the war.

Costs continued to mount. Political differences had not been solved by negotiation, only removed from sight. Housework differences, which once had been solved by tenuous truce, again reared its ugly head since each felt that "if the other was going to be like that," he or she wasn't about to give as much as previously. Money problems also again came to the fore, as Sally now felt she had greater reason to pursue a more independent path. As she made financial decisions independent of her husband, Bill felt greater costs. When Bill tried to increase his rewards by making Sally stick to earlier agreements, Sally felt greater costs.

Each became increasingly unwilling to bear the rising costs of keeping their marriage alive, especially since their rewards were simultaneously decreasing. Their love life was especially hard-hit. Bill and Sally still made love with each other, but something seemed to go out of it. They later said that at this point in their marriage they felt a certain "spark" had died out. Their lovemaking decreased in intensity, and finally let up in frequency, for sexual relations within marriage had become increasingly costly to both Sally and Bill: They reminded them of how good things had once been between them, bringing the punishing aspects of their day-to-day lives into bold relief with past shared pleasures.

As they withdrew from marital sex, both Sally and Bill experienced sexual deprivation. When Bill had been in such deprived states prior to his meeting Sally, he had engaged in sexual relations with a number of girls. He had found these amorous activities extremely rewarding, and when he now found himself in a similar state, he repeated behavior for which he had previously been rewarded. Sally, in contrast, had engaged in sexual relations with no one other than Bill, and when she was deprived she did not have the same tendency to seek extramarital sexual partners. Frustrated during a particularly rancorous quarrel, Bill thought he would "take the wind out of her sails" by letting her know that he was seeing other women. This news shocked Sally, making her upset and angry. Out of her anger she struck back at Bill by seeking sex outside of marriage, finding aggression against him rewarding at this time. She did not by any means explain her act in terms of a frustration-aggression proposition, however, but spoke of it as "tit for tat" and "what's good for the goose is good for the gander."

As long as the rewards each felt he or she was receiving from the marital relationship were greater than their perceived costs, the marriage was in fairly good shape. When, however, the costs they experienced neared what they felt they were getting out of the marriage, the marriage was threatened. When they felt the costs were about the same as the rewards, it then took but one of them to perceive an alternative felt to be more satisfying than the marital partner. In this case, it was Sally who made the break after she met a man who shared both her political views and her ideas on marital roles.

It should be emphasized that, like evaluations of rewards and costs, acting on perceived potentially satisfying alternatives has a historical and cultural base. It was not many years ago in the United States that alternatives to an unhappy marriage were generally unavailable. An unhappily married person felt he or she had to stick out marriage for life. The costs of being divorced were perceived as being greater than the costs of sticking out a marriage. Especially was this so for the wife, for a divorced woman was perceived by most people as living in a shameful state, and as perhaps being morally loose. Additionally, for women the alternatives were especially stark since women had few employment opportunities outside the home.

From the example of Sally and Bill we can see some of the advantages of jointly using the analytic tools of the sociological imagination and social exchange theory. The sociological imagination alerts us to structural aspects of society which permeate the lives of individuals and place constraints on their behavior. By examining Bill's and Sally's varying social backgrounds, we are able to uncover underlying causes for their contrasting orientations and approaches to the contingencies of modern life. They learned different basic frameworks for interpreting events occurring in society and for guiding their own behaviors in everyday life, frameworks which later led to pitched conflict when they were juxtaposed in the crucible of marriage. But discerning structural bases for frameworks of social constraint is insufficient for understanding the intimate realities of social life. It is social exchange theory which we can better bring to bear on the dynamics of human interaction, sensitizing us to perceived costs and rewards and the vigorous interplay between them. The sociological imagination is also relevant for understanding interpersonal dynamics, however, because ideas of rewards, costs, and distributive justice are culturally relative, as well as varying among groups in a pluralistic society. We need to use the sociological imagination to understand the cultural and subcultural framework or structure which leads people to find different things rewarding and to differ in their ways of evaluating costs, as well as to aid us in determining what goes into the make-up of someone's particular sense of distributive justice. The sociological imagination and social exchange theory are thus mutually explanatory, the one sensitizing us to larger social constraints on human behavior and the other to the ways in which those constraints are played out in people's lives. These perspectives complement one another and can advantageously be used side by side to help explain why people do what they do.

4

Social Control and Social Change

chapter 14

Jtaging Reality: Jocial Control and the Legal Jystem

In the last chapter we dealt with relations between people where a sense of distributive justice underlies the interaction, where people interact in "free-choice" situations and feel that their costs in an interaction is or should be fairly proportionate to their return. We saw how this idea of distributive justice gives shape to many of the ways people deal with each other. In this chapter and the next we shall focus on situations in which the idea of distributive justice is generally not the basis for interaction, situations which are more "forced" in nature. We shall examine larger societal structures in which various devices are used to bring people into line regardless of their own wishes and sometimes against their own interests. As we examine ways in which the legal and political institutions are used to enforce the desires of those in power, we shall focus on the members of society who are on the "receiving end" of these uses of social institutions. Keep in mind that we are taking but one particular view of the uses to which these institutions are put, that we are consistently examining these two social institutions within this single framework, and that there are any number of alternate frameworks which could be utilized for such an analysis.

A particularly disenchanting view of life in society centers around the deceitful aspects of the ways people deal with each other, the ways by which people are conned into conformance of behavior or belief. Conning involves the fraudulent staging of reality in order to dupe others (Goffman 1952). It is a distortion of reality in order to gain one's own ends over against the wishes of others. Thus **conning** is fraudulently distorting reality in order to manipulate others for the sake of

Distorting reality is a common feature of everyday life, practiced by individuals in their interactions with others and by the institutions of society in the enforcement of social control. As this cartoon shows, some forms of reality distortion are more socially acceptable than others.   (Courtesy of *Adventure*. Cartoon by L. Herman.)

self-interest. Before examining reality distortion on the institutional level, I wish to first illustrate the pervasiveness in society of this type of staging reality by briefly looking at conning and everyday life.

Distorting reality for one's own self-interest is a common, recurring feature of everyday life, a regular part of living in society. As we saw in Chapter 8 with the example of the teenager giving answers which did not match reality in order to be able to use his parent's car, conning frequently occurs on the interpersonal level. Conning is also present in the simple case of a woman wearing "falsies" in order better to attract members of the opposite sex. This particular conning device is used within the context of major American values. When we discussed cultural values in Chapter 3, we did not explicitly deal with personal attractiveness or beauty, but this value is highly interconnected with some of the others, especially those of romantic love, heterosexuality, and youthfulness. It is a goal sought after by most Americans. In this frequently elusive goal, size and shape of the bust become central for American women as they engage in the social presentation of self. Bust size and shape is a major part of the self-presentation of women, a major means by which they manage impressions. Americans have developed a sort of breast fetish, and as American women drink their Carnation and Sego and watch the scales, they are also alert for any mammary changes. As breast size and shape have become a vital concern in self-presentations, it has become widely accepted that women who are not amply endowed by nature need not suffer in their competing presentations, but through the wonders of modern technology they can make up any void left by nature. The person who wears "falsies," however, is using con. She is fraudulently distorting reality in order to manipulate a victim for her own self-interest.

Besides "standard" techniques used in interpersonal relationships to distort reality, conning of individuals by other individuals sometimes becomes the "stock in trade" of workers in service occupations. This occurs in the well-known case of automobile mechanics who charge customers for work never performed and in the lesser known instance of cabdrivers who place a 2-by-4 under the forward part of their cab's rear seat in order to increase its tilt so that at the end of their shift they can collect the loose change that has fallen from their passengers' pockets. Cabbies also sometimes con others by charging what might be called a "use tax" for their cabs, extorting money from passengers who wish to use their cab for deviant sexual activities (Henslin 1967; 1971).

"It'll come to about forty-five dollars. But that doesn't include parts and labor."

The distortion of reality for one's own gains has become the stock-in-trade of many service occupations.   (Courtesy of Cartoon Features Syndicate. Cartoon by George Dole.)

Individuals also sometimes con organizations and bureaucracies in order to "beat the system." Sometimes such conning is primarily an individual matter, as the actions of a student I know who graduated from college but due to economic recession could not find a job to his liking. He then re-enrolled in college in order to continue collecting his G.I. benefits of $240 a month, with his tuition paid by the state of Illinois. A few days after enrolling, he stopped attending classes. He lived on the $7-a-day income he cleared from his student janitorial job, banking his G.I. check. After repeating this for two quarters, he had saved enough to go to Europe.

Sometimes conning by individuals in order to "beat the system" takes place only with the cooperation of others and becomes so recurring that it receives a special name to designate it. This is the case with "rocking." An individual who is already drawing unemployment compensation goes to work, but his employer does not record his wages, allowing him to continue to collect his unemployment. In one variation of rocking, at an agreed-upon date the employer reports the employee's wages, terminating his unemployment payments. But he reports the wages at a higher rate than he is paying, both making up for the time he did not report them and making the employee eligible for future higher unemployment compensation because of his higher wages. The employee then repeats this process, "rocking" back and forth between working at jobs and drawing unemployment. With sufficient cooperation and connivance from others, a person playing this con game can actually remain continually employed at his job while increasing his remuneration through nonexistent unemployment periods.

In addition to individuals conning other individuals or conning organizations, either singly or with the cooperation of others, the institutions of society are also used to con people. Central to viewing conning by institutions is an idea contrary to what most of us learn early in our socialization process. This central idea is that the institutions of society do not exist primarily for the welfare of the majority of the citizens, but that they serve as the major means for maintaining order in society and for consolidating or protecting existing power relationships. As the use of force is frequently self-defeating because it can stimulate or bring into play oppositional force, which may tend to upset precarious social equilibrium, force is ordinarily used only as a last resort to elicit compliance. Much more common than force is the use of subterfuge to create and maintain definitions of reality which then control both the perceptions and the behavior of vast numbers of people. It is the use of subterfuge as a conning device to maintain social order by enforcing conformance on the part of the citizenry and to consolidate or protect power relationships which we shall now examine.

The legal system lends itself extremely well to being analyzed within the framework of "conmanship." Although our courts are supposed to be an adversary system centering around combative trial-by-jury in which the accused defends his innocence and a prosecutor attempts to prove his guilt, this conception is a long way from matching the facts. The overwhelming majority of convictions in criminal cases, approximately 90 percent of them, merely involve the sentencing of an individual after court personnel have already negotiated a guilty plea (Blumberg 1967:18). What is supposed to be a trial is in the typical case merely the perfunctory validation of pretrial interrogation and investigation.

What leads to our legal system being so different from what it is supposed to be and from the way it is usually viewed? This is primarily due to two major factors, production norms of the courts and an organized system of complicity.

Budgets for our judicial system are appropriated on the premise that we will not have to provide a trial for each defendant. If each person accused of a crime were to receive an adversary trial, it would be necessary to literally multiply our current court personnel and budgets. Accordingly, in order to function within its contemporary budgeting, each court must "produce" a large proportion of guilty pleas in the cases coming before it. This results in "production rates" being informally agreed upon. No specific number or percentage is established, but the goal is to negotiate as many guilty pleas as possible in order to cut costs and keep the courts running.

In order to cut through large caseloads, the major strategem employed is **plea bargaining.** All court personnel, including judges, exert both implicit and explicit pressure to get the defendant to plead guilty and avoid trial. In exchange for pleading guilty and saving the State the expense and effort of a trial, a defendant's charge is "reduced." Not only do the police have discretion when it comes to deciding whether or not to arrest someone and deciding what to charge him with, as we covered in Chapter 12, but so do prosecuting attorneys. Prosecutors especially utilize their discretionary power in order to expedite the judicial process by inducing guilty pleas. At the prosecuting attorney's discretion, a defendant can be charged with crimes carrying relatively light sentences or crimes carrying heavy penalties. If the defendant cooperates with the prosecuting attorney and enters a guilty plea, he may be promised a reduced charge. His charge, for example, may be reduced from burglary to breaking and entering, or from first to second degree murder or even to homicide.

A major reason other than court costs that the prosecutor is willing to make this exchange is a possibility which is never stated to the defendant, the possibility that the State might lose the case by the jury returning a "not guilty" verdict. This would be embarrassing to the record of the prosecuting attorney, who frequently has state-wide and sometimes national political aspirations and needs to maintain the highest conviction rate possible. It is not too surprising that 90 percent of our criminal cases are decided by plea bargaining when we realize that in this process of negotiation there hangs over the head of the accused like the mythical Sword of Damocles the sanction of a potentially harsh sentence as the viable alternative to pleading guilty.

Even the *defense* attorney is intimately involved in this "behind-the-scenes" manipulative process of eliciting guilty pleas. To understand the collusion of defense attorneys, we must examine the attorney's relationship to the court. While the lawyer's relationship to his client is transient (seldom in criminal cases will he have the same client again), ephemeral (it ordinarily occurs over a short period of time), and often superficial (he typically reveals little of himself to the client), his relationship with major court personnel is ongoing and extensive. He deals with the same people over and over again within the setting of the court, and he ordinarily sees at least some of them on a social basis. Some are personal friends; others are "friends of friends." The defense attorney not only desires their professional respect which he would risk if he were to frequently "cross" them, but he is also professionally dependent on them as a member of a highly interlocking, interdependent system.

The defense attorney needs the cooperation of court personnel because they exert great effect on the performance that a lawyer is able to manage. He needs their good graces both in order to gain information from them and to elicit their cooperation with such things as his motions for postponement. Judges need not grant and opposing attorneys can fight motions for the postponement of a case if they so desire. This can affect the attorney's career by making him present before the court a public appearance for which he is not well prepared. It can also force him to turn down a more remunerative case which would demand his time for trial preparation. Court personnel are also in a position to convey to the client the impression that his lawyer possesses inside information that will help his case. This greatly aids the attorney in managing the impression of an "all-out" performance for the accused, as well as helping him justify his fee. Collecting his fee is frequently a troublesome matter, and the defense lawyer sometimes even needs the cooperation of the court to do so. He is given more leverage in collecting his fee if, for example, a judge will adjourn the case and keep the accused incarcerated for a longer period of time (Blumberg 1967:30).

In return for such vital cooperation from other court personnel within this tightly interlocking judicial network, defense lawyers produce guilty pleas. Although they do not do so because of any formal agreement, there is an informal, tacit arrangement which all parties understand and accept and from which all parties benefit—except, of course, the accused. It is especially here where we find con in the judicial system: In return for personal and professional favors from the court, the lawyer whose duty it is to provide the best possible defense for the accused is most frequently the person most instrumental in convincing the accused to plead guilty. A random sample of the cases coming before one of the largest criminal courts in the United States which deals only with felonies demonstrates this anomalous situation. Defendants were asked to indicate the person who first suggested to them that they plead guilty. They were then asked who was most influential in their decision. The results are presented in Table 14.1.

Thus, contrary to common assumption, it is not the police by forcing confessions or the district attorney by various pressures who are most instrumental in inducing the accused to plead guilty. It is, instead, the person who is paid to defend him, the defendant's own counsel, who most often brings this about. This is one of the major conning aspects of our judicial system. A fraudulent definition of reality is presented the accused through the collusion of court personnel. Biased information is given the accused, even by the person he pays to defend him, in order to elicit his cooperation in avoiding a trial and thus maintaining the smooth functioning of the judicial system—which will find him guilty as charged.

Table 14.1 Role of Agent-Mediators in Defendant's Guilty Plea

Person or Official	First Suggested Plea of Guilty	Influenced the Accused Most in His Final Decision To Plead Guilty
Judge	4	26
District Attorney	67	116
Defense Counsel	407	411
Probation Officer	14	3
Psychiatrist	8	1
Wife	34	120
Friends and Kin	21	14
Police	14	4
Fellow Inmates	119	14
Others	28	5
No Response	8	10
	724	724

Source: Table 2 in Blumberg 1967:36. Reprinted by permission of the author and publisher.

It is also of high interest to note that the fee which defense lawyers set often bears an uncanny relationship to the net proceeds of the offense lodged against the accused (Blumberg 1967:26). By manipulating his client's anxieties concerning the outcome of the trial, the lawyer lays firm groundwork to insure a minimum of haggling over his definition of the situation and over the prompt payment of his fee. The lawyer convinces the accused that he must follow his instructions to the letter, which greatly aids the lawyer in influencing guilty pleas and insures the future cooperation of court personnel in the advancement of his professional career.

These same behind-the-scenes factors operate to mitigate the adversary system when it comes to criminal cases involving indigents, persons who cannot afford to pay for a lawyer and for whom the court assigns a public defender. Because public defenders are also inextricably caught up in the intricate interdependency of the court system, they provide far less defense of the accused than the popular ideas current in American society and broadly popularized by the Perry Masons of the mass media. On the contrary, although public defenders are an essential part of the charade of defense, their activities belie the charade. A sociologist who studied the public defender's office reported that:

> . . . the district attorney, and the county which employs them both, can rely on the P.D. (Public Defender) not to attempt to morally degrade police officers in cross-examinations; not to impeach the state's witnesses by trickery; not to attempt the exposition of the entrapment method of narcotic agents; not to condemn the community for the "racial prejudices" that produce our criminals . . . ; in sum, not to make an issue of the moral character of the administrative machinery of local courts, the community, or the police. He will not cause any serious trouble for the routine motion of the court conviction process (Sudnow 1965:273).

But additional variables enter the picture in cases involving indigents which even further decrease the likelihood of anything like a defense of the accused. First of all, compared with the prosecuting attorney's office, the public defender is grossly understaffed and operates under a much more restrictive budget. Moreover, public defenders ordinarily do not have as much trial experience as do prosecutors, which is not infrequently the critical factor in deciding the outcome of a trial. In some cases the turnover in a public defender's office is so great that the accused is interviewed by one lawyer and, when his case comes to trial several months later (during which time he has been kept in jail for lack of bail money), he is defended by a different lawyer, one who has not even talked to him. In the courtroom this second lawyer is forced to defend his client on the basis of notes hastily written by the first lawyer. Additionally, the prosecutor's office is assigned investigative personnel by the police department, but, needless to say, no such investigators are assigned to work up evidence on behalf of the accused (McCart 1970). Considering such significant variables, it is no exaggeration to observe that the deck in this con game is stacked against the indigent.

Subverting our adversary system of justice not only works to the detriment of the poor. The same process is also frequently wielded on behalf of the influential of society. When the crimes committed by the rich or the politically powerful are of such a flagrant nature that they cannot be overlooked, the legal system is often put into effect in such a way that the *appearance* of justice is managed while the accused go through only a wrist-slapping gesture. Perhaps the most widely celebrated case of this sort in our recent history was that of Spiro Agnew. In return for a plea of *nolo contendere* (no contest) and resignation from the Vice Presidency, Agnew was able to avoid what probably would have been a lengthy prison sentence on such charges as bribery, corruption, and income tax evasion. Instead he received merely a $10,000 fine and a "self-administered" three-year probation (Associated Press, October 1973). Similarly, a wealthy executive who defrauded the American public of *two hundred million* dollars through stock swindles was able to trade his guilty plea for the sentence of a year in jail, making him eligible for parole after serving but four months of his sentence. He was, moreover, given no fine whatsoever (Associated Press, October 12, 1973). To better see the legal con in such cases involving the rich and powerful, compare these sentences with the multiple-year prison terms regularly meted out to offenders from the poorer sectors of society who are found guilty of stealing a thousand-dollar automobile.

In addition to conning aspects built into the legal system which work for or against the accused, depending primarily upon his social standing or his "connections," a second major conning aspect of the legal system is its use to control behavior offensive to those who wield power. We shall now briefly look at this conning aspect of the legal system.

The legal system itself is one of the primary means of social control in modern societies. By means of the legal system, the powerful in society make their voice thunderously heard, and we all respond. Those who are in a position to pass laws are never equally responsive to everyone in society. Rather, they differentially react to pressure groups and special interest groups. Tax breaks, for example, are granted the favored few, and between oil depletion allowances and tax-free municipal bonds some persons with incomes over a million dollars a year are able to avoid paying even a cent in federal income tax. As we have seen in the case of juvenile delinquency, the legal system is discriminatory in favor of whites, females, and middle and upper class persons. We could analyze many aspects of the legal system, perhaps the legal system itself, within the context of conmanship, but what I wish to concentrate upon in the rest of this chapter is legal conning in the areas of morality and political dissent.

Acts which do not pose a threat to the social order but which are offensive to the influential of society are sometimes made illegal in an attempt to legislate morality according to the views of those who hold power. I referred in Chapter 9 to the category resulting from legislating morality as moral crimes. They are also called **victimless crimes,** because, unlike crimes where someone is unwillingly acted upon or against by others, moral crimes involve consensual acts. Because people are agreeing to engage in particular acts with each other, there is no victim in these legal violations. The act, however, is abhorrent to persons who are in a position to influence laws, and laws have been passed which make the act illegal. Victimless crimes include gambling, drunkenness, the use of certain drugs, particular forms of sexual behavior between consenting adults, obscenity, pornography, and vagrancy.

Not all such behavior is made illegal, however, just those which offend legislators or groups which are in a position to influence legislators. For example, obviously not all sexual behavior between consenting adults becomes proscribed by law. But sexual behavior such as homosexuality and prostitution, which offends the moral standards of persons or groups who wield power or those who are capable of organizing and influencing those who do wield power, becomes proscribed by law. When the legal system is used to enforce this type of control, criminal law then becomes a substitute for education, persuasion, and custom in maintaining moral standards.

The conning aspect of making crimes of such acts is that the people involved are consenting to the particular behavior. They are not unwilling victims of the actions of others. The concept of crime generally carries with it the idea that someone is forcing himself on others. For example, it is no crime if one person tells another that he can have some of his money. We call this lending or gift-giving, and there is no law against it because there is no victim in the act and it is not offensive to those in power. It is a crime, however, if someone takes another's money by force or gains it by trickery or fraud. These are two entirely different sitations: The one involves consent and has no victim, while the other involves some sort of force or fraud directed against a victim.

Victimless crimes, in contrast, are acts that violate the symbolic system of persons who are in a position to influence laws; that is, because

The major victimless crime in the United States in terms of arrest statistics is public drunkenness. More arrests occur in the United States for this offense than for any other.   (Courtesy of Wide World Photos)

some particular act offends their morality, they use their political power to pass laws to support their own system of values. It would be the same if persons in a situation to influence or pass laws found borrowing money to be offensive to their morality and were to then pass laws making it illegal to lend or to borrow money. Given a particular value system, this would not be so farfetched as it may first sound. At one time, for example, the Western world had laws making it illegal to loan money at interest. It was not illegal to loan money, but to collect interest on the money loaned was the crime of usury. Heavy penalties were attached to usury because collecting interest on money was considered to be a form of theft, gaining money without working and at the expense of someone in a position so unfortunate that he had needed to borrow money.

Although we do not have this particular law, since the orientation of the influential of society has changed from a theological one to crass materialism, we do have many other laws on the books which make specific acts illegal simply because particular groups find them *morally* offensive. Consequently, millions of persons who do not victimize others come to be defined as law violators, as criminals, because their particular behaviors offend society's influential. *Our victimless crimes represent the legal system used as a buttress to enforce the values of persons who are in the controlling sector of society.* This is what I am referring to when I say they are part of a legal con game.

To make clearer what is conning about victimless crimes, think what it would be like if the contemporary power situation were reversed. As we saw in Chapter 10, homosexuality is a developed sexual preference for members of one's own sex. What if persons with a homosexual preference were in control of society instead of the currently reversed situation? Homosexuals would then be in a position to pass laws favoring their particular sexual orientations. They could make heterosexual acts illegal solely on the basis that they found such acts offensive. The stigma of illegality could be applied to heterosexual acts even though they involved consenting adults making love in private, as with our contemporary laws banning sexual acts between homosexuals. The con of such laws would be that simply because homosexuals were in power they utilized the legal system in an attempt to force others to conform to their own sexual preferences. By legal power they would be punishing and attempting to eliminate behavior not in line with their own brand of morality, *not* because the act harms society, but because of their own values.

To continue our most hypothetical example, homosexuals would then be able to muster the legal system, with its powerful network of police, courts, and jails, in order to punish heterosexuals and perhaps attempt to stamp out heterosexuality. The legal system could also be used to harass any persons who were even *suspected* of heterosexuality. As sexual orientations do not develop simply because laws proscribe behaviors, although laws are able to affect sexual orientations by changing the ways people interact with one another, the passing of laws prohibiting heterosexuality would no more stop heterosexuality than our current laws stop homosexuality. Heterosexuals would then meet on the sly, hold hands, kiss, pet, and covertly copulate in fear. Heterosexuals would find greater tolerance in some occupations, and these occupations would become "tainted" with heterosexuality. Anyone inclined to work in these occupations would be suspected of being a heterosexual. Heterosexuals would also probably develop subterranean institutions such as the "straight" bar. Although the police probably would be paid off to allow heterosexual activities to continue on a clandestine and semicontrolled basis, the threat of heterosexual crackdowns would always be present. Moreover, the symbol of heterosexuality could be brought out at any time in order to besmirch the reputations of those who appeared to threaten the status quo, as well as to blackmail wealthy and influential heterosexuals.

It is con, in other words, whenever the legal system, which in principle is supposed to protect all citizens equally, is used to foster and enforce any particular group's brand of morality—whether it is heterosexuals who are in power and pass laws against homosexuals, or those who prefer caffeine, nicotine, and alcohol versus those who prefer marijuana, hashish, and LSD.

A major victimless crime in contemporary society is public drunkenness. I am not referring to acts of vandalism, robbery, or assault committed by a person who is drunk: Such acts are not consensual but involve forcing oneself on other persons or on their property. Public drunkenness simply refers to someone being drunk in public, and more arrests occur in the United States for public drunkenness than for any other offense. Of our approximately seven million annual arrests, about 1,400,000 are for public drunkenness (*Crime in the United States*, 1972, Table 34). In Seattle, Washington, 70 percent of all police man-hours are spent dealing with this type of offense, while 80 percent of Seattle's jail population is made up of chronic alcoholic offenders (Spradley 1970:17).

The treatment which alcoholics receive in our legal system especially underlines its conning aspects. Alcoholics are seldom represented by a lawyer when they are brought into court, and 97 percent of persons arrested for public drunkenness are convicted. In line with the material we earlier covered on the production norms of our judicial system, it is not surprising that almost all these convictions are based on guilty pleas. After being convicted, alcoholics are typically placed in jail where they merely serve custodial time. Rarely does any court or jail system attempt to rehabilitate them. When they are released, alcoholics are typically flat broke. Their release can only involve the sarcastic expectation that they "have learned their lesson," because, even though they are broke, on the same day that they are released they are expected to not only remain sober but to also find both a job and a place to live.

Further conning aspects of the legal system become apparent when we examine how our bail bond system is applied to persons accused of public drunkenness. By forfeiting a $20 bail, a person convicted of public drunkenness can typically avoid going to jail. In some cases he is even able to avoid a six-month jail sentence for $40. Measured in these terms, the life of someone who does not have access to even this small amount of money is worth the pittance of 22 ¢ a day. Many chronic alcoholics consequently serve lengthy jail sentences because they cannot pay the ransom demanded for their freedom.

Our bailing system starkly discriminates against the poor in society, not just poor alcoholics. Persons with money can bail themselves out of jail while awaiting trial for all minor infractions (misdemeanors) and almost all serious infractions (felonies), while those who do not have the money or collateral for bail must remain in jail while they await their trial date. It is not unusual for a person from the poverty sector of our society to spend many months in jail in lieu of a few hundred dollars bail money. When his trial belatedly arrives, he is sometimes found not guilty of any wrongdoing (although this is unusual given our plea bargaining system), and in some rarer circumstances it turns out that he was the victim of mistaken identity. Yet, the accused was forced to spend months in jail awaiting his trial simply because he could not afford bail. No middle class or wealthy person undergoes the deprivation of freedom of movement due to jailing simply because he does not have money. Only our poor are such con victims of our legal system.

Another major conning aspect of our legal system is that it sometimes serves as the means of punishing persons whose political activities bring them into disfavor with the more powerful in society. We noted a rather startling example of this in Chapter 11 concerning Mrs. Henrietta Wright, the black lady who registered to vote in Mississippi and was subsequently beaten by representatives of the law and through legal manipulations was forcibly incarcerated in a state mental hospital. It is important to note that this use of the law was not individualistic, that is, this was not simply an isolated case which depended on the idiosyncracies of a particular sheriff. The registration of Mrs. Wright, rather, represented a direct threat to white political supremacy. Consequently, the local legal machinery was brought into play in order to publicly punish the individual who represented the posed threat and to serve as a warning to any others who might similarly wish to upset the status quo. As those in power are not only able to pass laws which best serve their class interests but are also able to muster the legal machinery to enforce those laws, it is not unusual for the legal system to be wielded as a weapon against persons who in some way threaten those who are in power.

If officials desire to punitively and defensively use the legal system but are unable to find laws which directly apply to the perceived threat, the legal system becomes part of "straight con." In this use of the law, in order to put him out of circulation an individual is arrested on one charge when he is really wanted for other activities. It is not unusual, for example, for persons who are labelled "radicals" to be arrested on drug charges if authorities are unable to arrest them for their political activities. Similarly, the Internal Revenue Service established a special squad which was assigned the specific task of checking the federal income tax returns of "radicals" (Associated Press, January, 1972). As was revealed in the Watergate investigations, the Nixon administration even drew up an "enemies list" consisting of persons who had fallen into political disfavor. Against these persons the Internal Revenue Service and other legal and administrative machinery were to be mustered. In one particular case of this type of legal con, orders for special tax audits were directed against two staff members of *Newsday* simply because they had written an article unfavorable to a personal friend of the then President of the United States (NBC News, June 26, 1973).

It is con when people who threaten entrenched power establishments are investigated or arrested under the guise of law and order, under the guise of the dispassionate enforcement of equalitarian laws for the

As the Watergate investigations starkly demonstrated, the legal-political system lends itself well to the illegitimate exercise of power for the attainment of personal goals. (Courtesy of Wide World Photos)

protection of the community. When people are arrested not because of legal infractions but because the powerful manipulate the law in order to maintain their vested power interests, that is con. Charles Koen was such a victim in this legal con game. Koen was a black clergyman of the National Baptist Convention. If this were all, he would have had no legal problems. He was, however, also a leader of the Black Liberators of St. Louis. Koen attempted to develop black consciousness and to politically mobilize blacks to fight racial discrimination in the City of St. Louis. The city administration moved powerfully against him, primarily by means of the St. Louis Police Department. Although they desperately tried, the administration found that they were unable to associate Koen with illegal activities. The police then arrested him on the charge of "driving with an unlighted license plate." After taking him into custody under this subterfuge, the police severely beat him in the basement of the Lucas Avenue Police Station. Consequently, Koen had to be hospitalized for several months (*St. Louis Post-Dispatch,* October 6, 1971).

Persons who are employed by the legal system are almost powerless to change its conning aspects. In most instances they cannot even refuse to cooperate with its con, except by seeking employment elsewhere. This dilemma faces them even when the tasks they are assigned strike directly against their own class and personal interests. In the illustration I used in Chapter 9 of the Heidelberg demonstrations, for example, when the orders to break up the demonstration by force were handed down by the city administration, the police obediently responded—even though their own sympathies appeared to lie with the demonstrators.

Members of the working class are regularly used for purposes of repression by those who wield power. The Kent State students, for example, were not shot by politicians, but it was a politician who felt threatened by the student disruptions who ordered out the National Guard. At Jackson State it was the State Police who did the legal killing. Carnage at both Jackson and Kent State was carried out primarily by members of the working class, but it was power unleashed by persons who were attempting to maintain the status quo of power relationships.

What can a policeman do but obey? To do otherwise is to severely threaten those persons established in power. Consequently, even the threat of disobedience invites speedy and effective retaliation—again carried out by members of the working class at the orders of the powerfully entrenched. Yet, the typical "I must follow orders" reply is certainly reminiscent of Eichmann. Even those at or near the top of political power are able to locate someone to whom they can demur in responsibility.

The con games of the law involve a hierarchic cast of characters. Some are willing partners because they believe the symbols manipulated by those over them. Others are unwilling players because they perceive that the acts of repression in which they become involved have a class interest which is not their own. Both, however, are the co-opted.

Yet some co-opted role players do attempt to directly confront the system of repression in which they are playing an active part. Renault Robinson is a particular case in point. He is a black who compiled a distinguished record on the police force of Chicago. He was awarded citations for outstanding service and gained a reputation as a "Cinderella policeman." (Seldom are sex and race categories irrelevant in American life, but the application of this term to Robinson was one of those rare examples.) Robinson later became convinced that the Chicago police force was being used to enforce racial discrimination. He felt that mere protest would do little good, so he formed an organization to combat racism on the police force. After he founded the Afro-American Patrolmen's League, however, his occupational situation changed abruptly. He soon found himself in serious and continuing trouble with administrative authorities in the police department. He was written up by his superior officers on such "serious" charges as not wearing his hat while exiting from his police car. It was not long after he founded the organization that he was suspended for infraction of departmental rules (Hall 1970). Later, at the U. S. Justice Department, while he was passing out a copy of the League's complaint in which he alleges racial discrimination in the Chicago Police Department, he was arrested for "disorderly conduct." The charge of disorderly conduct was dropped after a few hours, only to be replaced with the charge of "conduct unbecoming a police officer" (*The Brief*, January, 1972).

Such are the conning aspects of the legal system. It is employed to enforce the particular morality and class interests of those who are in power. In order to stabilize the social system and maintain relative power positions, it is quickly and forcefully brought into play when the vested interests or the status quo of those in power are threatened. It is consistently used to discriminate against the poor and minorities of our society. Because of the interdependence of the network of social relations in the court system, the adversary system which is held as the ideal is a far cry from an adequate picture of reality. In the next chapter we shall examine similar conning aspects of the political system as it is used for purposes of social control.

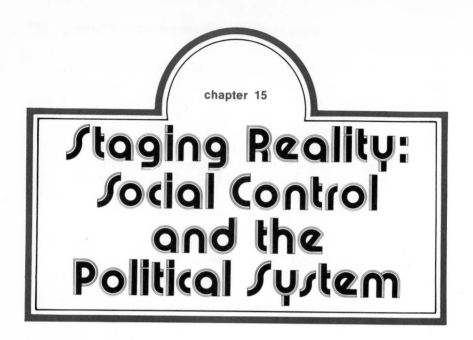

chapter 15

Staging Reality: Social Control and the Political System

The second major social institution which we shall analyze within the framework of reality distortion and social control is the political system. I am not referring primarily to an office-seeker making promises during his campaign and forgetting them during his tenure in office, although this perspective certainly also applies. I wish, rather, to emphasize the subterfuge inextricably intertwined with the political exercise of power, the conning aspects of the political presentation of self which inhere to politics as it is currently practiced in the United States. We shall again focus on reality distortion as it relates to the extremes of the economic spectrum, the nation's poor and the nation's wealthy, looking specifically at scapegoating, the differential treatment of the rich and the poor at the hands of politicians, the use of statistics as a mechanism to stage reality, political subterfuge in playing the war game, the manipulation of ideology to structure reality for vast numbers of people, and "cooling out" techniques designed to facilitate the continued exercise of political power.

Politicians are quick to project responsibility and blame away from themselves during times of a nation's external or internal difficulties. If they are able to latch onto a **scapegoat,** that is, if they can present a diversionary source on which they can focus reasons for the problems confronting them, they can divert attention away from themselves and make others the responsible agent. Not just any group can serve as a scapegoat, however, and here is where reality distortion comes in. Scapegoats appear to be chosen on the basis that they (1) are politically weak, since pinpointing blame on a powerful group is likely to have negative consequences for the politicians' remaining in office; (2) possess an ostensible characteristic, that is, the group must be marked by a trait which the politicians can make the public believe is in some way connected with, causing, contributing to, or aggravating the particular problem; (3) are unpopular; and (4) preferably do not represent the values of the dominant group, or, more preferably yet, are even notably lacking or antithetical to some major cultural value.

When the United States experienced economic setbacks in the late 60's and early 70's, politicians located a scapegoat that met these qualifications, the nation's poor. Politicians did not choose those who were merely "not too well off," but they chose those who were living in extreme poverty, those at the bottom of the economic barrel who eked out their existence on a hand-to-mouth basis. Welfare recipients met each of the qualifications for the role of scapegoat since (1) they were politically weak, not organized as a political group with the capacity to deliver bloc votes; (2) their ostensible characteristic was that they were costing money while the nation was experiencing monetary difficulties, supposedly endlessly absorbing our financial resources; (3) aspects of disrepute and shame are associated with being on a welfare list, with persons receiving welfare typically looked down upon (they are *moral* violators, as we discussed in Chapter 3); and (4) welfare recipients, at least in popular imagery, do not match the major American value of hard work, at least work in direct exchange for a paycheck.

While politicians did not go so far as to blame the poverty-stricken for causing our economic recession, they indicated not only that welfare recipients were "eating up" the nation's resources without making an economic contribution themselves but that a large proportion were able-bodied persons who were on welfare simply because they did not want to work. The then Vice President of the United States said, "Maybe you should send interior decorators over to all those deadbeats' apartments—to paper the ceilings with help-wanted ads" (Royko 1971). This statement, while crass, is also quite subtle. Hidden within it is the implication that most of us are doing our best to help the economy, but while we are working hard others are irresponsibly taking a free ride off our efforts. During an economic crisis so great that the United States had to take the severe, unprecedented steps of devaluating the dollar and placing price and profit controls on a "peacetime" economy, this statement indicated that welfare recipients are people who refuse to work and thereby drain our resources and contribute to a rapidly deteriorating economy.

By focusing blame on a group as disorganized as welfare recipients, a group so weak in resources that even when openly attacked they pose neither political threat nor even discomfort to the dominant power structure, politicians had found themselves a ready scapegoat. Others were then able to blame the poor of the nation for their difficulty in finding jobs and their problems in meeting higher taxes. Successfully avoided by such scapegoating is placing fault on political leaders, those persons who (1) make the decisions which directly affect the employment rate and (2) by their votes directly decide taxation.

Not only does such scapegoating take the heat off politicians, but, very importantly, it also maintains divisiveness among the poorer groups in society. This is highly desired by politicians lest dissident groups in society gain a collective consciousness by which they identify with one another and through concerted effort replace their politicians with leaders who more accurately reflect the needs of the less wealthy.

A rather intriguing related conning aspect of the Vice President's statement about welfare recipients is that it was made at a gathering of Illinois farmers. What is intriguing about this is that some farmers themselves receive a substantial annual income from the Federal Government. American farmers over-all have been paid approximately four *billion* dollars a year for *not* growing crops on their land (*USDA Economic Research Services*, 1970:64; *The Farm Index,* March 1973:3). Without stretching the concept too far, one could look at farmers' subsidy payments as a form of welfare. Some corporate farmers have even managed to draw over four million dollars a year from the government, simply for not growing crops (*Congressional Quarterly Weekly Report,* April 1971:839) (cf. Schultze 1971). One might say that such recipients are playing a rather remarkably successful welfare game. Americans, however, have a tradition concerning the land and those who farm it which goes back to the founding of this nation, and politicians usually take care not to openly offend the farmer. Additionally, farmers are fairly well politically organized, and with their effective lobbying in Washington they are sometimes able to swing key states in Presidential elections. Urban welfare recipients, in contrast, have no venerable traditions surrounding them and are politically unorganized. As such, they are much more likely candidates for the scapegoat role.

Similarly, during his terms in office as the Governor of California, Ronald Reagan was one of the foremost outspoken critics of welfare recipients. Yet, Reagan himself is a wealthy man who ungrudgingly takes what he can from the government. 1970 provides a good example: Although Reagan sold his 236 acre ranch to Twentieth-Century-Fox Studios for a reported 1.93 million dollars, and although he owned one home in Pacific Palisades, California, and leased another in Sacramento for $1,250 a month, and although he received a taxable government salary of $44,100, yet Reagan paid no California income tax for 1970 "because of business reversals" (*Globe-Democrat,* May 5, 1971). Another

Politicians are not unknown to publicly present one face while privately presenting another: That which is given for public consumption does not necessarily match either true feelings or private behavior. (Courtesy of Wide World Photos)

outspoken critic of welfare recipients, Richard M. Nixon, was paid a salary of $200,000 each year he was President. For the years 1970, 1971, and 1972, he declared a total income of $794,104.85. Yet he attempted to pay only $5,869.01 in taxes over this three-year period, claiming enormous exemptions because he had donated his Vice Presidential papers to the government. These documents had been typed on government typewriters, on paper paid for by the government, by typists whose salaries had been paid by the government (*St. Louis Post-Dispatch*, December 9, 1973).

By drawing attention to the formal welfare system and its recipients, politicians are able to lower the visibility of the recipients of many forms of government payments, payments made to persons who are closer to the politicians' own purse strings, the nation's wealthy. By castigating the welfare system, they attempt to keep the public thinking that it is only the poor who collect welfare in the United States. If we take a closer look at the matter, however, it becomes apparent that the rich also receive welfare. But they do so with a major difference—when the wealthy collect welfare they garner it at a very hefty rate indeed.

Their huge tax breaks operate like governmental subsidies (Bartlett 1973:109). According to an announcement by President Nixon in January 1971, for example, the United States Treasury proposed to give a three-billion-dollar tax break to businesses and corporations. Moreover, this tax break would have been accomplished simply by administrative action, thus bypassing the obstacle of trying to get legislation through Congress. This tax cut, unabashedly designed to benefit the wealthy, could be brought about simply by revising the federal income tax rules for depreciating machinery and equipment. By permitting businesses to speed up their depreciations, billions of dollars in tax savings would accrue to a very limited but politically powerful segment of our society, primarily to our large manufacturing and mining industries and to some utilities. Moreover, it is estimated that this tax break would cost the government *forty billion dollars* during its first ten-year period ("Common Cause Report from Washington," *1,* May 1971, p. 10).

To catch a glimpse of the far-reaching conning involved in this proposal, we can note that it was made *at the same time* that government spokesmen were saying we did not have sufficient funds to end hunger, to clean up the environment, to build mass transportation, or to rejuvenate our cities. This is what is meant by the phrase "political con."

In the same vein we can examine the B-1, the proposed manned strategic bomber, which was scheduled to cost in just its first year 370 million dollars for engineering development alone. This sum represents more money than the government was scheduled to spend for all of its urban mass transit programs. According to the director of the Federation of American Scientists, even though this plane would cost so much money, it was probably already outmoded:

> No really essential task of destruction can be reliably assigned either the B-1 or B-52 because the survivability and penetrability of neither can be ensured. While the B-1 is taking four hours to fly 6000 miles . . . eight successive missile salvos—four on each side, and each "answering" the other—could take place. The war may well be over before the bombers arrive (*St. Louis Post-Dispatch,* January 19, 1972).

While playing this con game, politicians were silent regarding the beneficiaries of the B-1 proposal, the favored corporations and their wealthy stockholders who would be the recipients of millions upon millions of dollars. Although they remain silent concerning the wealthy and politically influential who turn handsome profits from our vast military expenditures, our politicians are quick to publicly point an accusatory finger at welfare recipients as the undeserved financial beneficiaries of government action, self-righteously proclaiming that they should be ashamed of themselves for accepting government handouts.

What they conveniently conceal in their sweeping statements is that the average recipient of Aid to Dependent Children receives but $1.40 a day to live on, the average payment for Old Age Assistance comes to $2.57 a day, and the average payment for Aid to the Blind is $3.53 a day (*Statistical Abstracts of the United States,* 1972: Table 486).

At the same time that the government proposed tax breaks for the nation's wealthy which would run up to 40 billion dollars and the development of a plane we probably don't need but which would also cost billions more, the Washington administration opposed legislation which would appropriate 90 million dollars to develop a cure for a disease from which 50,000 Americans are now dying. This is the fatal blood disease of sickle-cell anemia. In addition to the 50,000 Americans who are now dying from it, another two million Americans carry the sickle-cell anemia gene. If someone carrying this gene marries another person with the same trait, their children will have a 25 percent chance of being born with the fatal sickle-cell disease (*St. Louis Post-Dispatch,* November 12, 1971; November 15, 1971).

With the vast amounts of money being spent by the Federal Government on its practically countless programs, how could the Executive branch of our government possibly oppose such humanitarian legislation? The answer is an essential part of the political con game American style: Sickle-cell anemia almost exclusively strikes blacks. Almost all whites are immune. Thus, there was little political threat in opposing this legislation. The President made his position crystal clear with the simple pronouncement that "programs have been established to meet all the objectives of the proposed legislation." Over his objection, Congress later passed a 115-million-dollar appropriation for diagnosis, prevention, and treatment of sickle-cell anemia (*Congressional Quarterly,* May 13, 1972:1110).

A favorite ploy in the political con game is to use official statistics for purposes of subterfuge. For example, Daniel P. Moynihan, a Presidential assistant, stated that great breakthroughs had been made in minority incomes during the 1960's. He pointed out that in 1960 only 15 percent of black and other minority families earned $8,000 or more but that this had jumped to 32 percent by 1968. What he said was true. What he failed to indicate, however, changes the picture entirely. Over this same period of time the proportion of white families with an annual income of $8,000 or over increased from 39 percent to 58 percent. By his use of statistics Moynihan hid the fact that the differential between minority and white family incomes *increased* during this period. The black-white differential in 1960 was 24 percent (39 percent − 15 percent), while by 1968 the differential had increased to 26 percent (58 percent − 32 percent) (Cook 1970:146).

The income gap between blacks and whites has also continued to increase since 1968. Whites averaged $3,577 more than blacks in 1968, while by 1972 their lead had increased to $4,685. The average difference between black and white income has now grown to such an extent that it is greater than the minimum amount ($4,275) a family of four is expected to live on and still *not* be living in poverty. Unfortunately, 33 percent of blacks and 9 percent of whites live below the official poverty line (*New York Times*, July 23, 1973:1 and 17).

Statistics lend themselves well to the political con game because, as in the example cited, they can be fairly easily manipulated to distort reality for purposes of social control. As the essence of a con game is to manipulate presentations in order to foster a definition of reality which does not "square" with the facts and in this way to be able to gain or to maintain control over others for the benefit of one's own ends, for political con statistics become a useful tool for subterfuge.

Similarly, the government manipulates the statistics which are supposed to accurately represent the nation's unemployment rate. Things look better to the public and life is made easier for politicians the lower the unemployment rate can be shown to be. The better things look, the less unrest among the public. Accordingly, the government manipulates the official figures on unemployment that it publicizes through its Bureau of Labor Statistics. In order to decrease the proportion of the population listed as unemployed, one need merely count fewer unemployed. For example, in the late 60's the Department of Labor began excluding from the category of unemployed persons who work only ten or twenty hours a week, persons who are on strike, and persons who are missing from work because they are ill. As the category of unemployment is now being used, to be employed is not the same as to be engaged at work. In fact, by manipulating unemployment figures in this way, we end up with the Kafkaesque situation wherein an increase in the number of people out of work due to a strike could contribute to an immediate decrease in the official unemployment rate for that area. This could have a drastic effect on such communities as Detroit (Leggett and Cervinka 1973).

One of the most revelatory aspects of the political con game played on the American public and on other nations was disclosed when the United States government announced an offer of 2.5 billion dollars to North Vietnam for postwar reconstruction as part of a 7.5-billion-dollar program for Indochina. Why would we make such an offer since these are the same people whom we said we would "bomb back into the Stone Age?" We never did gain our well-publicized desires of political and military victory in Vietnam, even though American casualties ran somewhere around 50,000 and Vietnamese deaths soared into the

Official statistics, such as those on unemployment, lend themselves well to manipulation for the purposes of both maintaining the social order and preserving one's position in power. (Courtesy of Wide World Photos)

hundreds of thousands, in addition to the uncounted and perhaps uncountable wounded. Yet the President announced that "We remain prepared to undertake a major reconstruction program throughout Indochina, including North Vietnam, to help all those people to recover from the ravages of a generation of war" (*St. Louis Post-Dispatch*, January 28, 1972).

Following the idea of reality distortion and social control, one would look for conning aspects in such an announcement. One would ask how the United States, having failed in its professed goals of military victory, could best extricate itself from a degrading and demoralizing morass and yet save some face. Such an offer of money would be one answer. It might help swing back onto our side world opinion, which had been almost uniformly opposed to our role in Vietnam. It makes us appear generous to our enemy.

But a more fundamental question is whether they ever were our enemy in the first place. If the leaders of the government of the United States had been sincere in their professed reasons for the United States involvement in Vietnam, it does not appear that they ever would have made such an offer. Supposedly we were there to "fight communism," to "make South Vietnam free," and to "protect the free people of South Vietnam." As military victory was never achieved, but instead a peasant people incredibly withstood the heaviest bombardment ever inflicted on any nation in the history of the world, a bombardment backed up by perhaps the most powerful military force the world has ever known, and as political victory also proved elusive, why would the United States ever make such an offer? Would not two and a half billion dollars strengthen the very enemy over which the United States spilled so much blood in attempting to defeat? So it would seem, until we question whether the leaders of the United States ever desired military victory in the first place.

A group of persons extremely disenchanted with the political scene in the United States repeatedly stated during the war that the United States became involved in Indochina for reasons far disassociated from goals of political or military victory. Persons of this more radical persuasion said that the goal of the United States, despite official political pronouncements, never was to achieve victory. Although the view was quite unpopular, they said that the goal instead was profit for a select segment in our society, especially for the industrial leaders who head up our various armaments industries (Reynolds 1972). The interests of our top industrialists have coalesced with those who head our military, those who already desire war that they might use their training, test their strength, develop new combat strategies, and increase their own personal power through promotions and the wielding of authority over larger and larger numbers of soldiers and a burgeoning budget. With the interests of these two powerful groups intermeshed, they were able to bring enough pressure to bear on the political leaders such that the military's desire for war and the industrialist's desire for profit through war could be made a reality—so much so that they were even able to bypass Congress and avoid the necessity of securing a declaration of war, even though this war both lasted longer and cost more than any previous war fought in the history of the United States (cf. Mills 1963).

It appears that the offer of postwar reconstruction money greatly supports this thesis of reality distortion: If communism were the enemy we had been fighting these many years, and at such a dear cost in lives, material, and morale, why would we ever offer an amount of money which could only strengthen our enemy? Unless, of course, the reasons presented for the war were subterfuge, being created only for public consumption. If that is so, when our political leaders found they could no longer bear the cost of the divisiveness produced by the war, a divisiveness perhaps unequalled in spirit and bitterness since the split caused by the Civil War, and were forced to pull out their armed forces, this announcement then represented a new scheme whereby more billions could be spent, a spending program which would continue to primarily profit the wealthy in American society. It would be they, after all, who would produce the goods, at a profit, which would be used to "build up" the very country from which they made a handsome profit in the billions expended to destroy it. From this perspective, one would say that if the top wealth holders in American society cannot continue to increase their wealth through bombing, then they will attempt to do so through repairing the results of their bombing.

A rather fascinating side con game that was played in this financial offer by the United States centers around the way in which the offer was made. At the Paris peace talks, Hanoi had presented a secret nine-point settlement plan to end the war. The response of the United States totalled only eight points because the payment of reparations "would be an admission of guilt by the United States." In its place, the United States "outlined separately" this postwar reconstruction plan (*St. Louis Post-Dispatch*, January 28, 1972). Thus, in this political staging of reality we were willing to pay reparations only if the label of reparations not be attached to our payments.

As revealed by the House Impeachment Hearings, reality distortion for conning purposes was involved in almost every phase of our military campaign in Indochina: President Johnson campaigned against Barry Goldwater on a peace platform while behind the scenes he was busily making plans for waging war in Veitnam; when President Johnson announced to the nation that he was not changing policy by sending 50,000 troops to South Vietnam, he was, in fact, both making an abrupt about-face in our policy and was actually sending 100,000 troops; President Johnson further successfully deceived Congress and most Americans as he pushed through the Tonkin Gulf Resolution in the attempt to legitimize his military activities; and President Nixon ordered fake bombing reports to conceal from Congress and the American public what was later to be called his "secret war" in Cambodia (*House Impeachment Hearings*, July 30, 1974).

The man who under both these Commanders-in-Chief headed our armed forces in Indochina similarly distorted reality for public consumption. General Westmoreland regularly announced to the nation optimistic reports of our military involvement, regardless of how the situation was deteriorating. He continuously reported that we were doing excellently, but always added that we needed a few more thousand troops to wind up the job. When he failed to achieve military victory even after a half million American soldiers had been sent to South Vietnam, in the inexplicable way of politics he was rewarded by being promoted to head our Joint Chiefs of Staff. In line with the view that military victory was never our goal, however, his promotion makes sense. After our stunning military and political failures, Westmoreland followed up a visit he made to Vietnam in 1972 with a somewhat predictable statement that "the situation in Vietnam is gratifying because of the progress we have made on the economic and social fronts" (Mutual Broadcasting System, January 9, 1972).

We could similarly examine our other social institutions for distortions of reality for purposes of social control. For example, our educational institution sometimes teaches a white value system in the guise of books which are supposedly intended only to teach reading skills (Kozol 1967). In the economic institution, General Motors was forced to recall seven million Chevrolets because of defective engine mounts. The repairs cost them an estimated 35 million dollars. When recalling them, however, General Motors refused to admit that there was a safety factor involved even though according to government experts the defective engine mounts might cause the accelerator to stick or the vacuum hoses for power-assisted brakes to be pulled loose, affect automatic and manual transmissions, and cause a car to go out of control (*St. Louis Post-Dispatch*, January 19, 1972). The auto industry also fraudulently distorts reality when it widely advertises its safety campaigns but at the same time emphasizes power in its automobile advertising (O'Connell 1967). Con is also present when polluting becomes profitable, when the industries which pollute the environment are paid for cleaning up their own pollution (Gellen 1970). The medical institution can similarly be viewed as having fraudulently distorted reality when tooth-and-nail it fought Medicare on the basis that Medicare would lower the quality of health care—when the medical profession's concerns actually centered on the autonomy of the medical profession, and after the passage of Medicare doctors happily profited from the legislation.

The distortion of reality by social institutions ordinarily takes place within an ideological framework. That is, **ideology,** reasons which match a general framework of belief and morality and which defend or support actions, is used in order to make actions acceptable to people who might otherwise object to them. For example, Lyndon B. Johnson defended the involvement of the United States in Vietnam by manipulating the concepts or symbols of democracy, freedom of elections for the South Vietnamese, and the protection of the integrity of a nation. Spokesmen in his administration followed up these positive symbols with the use of negative ones when they warned against "the yellow peril," tying into a combined ideology of racism and anti-communism. Similarly, the medical profession defended its stand against Medicare by using the ideology of "quality" of medical care, saying that quality would be threatened if the proposed legislation were to pass. In such ways, specific actions are placed within general frameworks in order to justify the actions. Ideology thus serves as a justifying device to make actions acceptable to others: It is a significant part of the political presentation of self.

The major advantage of using an ideological framework is that, like statistics, ideology readily serves to distort perception. Staging reality becomes connected with the major symbols into which people have been socialized. Manipulating ideological symbols can camouflage issues, conceal motivation, and provide a conceptual framework for coming up with the "right" interpretation. Ideology, successfully utilized, orientates people; that is, ideology is able to direct the thought and perception of those for whom the message is intended. Using ideology as an orientational device allows political leaders to give shape to the views of their people. By the skillful use of ideology citizens can be much more easily led into submission and into cooperative acts which serve to maintain the social order than they can be through the use of sheer force.

A major factor which enables ideology to play this role in bringing about submission and cooperation is its orientating function in perception. Ideology, like any conceptual system, as we covered in Chapter 4, provides a framework for interpreting events. Ideology directs people to perceive events in some specific way, to focus on certain things rather than others. Ideology is a critical tool for politicians because it both leads people to overlook conflicting information and provides a ready explanation for conflicting facts which do come to their attention. Ideology thus leads to **selective perception;** that is, ideology provides a conceptual framework which sensitizes an observer to the existence of certain events or information but desensitizes him to others.

Selective perception is brought about, for example, by the American ideology that "anyone can succeed." While most people do not perhaps believe that everyone has an equal opportunity to become President of the United States or of General Motors, our ideology teaches us that anyone can become financially successful if he or she but puts forth the proper effort. This ideology was once put in the following form by testimony before the Special Tax Study Committee of the House Ways and Means Committee:

Our country has grown great by the chances we have offered to every country boy and workingman to build himself up by his industry and thrift to as good a position as his capabilities justify. Our great productivity results from the work of men who have made their own ways to the top (Eisenstein 1961:58).

At first glance, this statement appears to be a defense of the working class, or at least of working class men. It says that our country is great because 1) working class men 2) are able to climb the social class ladder 3) to the limit of their capacities, and 4) that this leads to high productivity. By juxtaposing in just two sentences the key ideological symbols of great country, equality of opportunity, country boys, workingmen, self-development, industry, thrift, good positions justified by ability, productivity, and making one's own way to the top, the speaker selectively channels our perception. We become guided into perceiving the world according to the terms and images indicated by this ideology.

This particular statement, however, was not made by members of the working class. On the contrary, it was made before Congress by a group of prominent industrialists, bankers, and tax lawyers who were arguing against a progressive income tax. They were attempting to provide a conceptual interpretation of events which would further their own position in the social class structure by leading to a lowering of their share of income taxes. In this attempt, they were constructing reality by tapping for their own self-interests the basic American ideology of hard work and success and thereby making the fantastic identification of themselves with the working class. Not incidentally, they also simultaneously defended our social class divisions: Their own positions of affluence are justified by industry, thrift, and ability, as well as the lesser positions for those with "lesser capabilities."

The ideology of success, coupled with its interconnected corollary that "we are living in an era of abundance and affluence," leads us not to see that the average American owns nothing more than the clothes on his back, a second-hand car, and household goods consisting of little more than a few glittering gadgets. The average total life's accumulation of 89.6 percent of our population is less than $20,000, which sum includes the value of their home and all their property. In fact, 68.4 percent of our population (included in the above figures) leave a gross estate of less than $10,000, while 28 percent (also included in the above figures) leave an estate less than $1,000. The average estate size for 50 percent of Americans is only $1,800, barely enough to cover cheap furniture and clothes, an old T.V., and a run-down car. In sharp contrast, 1.6 percent of our population owns 32 percent of all the privately owned wealth in the whole country. This 1.6 percent owns 100 percent of state and local bonds and 82.2 percent of all stock. The other 17.8 percent of the stock is thinly spread over 15.4 million people. Moreover, one-half of one percent (included in the above figure of 1.6 percent) owns 25 percent of the total national wealth (Lundberg 1968:1–18).

Is there room at the top? Looking at these figures one would conclude that if there is any room at all it certainly isn't ample. Except for a few Texas oil-lease speculators and wildcatters who have made it big since World War I, a select few entertainers such as Bob Hope and Billy Rose, a handful of fortunate inventors, and some politicians who have been on the take, it is almost impossible to move into the realm of the rich. But our ideology would have us believe quite differently. Our ideology is extremely effective, guiding us to selectively perceive the world around us. As such, ideology serves well as a device for distorting reality and maintaining social control.

Conning is frequently accompanied by "cooling-out" techniques by which those who have been conned are "adjusted" to their loss (Goffman 1952). If a "mark" or victim can be adapted to his loss, he is said to be cooled out. One technique, as indicated, is to manipulate symbols which detract attention from the fact that someone has been conned. If the individual or group does not recognize that conning underlies his loss, or, better yet, does not even recognize that a loss has taken place, discontent and public outcry can be avoided. This technique diverts attention from problems that could become public issues and tend to create disorder in society.

We can examine cooling-out techniques by referring to several of the situations we have analyzed in this and the previous chapter. One technique for cooling people out, as was indicated, is keeping people in ignorance. Although public defenders' offices are underfinanced and understaffed compared with the financial outlay and personnel of prosecuting attorneys' offices, this situation receives little publicity. The greater the ignorance which people have of reality distortions, the less the cooling-out that is necessary. For persons who get caught up in the legal system and receive less than adequate services and defense from the public defender, this very underbudgeting and understaffing serves as a cooling-out mechanism. The accused might be told "there is nothing that can be done to change the system" and "we are doing our best with what we have." It might admittedly be a poor system, but if those assigned to help are doing their best, how can one complain? In this way the structural causes that undermine the adversary proceedings are overlooked because of the existing effort to help the poor. The feeling that "it certainly is better than nothing" directs thought, perception, and action away from the causes built into the system which lead to the public defender being underfinanced and understaffed in the first place.

Those who fail to receive a defense under this system but are instead manipulated into making a guilty plea can be cooled out by the consoling thought that "it could have been worse." Defense lawyers are quick to cool out malcontented clients with the statement that if the defendant had pled not guilty he might have been found guilty of the more serious charge which would certainly have been levelled against him, and he would, accordingly, be worse off than he now is. For the poor who must await trial in jail because they cannot come up with the required bail there is the thought that their lawyer will request the judge to count the time they have spent in jail awaiting trial as part of their sentence. People who have never personally found themselves victims of the judicial system but who become concerned about it can be cooled out concerning the bail system by the thought that the accused is "probably guilty anyway." Why else would the police arrest him?

Persons who have been arrested for violating the moral standards of those who have been able to influence the passage of laws need special cooling out. Those accused of victimless crimes must be brought to think of the law as moral, as just, and as existing for the welfare of society. They should think of themselves as immoral, as bad, and as wrong for having become involved in the particular act. If they can be brought to the point of accepting this ideological framework which justifies the existence of moral laws, they can then be easily cooled out. To bring about these changes in self-concept and in ideas of the law necessitates much teamwork. Court personnel, including judges and lawyers and especially probation officers and various counselors such as psychiatrists, must present a unified staging of reality. When the offender "sees the light" and expresses a desire to reform his evil ways, he can then be rewarded by a light sentence or perhaps by probation, but with the warning that if he appears in court on a similar charge "the book will be thrown at him."

When it comes to conning on the political scene, cooling out is also necessary. For example, when two and a half billion dollars is offered "the enemy," what does one tell the families of approximately 50,000 G.I.'s who have died in Vietnam? How does one account for this offer to the families of the hundred and fifty thousand or so young men who are now spending the rest of their lives maimed, crippled, or disfigured? Or what does one say to the countless who have come back whole in body, but whose ideas of themselves will never be the same because of acts they don't even wish to discuss? How does one continue to convince parents that the sacrifice of their sons was worth it, or even that these deaths were a sacrifice for "the cause"? Effective cooling out is especially necessary when the victimizing involves losses that are not easily accepted and involve large numbers of people. There is political danger to the equilibrium of society in such cases. Fortunately for the politicians, in this case the desire to believe that the loss of a son in battle was a sacrifice for a larger cause to benefit society is quite strong, which makes the job easier. Facilitating the matter further is the social isolation of these families, that is, they are not banded into a group, which might change the level of their consciousness, but they live as individual families largely thinking of themselves as having suffered an individual loss. If they were to see themselves as collective victims of a profit-seeking system, the political order might be severely threatened. Cooling out in this case probably also means to encourage such individuated thinking. The national publicity given the wives of prisoners-of-war and their pressures on the government's policy in Vietnam is a case in point of what can occur when the consciousness of the individual is expanded to see himself as one of many in a situation with common causes.

As indicated, ideology itself serves as a cooling-out mechanism by directing perception, thought, and action. The unemployed, for example, must continue to think that there is room at the top. It would probably be politically dangerous for the unemployed to begin to think of their unemployment as due at least in part to the deliberate policy of the government, to realize that our federal administrators view the economy as being able to "afford" a certain proportion of unemployed. If people come to the conclusion that they are unemployed not because of bad luck but because they form part of the expendables of the economy, this change in consciousness could very well upset the stability of society.

Consequently, specific devices are used for cooling out the unemployed. These include unemployment compensation that keeps bodies alive, but at the poverty level, and job retraining that keeps hopes alive, but typically means that people are being trained for nonexistent jobs. It also means publicizing tax information in such a way that the majority never come to the realization that exclusive of welfare payments the very poor pay about 50 percent of their income in taxes, while those persons with annual incomes in excess of $1,000,000 enjoy loopholes purposely included for their benefit and pay only approximately 27 percent of their income in taxes (Bartlett 1973:122–123). In light of the great potential cost for failing to cool these people out, it is not surprising that severe economic recessions or depressions bring with them far-reaching steps for dealing with the poor and the unemployed. When large numbers of people refuse to be cooled out by the existing mechanisms, the situation becomes too volatile for the stability of a government to allow it to continue unchecked. Once collective consciousness arises, it can easily be directed against political figures who are perceived as the cause of the problems.

To conclude this analysis, I wish to look at just two of the many cooling-out devices used by the government. These two were used by the government in its dealings with the coal industry. As is common, it was not at first known that these were cooling-out devices, for they appeared to serve more open and legitimate purposes. The first involves a "hot line" set up for coal miners. In 1970 safety violations in coal mines once again became an issue, as they have intermittently over the years. The Bureau of Mines then set up a "hot line" whereby coal miners could anonymously report safety violations. A miner could call a certain number collect, and his incoming call would be taped. During a two-month period in 1971, however, the Bureau of Mines personnel did not even bother to check these tapes. This two-month period was during coal mining's most dangerous season, the fall-winter months when atmospheric conditions increase the risk of mine explosions. The reason that the tapes were not audited was not that the "hot line" was not being used. Nor was it because the incoming calls were insignificant, since during the first four months after the "hot line" was installed thirty-three calls were recorded, thirteen of which resulted in investigations being completed, and three of which resulted in orders closing unsafe mines (*St. Louis Post-Dispatch,* December 25, 1971). As long as no one knew that the calls were not being monitored, however, this device capably served as an efficient cooling-out technique.

Fines are a second cooling-out device used by the government in their intriguing dealings with coal companies. Pittston Coal Company is the third largest coal producer in West Virginia. In their relentless pursuit of profits, Pittston has run up an unenviable record of safety violations. As a consequence of these violations, the Federal Government over the past several years has fined Pittston Coal Company more than two million dollars. On the face of it, this sounds as though the United States government has carefully looked after the health and welfare of coal workers by taking a tough stand against this company. A levied fine which does not have to be paid, however, no matter how steep it may be, is but a scrap of waste paper. And that is how it was in this case. These fines merely served to cool out interested persons. After all, as the company had been fined for its violations, "justice had been done." Pittston, however, did not bother to pay anything—until ABC-TV uncovered and publicized this fact. The remarkable con in this fascinating cooling-out device includes the membership of a man named Morton on the Board of Directors of the Pittston Coal Company. He, not so incidentally, just happened to be the brother of the then Secretary of the Interior, Rogers C. B. Morton (Archibald 1973).

The consequences of failing to enforce safety standards in coal-mining operations can be horrendous. They involve far more than the convenience and comfort of miners. Violations can and do result in death, sometimes in mass slaughter. This appears to be the situation in this case, for the West Virginia attorney general's office is suing Pittston for approximately $50,000,000 in connection with the Buffalo Creek flood of February 1971, which claimed the lives of 125 persons (*St. Louis Post-Dispatch,* December 13, 1973).

Conning, with its related subterfuge and cooling-out devices, is an endemic feature of the contemporary political-economic system. The political distortion of reality is geared to maintaining equilibrium in society. It is directed from the top downwards in order to keep the precarious balance between conflicting groups from being upset. Distorting reality helps maintain a current social order by consolidating and protecting existing power arrangements. Groups in control wish to maintain that control and the benefits they derive from their elite position. The distortion of reality is one of their major means of doing so. Cooling-out techniques also help maintain the status quo by preventing the development of a collective, revolutionary consciousness which might otherwise be directed against political-economic leaders or against other social institutions.

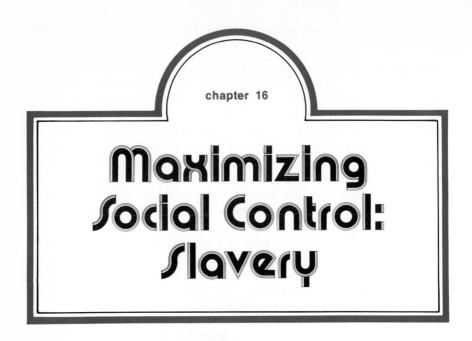

chapter 16

Maximizing Social Control: Slavery

As we analyzed social control aspects of the legal and political institutions in the last two chapters, we focused on ways by which reality is fraudulently distorted in order to maintain the status quo. We especially examined ways by which the powerful in society use social institutions in order to maintain their positions of power. As we saw, this use of social institutions in staging reality for purposes of social control is extremely effective. Reality is managed for large numbers of people who are brought into compliance with the wishes of a few. We shall now turn to an analysis of a social institution in which social control once reached its maximum, wherein physical coercion was regularly used to elicit compliance with the wishes of the more powerful.

In order to develop an adequate sociological imagination for understanding many contemporary events in the United States, it is necessary to understand slavery. Slavery was not simply a superficial characteristic of life in the New World. On the contrary, slavery was an essential part of that life. Slavery was so fundamental that it has left an indelible mark on the culture of the United States. Consequently, even though this aspect of our history officially ended well over a century ago, it continues to exert far-reaching effects on contemporary life.

Blacks are not a group of people who were simply "added on" to a vibrant white society, as so many suppose because of the traditional lack of accurate coverage of this subject in the United States school system. Rather, blacks have played a continual role in the history of the Americas. The first black of whom we have record in the New World is Pedro Alonzo. He sailed with Columbus and was captain of the Niña. Blacks were with Balboa when he explored the Pacific, with Cortez in Mexico, with Ponce de Leon in Florida, and with Coronado in Mexico. It was a black, Estevanico, who discovered the Zuñi Indians (Redding, 1950:11).

Black slaves had already been imported from Africa to Europe fifty years before the discovery of America. Trading in black slaves began in 1442 with the Portuguese. By the end of the fifteenth century Portugal controlled large parts of Africa and was supplying slaves to Spain. Spain then entered the slave trade in 1517, England followed suit in 1562, with France, Holland, and Denmark soon casting their lot on the side of the forceful expropriation of human beings. Trading in black bodies became so profitable that eventually a thousand ships were engaged in this enterprise, with voyages frequently netting $30,000 to $50,000.

The basic reason for slavery in the New World was an economic one. If slavery is an option open to countries, as it was in the fifteenth to nineteenth centuries, slavery will be used when it is profitable, rejected where it is not. At that time, slavery became profitable with the rising standard of living in Europe. The use of tobacco spread among the European population. Tobacco production took many acres, and prior to mechanized farming it demanded the use of a vast army of cheap, docile workers. Coffee, tea, and chocolate also became popular drinks, stimulating the demand for cane sugar. Cane sugar production also required a plentiful supply of cheap labor. The New World became the primary source for meeting these changed tastes of Europeans, becoming a sort of agricultural periphery to Europe. Plantation owners and developers, primarily in Latin America (especially Brazil) and the West Indies, in their pursuit after wealth turned increasingly to slaves as the source of their labor.

Basically, a triangle of trade was involved. Goods were manufactured in Europe and shipped to West Africa where they were traded to Africans for African slaves. The African slaves were then shipped to the New World where they were used to produce crops, which were, in turn, shipped back to Europe. From a cold, economic point of view, then, "the history of transatlantic slavery can be written in terms of sugar, tobacco, cotton, rum, and similar commodities" (Gann and Duignan 1972:319).

Contrary to common assumption, the main beneficiary of the trans-Atlantic slave trade was not the Thirteen Colonies. It is estimated that this territory received only approximately 4.5 percent of the slaves exported from Africa, with 1.8 percent going to Europe, and over 90 percent being sent to subtropical and tropical America, which extends from Brazil to the Caribbean. The main development of slavery took place outside the territory which later became the United States. The primary plantation economy for Europe was Latin America and the West Indies. Here sugar had to be grown on a large scale in order to be profitable, and most small holdings were gradually absorbed into large plantations (Gann and Duignan 1972:319–320). By 1715 there were approximately 60,000 slaves in the American colonies, but in just sixty years, by the time of the Revolution, this number had increased to over half a million (Redding 1950:12).

The monopoly in trading in black slaves eventually passed from the Portuguese to the Spanish, then to the Dutch, to the French, and finally to the English. The English turned their vast organizing talents to slave trading and founded the Company of Adventurers of London and the East India Company. Several times as many African slaves were eventually transported in British ships as in the ships of all other nations combined (Redding 1950:17).

Blacks were brought to the New World in chains from the west coast of Africa, from Cape Verde, Biafra, Gambia, the Gold Coast, the Ivory Coast, and the Grain Coast. Slaves came from four major groupings: the Negritians, the Fellatahs, the Bantus, and the Gallas. They came from such tribes as the Bassutas, Efik, Fulahs, Ibos, Makalolu, Mandingos, Senegalese, Wysyahs, and the Zandes. These were not simply primitive peoples, as goes the common legend in the United States. They came both from tribes which were simply organized and from tribes which had complex socioeconomic institutions. The schools and universities of kingdoms such as the Melle and Songhai had attracted scholars from Asia and Europe at the end of the Middle Ages. Various political systems existed among these peoples: Some were marked by monarchies, others by aristocracies. They had courts and kings, chiefs and headmen, craft and trade guilds, usually the common ownership of land, and a monetary system based on the cowrie shell. In some areas, such as the Niger Delta, lived millions of people who were divided into hundreds of small independent tribes (Redding 1950:14).

Europeans did not introduce slavery to Africa. Africans had themselves practiced slavery from antiquity. Slaves had been imported to Egypt and Carthage from Nubia and the Sudan. East Africa had been an important supplier of slaves, sending its human merchandise to Turkey, Arabia, Persia, India, Indonesia, and even China. Slavery was also a part of the social organization of Africa itself. Persons captured in battle or in raids were subject to slavery, as were persons convicted of crime and victims of political intrigue. Voluntary slavery also existed. Among the Ibo, a person might offer himself as a cult slave to a local deity or even pawn himself in repayment of debt.

But this was a different kind of slavery than the trans-Atlantic trade. Slaves rarely became part of labor gangs used to work large estates.

Slaves were used as soldiers, domestic servants, concubines, eunuchs, palace retainers, wrestlers, craftsmen, as well as field hands when the economy was so organized. The fate of a slave was subject to immense variation. In some societies, he might receive the harshest treatment, while in other societies, such as the coastal communities of Nigeria and the Ila of what is now Zambia, a slave was practically absorbed into the owner's family. In Nigeria the wives of the owner would become "mothers" to the slaves. Slaves were typically treated with kindness and had the right to acquire wealth. The difference between slave and citizen in African practice was typically one of degree rather than kind (Gann and Duignan 1972:316–317). A slave in Ashanti society, for example, was able to marry, own property, own a slave himself, serve as a witness, and to become heir to his master (Elkins 1963:96). I don't want to leave the impression of idealized African slavery, however, for people seldom find the status of slave, regardless of how benevolent it may be, preferable to the status of free men.

The colonists in what later became the United States did not first look to Africa as their source of forced labor. Indians lived nearby, and it was easier to enslave their red neighbors than to transport black slaves thousands of miles. Quite significantly, it was also cheaper. Unfortunately for the colonists, Indians did not work out well as slaves. They demonstrated a high degree of unwillingness to remain in forced labor for whites. They also exhibited a high mortality rate, which further cut down their desirability as slaves. Moreover, this "new land" was not new to them, and when they escaped from enslavement they were able to survive, eventually finding their way back to their own people.

In contrast to the idealized story of the origins of the Colonies with which we are so often presented, the colonists themselves were frequently reluctant to perform the required physically demanding heavy labor. In 1610 in the Virginia Colony, for example, Captain John Smith had to organize the settlement into a working force, marching the men to daily work in squads and companies under the command of armed officers. In 1618 the colonists petitioned King James I to send them vagabonds and condemned men as indentured servants (Redding 1950:23). Indentured servants were persons who had signed a contract binding them to service for a stipulated period of time in return for their passage to the New World. After an indentured servant had fulfilled the years of service called for in his contract, he was then able to take up land as a free man. Others were "redemptioners," persons who had arranged with the captain of the ship to pay for their passage after they arrived in the New World. If they were unable to meet their payment, they were sold by the captain of the ship to the highest bidder. The importation of indentured servants was extensive. About a quarter million indentured servants came to the United States during the colonial period, with perhaps half of all English immigrants being indentured servants (Williams 1966:9–10).

Perhaps the decisive factor in the move from white indentured servants to black slaves was that for what it cost to procure the services of a white indentured servant for two years one could buy a black for life. The reason for the enslavement of blacks was not racial, but economic. It did not have to do with the color of the laborer, but the cheapness of his labor. Both Indian slaves and white servants gave way to the superior endurance and capacity for labor of the blacks (Williams 1966:19–20). The need was for cheap labor, and race was irrelevant.

Because of the sketchy records from this period, it is difficult to say when the first slaves were brought from Africa to the Colonies. Perhaps they were brought by a Spaniard in 1526 to a new colony in the South (Redding 1950:21), or perhaps it was not until 1619 that the North American colonies received their first slaves (Gann and Duignan 1972:320). At any rate, the importation of slaves into the Colonies began slowly. This was because the plantation economy of the South itself grew at a slow pace. Additionally, however, the colonists appear to have at first preferred white indentured laborers to black slaves. Colonial legislatures even passed a series of laws designed to prevent or hinder the importation of slaves (Gann and Duignan 1972:321).

Economic needs, however, changed rapidly. In about 1680 rice and indigo began to be grown on a large scale in South Carolina. At the same time tobacco production was expanded in Virginia. Small independent farms gave way to plantations of hundreds and even thousands of acres. Virginia and Maryland became the tobacco colonies, while South Carolina and later Georgia became the rice colonies. Indentured servants could no longer meet the vastly increased labor requirements, and the southern colonies turned increasingly to Africa for satisfying their ever-growing need for cheap labor. In general, at the limits of the temperate zones the cultivation of these crops became impractical, and with it the practicality and desirability of slave labor also diminished. Although slavery was primarily a southern institution, the northern colonies also profited handsomely from it. They shipped manufactured goods to the developing market in the South and built many of the ships which both brought the slaves from Africa and transported the South's agricultural goods to its European destination (Gann and Duignan 1972:321).

Cotton production was at first primarily a by-product of southern agriculture. It took too many people too long a time to remove by hand the seeds from cotton to make it very profitable. Although British textile manufacturers were undergoing mechanization at this time and

The invention of the cotton gin in 1793 allowed the South to take competitive advantage of the expanding market for cotton. Slave importation increased on a large scale, making slavery a cornerstone of the South's economic system. (Courtesy of Wide World Photos)

had developed an increased need for cotton, the South could not take advantage of the market. The invention of the cotton gin in 1793 signalled a drastic change in the South's competitive position and ushered in social changes significant to the history and culture of the United States. The cotton gin allowed the South to meet a large proportion of the growing need for cotton, as unskilled slaves were able to run the machine. As cotton production became a staple crop, the price of slaves increased, as did the size of plantations. Southerners became more convinced than ever that slaves were essential to their economic well-being, and importation of slaves rapidly increased (Gann and Duignan 1972:321).

The European slave traders depended almost without exception on indigenous suppliers of slaves. It was not uncommon for African rulers to increase their power by slave-trading with Europeans. Dealing in slaves allowed them to acquire imported weapons, providing them a military advantage over their rivals. They could, in turn, utilize the advantages gained from slave-trading to increase their participation in this enterprise. In the kingdom of Dahomey a highly centralized monarchy ran the slave trade as a state enterprise. Dahomey carried on an extensive slave commerce with Brazil but was unable to secure a monopoly in slave traffic because of competition with the Yoruba. In areas of minor city-states, slave trading was carried on by leading merchants who were required to equip at least one war canoe for their respective city. Inland kingdoms also began to participate in the slave trade as caravans penetrated deeper and deeper into the interior of Africa.

The coastal peoples seldom supplied slaves from their own tribes. They were, rather, involved in an extensive transport network. They purchased captured prisoners from tribes in the hinterland. These tribes sold some people from their own regions but depended on their main supply from peoples still further in the interior. Most slaves were drawn from an area which reached inland from the coast for several hundred miles, primarily from the forest belt and to a lesser extent from the grassland beyond the forest (Gann and Duignan 1972:323–324).

The newly-made slave was filled with shock. His first shock resulted from capture itself, as he was typically taken in a war or a raid upon his village. His next shock came from being marched to the coast, a tortuous trek which took many weeks. Men, women, and children were driven like beasts. They were chained together neck and foot and forced to march near exhaustion under the glaring sun of the steaming jungle. A large proportion of the captured died on these long forced marches. The newly enslaved's next shock was being sold to European slavers. They were taken from the pens at the trading station, examined, and those found acceptable were branded, given numbers inscribed on leaden tags, and then herded on board ship. Then came the shock of the dreadful Middle Passage, the trans-Atlantic voyage which lasted about two months. Slaves were manacled together wrist-to-wrist, ankle-to-ankle, and packed in holds so confining that sitting upright was impossible (Cheek 1970:3). These holds have been described as filled with filth, prestilence, cruelty, disease, and death (Elkins 1963:98–101). They were chained together in their own excrement and blood for this tortuous voyage to the New World, and another large proportion died during this last phase of their journey (Redding 1950:13; Gann and Duignan 1972:325).

Slavers had two schools of thought regarding transporting slaves. These have been called the "loose packers" and the "tight packers." "Loose packers" argued that they could reduce mortality and receive a higher price for each slave by giving them a little more room, better food, and a certain amount of liberty on the Middle Passage. "Tight packers" held that even though they lost more slaves by cramming the vessel full the net receipts were greater from their larger cargo. This argument continued as long as slaving continued, but after 1750 the "tight packers" dominated the trade (Gann and Duignan 1972:325).

Conditions on a slave ship are reported by Olaudah Equiano, the son of a village elder. He was kidnapped at an early age and served as a slave on a Virginia plantation. He was later purchased by a Philadelphia merchant who allowed him to buy his freedom. He published his autobiography in 1789, and this is what he had to say about his introduction to the ship which carried him to the New World:

> [I] was filled with horrors of every kind, still heightened by my ignorance of what I was to undergo. I was not long suffered to indulge my grief; I was soon put down under the decks, and there I received such a salutation in my nostrils as I had never experienced in my life: so that with the loathsomeness of the stench and crying together, I became so sick and low that I was not able to eat, nor had I the least desire to taste anything. I now wished for the last friend, death, to relieve me; but soon, to my grief, two of the white men offered me eatables, and on my refusing to eat, one of them held me fast by the hands and laid me across I think the windlass, and tied my feet while the other flogged me severely. I had never experienced anything of this kind before, and although, not being used to the water, I naturally feared that element the first time I saw it, yet nevertheless could I have got over the nettings I would have jumped over the side, but I could not; and besides, the crew used to watch us very closely who were not chained down to the decks, lest we should leap into the water; and I have seen some of these poor African prisoners most severely cut for attempting to do so, and hourly whipped for not eating. This indeed was often the case with myself (Equiano 1967:26, as quoted in Cheek 1970:41–42).

The captives neither willingly nor passively endured such hardships and torture. Suicide was not uncommon, and slavers had to be constantly vigilant lest they lose their profits through self-inflicted death. At times a group of slaves would together snap their chains and hurl themselves overboard. Slaves would often refuse to eat while they were being transported, preferring to die from hunger than face further tortures of slavery. Because self-willed starvation became such a common practice among slaves, a special compulsory feeding device known as the *speculum oris,* or mouth opener, became standard equipment on slave ships (Cheek 1970:3). The *speculum oris* "looked like a pair of dividers with notched legs and a thumbscrew at the blunt end. The legs were closed and the notches were hammered in between the slave's teeth. When the thumbscrew tightened, the legs of the instrument separated, forcing open the slave's mouth; then food was poured into it through a funnel" (Gann and Duignan 1972:324).

The captives also actively rebelled and fought for freedom whenever they could. We have accounts of over 150 mutinies or revolts by the slaves as they were being transported from Africa. Although unlikely, slave mutinies were sometimes successful. If a successful mutiny took place while they were still in African waters, the ship was often steered ashore, looted, and demolished (Cheek 1970:3).

Punishment for even small offenses was severe. The British used a flogging instrument for ordinary offenses which was capable of taking the skin off a horse's back. Under the Black Code the French allowed punishments that included hamstringing, branding, and flogging. Anyone involved in mutiny was put to death by slow, sadistic means (Redding 1950:17). For attempting to revolt on the American slaver *Kentucky,* 47 slaves were killed in the following manner:

> They were ironed or chained, two together, and when they were hung, a rope was put around their necks and they were drawn up to the yardarm clear of the sail. This did not kill them, but only choked or strangled them. They were then shot in the breast and the bodies thrown overboard. If only one of two that were ironed together was to be hung, the rope was put around his neck and he was drawn up clear of the deck and his leg laid across the rail and chopped off to save the irons (as quoted in Redding 1950:29).

For those who survived the initial tortures of slavery, the next shock came when the formerly free landed in the New World. Here the newly imported slaves were sold at a public auction where prospective buyers could poke and prod any part of their bodies in order to make certain they were getting their money's worth.

I have emphasized the shock and brutality of capture and transportation because, first of all, it was characteristic of slavery in the New World, and, second, the fear, shock, and depersonalization the slaves underwent was extremely significant for what happened when the slaves entered the Colonies. It had a tremendous effect on their adjustment to a radically different life. Much of the past of the individual had been annihilated. Nearly every connection with his former life had been brutally severed. The slave still remembered his family and kinship arrangements, his language, his tribal religion, and the name he had once been given. But little of these memories and self-identification carried meaning for the life which he was now to enter. His old values, expectations, and way of life were no longer operative in this unreal world which he had so brutally entered against his own

With its shock, brutality, and depersonalization, with the negation of old values and the re-placement of new ones dependent upon a master class, and with dependency centering around a rule-and-reward system initiated and controlled by masters, the enslavement of blacks in the United States has been compared by some scholars to both the treatment and the reactions of Jews in the Nazi concentration camps. (Courtesy of Wide World Photos)

desires. They no longer furnished him reliable guides for conduct in everyday life. Almost everything he had previously learned, his whole past, the sum of all his experiences, was made irrelevant in one fell swoop. His destiny was now committed to one man, his master. Upon the will of this one man depended his very existence—his food, shelter, and whatever else he would receive (Elkins 1963:101–102). With its shock, brutality, and depersonalization, with the negation of old values and the replacement of new ones dependent upon a master class, with child-like dependency centering around a rule-and-reward system instituted and controlled by masters, the enslavement of blacks in the United States was not unlike both the treatment and reactions of Jews at the hands of Nazi masters in their infamous concentration camps (Elkins 1963:104–133).

The numbers so enslaved are unknown, but the estimates run from 9,000,000 to 50,000,000. With what is known about European shipping capacity, it appears that 11,000,000 is probably as close as we can come to an accurate estimate (Gann and Duignan 1972:326) (cf. Franklin 1967:58–59; Kuczynski 1936:8–15; Meier and Rudwick 1970:36). Regardless of the actual total, the trans-Atlantic slave trade represents "the greatest forcible transplantation of human beings known to history until the mass deportations and expulsions initiated by the totalitarian regimes of the twentieth century" (Gann and Duignan 1972:327).

Once transplanted to the Colonies, what was the life of a slave like? Almost everything depended on the slave's master, as the master wielded absolute power over his slaves. Slavery in the United States was among the worst the world has ever known. The slave was removed from the protection of organized society, he was not recognized as a human being, he was totally cut off from his past, he was offered absolutely no hope for the future, his children could be sold, his marriage was not recognized, he could not legally be taught to read or write, he could not practice religion without the explicit permission of his master, and every legal obstacle was put in the way of the master who wanted to free his slaves (Glazer 1963:x–xii). As slavery continued, laws to control slaves grew steadily more rigorous, and finally, masters gained absolute control over the slave's person, and a master could "whip his slaves at will, cut their rations, crop their ears, brand them, pillory them" (Redding 1950:32). Slaves had no right of assembly; they had to carry a pass to leave their master's premises; they could not own property; they could not buy, sell, or trade; they were forbidden arms and even dogs; they could not sue or be sued; and they could not give evidence against a white person. Neither were they allowed to protect themselves from whites, even when attacked and their lives were endangered.

These conditions contrast sharply with slavery in the ancient world, in medieval and early modern Europe, and even with slavery as it was practiced in Brazil at the same time that slavery existed in the United States (Glazer 1963:ix). Although blacks in Brazil were slaves twenty years longer than blacks in the United States, blacks in Brazil are not cut off from their society today but are accepted by other Brazilians. The major reason given for the difference revolves around the difference in slavery in the two nations. In Brazil slaves possessed legal rights: A slave could legally marry, he was baptized and became a member of the Roman Catholic Church, his family could not be broken up by sale, and he had certain days set aside on which he could rest or earn money to buy his freedom. Brazilian slaves could also purchase their infants' freedom for a small amount of money when they were baptized. Brazilian slaves knew they differed from their masters only in degree, not in kind (Glazer 1963:x–xii). (For a contrary opinion of Brazilian slavery, see Gann and Duignan 1972:319; Rawick 1972:126.)

Not a great deal is known about the family life of slaves in the United States, but it appears that on some plantations the stronger, healthier males were used for breeding purposes, while on other plantations men and women were allowed to live in monogamous relationships. It appears that, in general, promiscuity was encouraged. Legal marriages between slaves were not allowed, and the common marriage ceremony for monogamous relationships consisted of jumping over a broomstick. Even where monogamy was permitted, the children born of slave mothers still belonged to the master and could be sold at will. Because slave-born children were economically valuable, a pregnant woman who was to be beaten for some infraction would sometimes be laid with her stomach over a hole in the ground and then beaten (Rawick 1972:58). It was not uncommon for slave masters to cohabit with female slaves. The offspring born from such sexual alliances were almost inevitably considered not free but slave. They were sold just as though they were not the sons and daughters of the slave master.

In addition to the paucity of records from this period, it is also difficult to describe the family life of slaves because it differed depending on whether the slave was a house slave, whether he was located on a small or large plantation, whether the slave had a paternalistic or oppressive master, whether he was a slave on a large plantation in an older, settled region of the sea coast or a slave on the new frontier plantations on the Mississippi River delta. It does appear, however, that rather than an isolated, nuclear family consisting of father, mother, and children being common that a generalized, extended kinship developed among slaves. Because both the father and mother usually worked in the fields, more elderly persons would take over the role of absent parents, and older children were given much responsibility for the care of their younger brothers and sisters (Rawick 1972:91–93).

Although the slaves were forced to abandon their African life, with the social institutions to which they had become accustomed, and adapt themselves to being slaves under white masters in a new land, they formed "an Afro-American way of life that combined the thought patterns of the African heritage with the social forms and social conditions of the new land" (Rawick 1972:xix). Essential in this adaptive process was religion. Religion kept alive the desire to struggle for freedom, as well as making their daily lives more bearable. The religion of the slaves, however, was not simply a transfer of Christianity from the white masters to the black slaves. When slaves accepted Christianity, they modified it according to patterns that they had brought with them from Africa.

For example, when slaves gathered for religious rites during times not approved by their masters, especially after dark, they typically inverted an iron pot in order to deaden the sound of their singing to prevent the masters from knowing they were gathering. An iron pot placed face down on a cabin's earthen floor does not itself deaden sound, but this practice was related to a belief slaves brought with them from West Africa. In West Africa iron pots were symbols of the gods who afforded protection to men and women. The iron pot was used in Africa as an aid to worship and was connected with good health and prosperity. In this way slaves adapted an item from their past which gave them courage to gather at prayer meetings after dark. They were thus able to develop their own community, even though such meetings were prohibited by their masters and made them subject to severe punishment.

Similarly, in West Africa it was considered natural to have personal relationships with the deities:

> The Yoruba god Elegba, or Legba, is an important deity throughout West Africa. He brings divinity down to earth, intervenes directly and often mischievously in the lives of men, acts as messenger of the other gods, and announces death. . . . He causes trouble for people who offend or neglect the gods, and he does good deeds for those whom the deities wish to aid. . . . He is a sort of West African Hermes, a messenger of the gods who relates the gods to men (Rawick 1972:47).

Conversion stories told by individuals who had been forcibly enslaved frequently contain an account of a "little man" who appeared to them during a sort of trance and helped in their conversion. Thus elements from African religion became mixed with elements from Christian religion, in this case the announcer of the death of the "old self" and the bringer of good fortune or salvation in the form of a "little man." Legba and the Holy Spirit became mixed together, with both being announcers of the will of god and both serving as a link between the world of human beings and the spiritual world.

In spite of severe prohibitions to the contrary, slaves appear to have regularly gathered for their own religious services. Sometimes these were held late at night in the slave quarters; at other times they took place in outdoor meeting places, frequently in a group of trees which were considered to have magical properties. Male and female slaves would crowd together to sing, to pray, to shout, and to "get happy." Often they would slowly dance in a circle with each individual's hand on the next person's shoulder (Rawick 1972:34).

These prayer meetings were extremely important for developing feelings of unity among the slaves. The religion of slavery served as a means of continuing significant forms of black culture brought from

West Africa, gave slaves the encouragement to offer daily resistance to their enslavement, to engage in slave strikes, and to work for the Underground Railroad. Slave religion was also significant in shaping slave revolts, as we shall note below (Rawick 1972:51).

The importance of religion for the slaves did not go unnoticed by their masters. Slaves were generally expected to go to sleep at 9 P.M. since they had to get up for work by dawn and sometimes by 3:00 or 4:00 A.M. When they were caught violating the rule against holding religious services, the resulting sanctions could be quite brutal. Whipping was an ordinary part of slavery, and the whip was liberally used in order to enforce compliance with the rules. The following, for example, is an account given by Ida Henry, a former slave:

> De patrollers wouldn't allow de slaves to hold night services, and one night dey caught me mother out praying. Dey stripped her naked and tied her hands together and wid a rope tied to de handcuffs and threw one end of de rope over a limb and tied de other end to de pommel of a saddle on a horse. As me mother weighted 'bout 200, dey pulled her up so dat her toes could barely touch de ground and whipped her (as quoted in Rawick 1972:62).

Night patrollers were generally poor whites. They were used by the masters to chase runaway slaves, to punish them, and, in general, to intimidate the slave population. It was the patrollers' duty to make certain that slaves were in their quarters at night and to check the passes of slaves who were off their master's plantation. Patrollers made liberal use of fear and physical brutality to maintain compliance. Slaves were sometimes forced to witness the punishment of others as an object lesson for themselves. Mingo White, an adolescent when the Civil War began, recounted the following:

> I 'members once ol' Ned White was caught prayin'. De drivers took him de nex' day an' carried him to de pegs, what was fo' stakes drofe in de groun'. Ned was made to pull off ever'thang but his pants an' lay on his stomach 'tween de pegs whilst somebody stropped his legs an' arms to de pegs. Den day whupped him 'twell de blood run from him lack he was a hog. Dey made all of de han's come an' see it, an' dey said us'd git de same thang if us was cotched (as quoted in Rawick 1972:60).

If a plantation had any size to it, an overseer was employed. It was his job to keep slaves in line and to maintain satisfactory production. Overseers sometimes chose a strong black male and assigned him the task of administering punishment to slaves who had gotten out of line. Overseers did not have an economic investment in the slaves, as did the masters, and they were generally less concerned than the masters about the physical welfare of the slaves. It was not unknown for them to beat slaves to death, but they had to answer to the slave owner for any losses they incurred.

Not all slave masters used such severe punishment, of course, but very few did not use some form of corporal punishment. The average slave master was probably not a villainous, brutalizing individual. From the records of this period, we even know that some had abolitionist sentiments. But even paternalistic and kindly slave masters were part of a villainous, brutalizing system. By owning slaves, even those who treated their slaves well helped perpetuate the basic system of slavery, a system which can hardly be called anything but evil (Rawick 1972:66). Men of goodwill who participate in a system of evil end up perpetuating an evil system.

Basically, slaves were either field slaves or house slaves. Those who were assigned to work the fields generally received rougher treatment than those who had the privilege of working in the "Big House." House slaves were usually given better food and better clothing than field slaves because they regularly worked in the presence of their white masters and their appearance reflected on the masters' prestige. The average slave did not starve, but neither was he lavishly fed. His usual diet consisted of cornmeal, sidebacon, and molasses (Rawick 1972:68). In addition, slaves were frequently allowed to keep a small garden to supplement their diet. Occasionally slaves were allowed to raise vegetables and chickens and sell these on the open market for spending money. This, however, was not typical.

Contrary to current mythology, blacks did not passively accept their oppressed and exploited status. On the contrary, through their daily resistance to slavery they prevented themselves from becoming total victims of their oppressors. From being frightened, shocked human beings who had been savagely thrown among a strange people who did not even speak their language, when the opportunity came hundreds of thousands of slaves began a general strike. They deserted the plantations and destroyed the South's ability to supply its army. Over two hundred thousand blacks joined the Union Army, allowing the North to take the military initiative after the battle of Gettysburg and win the war (Rawick 1972:96). How did men and women who became culturally disoriented through being brutally brought across the Atlantic in the holds of slave ships and dumped as captives among hostile strangers come to take part in striking off their own shackles?

Knowing what slavery is like, it seems needless to say that no one would enjoy being a slave. Yet the myth has been perpetuated that blacks, though deprived, were relatively content with their lot in life.

The image of the happy-go-lucky, carefree negro being provided his needs in life by a benevolent, though perhaps strict, master still persists. Though there were kind masters to whom their slaves became devoted, some even refusing to leave their plantations after the abolition of slavery, such situations were far from typical.

Blacks did not like slavery any more than whites would enjoy being enslaved and having another as the total master of one's fate. As early as 1663 black slaves in Gloucester County, Virginia, joined in a conspiracy to rebel with white indentured servants. The plot was discovered, and the ringleaders were drawn and quartered. Their bloody heads were impaled on posts for the public to gaze at and to serve as an object lesson to other slaves and indentured servants. In 1687 the leaders plotting a slave revolt in three Virginia counties were also discovered and put to death. By 1710 slaves had been involved in a dozen revolts from Virginia and Maryland to New Jersey and Massachusetts.

Besides revolts, slaves would sometimes use arson as a form of retaliation. In 1712, slaves set fire to buildings in New York, then killed nine whites who attempted to put out the flames. Nearly twenty slaves were apprehended and sentenced to die, one being put to death "by slow fire" (Redding 1950:28–29). Another form of slave rebellion was the killing of their oppressors, and in Virginia alone thirty-one slaves were executed between 1786 and 1810 for killing their masters and overseers (Cheek 1970:17, 20).

Most resistance to slavery by blacks was not of such dramatic scope as armed rebellion or arson, however, but it was a sort of daily disaffection—mocking, being passive, dawdling, pretending to be sick and not to understand, or see, or hear. It was primarily a form of passive resistance continually carried on by the slaves in rejection of their own bondage. Slaves would run away when they had the chance, stealthily leaving the plantation and heading North for desired freedom. Running away became so common that the listing of runaway slave advertisements became a regular feature of southern newspapers. Another act of resistance was sabotage in the form of breaking tools. Slaves "accidentally" broke so many hoes, for example, that a heavier and work-slowing hoe had to be substituted. This, in spite of the fact that the hoe was one of the basic tools of West African agriculture (Cheek 1970: 17, 20).

When the Revolutionary War broke out, blacks fought on both sides. Some slaves in New England were freed to fight, while others fought as substitutes for their masters. The first American to die in the Revolutionary War was Crispus Attucks, an escaped slave. Another slave, Peter Salem, killed the British major Pitcairn at Bunker Hill. Lord Dunmore, the Royal Governor of Virginia, promised freedom to blacks who would fight for the British, and he armed slaves to fight against their masters. George Washington at first opposed the enlistment of blacks in the Continental Army, but as the military situation deteriorated he gave in and allowed freed slaves to fight with him. As the war situation grew still more desperate, the Colonies themselves further relaxed their enlistment policy, and whole battalions of blacks enlisted in New Hampshire, Massachusetts, and Rhode Island. Others were promised their freedom and served from Maryland, New York, Virginia, and North Carolina. Blacks served throughout the war—at Ticonderoga, Bemis Heights, Stony Point. They were with Lafayette. Rhode Island blacks "sacrificed themselves to the last man" in defense of an important position at Point Bridge, New York. A black, Mark Starlin, commanded the Virginia naval vessel *Patriot*. Other blacks served on the *Royal Lewis,* the *Tempest,* and the *Diligence.* Blacks crossed the Delaware with Washington and died at Valley Forge. The only woman who bore arms with the Continental Army was a black, Deborah Gannett.

Black participation in the Revolutionary War was a travesty on justice, however, since slaves fought to win for others a freedom which they themselves could not enjoy. This became apparent beyond all doubt when after the Revolution the Constitutional Convention was held in 1787. Major issues facing the Convention were the taxation of imports, proportional representation, and slavery. Benjamin Franklin brought with him an anti-slavery resolution prepared by the Pennsylvania Society for Promoting the Abolition of Slavery. The debate dragged on for four months, and when the Constitution was finally agreed upon "the humanitarian light of the revolution was blown out in fearful compromise" (Redding 1950:44). A slave was to be counted as 3/5 of a person for purposes of representation and taxation; slave importation was to be allowed until 1808; and escaped slaves, even though they had fled to a nonslave state, were to be returned to their masters. Such was the payment returned to blacks for their sacrificial service in helping the Colonies gain freedom from England.

Slaves were forced to continue their fight for freedom in this land where justice was so prized that people were willing to die rather than be taxed without representation. The largest slave revolt in the United States was organized by Gabriel Prosser. He planned the revolt for months with the aid of his wife, his brothers, and another slave, Jack Bowler. He recruited somewhere around a thousand slaves, some of whom had gained military skills in the Revolutionary War. His plan was to attack on the night of August 20, 1800, to kill the whites in the neighborhood of the plantation on which he was a slave, with the exception of the French and the Quakers. He then planned to take over the city of Richmond. By setting fires as a diversionary tactic, he planned on seizing the arsenal and State House and then establishing a black monarchy. Their flag was to bear the legend "liberty or death." On the appointed night, approximately a thousand slaves rendezvoused six miles from Richmond, but a tremendous wind and rainstorm came up which swept away bridges, blew down houses, turned the roads to mud, and made progress to Richmond impossible. The insurrectionists pledged to rendezvous later, and then scattered. They had already been betrayed, however, and troops were waiting for them in the city of Richmond. When the scope of the conspiracy later became known, the city and state went into a panic and martial law was declared. Blacks were arrested indiscriminately by the militia, and some were hanged as soon as they were caught. Prosser escaped, but he was again betrayed, and on October 7, 1800, he was hanged with fifteen others before a wildly cheering mob (Redding 1950:48–50).

In 1804 slaves rebelled in Haiti under the leadership of Toussaint L'Ouverture. They killed perhaps 2000 whites and destroyed hundreds of sugar, coffee, cotton, and indigo plantations. Under his leadership they defeated the British, the Spanish, and finally the French. After a ten-year revolt France reluctantly granted freedom to all slaves loyal to France, and Haiti became a black republic (cf. Cheek 1970:23; Redding 1950:46–47). The lesson was not lost upon whites on the continent, who became fearfully aware of the potential retaliatory power of the slaves in their midst.

Why were there not more slave rebellions in the South? There was, first of all, ordinarily great distance between plantations. This made it difficult to assemble large groups in order to organize, plan, and then carry out insurrection (Cheek 1970:8). Some slaves were also rewarded with being chosen as house slaves, and were reluctant to risk their higher status and their better physical treatment. Others hoped for such a "lucky break," and along with those who had attained these positions felt they had less to gain by rebelling. Safety valves were also sometimes added to the American form of slavery in order to prevent explosive slave outbreaks, with slaves sometimes being permitted to hold religious services, to keep a garden, or to hire themselves out for wages. On holidays, especially at Christmas, slaves were encouraged to overeat and get drunk.

A primary factor, however, in increasing the difficulty to plan and organize rebellions was the Machiavellian way the slavery system was set up to discourage intimacy, communication, and solidarity among slaves. When they arrived from Africa, lines of communication were crippled by the practice of separating from each other slaves who spoke the same native tongue and attempting to put on the same plantation only slaves who spoke different African languages. Further, kinship groupings were purposely disrupted by encouraging promiscuity, by forbidding marriage, and by selling children born in slavery for servitude on distant plantations. The communication and trust so essential for carrying out a rebellion was also significantly blocked by encouraging and rewarding spying (Cheek 1970:8). A century or so later the Chinese communists applied a similar technique to their prisoners. Coupled with a reward system controlled by the captors, the encouragement of spying on one's own fellows in order to attain deferential treatment was found to be a highly successful technique for breaking down prisoner solidarity among American POW's in Korea. It appears that this technique was also successful when used by American slave masters.

The extensive police system set up in the South was also significant in helping prevent slave revolts. The patrollers were constantly at work, eager to wreck bloody vengeance on the slave populace at the first sign of resistance. The South at this time was like an armed camp, with manned towers, patrollers with guns, passes being checked, fear endemic and rumors flying. Immediately following a slave revolt, blacks, both men and women, would be strung up in chains. Their heads would be sliced off and attached to poles for public display. Slaves learned quite early what the penalty would be if they rebelled (Cheek 1970:9).

Slaves had to rely primarily on indirect techniques, the passive resistance and noncooperation discussed above. But when the opportunity came, slaves fought, and fought hard. The victory of the North in the Civil War was greatly aided by the service of blacks. In addition to the 200,000 blacks who served in the Northern Army, the 29,000 blacks serving in the Union Navy made up one fourth of the entire navy enrollment. Tens of thousands of other blacks worked for the army as laborers and teamsters. Additionally, thousands of slaves risked their lives by engaging in strikes upon the plantations, refusing to work to supply the southern system. A strike anytime carried heavy penalties, but a strike during war was easily viewed as treason. The abolitionist movement was dominated by freedmen (former slaves or descendants of former slaves) who provided homes, churches, and food for abolitionist lecturers. The slave community also helped the northern war effort and demonstrated solidarity with the cause by aiding Union soldiers who had escaped from southern prisoner of war camps (Rawick 1972:111, 114).

It is important to emphasize that slavery in the United States was not at first based on racism. Slavery was initially based on perceived economic necessity, as I have outlined, on the necessity people felt for cheap labor to work the sugar plantations in Latin America and in the

Caribbean and the tobacco and cotton plantations in the Colonies (Williams 1966:23). Any cheap labor would do: It did not by any means have to be black labor. It was only after Indians failed as slaves and there were not enough white indentured servants to satisfy labor needs that the colonists turned to the black labor supply.

The first blacks brought to the Colonies were not slaves in the same sense as were blacks who were later imported. The first blacks were indentured servants. Like indentured whites, after serving the required period of indentureship these blacks were able to claim land. Anthony Johnson, for example, was a black who himself imported 500 indentured servants and on the basis of their headrights was granted 250 acres (Redding 1950:133).

As slavery gained more of a foothold in the Colonies, the economic system of the South began to depend increasingly on slavery. To maintain slaves in their slave status, by 1640 newly imported blacks were removed from their indentured status and placed in perpetual or lifelong servitude (Redding 1950:23). Both religious and secular teachings were developed to support the changed status of blacks from indentured servants to perpetual slaves. These teachings centered around the view that whites were inherently superior to blacks. As blacks were demonstrably heathen, the Christian precepts of kindness, charity, and humane dealing did not apply. To forestall escape from slavery by conversion to Christianity, it was also decreed that "Baptism doth not alter the condition of the person as to his bondage or freedom" (Redding 1950:25). Blacks became categorized as a people inherently inferior to whites and thus as persons who had less rights than whites. *Racism, then, was the consequence of slavery rather than slavery being the consequence of racism.*

Why should racism have developed from slavery? As I have presented above, racism, like slavery, was based on economics. The need to maintain cheap labor led to a rationale for keeping blacks in perpetual slavery. A contrary view has also been advanced (Rawick 1972:125–149). It is theorized that Europeans, with their peasant background, were once quite similar to the slaves they later imported. When their livelihood had been agriculturally based, they were more expressive, both emotionally and sexually. Work was a rhythmic part of their lives, blending in with other activities. With industrialization, work became separated from other aspects of daily life. Industrialization requires steady output on the part of workers. When machines must be run, workers must be able to be depended on to be present. This requires the repression of nonrational desires, subordinating them to work. Sexual desires, consequently, became more restrained, and a sort of new personality emerged in response to the new organization and dominance of work. Previous behavior patterns (nonrational expressivity) became defined as sinful, while their opposites (controlled emotions) were made into virtues. When the English met the Africans, it was like a reformed sinner uncomfortably confronting someone who is contentedly engaging in behavior one has just overcome. The English congratulated themselves on being both different and superior. They then looked at blacks who were both emotionally and sexually more expressive as inferior to them.

Regardless of the exact process by which racism emerged from slavery, its emergence has profoundly affected the life of the nation. When slavery ended in the United States, racism became the means by which relations between the races were regulated. This new racism called for the *segregation* of blacks from whites, which was in marked contrast to the social contacts which had been allowed masters and slaves during slavery. When white dominance of the South was threatened by blacks following the end of the Civil War, the Ku Klux Klan sprang up in order to preserve white institutional superiority. The Ku Klux Klan fostered and enforced racism in many areas of social life. One of their aims was to prevent white males from having sexual relations with black females, an act which during slavery had been quasi-sanctioned (Rawick 1972:145). Eventually a whole system of racist laws was passed in order to minimize contact between blacks and whites in almost every walk of life.

This racism is the primary legacy we have inherited from our slave past, a racism which so thoroughly pervades American culture that it still affects us all. Though institutionalized slavery is long gone, its legacy remains. It is to an examination of that legacy of racism to which we shall now turn.

chapter 17

Maintaining Social Control: Racism

Although the end of slavery in the United States was anything but the end of racism, a major difference exists between racism during slavery and racism following slavery. That difference centers around the idea of "equality." Racism during slavery had no overlay whatsoever of ideas of equality between blacks and whites. Blacks under slavery were not even considered human: They had no constitutional rights, and they were bought and sold on the open market as though they were cattle. Whites considered themselves superior and were dominant, while blacks were considered inferior and were subordinant. There was no question of blacks and whites being on the same plane, just as today we do not question whether dogs or farm animals belong on the same level as human beings. Blacks were private property, imported for the sole purpose of serving the superordinant whites.

Racism in the United States today, however, operates under the veneer of equality. Blacks have constitutional rights equal to all other people in our society: Color is no longer a legal basis for differential and discriminatory treatment. Yet, since the end of slavery blacks have traditionally been treated as subhuman, and even in our present era racism remains one of the fundamental forms of social control in American society. It is not as though we still have "remnants" or "pockets" of racism within our society. Rather, our society is thoroughly racist from beginning to end. Whites in general still consider themselves to be superior and are dominant, while blacks are still considered inferior and remain generally subordinant to whites in all walks of life.

Any person growing up in the United States learns racism as a normal part of becoming an American. **Racism** is the association of be-havioral characteristics with racial, ethnic, or other social group mem-bership. Although in the United States preconceived notions of what others are like are frequently based upon skin color, racism is by no means this limited. For example, imputing behavioral characteristics to people because of their social group membership is also commonly done in the case of sex. We shall, however, deal with that form of rac-ism in the following two chapters. We shall focus in this chapter on the more common connotation of the term, that of imputing behavioral characteristics to people on the basis of skin color.

Having a racist orientation is by no means limited to whites or to members of any particular race. We all learn to categorize others as possessing particular attributes on the basis of their skin color. This leads whites to expect certain behaviors from blacks they have never even met, expectations based upon their presumed racial character-istics. Blacks also learn a similar racist orientation to life as they grow up in American society. They learn to think of whites, even whites whom they have never met, as having certain characteristics *because* they are white.

Certainly we do not all learn to treat people badly on the basis of race, and not all of us learn to hate or to refuse to associate with others solely on the basis of skin color. But because race is a major concept in American culture, all of us learn to categorize people on the basis of race. As part of the very air we breathe, while we are growing up in our society we learn a racial consciousness which has as its fundamental proposition that people of other races possess certain characteristics *because* they are members of a particular race or *because* they have a par-ticular skin color. Within this framework of racial consciousness, while we are still children we learn to place others into racial categories. We learn to think of a person as a black, as a white, or whatever. We then tend to hold expectations of other persons based on how we categorize them by race.

Contemporary racism in our more "enlightened" era is often covert. It is a non-conscious orientation which subtly, but thoroughly, pervades our thinking, our way of looking at the world, and especially the ways by which we categorize and react to others. Stereotypes of persons of other races abound, and although through experience many of us learn that stereotypes only imperfectly match reality, even when we reject racial stereotypes part of their emotional and cognitive content is likely to remain. Every time the picture of a black is linked with a vio-lent crime in our mass media, subtle and not so subtle ideas of racism are reinforced in the minds of whites. Every time a ghetto black is roughed up or even "stopped for suspicion" by a white policeman, subtle and not so subtle ideas of racism are reinforced in the minds of blacks. Such is the nature of American society. We grow up surrounded by racism to such a pervasive degree that it is almost impossible for a member of our society not to hold preconceived notions of what others are like solely on the basis of their racial membership.

As we have previously covered in several other contexts, the ways by which we categorize the world influence not only our ways of thinking about the world, but also, ultimately, our ways of acting towards our world. Our categories of thought are the fundamentals of our symbolic system. These categories help determine what we perceive, what we feel, and how we act.

So it also is with relationships between races. If we learn to apply particular conceptualizations to persons with certain racial or ethnic characteristics, we then tend to perceive the very characteristics called for by the conceptualization. For example, if whites are taught that blacks are dirty, ignorant, and lazy, they tend to perceive these characteristics when they see blacks. If blacks are taught that whites are untrustworthy, selfish, and bigoted, so they tend to see whites. The same with our other common racial conceptualizations or stereotypes, whether Orientals are thought of as sneaky, Indians as drunkards, Chicanos as dumb, Puerto Ricans as immoral, or Jews as greedy. If such characteristics of others are widely agreed upon by members of one's own group, we then tend to feel that there must be a solid basis for ascribing those characteristics.

We learn to think of others in terms of race, which prepares us to perceive the characteristics called for by racial stereotypes. In the absence of extensive, intimate interaction with members of other racial groupings, it takes but few positive cases to confirm such negative conceptualizations. For someone who does not become well acquainted with members of other racial groupings, the stereotype is confirmed by a single unemployed black, discriminatory white redneck, cheating Japanese, drunk Indian, illiterate Mexican-American, Puerto Rican pimp, or Jewish pawnshop owner. And in our racially divided society, few of us ever get to know members of other racial groups well. Few of us become involved in interracial interaction that goes beyond the school, the job, or participating in sports. Some of us never even get beyond racial presentations on television. It is rare in our society for members of one racial grouping to gain intimate firsthand experience with members of other racial groupings in such a way that they are able to transcend experiences at work or school, in sports, or on television. As our society is presently constructed, few of us are able to participate with members of other racial groups as they pray at church, socialize at their clubs, drink at their bars, or are at home eating meals, relaxing with their families, planning for the future, dealing with family crises, and otherwise handling the joys and sorrows of intimate life.

As long as we attribute behavioral characteristics to people on the basis of their racial membership, we have a racist orientation. This is true even though the characteristics which we ascribe and perceive are positive, such as blacks being naturally rhythmic, Indians having the ability to perceive sham, Orientals being thrifty, whites industrious, Chicanos religious, Puerto Ricans loyal to their families, or Jews being intelligent. Regardless of whether the characteristics ascribed are negative or positive, it is racism as long as the basis for ascribing characteristics is membership in a racial or ethnic group.

And how can we not so ascribe and perceive characteristics when from birth we are constantly surrounded by such ideas? Only by contrary experiences can we overcome categorizing people on the basis of race, and our society is structured in such a way that intimate interracial contact is held at a minimum. Lack of informal contact breathes life into stale stereotypes. Having grown up in a society as racist as ours, for most persons it is perhaps only possible to partially overcome this way of thought. And even when individuals attain nonracist ways of categorizing the world, the social institutions of American society retain their vigorous contemporary forms of racism and continue to further racist thought, perception, and practices among our people.

One of the most negative aspects of racism is discrimination by members of one racial grouping which has greater power against those having less power. As we covered in Chapters 3 and 16, whites in the United States have not solely directed their discrimination only against blacks. The American Indian was the first to feel the lash of racism from those who were later to be called Americans. Although Indians befriended the first settlers and helped them survive the harsh New England climate, Indians were later reacted to on a racial basis. They became categorized as inferior to whites, their enslavement was attempted, their lands were taken, and they were forcibly driven westward. When they did not want to leave their tribal lands, they were forced to do so at gunpoint. They were systematically exterminated as the Anglos continued their relentless westward trek. They were eventually secluded by the interlopers to areas called reservations, where they were forced to live as aliens in the land which had for centuries been their home. When reservation lands later became desirable to whites, even though they had been assigned by the Congress of the United States in perpetuity to the Indians, the treaties were systematically broken and under the superior firepower of the U.S. Cavalry the Indians were forced to even less desirable areas. After their traditional means of livelihood had been exterminated by the whites, they were then left to exist in despairing poverty.

Racism has taken many forms in the United States. During World War II, in an action sanctioned by the Supreme Court, solely on the basis of their racial ancestry Americans whose loyalty had not been disproven were rounded up and interred in concentration camps. (Courtesy of Wide World Photos)

While whites did not enslave Orientals, their immigration to the United States was encouraged so that they might supply the labor so direly needed in the Anglos' frenetic expansion westward. Unskilled labor in vast quantities was especially needed for building railroads to the West. When the railroads were completed, Oriental labor was no longer needed, and as we covered in Chapter 3, Orientals became another racial outgroup. The outcry of "Yellow Peril" replaced their earlier welcome. Legislation was directed against further Asiatic immigration. Violent riots against persons whose skin color was yellow exploded in western cities. In World War II, concentration camps were set up for Americans of Japanese ancestry. These Americans, whose loyalty had not been disproven, were forced to sell their businesses at tremendous loss, quit their jobs, leave their schools, uproot their families, and were then interned in concentration camps—solely because of their racial ancestry. This barbaric action directed against a people because of their race was later sanctioned by the Supreme Court of the United States.

Similarly, Chicanos, or Mexican-Americans, have been victimized by our endemic racism. Chicanos also have never been physically enslaved in the United States, nor have they been placed in concentration camps because of their ancestry. But they also have suffered from a long history of social discrimination and economic exploitation. About five and a half million Chicanos form a largely invisible minority group in our midst. Most of them live in the southwestern part of the United States, where they are systematically discriminated against in jury selection, at the hands of the police, in voting, in employment, in housing and in education. Chicanos experience an additional aspect of contemporary racism. They are subject to harassment and humiliation at the whim of immigration authorities. This sometimes takes the form of forceful invasion of their homes and search and seizure in public places (*Civil Liberties, 299,* November 1973). Chicanos are also ordinarily segregated into barrios, or slums, which are as equally depressing as those in which inner-city blacks live. The latest group to experience discrimination on the basis of race is the Puerto Ricans. They live primarily in the New York City area and are discriminated against not only by whites but also by blacks.

Although racism in the United States is directed against many groups, in this chapter we shall focus primarily on racism and blacks because blacks are the largest minority group which directly and consistently feels the effects of racism today. It should be kept in mind that what is true of racism directed against blacks also applies, with some modification, to a number of other minority groups in the United States.

As is well known, the so-called "separate but equal" doctrine prevailed in the United States until the Supreme Court made its landmark decision in 1954. Blacks and whites were taught in segregated schools. These schools, although separate, were supposedly equal. The Supreme Court of the United States rejected this doctrine and practice in 1954 on the basis that racial segregation means racial inequality. It is perhaps not insignificant that part of the argument heard by the Supreme Court was presented by the then Secretary of State, Dean Acheson, who spoke of the embarrassment in international relations caused by the doctrine. He said:

> The continuation of racial discrimination in the United States remains a source of constant embarrassment to this government in the day-to-day conduct of its foreign relations; and it jeopardizes the effective maintenance of our moral leadership of the free and democratic nations of the world (Bennett 1965:220).

A year later the Supreme Court ordered the desegregation of public schools "with all deliberate speed." As has been often noted, this ruling was carried out with more "deliberateness" than "speed." By the fall of 1968 only 23 percent of black students attended schools with a white majority. Even after fourteen years, in the eleven states of the old Confederacy the percentage of blacks in majority white schools was only eighteen, while in the northern and western states integration was somewhat higher, but it was only approximately 27 percent. Mississippi ranked last among the fifty states with 6.7 percent of its black pupils in majority white schools. Following intensified pressures from the federal government, racial integration in southern schools jumped to 84 percent by 1970. At the same time, however, integration remained at a steady rate of 27 percent in the northern and western states. Some of the larger cities in the North even experienced declines in the percentage of blacks in majority white schools. In St. Louis, for example, where blacks make up 65.6 percent of the school population, the percentage of blacks in majority white schools declined from 7.1 to 2.5 percent. From 1968 to 1970 declines were also recorded in most major cities in the North including Kansas City, New York, Chicago, Detroit, Philadelphia, Cleveland, Milwaukee, Columbus, Indianapolis, Boston, San Francisco, Cincinnati, Seattle, Minneapolis, and St. Paul (*St. Louis Post-Dispatch,* June 18, 1971; *Statistical Abstracts of the U.S.,* 1972, Table 180). Another way of understanding these figures is to note that only one third of all black students across the country attend schools in which whites compose the majority, while over a third of our black students attend schools which are from 95 to 100 percent black (*Statistical Abstracts of the U.S.,* 1972, Table 184).

Racial segregation in schools of the North is a form of *de facto* segregation. Segregation in the North today is not based on a dual school system for blacks and whites, but it is largely due to our prevailing racial segregation in housing. When school districts follow neighborhood lines, racially segregated neighborhoods lead to racially segregated schools. Gerrymandering of neighborhood boundaries, however, in order to maintain racial segregation in the public schools is not unknown.

Expenditures per pupil vary widely from school to school within urban school systems. Even today, schools which are predominantly black tend to spend less per pupil than schools which are predominantly white. Disparities in instructional appropriations sometimes amount to as much as a two-to-one racial imbalance—and the direction of the imbalance does not favor minority students. Such disproportionate appropriations, as in the Chicago public school system, regularly operate to the disadvantage of students from poor neighborhoods, whether they are white or black (*The Brief,* May and November 1971). The courts have been examining this inequality in per-pupil expenditures. In Washington, D.C., the courts have ordered the district school board to equalize per-pupil expenditures among all Washington, D.C., schools within a variation of no more than 5 percent (*Civil Liberties, 282,* December 1971). Thus "equality" when applied to the education of minority groups in the United States' public schools does not exist even today. Our public schools are part and parcel of the racist and social class discriminatory system which pervades the United States.

Texts used in public schools have also come under fire for being part of the racist orientation of American life. When gains attained by civil rights activists are mentioned in social studies texts, they are frequently pointed out as being part of the inevitable justice and progress of the democratic system, not as gains made through the bitter and often bloody struggles of those who have been systematically discriminated against and others who have joined in those efforts (Kane 1970:78). Even the way in which we are taught to read in the American public school system frequently socializes us into a racist approach to life. The texts by which reading is taught sometimes promote racial prejudice and racial stereotypes. Children's readers are supposedly devoted to teaching the value-free subject of reading. They sometimes, however, present whites as leaders, members of a "sturdy race," and as persons who are doing good things for blacks, while blacks are pictured as a less knowledgeable, subordinant people. In a reading text which was widely used in the Boston public school system, for example, black was depicted in negative terms, while white was associated with positive attributes (Kozol 1967).

I.Q. testing is something which American school children at an early age learn to take for granted as part of school life. We usually begin testing I.Q.'s when children enter the first grade and continue intermittently thereafter. Few of us ever question the necessity of such testing, much less critically examine the tests themselves. Only now are the social class and racist implications of our intelligence testing becoming generally apparent. The I.Q. tests commonly used are administered in standard English and heavily emphasize middle class experiences. The social class bias includes asking children from poverty homes questions about writing checks, when their parents have no bank account. They are expected to know the color of jewels which they have never seen and perhaps have never heard of, as jewels are, to put it mildly, certainly not one of their major possessions. They are also expected to be knowledgeable about the authors of a classical literature to which they have never been exposed. Since blacks, Chicanos, Indians, and Puerto Ricans are more likely to be poor than are whites, these tests not only

favor the middle class and wealthy, but in doing so they also disproportionately discriminate against nonwhites.

The standardized English in which the tests are given biases in a similar way. Spanish-speaking children actually take an intelligence test in
a foreign language, since many of them do not learn English at home.
A similar situation holds for blacks. Although blacks learn English at
home, it is a form of English which differs markedly from the standard
English spoken in white middle class homes. It is not simply that blacks
learn a different pronunciation of the same English, but Black English
is in itself "a bona fide language system with its own rules of grammar,
vocabulary, and structure" (Haskins and Butts 1973:40). I.Q. tests,
however, are standardized for the middle and upper class experiences
in learning the English language, and they are consequently culturally
biased against minority children. As a result, minority children are
disproportionately classified as slow learners and even as mentally retarded. Nine Chicano children who had been classified as mentally retarded brought suit against the state of California on this basis. When
they were retested in Spanish, eight scored *above* the mentally retarded
level. They achieved even higher scores on a nonverbal intelligence
test. The settlement provided for retesting 22,000 California Chicano
children who had been declared mentally retarded on the basis of
English-language I.Q. tests. Additionally, part of the settlement
directed the state to seek ways to measure intelligence which are free of
cultural bias (*The Brief,* February 1971).

The results of racism are devastating. Not only are blacks, like other
minority groups, discriminated against in education, but contemporary
racism also rears its ugly head in housing, employment, income, the
criminal justice system, the military, and medical care. The legacy of
slavery has been passed on to these and many other areas of contemporary American life.

When blacks were slaves, they lived in one-room shacks. Although
their housing has improved considerably since that time, this legacy
from slavery has remained with us, and blacks are still disproportionately characterized by inadequate housing. In our urban areas, blacks
are generally shunted off into the decaying inner-city, where housing is
markedly inferior to that of the newer suburban areas to which whites
are frantically fleeing. Proportionately far fewer blacks than whites are
assisted by the Federal Housing Administration (FHA). Less than 2
percent of all housing with mortgages insured by the FHA since 1934
and by the Veterans Administration since 1944 have gone to nonwhite
families. FHA insured housing has provided about ten million units for
persons from middle and upper incomes, while it has produced less

than one million units for the disadvantaged. Blacks in the city of Chicago were able to occupy less than one half of one percent of the 280,000 new homes constructed there during the 1950's.

Density is another indicator of relative housing conditions. In 1900 both blacks and whites averaged 4.8 persons per housing unit. By 1950 the density per housing unit for whites declined to 3.3 persons, while for nonwhites the decline was only from 4.8 to 3.9. By 1960 blacks generally found themselves living in more seriously overcrowded conditions than they had experienced in 1950. (Comparable figures are not available for 1970.) Probably the worst overcrowding occurs in Harlem. It has been estimated that if the rest of New York City was as densely populated as some of Harlem's worst blocks the entire population of the United States could fit into just three of New York's boroughs (Willhelm 1970:109–111; *Statistical Abstracts of the United States,* 1971, Tables 1109 and 1110; 1972, Table 1155; *General Population Characteristics, 1970 Census,* Tables 2 and 6).

Urban renewal has sometimes been hailed as the panacea for such overcrowding. But urban renewal has also been called by its critics "negro removal," and with good reason. When slum dwellings are cleared out, thousands of poor families are displaced. What typically happens is that the displaced families move into adjacent slum areas, merely adding to the overcrowded conditions there. Moreover, if new homes are built in place of the old ones, they are ordinarily beyond the means of those who have been displaced. This applies not only to blacks, but also to Italians, Jews, Poles, Irish, Albanians, Ukranians, Greeks, and Gypsies, as in the case of an urban renewal project in the city of Boston. In this particular case, rent for the new dwelling units increased to *twelve times* the rent charged prior to the urban renewal project (Gans 1962:308–317).

When blacks attempt to leave the inner city, they encounter considerable obstacles purposely placed in their path in order to keep them confined to the ghetto, to the "new reservations." In the St. Louis suburbs, for example, construction was begun on a moderate income 214-family housing project. In order to gain the power to pass zoning laws to keep out blacks, the suburban area in which it was to be built incorporated as the city of Black Jack. Black Jack then rezoned the area, banning the project (*Civil Liberties, 282,* December 1971). Another case in a different St. Louis suburb which has been personally reported to me involved a wealthy black. He had amassed much money through many years in the junk business, and he purchased a lot in an exclusive suburb of St. Louis. This suburb was inhabited solely by wealthy white professional and business people. He was about ready to start construction on his dream home when he was informed by city officials that he must sell his property because the city had just decided that it should be turned into a playground. He was told that if he didn't cooperate the city would begin condemnation proceedings. He thought it over and acquiesced in the face of this show of white power. After he disposed of the property, however, no such rezoning was attempted.

Obstacles to adequate housing for blacks are not always this dramatic, of course. Pressure to contain blacks and other minority group members within particular areas of a metropolitan area is usually much more subtle. A fairly common real estate practice used for this purpose in the United States is double listings. In double listings a realtor carries two sets of books, one for "desirable" clients and one for "undesirables." Dwellings in areas from which "undesirables" are to be excluded are not listed in the offerings shown members of minority groups. When a single listing is used, realtors who desire to discriminate against minority groups frequently use two sets of prices. One is the officially listed price which they show everyone. Nonwhites are told that the price is firm, while clients deemed "desirable" for the neighborhood are privately informed that they would be able to purchase the home for several thousand dollars less. Similarly, "private listings" are used in order to get around real estate sales laws. A large suburb close to the university at which I teach avoids integration by keeping most of its listings private. They are "private" only to certain categories of persons, however, and public to the rest. Persons who desire to purchase or to rent dwellings learn by word of mouth whom to see. As these persons are not officially realtors but are simply "handling things for friends," by means of this simple technique they bypass laws forbidding racial discrimination in housing.

On the other hand, steps taken to geographically contain blacks in our contemporary United States are sometimes even more dramatic. In the area in which I am teaching, for example, a black woman recently bought a home in a previously all-white neighborhood. It did not take long before she began receiving telephone threats. Cars staffed by white men began to slowly drive by her home. The police refused to assist her even after her children's lives were threatened. Her garage was burned down, and for her own and her children's security she was forced to keep armed guards inside her home at all times. The pressure continued, finally became too great, and she moved. It should be noted that this incident occurred in Illinois, one of our northern states in which we supposedly have less prejudice and discrimination and greater opportunity for blacks. It should also be noted that in our contemporary United States such an incident is by no means an isolated one.

Blacks also face discrimination in employment because they are black—and not only on the part of management. Even labor unions discriminate against black membership, jealously preserving for whites apprenticeship programs which lead to employment in the higher paying crafts. Although the American labor movement supposedly stands for all laboring people, since their founding labor unions have systematically discriminated against blacks. White labor has been fearful of black gains at its expense and has systematically excluded blacks from its membership. During World War I production demands in the face of a tightened labor market forced changes in this area:

> The war economy required the hiring of nonwhites in previously all-white jobs, thus encouraging a black exodus out of the South's agricultural economy into the North's booming industrial market. The economic needs of America's war efforts and harsh economic circumstances made worse by the cotton boll weevil plague and washouts of cotton crops by widespread floods, enticed Negroes by the millions to migrate to the less-abusive North. Many Negroes traded the mule and hoe for employment in Northern factories: 300,000 entered manufacturing; 100,000 joined the ranks of transportation and communication workers; almost 75,000 became miners. . . .
>
> . . . The economic dislocation of the war brought in its wake not only a black migration but also a black awareness. Race consciousness developed among Negroes in readjusting to new economic and unfamiliar racial conditions. This two-fold alteration instilled a degree of restlessness within the Negro mass that would set the stage for the entrance of Garveyism in the 1920's. DuBois headlined his newspaper, *Crisis:* "We return! We return from fighting! We return fighting!" The tone alarmed whites.
>
> Perceiving a threat to their racial domination, whites met blacks in vicious and bloody race riots that swept across the cities of the nation. In the countryside, whites confronted Negro recalcitrance through terror lynchings. Twenty-six race riots erupted during the Red Summer of 1919; 83 lynchings occurred in 1919. Such physical assaults provided visible proof of White America's determination to rule over Black America. Whites returning from the war front replaced the Negroes who had taken over their jobs during their absence. Negroes vanished from the industrial work force as the manpower shortage of the war vanished. The government cleansed itself of black inroads made during the war years; Negroes, for example, were removed as postmen and policemen. Labor unions expressed boldly and pressed vigorously against Negro employment (Willhelm 1970:68–70).

Only recently, with the forceful prodding of the federal government by threatening to withhold funds from building projects, have blacks

Although power confrontations have been successful in ridding our society of its most glaring, overt forms of discrimination, racism is still deep-rooted in our social institutions: It sometimes takes little to bring into the open such feelings of racial bias and superiority. (Courtesy of Wide World Photos)

been allowed to enter certain skilled building and trade unions. Even into the 1970's, many labor unions and construction companies have maintained their racial discrimination, with some being forcefully desegregated by means of law suits and picket lines. Some contractors doing business with the federal government have been ordered to hire only blacks until their labor force reaches an assigned arbitrary "racial balance." In one situation brought to my attention by a laborer working on the project, a Washington, D.C., contractor has attempted to forestall compliance by working his present white employees overtime. This avoids the necessity of hiring new workers. Though this action presents mounting problems for him in production scheduling and job completion, this contractor's racism is so deeply embedded that he would rather put up with these difficulties than hire blacks. Under these conditions, however, and with worker attrition, he is engaged only in a holding action.

It is not only in hiring that blacks face economic discrimination, for once on the job the racial equation still operates. Racial discrimination in promotion practices, for example, occurs in both private business and in our governmental bureaucracies. In one case which reached the courts, for example, more than $30,000 was awarded to fourteen persons who had been found victims of racial discrimination in promotions in just the Washington, D.C., Department of Licenses and Inspections (*Civil Liberties, 282,* December 1971). In another suit Detroit Edison was found guilty of deliberate racial discrimination in both hiring and promotions. Detroit Edison was assessed $4,000,000 for restitution and punitive damages. They were also ordered to begin a compensatory hiring and promotion program (*Civil Liberties, 299,* November 1973).

Though unions and mangement are traditional enemies, much of this enmity today is merely contrived appearance put forward for public consumption. The interests of big unions and big business have increasingly coalesced, similar to the merged interests between the top echelons of the political, industrial, and economic sectors of our contemporary society (cf. Mills 1959a, Henslin and Reynolds 1973, and Leggett 1973). Part of these reciprocal interests of businesses and unions centers around maintaining white dominance. In the Detroit Edison case, for example, the Utility Workers of America was also levied $250,000 damages because the union had encouraged the company's discrimination against blacks.

Automation also makes its effects felt on a racial basis. With the blooming of automation, the unemployment rate of unskilled workers will continue to increase. As machines take over jobs previously performed by people, persons without specialized skills find themselves with little to market. Since blacks are numbered disproportionately among the unskilled, blacks will continue to be disproportionately affected by automation.

Although it may sound as though it is taken from some utopian scheme, it has been estimated that the day will come when only 2 percent of the population will be needed to produce all the manufactured goods our total population needs. That day may not be far off as Ford Motor Company now takes only six men to produce a single car while it took 104 men for the same task in 1910; petroleum companies can reduce their work force from 800 to twelve by applying automation; the American Electric Power computer in Canton, Ohio, automatically weighs the cost of fuel at each plant during a surge in power demand, the cost of transmitting power, the efficiency of each unit, and decides from where the extra power should come; a bakery is now in operation which takes grain into a silo and processes it entirely by automation into bread untouched by human hands—and it is possible that a single plant with but a single worker can produce all the bread needed in Southern California. Whereas only two computers were in use on the production lines and offices of American manufacturers in 1953, by 1956 there were 570. This number then jumped to 20,000 in 1964, to 56,000 in 1968, and on to 70,000 in 1970–71. Their annual expansion rate is estimated at 30 percent. There is nothing indefinite about the trend (Willhelm 1970:186–193, 202, 262–266; *Britannica Yearbook of Science and the Future, 1972*:223).

Whether such changes represent a utopian dream coming true or not, for displaced workers it can well be a nightmare. And unless retraining is given these workers, both white and nonwhite, *or* unless a means of production and distribution is worked out which insures consumer rights for all, the nightmare is well on its way. As usual, nonwhites are feeling it first and feeling it hardest. In this case, nonwhites are disproportionately members of the work group which is now needed only partially and only for a short time, while whites, who make up the vast majority of white collar workers, are fighting to keep their own jobs, and in this battle they are doing their best to keep nonwhites out. Consequently, nonwhites are rapidly becoming defunct workers stripped of their economic utility (Willhelm 1970). During our 1970's recession, for most people jobs became much harder to obtain. From 1970 to 1971, however, (the latest figures available), while the number of employed whites increased 534,000, from 70,182,000 to 70,716,000, the number of minority employees dropped 42,000, from 8,445,000 to 8,403,000 (*Statistical Abstracts of the United States*, 1972, Table 367).

The unemployment rate of nonwhites averages about twice that of whites. This is illustrated by Table 17:1. (Cf. *New York Times*, July 23, 1973:1 and 17.) Differential unemployment by race exists not only for

Table 17.1   Average Annual Unemployment Rates by Race, 1950–1972

Period	Blacks and Other Minority Groups	Whites	Unemployment Ratio of Blacks and Other Minority Groups to Whites
1950–1954	6.8	3.7	1.8
1955–1959	9.6	4.4	2.2
1960–1964	10.8	5.1	2.1
1965–1969	7.2	3.4	2.1
1970	8.2	4.5	1.8
1971	9.9	5.4	1.8
1972*	10.2	5.1	2.0

* Estimated.

Source: Computed from Social and Economic Status of the Black Population in the United States, 1971, Current Population Reports, 1972, p. 52.

the unskilled. It applies to all categories of employment, including professional, clerical, and sales workers, craftsmen, proprietors, managers, and foremen, as well as to laborers and household workers (Willhelm 1970:206).

The pervasive discriminatory practices directed against nonwhites in employment and in related sectors of American society lead to a large disparity in income by race. The median (average) family income of blacks in 1971, for example, was $6,993, while for whites it was over *50 percent greater*—$11,018 (*Statistical Abstracts of the U.S.*, 1973, Table 540). Similarly, while 50 percent of white families have incomes over $10,000 a year, only 26 percent of nonwhite families reach this income level (*ASA Footnotes, 1*, February 1973). These startling differences between white and nonwhite income in the United States hold

Table 17.2   Income for Quintiles and Highest 5 Percent of Families, White and Nonwhite, 1968

	Income		Difference (White minus Nonwhite)	Ratio (Nonwhite [to] White)
	White	Nonwhite		
Lowest quintile *	$ 5,015	$ 2,721	$2,294	.54
Second quintile	7,699	4,885	2,814	.63
Third quintile	10,277	6,805	3,472	.66
Fourth quintile	14,000	10,049	3,951	.72
Highest 5 percent	23,217	16,600	6,617	.71

* A fifth, or 20 percent, of some grouping

Source: Modified from Harold W. Guthrie, "The Prospect of Equality of Income Between White and Black Families under Varying Rates of Unemployment," The Journal of Human Resources V, 1970, p. 436.

Table 17.3 Income by Race and Education, 1970

Level of Education	Income		Dollar Difference (White minus Black)	Percent Difference (White Higher Than Black)
	Black	White		
Elementary	$ 4,930	$ 6,933	$2,003	45%
High School	7,492	10,579	3,087	41%
College	11,573	14,127	2,554	22%

Source: Computed from *Statistical Abstracts of the United States,* 1972, Table 531.

true for *all* levels of income. At the lowest income level, nonwhites receive approximately half the income of whites, while at *no* level does nonwhite income ever equal that of whites. Even where nonwhite income comes closest to white income, it still remains less than three-fourths that of whites, as is illustrated by Table 17.2.

Racial disparity in income also holds true for *all* levels of education. Regardless whether a person has only an elementary education or whether he has gone on to high school or even college, whites on the average are consistently paid more than blacks. As can be seen from Table 17.3, this difference is both consistent and considerable. Note that blacks who go on to college earn only about 10 percent more than whites who have gone only to high school ($11,573 versus $10,579), while when we reverse the matter and compare whites who go on to college with blacks who have gone only to high school we find that the difference jumps to almost 100 percent ($14,127 versus $7,492).

I have covered some aspects of racial bias in our judicial system in Chapter 14, but the racial basis of discrimination in our judicial system is made more starkly clear when we examine the race of prisoners executed in the United States (see Table 17.4). Race makes a difference in a person's chance of being executed, and, not surprisingly, we find that the difference does not favor blacks. While blacks comprise perhaps 11 percent of the population of the United States, about 49 percent of those who have been executed for murder have been blacks. When it comes to executions for the offense of rape, the racial bias takes on

Table 17.4 Prisoners Executed in the United States, 1930–1968

Murder				Rape			
Whites	Blacks	Others	Total	Whites	Blacks	Others	Total
1,664	1,630	40	3,334	48	405	2	455
(49.9%)	(48.9%)	(1.2%)	(100%)	(10.5%)	(89.1%)	(0.4%)	(100%)

Source: Based on figures contained in *NPS Bulletin, National Prisoner Statistics, Capital Punishment, 1930–1968, 45,* August 1969, United States Department of Justice, p. 7.

even more immense dimensions. Almost 90 percent of the persons who have been executed in the United States for the offense of rape have been blacks. This racial discrimination in state-inflicted death has made it traditionally more likely for a black than a white to be executed even though each has committed the same offense.

Racial discrimination in death is geographically based. Of the 405 blacks executed for rape in the United States, the overwhelming total of 398 have been executed in the South. No blacks have been executed for rape in the East or the West, while only seven blacks have been executed in the North Central states. At the same time, 43 of the 48 whites executed for rape have been executed in the South. Three of the other five whites were executed in the North Central states, while the other two were executed by the federal government. Thus, while it has been much more likely that an individual convicted of rape would be executed for his crime in the South than in our other states, this has been disproportionately true of blacks. The racist dimension comes into even sharper focus when we note that blacks have traditionally been excluded from serving on southern juries (*Civil Liberties, 282,* 1971). With the 1972 Supreme Court decision declaring capital punishment to be cruel and unusual, perhaps such lethal racial discrimination will now become but a mere relic of a barbarous past.

Racial discrimination resulting in involuntary servitude and death is also reflected in the military's treatment of blacks. Blacks are consistently inducted into the armed services at a rate higher than their proportion in the population. From 1961 to 1966, for example, the proportion of blacks inducted into the army ranged from 13 to 18 percent. About 14 percent of the army's enlisted men who served in Vietnam were black, but about 22 percent of the army's casualties were black. Blacks were disproportionately assigned to primary combat units in Vietnam, and it was these which bore the brunt of combat casualties (*Congressional Record—Senate,* June 14, 1967, pp. 15764, 15765).

Although blacks accounted for more than their share of American servicemen in Vietnam and an even greater share of battle deaths, a disproportionately small number of blacks served as officers. Even at the end of 1970 only 1.7 percent of our total officers in the armed forces were blacks (Rowan 1971) (cf. Willhelm, 1970:90).

The racist basis of blacks being disproportionately drafted and killed in our latest armed conflict becomes more apparent when we examine the racial membership of draft boards in the United States. Just as it is primarily whites who serve on juries and decide who will die or be imprisoned for violating criminal law, so it is almost exclusively whites who serve on draft boards and make similar decisions. In Mississippi, for example, only one in 300 of those sitting on draft boards is black, while in Alabama, Arkansas, and Louisiana not a single black has participated in the judgment to draft blacks. This is so in spite of the fact that blacks constitute almost a third of the total population of those states. In fact, in only three states has the percentage of blacks on draft boards been higher than 3 percent. Even in California, supposedly one of our more progressive states, the percentage of blacks on draft boards is only 1.6 percent (*Congressional Records—Senate*, November 18, 1969, p. 34730).

One of the major differences between the poor and those from the middle and upper classes is that the poor not only receive less adequate housing, education, and employment, but they also receive poorer medical care and more frequently suffer from inadequate diets. As we covered in Chapter 2, these aspects of poverty lower the survival chances of children born to poor parents. Since blacks are disproportionately poor, their mortality rates are higher than whites. Although there is some question about the quality of the data used in making such conclusions (Zelnik 1969), mortality rates across the United States run approximately twice as great for black infants than for white infants. Infant mortality for whites is about 21.6 per thousand, compared with the much higher rate of 41.1 for nonwhites. For American Indians the infant mortality rate is approximately 37.6 per thousand live births, very close to that of blacks and considerably more than the comparable rate for whites (*HSMHA Health Reports, 86,* March 1971, p. 237). This differential death rate also goes in the same direction when it comes to adults, with nonwhites showing a consistently higher mortality rate than whites (*U.S. Department of Health, Education, and Welfare: Mortality Trends in the United States, 1954–1963,* June 1966, p. 7; *U.S. Department of Health, Education, and Welfare, Socioeconomic Characteristics of Deceased Persons, U.S., 1962–1963,* February 1969, p. 13; *New York Times,* July 23, 1973:1 and 17).

The pernicious effects of racism combine to form an ever-tightening circle. A black born in the United States is caught up in a racist cycle which surrounds him from birth and makes his life similar to that of a one-legged man running a hundred-yard dash. A black is typically born into a family whose average annual income is considerably lower than whites. He is likely to receive inferior medical care. His diet may be less than adequate. The education he receives is generally inferior due to differential funding, as well as such factors as less experienced teachers. With the substandard education he receives, he is less equipped for the jobs that are available, and if a job is available an employer is likely to hire a white over him. If he does get a job, he is liable to face discrimination in both promotion and salary. The "last hired, first fired" syndrome is still at work. His activities are more likely to

Those who compete for success after beginning life in impoverished circumstances are caught up in a despairing cycle which makes their success most unlikely.   (Courtesy of Wide World Photos)

come to the attention of the police. If arrested, he is more likely to receive discriminatory treatment at the "bar of justice." Accordingly, he is
disproportionately likely to end up on welfare. And with all of this,
whites are more likely to blame him for his life situation than they are

the social system which produces racial prejudice and discrimination. There's hardly a way that he can win.

There are exceptions, of course. Some blacks are born wealthy; others receive opportunities to develop rare talents; while some of average ability and from poor parents do receive breaks. For a few others, the current racial situation is working in their favor. In some rare instances it is even a decided economic advantage to be black. For example, this is true for certain academic positions today, since some universities have begun to specifically recruit blacks for academic openings. Many departments in American universities have come to the point where they desire a black on their faculty, if for no other reason than to demonstrate that they are not prejudiced. With the public educational system being middle class and working to the disadvantage of the poor, only a limited number of blacks are available for these positions. As the current demand for black academics is greater than the supply, the pay offered is frequently higher for a black than for a white in the same position. Such "reverse racial discrimination" is indeed an exception, however, and in the typical situation it is not difficult to project the winner of a hundred-yard dash in which only some are running one-legged.

Relations between the races in the United States, although differing in many respects, are similar to the caste system of India. Due to an accident of birth, we all become members of racial groupings that have highly differentiated social boundaries. We grow up within the confines surrounding our racial grouping. We learn negative ideas about other racial groupings and positive ideas about our own group. If our racial grouping is in the minority, we also learn the negative stereotypes pertaining to our own group. With but rare exceptions, we marry within our own racial grouping and are forever barred from joining any other. Similar to the caste system of India, then, in our contemporary United States one is born into, marries into, and lives out one's life as a member of a particular racial-ethnic-social group.

Membership in a racial group supposedly imparts an indelible mark which is taken as the justifiable basis for almost all social relationships. In the early 1800's, for example, "a free man of colour" by the name of Daniel Reed emigrated from the island of Santo Domingo and settled in Washington County, Alabama. He purchased from slavery a woman named Rose, then petitioned and won from the Alabama legislature the right to emancipate his first two children. Four of their five daughters later married white men (the fifth never married), and most of their 2,500 or so descendants still live in the same area. "Whites" in the area call them Cajuns and say they can still recognize their "Negro blood." In about 1929 Mrs. Barbara Young, a direct descendant of Rose and Daniel Reed, tried to get her children enrolled in a white school. She lost her case in court on a judge's ruling that her children were black because they "are 1/64 black and 63/64 white, or going back to the starting of this analysis, out of 63 white ancestors, one, or the 64th ancestor, was a Negro" (Severo 1970:86).

Seldom was racism in the United States more bizarre, and seldom has it been more similar to the racism practiced in Hitler's concentration camps, than in a recently publicized 40-year experiment performed on unsuspecting black men. In 1932, the United States Public Health Service began an "experiment" to determine the effects of untreated syphilis on the human body. The experiment was initiated by John R. Heller, a man who should go down in history as one of the most infamous medical doctors of all time. Heller was the assistant Surgeon General in the Venereal Disease Section of the U.S. Public Health Service. Four hundred black men (later supplemented by another 31 men) from Tuskegee, Alabama, and surrounding Macon County were recruited for the study. They were not informed that they had syphilis, but were told that they were being given a blood test or blood treatment. As incentives to cooperate in the program, these men were given free transportation to and from hospitals, free hot lunches, free medicine (for diseases other than syphilis), free burial (after a required autopsy), free hospital care, and $100 for their survivors. (If these are benefits, then one can consider the Jews of Auschwitz as having received free room and board.) These men were also led to believe that their participation made them members of "Miss River's Lodge," a cross between a social club and a burial society. They met once a year when the "government doctor" dispensed free medicine.

Four years after the "experiment" began, doctors gained at least part of the knowledge they initially sought. By 1936 they were able to compare the mortality rate of untreated syphilitics with their control group of nonsyphilitics. They found that 28 of the 92 autopsied syphilitic patients had died as a direct result of untreated syphilis. At this same time they found that more syphilitics than persons in their control group suffered from such conditions as arteriosclerosis, abnormal conditions of the lymph nodes, and loss of vision.

Yet the "experiment" was continued. Even after penicillin became common in the 1940's and its use could have saved the lives of a number of these persons, the drug was denied them. The 28 direct deaths from untreated syphilis reported in 1936 is 30.4 percent of those who died at that time (28/92). If this proportion held true for the rest of the sample, then of the 357 deaths approximately 108 men died as a direct result of their untreated disease (*New York Times*, July 26–September 13, 1972).

It is almost impossible not to draw the conclusion from this "experiment" that the subjects were chosen because of their low social value. I cannot say for certain that these blacks were considered by their experimenters to be subhuman and therefore not deserving the treatment given to human beings, but it certainly was inhumane treatment that they received.

Following his demonic plans, Adolf Hitler not only used medical experimentation in which non-Aryans were the victims of Aryan doctors, but he also "saw involuntary sterilization as a legitimate weapon in the elimination of undesirable races and the preservation of Aryan purity" (*St. Louis Post-Dispatch,* July 4, 1973). Events have taken place in the United States which uncomfortably smack of a similar orientation. In one case, a 13-year-old Illinois girl under the "protection" of the Illinois Department of Children and Family Services was sterilized in Texas. In another, 12- and 14-year-old sisters in Alabama were sterilized after their mother marked her X on forms she thought simply authorized immunization shots for her daughters. In both cases, those involuntarily sterilized were black girls (*St. Louis Post-Dispatch* July 4, 1973; July 14, 1973). These publicized cases probably only represent the scandalous tip of an immense iceberg since between 1960 and 1968 "The Eugenics Board of North Carolina" ordered the sterilization of 1,620 women, more than half of whom were under 20 years of age, and, needless to add, almost all of whom were black (*Civil Liberties, 301,* March 1974).

A final bizarre case of serious consequences resulting from discriminatory treatment on the basis of race which deserves mention is that of Dr. Charles Drew. Dr. Drew invented the process of separating plasma from blood. This process was a medical breakthrough which transformed operative and postoperative care throughout the country and throughout the world. Countless lives were saved by his unique contribution to medicine. In 1950 Dr. Drew was injured in a car accident in North Carolina. The hospital in Burlington, North Carolina, to which Dr. Drew was taken was "For Whites Only." Hospital authorities refused to admit him to their hospital because he was a black, and Dr. Drew bled to death (Drotning 1969:190).

The question of why we have riots is frequently asked by students and the public alike. With both our pervasively subtle and our overtly explicit racism, the question should perhaps not be, "Why riots?," but, "Why not more riots?" With racial discrimination having a centuries-long history in the United States, with racism in many ways affecting each American and bringing with it such dire negative consequences for those against whom it is directed, it is surprising that we have had so few riots. A people as systematically exploited as blacks might well have rebelled with greater frequency. Not only are the conditions that I have but briefly covered conducive to rioting, but when poor blacks are jammed together in the inner city in crowded, debilitating conditions, while others easily witnessed by them through the medium of television possess so much more, it takes but a spark to ignite the essential ingredients already present.

Blacks who are aware of causes of their denigrated position face the essential dilemma of the exploited: whether to cope with the rejection of the majority with the hope that ameliorative action will bring rewards by working within the system or to lash out and destroy that in the environment which is oppressive and hated. The more than one hundred major riots which took place between 1964 and 1967 were largely unplanned, unorganized, and unscheduled, but significantly they involved a high degree of community participation. In the Watts riot, for example, about 22,000 persons, 15 percent of Watts' black adult population, actively participated in the riot, while another 35 or 40 percent, about 51,000 persons, were active spectators. It is extremely significant to note that during the rioting two groups were singled out for attack. These were the police and businesses, two direct representations of white entrenched power. Largely ignored were libraries, schools, and civic buildings (Boskin 1969).

People who fail to understand why riots occur, or why they have a community base, lack understanding about the cause of riots to the same degree that they fail to grasp the implications of racism in the United States. Race riots are not simply wanton acts of violence, but the last resort of discarded and disregarded masses who feel that they have had no chance in the past, that they have no prospect for the future, and that there is no recourse in the present. Experiencing racism day in and day out can lead to a violent repudiation of that society which forces hopeless compliance to a racist way of life. Rioting is a retaliatory action by which an anguished people express their utter contempt for the society which has rejected them on the basis of color (Willhelm 1970:311–312).

Similarly, if one understands racism in the United States, one can also understand the rise of black power in the late sixties. With great hopes, black leaders such as Roy Wilkins, Bayard Rustin, Martin Luther King, Jr., and A. Phillip Randolph proclaimed a moratorium on direct-action demonstrations in order to minimize the "backlash" in the 1964 election. This helped give Lyndon Johnson's 1964 victory the highest plurality of votes the country had ever known. Under Johnson's direction, however, the result was primarily paper victories. Consequently, black leaders suffered a loss of confidence within their own communities, and they stood discredited in the eyes of black activists. At this point, proponents of black power quickly moved to fill the void (Willhelm 1970:221–222).

With the loss of confidence black leaders suffered in the 1960's, black-power advocates such as Eldridge Cleaver (shown here) quickly stepped in to fill the gap. (Courtesy of Wide World Photos)

Racism is a powerful means of social control. It pits group against group in an interlocking system of subservience and dominance. One group tenaciously holds its position, while another attempts to wrest what it can from the first. Persons not in any position of superiority in society, even victimized themselves, cling to their color and point with pride that they are not one of "them." The "thems" do the same. People identify with their own racial grouping, rather than identifying with others who are in similar class positions. Thus divisiveness is enforced, and the status quo made secure.

In the next chapter, we shall examine a related form of social control which goes back millennia further than that between the races. As we analyze traditional social relationships between the sexes, we shall focus on both discrimination on the basis of membership in a social group and the contemporary widespread attempt to drastically change the status quo, an attempt which holds the possibility of reshaping our society.

chapter 18

Challenging the Status Quo: The Women's Liberation Movement

Burning bras. Marches on Washington. High-pitched voices raised in shrill protest. Shouts of "Male chauvinist pig!" The biological sign for female, surrounding a clenched fist. Counter-protest from both men and women who say women have never had it so good. What is it all about?

Why do some women feel oppressed, while others feel they are the privileged sex? *Are* females oppressed in today's society? Or are they the privileged ones? What has happened to this generation of women, or to some of them, that they feel the need for liberation? Their mothers were content; why aren't they?

These questions and the related protest activities center around two major issues: the proper relationship between the sexes and whether or not women are currently discriminated against on the basis of their sex. In this chapter we shall deal with these issues, while in the next we shall deal with the questions of why this generation of women and why not all of them.

The question of the proper relationship between the sexes did not by any means originate with this generation. Some of the earliest writers in the Western world dealt with this issue. Plato maintained that males and females possess equal innate capacities, but he represents what has traditionally been a minority view in the Western world. He said:

I conclude then, my friend, that none of the occupations which comprehend the ordering of a state belong to woman as woman, nor yet to man as man; but natural gifts are to be found here and there, in both sexes alike; and, so far as her nature is concerned, the woman is admissible to all pursuits as well as the man, though in all of them the woman is weaker than the man (*The Republic,* 455E).

The more common view has been patterned after Aristotle, who felt that the physical differences of the sexes were part of a divine plan which should be matched by correspondingly different social roles. From the greater physical strength of males, Aristotle concluded that Providence intended men to be more actively involved outside the home and women to be more quietly passive within the home. As he put it:

For Providence made man stronger and woman weaker, so that he in virtue of his manly prowess may be more ready to defend the home, and she, by reason of her timid nature, more ready to keep watch over it; and while he brings in fresh supplies from without, she may keep safe what lies within. In handicrafts again, woman was given a sedentary patience, though denied stamina for endurance of exposure; while man, though inferior to her in quiet employments, is endowed with vigour for every active occupation (*Oeconomica I, III,* 4).

In traditional Christianity separate roles for males and females are also thought to be proper. Underlying these expectations are theological conceptions of creation. St. Paul put it this way:

A man should certainly not cover his head, since he is the image of God and reflects God's glory; but woman is the reflection of man's glory. For man did not come from woman; no, woman came from man; and man was not created for the sake of woman, but woman was created for the sake of man (I Corinthians 11:7–9).

These sex-linked roles are taught as being what God desires for a life pleasing to Him. When these teachings involve marriage, the man is given stringent obligations towards his wife, especially concerning love. The wife, however, is placed into a definitely subservient role, one in which she is expected to be obedient:

Wives should regard their husbands as they regard the Lord, since as Christ is head of the Church and saves the whole body, so is a husband the head of his wife; and as the Church submits to Christ, so should wives to their husbands, *in everything* (Ephesians 5:22–23; emphasis added).

"I don't remember. Were you the rib or me?"

Theological teachings of Christianity, Judaism, and Islam deprecate women in favor of men. These teachings permeate culture, leading to both conscious and nonconscious discriminatory ideology. (Courtesy of *Harper's.* Cartoon by D. Wilder.)

The religious heritage that woman is a lesser being than man is not by any means limited to Christianity. It is also especially pronounced in the Jewish religion. The following, for example, is prayed each morning by male Orthodox Jews:

Blessed art Thou, oh Lord our God, King of the Universe, that I was not born a Gentile. Blessed art Thou, oh Lord our God, King of the Universe, that I was not born a slave. Blessed art Thou, oh Lord our God, King of the Universe, that I was not born a woman.

Nor is a theological view which deprecates women limited to Western religions. The Koran, the sacred text of Islam, also baldly proclaims male superiority:

Men shall have preeminence above women, because of those advantages wherein God hath caused the one of them to excel the other (*The Koran*, IV:58).

These statements from three of the world's major religions form a set of related beliefs which yields a particular picture of reality. Why do we find in religion an ideology of inherent, God-given male superiority? For a devout religious believer, the answer typically given is that God has inspired the writing, which accordingly represents revealed truth. The sociological approach contrasts sharply with this: The sociologist views religious writings as part of human culture. Because people from each culture tend to be ethnocentric in their view of the world and of their own place in the world, it is easier to view the sacred writings from other cultures as cultural products than it is one's own. Thus, it is easier for those from a Christian background to view the Koran as a cultural literary production than it is their own holy writings. These same ethnocentric "cultural blinders" operate when Jews view theirs and when Muslims view theirs.

Following the sociological perspective, we would interpret the quotations just cited as part of an ideology or belief system which supports a particular relationship between the sexes. In other words, the sociologist would interpret such statements as theological reaffirmations of the status quo. In particular, he would view such statements as codified positions on existing power relations, positions which have been put forward under the concept of spiritual revelation in order to maintain traditional male supremacy. From this point of view, it is not surprising to note that males are the dominant sex in the three cultures represented by these writings. It is equally unsurprising to find that the major prophets and historical religious leaders of these three religions are also males. Male dominance in both religious and secular society is being buttressed by such theological pronouncements. By teaching as revealed truth the innate superiority of males over females, they provide divine underpinnings for male dominance in social relationships. If females ever complain about their lesser status and subservient roles, males are able to simply point to both Scripture and tradition and assert that God wants it that way. Who can argue with God?

Such teachings concerning the natural superiority of the male were once **conscious ideologies,** that is, they were openly believed, openly discussed, and openly taught. A discriminatory ideology of the sexes marked all social relations. Most people believed, and believed firmly, that the male's biological endowment of greater physical strength was an outward sign of an innate male superiority which separated the sexes. Roles between the sexes were overtly predicated upon this and similar supporting beliefs. People accepted these basic teachings as part of the divine ordering of nature. They provided the ideological base for traditional discrimination against women in all walks of life. Woman had a place—and it was not part of the man's world. It was up to men to run the institutions of society—because God had so ordained it. It was up to men to see that women's ambitions did not become too great—because God had so ordained it. It was up to men to protect the weaker sex who stayed ignorantly at home with the children—because God had so ordained it. In this way a theological rationale was provided for a basic separation of the sexes in society, with males being continually maintained in their ruling position.

The Victorian woman is currently thought of as having lived her life on a sort of protective pedestal. Her innocence, her genteel leisure pursuits, and the graciousness with which she was treated by men sometimes make contemporary men and women yearn for that better day in the distant past. Something may indeed be enviable about the admiration and concern with which gentlemen during that period treated their ladies. What most of us don't realize, however, is that this aspect of the Victorian past primarily applied to the aristocracy of that period. The feminine pedestal was a far cry from the everyday realities of most Victorian women. Most women were not privileged to be genteel ladies but were members of the working class, while most men were not privileged to be gentlemen but were also members of the working class. And a hard-working class it was. Reality was sometimes as unbelievable to modern ears as this account given by a woman who worked in the coal mines:

> I have a belt 'round my waist and chain passing between my legs, and I go on my hands and feet. . . . The pit is very wet where I work, and the water comes over our clogs always, and I have seen it up to my thighs. . . . My cousin looks after my children in the daytime. I am very tired when I get home at night; I fall asleep sometimes before I get washed. I am not so strong as I was, I cannot stand my work so well as I used to do. I am drawn till I have had the skin off me; the belt and chain is worse when we are in the family way (Neff 1929:72).

In the early stages of capitalism and the Industrial Revolution, the working class was especially disadvantaged. Work was hard, hours were long, pay was low, working conditions did not even come close to contemporary standards, strikes were illegal, collective bargaining was illegal, and there were no job security, paid vacations, hospitalization, or social security. These conditions applied not only to men but also to women and children.

Though both men and women lacked many rights which we take for granted today, the situation for men was ameliorated somewhat by the possession of basic legal rights not granted women. Because someone was born with a particular set of sexual organs, *on that basis* he or she occupied a special legal status. For example, on the basis of sex one was granted or denied the right to vote. Women were frequently denied the right to participate in the election process on the ideological basis that voting was an unfeminine activity. An early female labor organizer replied to this objection in this way:

Of course you know the reason we are employed in foundries is that they are cheaper and work longer hours than men. Women in the laundries, for instance, stand for thirteen or fourteen hours in the terrible steam and heat with their hands in hot starch. Surely these women won't lose any more of their beauty and charm by putting their ballot in a ballot box once a year than they are likely to lose standing in foundries or laundries all year round (Millett 1970:70).

As women in increasing numbers left their traditional domestic roles and entered the labor force, it became more and more difficult for men to push back this burgeoning force for social change. When people of a particular class position possess power that people of another class do not have, they are not usually eager or even willing to give up or to share that power. Men were, in general, no exception. Although they were increasingly hard-pressed for justification, men were most reluctant to extend the privilege of voting to women. Even though Wyoming had granted the franchise to women in 1869, and although by 1890 approximately 19 percent of the total work force in the United States was composed of women, with this rising to about 24 percent in 1910 (McGovern 1968-69:320), American women in general did not gain the right to vote until the Nineteenth Amendment to the Constitution was passed in 1919 and ratified by the states in 1920 (Johnson 1970:31). This amendment had already been introduced in Congress in 1878. It was regularly before the legislators from that time on, but it took 41 years before it was finally passed.

The enfranchisement which the Nineteenth Amendment provided women was not a gift from men. It was the result of a long, hard-fought, and frequently acrimonious battle waged by female activists and male sympathizers (Catt and Schuler 1923). Various forces were aligned against woman suffrage, including the liquor interests, who correctly feared that votes for women meant votes for Prohibition. These liquor interests generously applied large sums of money to the cause of retaining the vote in male hands (O'Neill 1971:75).

The major opposition to the passing of the Nineteenth Amendment, however, came from the southern states. The primary objection raised by the southern legislators was firmly rooted in their opposition to voting by blacks. If the Nineteenth Amendment became law, black women would also become voters. As this amendment authorized the Federal Government to protect the right of women to vote, southern Democrats felt that the Federal Government might enforce the voting rights of

The movement by women to gain equal rights with men has been a long, hard-fought international struggle. After American women gained the right to vote with the passage of the Nineteenth Amendment to the Constitution in 1919, the movement lost steam, finally regaining strength in the late 1960's. Though styles of dress have changed, styles of redress remain similar.   (Courtesy of Wide World Photos)

black women. They felt that if this was done the government could hardly ignore the southern practice of keeping black men away from the ballot box (Johnson 1970:32). A good while prior to the passage of this amendment American women had already demonstrated their interest in political issues and had experienced their own potential political power through their leadership in the antislavery movement (Lutz 1968). Female participation and leadership in the Abolitionist movement may also have wieghed heavily on the male legislators' minds, for it was during women's participation in that movement that the first Women's Rights Convention was held at Seneca Falls, New York, in July of 1848 (Schneir 1972:5).

With the passage of the Nineteenth Amendment, women appeared to have gained equal rights with men. One of the last bastions of male supremacy had been overcome, but the Womans' Suffrage Movement then lost steam. Women entered the flapper era of the 1920's, where they gained greater sexual and occupational freedoms, fought a holding action during the Great Depression of the 1930's, then broke further occupational barriers in the 1940's with the high labor demand

(Courtesy of Wide World Photos)

arising from World War II, and then continued their participation in American society relatively quietly until the late 1960's.

During this period the ideology of male supremacy lost many of its overt characteristics, but belief in the innate supremacy of males had been thoroughly engrained into the consciousness of Americans. Beliefs in male supremacy and female inferiority had become a basic part of the American **Weltanschauung,** the general or overarching frame of reference by which people look at the world. It became increasingly difficult, however, to maintain a system of overt beliefs in the innate supremacy of males when this belief so sharply conflicted with the ideology concerning the equality of all Americans and with the increasing participation of women in the labor force. Maintaining the belief became even more difficult because the movement to liberate women was not by any means limited to the United States. Women around the world were bitterly and forcefully crusading for equality. Since belief in the innate inequality of the sexes had become rooted in the basic consciousness of Americans, when these beliefs could no longer be overtly maintained, they took a different form. The ideology did not by any means disappear—rather, it went underground. It maintained its foothold in the American belief system as one of the **nonconscious ideologies,** that is, it remained a part of the belief system of the American people, but it was no longer overt.

Some of our cultural sayings represent this change in ideology. We used to have the adage, "A woman's place is in the home." A woman

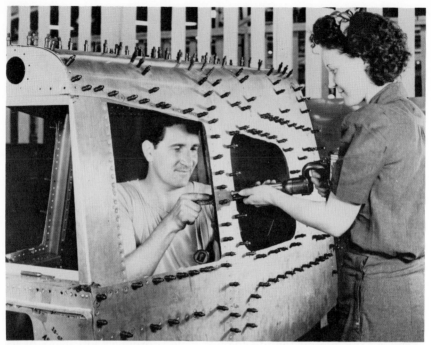

With so many men off to war and with the increased labor demands of World War II, American women broke many occupational barriers. As with black labor gains made during this same period, when the regular labor force returned, women were again placed in more subservient positions. (Courtesy of Wide World Photos)

should not, in other words, get out in the "real" world and compete with men. Although this particular statement of conscious ideological belief in what the social order of the sexes should be like has increasingly lost its hold and appears to be used with decreasing frequency, we today have sayings which express a more nonconscious ideological approach to the sexes. The vituperative exclamation, "Women drivers!" is a current and continuing example. This statement, which is usually prefixed by the word damn and uttered as one total profanity, expresses the conviction, contrary to empirical fact, that women are less adept at driving automobiles than men. This is part of a more general belief in American culture that women are less adept than men at handling mechanical things. Other common cultural sayings regarding the sexes are superficially complimentary, but underlining them is a nonconscious ideology concerning basic female inferiority. For example, "Behind every great man, there is a woman." This statement at first glance appears to be complimentary to women because it refers to certain behind-the-scenes power which women may possibly possess. It may also indicate, however, that the proper place for women is behind men. At least we have no cultural equivalent of, "Behind every great woman, there is a man."

Our nonconscious ideology is so pervasive that "even those Americans who agree that a black skin should not uniquely qualify its owner for janitorial or domestic service continue to act as if the possession of a uterus uniquely qualifies *its* owner for precisely that" (Bem and Bem 1970:22). We begin to be socialized into this nonconscious ideology while we are still infants. American parents typically encourage their male children to be aggressive, competitive, and independent, while they reward their female children for being passive, cooperative, and dependent. The nonconscious aspect of this basic approach to life is made evident when we note that in many instances parents are unaware that they are treating their infants differently according to the sex of the infant. In one study of 6-month-old infants, it was found that by this age girls were already being touched and spoken to more by their mothers than were boys. By the time these same children were 13 months old the girls were more reluctant than the boys to leave their mothers, they remained closer to their mothers during play periods, and they returned to their mothers sooner and more often than did the same-aged boys. When a barrier was set up to separate a child from his or her mother (and toys), girls tended to cry and motion for help more than the boys who more actively attempted to circumvent the barrier. The researchers suggest that the earlier differential touching and talking shaped these sex role behaviors (Goldberg and Lewis 1969).

An alternative interpretation of such early behavioral differences according to sex centers around the operation of sex hormones. Some researchers have discovered that there is hormonal imprinting of the brain which, through a complicated process involving the neural circuits in the hypothalamus, affects by the sex of the infant their degree of physical activity, aggressiveness, and attention span. This results in males being more aggressive and females being more attentive, passive, and compliant. But these early hormonal influences on behavior are adaptive to cultural patterns (cf. Bardwick 1971, Diamond and Young 1963, Levine and Mullins 1966, Money 1961, Witkin 1962, and Young, Goy and Phoenix 1964).

As we covered in earlier chapters, especially Chapter 7, conditioning into sex roles not only continues as children grow older, but it also becomes more explicit. Chemistry sets, trucks, and microscopes, for example, become "proper" Christmas gifts for boys, while girls tend to receive dolls, jewelry, and pretty clothing. If a boy does well in biology, he is likely to be encouraged to become a doctor or scientist. If a girl does well in biology, she is likely to be encouraged to become a nurse so that she will have an interesting job to fall back on—in case she ever needs to support herself. By the time they are in the ninth grade, 25 percent of the boys but only 3 percent of the girls are considering careers in science or engineering. By the time they apply for college, girls are scoring about 60 points lower on the math aptitude test on the College Board Examinations. That these scores are not due to hormonal factors can be demonstrated by noting that girls significantly improve their mathematical performance when the problems are reworded to deal with cooking and gardening. The abstract reasoning required for the solution, however, remains the same in either case (Bem and Bem 1970:24).

When a girl graduates from high school and enters college, we feel that she can make a "free choice" concerning her career. What is frequently overlooked is that by this time she has been subtly but carefully screened for 18 years to make sex-linked choices. When a baby boy is born, it is difficult to predict what occupation he will be in 25 years later. A number of possibilities are open to him—particularly, of course, if he is white and middle-class. But if the new baby is female, we can usually confidently predict how she will be spending her time 25 years later. Her individuality typically becomes irrelevant for making such predictions (Bem and Bem 1970:26, 115).

Aspects of the socialization process by which girls in American society learn to become *feminine* is illustrated by an excerpt (quoted by permission) from a woman's examination in one of my freshman courses:

The mystification of motherhood and womanhood by the school system begins in the fifth and sixth grades with a segregated program of sex education—two films on menstruation and free copies of books on the same, plus "good grooming" tips offered by sanitary napkin manufacturers. Written parental permission is obtained for this adventure, and the little girls are instructed beforehand to hide the pamphlets and refuse to tell their male classmates the subject matter of the filmstrips. When I was up for this initation rite, to make certain that no boys in passing by could see or hear any of the filmstrip the movie was shown on the condemned third floor of the school building. On film was a Walt Disney production with a Cinderella-like character romping animatedly into adulthood. The other, far more interesting, film was entitled, "You're a Young Lady Now!", a venture of the Kotex corporation. Its heroine was a 1950's-style bobbysoxer with an understanding mother who sits down with her and explains to her all the wonderful mysteries of womanhood—all happening now so that someday she can be a *mother*. Naturally, the young lady can hardly wait for the miracle to happen, which it does the very next day. Both mother and daughter are exceedingly proud and walk downstairs arm-in-arm to tell the father, who looks up from his newspaper in admiration. To the most naïve of sixth graders, the movie is pretty funny, but the school nurse in blue uniform who is officiating at the showing tells them to be quiet, that this is a serious matter, a matter of importance to everyone present. She warns them that they have been laughing at the wonders of *Womanhood*. The movie ends with "pointers on charm" and advertisements for the product. Perhaps the moral of the story is really to be demure and charming and buy Kotex, rather than be careful not to screw around because now you can be a *mother*, as I suspected at the time. A similar mysticism could be found in a required eighth-grade home economics class where the girls asked fearful questions about the pain of childbirth and the horrors of breast-feeding. Several expressed a desire to stay single, but the Home Economics teacher in her high heels quickly counter-socialized the mysteries by assuring her students that their fears were nonsense and they would, of course, all want to be mothers someday.

Little girls are urged to be ornamental. For most of my life I have been encouraged and prodded into wearing pretty clothes I had no desire for. During my childhood, I had too few books but many and various elaborate dolls. Because I was reluctant to don adolescent trappings and liked to think of myself as concerned with weightier things, I did not become a compulsive consumer of pink lipstick and nailpolish or get involved in devouring the parapoetics of advertising in girls' magazines. I felt the weight of peer-group scorn and sometimes feared that if I did not indulge in the paraphernalia of junior high school girls, I would be alone and miserable forever. I became the pariah of the seventh grade for my refusal to give up my undershirt for the harness of womanhood. It seems fortunate that I was still too interested in dogs, novels and treehouses to be seriously hurt by these rejections.

The mass media aimed at the adolescent girl are wonderfully adept at conveying the proper role of the young lady in society. An example is an ad in *Seventeen*, a nationally circulated monthly girls' magazine, for a product called "face-slicker." The two-page ad shows a Mod young man in purple velvet being leaned upon by a wearer of face-slicker. She looks innocent and "glowy," as the copy reads. The text ends with, "Makes you look as though you could just about add two and two. And even if your IQ is 140, you're like that inside, aren't you?" Articles and columns in *Seventeen* advise the reader to "think feminine," doff her own pride to the adolescent male ego, and to endear "that special boy" to her forever with Mushroom Cheese Casserole and Apple Blossom Punch.

The inevitability and great desirability of marriage as a woman's life's work is initially punctuated with the first doll—symbolic of the babies she will one day rear in the matrimonial partnership. I was smilingly told by a teacher that one day I would be happy just to be a good wife, squelching the new ambition I had rushed to her to disclose. I was told that I could not be a milkman because it was an occupation only for men. She offered me three alternatives: I could be a nurse, a teacher, or an artist (she had liked my paintings), but she assured me that I would someday choose wife-and-motherhood as the culmination of all my dreams. I decided then to work at becoming an artist. I was beginning to mistrust teachers.

Advertising and the mass media have deeply invested into the creation of a somewhat degrading housewive's culture—there is television programming created for them (The Guiding Light, The Secret Storm), and there are scores of magazines directed at this segment of the population. Jules Henry in *Culture Against Man* names the competitive struggle among the mass women's magazines as the best example of competition forcing the corruption of values. Much magazine advertising caters to the Self-Image of the housewife as dedicated Keeper of the Castle, and the articles are primarily concerned with the trivia of day to day housekeeping. The television image of the wife as a shrill-voiced bitch screaming about enzyme detergents and dull wash is extraordinarily insulting.

A fascinating aspect of dominant cultural belief systems or ideologies which are negatively directed against a minority group is that members of the minority group tend to adopt an attitude toward themselves which is similar to that expressed by the ideology. Although women are in the numerical majority in the United States, making up 51.3 percent of the population, they are a minority group as far as discrimination is concerned. Just as men are dominant and generally disparage female talent, so women also tend to look at men as having greater abilities than women. This was demonstrated by an experiment in which female college students were asked to rate a number of professional articles. Half of the women thought that the articles were written by men (the author was listed as John T. McKay), while the other half thought that the articles were written by women (Joan T. McKay). Except for the attributed authorship, the articles were identical. Moreover, the authorship was not pointed out to the readers. The students rated the articles on value, persuasiveness, profundity, writing style, professional competence, professional status, and ability to sway the reader. In all areas, lower ratings were given to articles attributed to female authors. This was true not only for articles from fields traditionally dominated by men, such as law and city planning, but it also held true for articles from fields typically dominated by women, such as elementary education and dietetics (Goldberg 1968:28–30).

Self-depreciating views of "housewife," the most typical role in American culture assigned members of this minority group, are also common. Married women who become conscious of their denigrated status and whose activities are primarily limited to the home sometimes undergo an extremely painful experience of awareness. The following is a quotation (quoted by permission) from an examination of a married woman in one of my introductory courses:

> Housewives are forced to denigrate their cultural contributions and lower them in our scheme of values. This same thing happens to female children. In materials used in the elementary grades to teach reading skills, mothers are always wearing an apron, while little girls endlessly fetch slippers for their fathers. Little boys are allowed dreams of becoming President, while little girls are carefully guided into thoughts of motherhood. Female children are taught to be subservient to males long before they enter school. They are taught this by their mother's role as housewife.
>
> After I graduated I was married and had my first child when I was eighteen. At this early age I found that I had already attained the goal that was set for me in life, and all that was before me was the occupation of housewife. My parents often reminded me that there would be no money for me to continue school, but that my brother would be allowed to go on to school if he wanted to because some day he would have to support a family. So it was with these values and goals that I had to become a housewife and be happy about it.
>
> Most housewives, black or white, don't look like the rest of the nation. We cannot dress like the younger single girls because of our constant maid-type duties. Sexy dresses would soon be ruined at the sink. If a housewife and a secretary were walking down the street together, it would only take one glance at the hair style and dress to know which was which. Just as the civil rights movement is a quest for identity by blacks, so the women's liberation movement is a quest for identity.
>
> The label *housewife* gives women a superficial identity. This label implies that they are needed to take care of a house and everything in it. Actually, any member or all members of the house could do the tasks that she normally does, and they could do them just as well. A

housewife is a cleaning woman, a cook and a maid, and she is supported totally by her husband, usually with the inference that she is unable to support herself. In our society a person who is unable to support himself usually has a very low opinion of himself, and so does the rest of society.

A housewife usually does not think of her job as being respected or prestigious. If she is asked what she does, her usual answer is, "Nothing," or, "I am just a housewife." However, if she gets a part-time or full-time job, her answer immediately changes. She then refers to her job as a teacher, secretary, etc. Although she still does her housewife chores, she no longer labels herself a housewife. As a housewife, there is little opportunity for learning or advancement. It takes very little brain power to learn to do dishes or the ironing, and there is no job you can advance to short of getting out of the business.

Although these types of issues lie at the root of the current women's liberation movement, the movement centers around much more than the dislike and repugnance some women feel at being shunted off into becoming household drudges because of the possession of particular reproductive organs. Almost all areas of contemporary American life are characterized by either pervasively subtle or marked overt sexual discrimination. The pervasiveness of sexual discrimination becomes apparent when we note that American women live in a world which is still so male-dominated that the word used to refer to both sexes is the masculine pronoun "he" (which part of our language may very well remain even though sexual equality is gained); when important events are covered on television and radio news, and even insignificant ones on late talk shows, a male voice and face are typically presented; and even the image of God in the Christian and Jewish religions is male (Wells 1973).

Discrimination on the basis of sex occurs in all the institutions of American society, from religion where most denominations still refuse to ordain women, on the basis that they are women, to the family, where women are regularly socialized to play traditional subservient roles. As we shall briefly examine, the legal, military, educational, political, and economic institutions are also not exempt from sexual discrimination.

Although legislation which discriminates against women has been easing, the legal institution remains one of our most sexually discriminatory institutions. Although female American citizens of the required age and residence have been allowed to vote since 1920, some of the changes designed to overcome basic legal sexual discrimination have been much more recent. Until 1966, for example, women were still denied the right to serve on juries on the same basis as men (Kanowitz 1969:28, 29, 47, 56, 92). Until 1970 not a single one of our states permitted abortion on request—even though it was widely known that such legislation would sharply decrease maternal deaths. The charge of sexual discrimination in such legislation is partially based on the almost exclusively male makeup of our legislatures (Henslin 1973:146). Until 1972 a woman with a taxable income was not allowed to declare a tax deduction for (the costs she incurred in) child care, although working men who employed a housekeeper to tend motherless children regularly received this benefit (*Civil Liberties, 284,* February 1972).

In spite of recent legislative changes, some of today's laws are strongly reminiscent of an earlier more sexually repressive era. As recently as 1971, for example, a woman in Nebraska was deprived of her right to property because she was found guilty of adultery (*Civil Liberties, 282,* December 1971). When a woman marries, still today she must by law assume the surname of her husband, regardless of her own preference in the matter. Similarly, her domicile or legal residence generally follows that of her husband. In California, Florida, Nevada, Pennsylvania, and Texas a wife must obtain court approval before she is legally able to engage in an independent business. In the Florida case a wife must petition the court, listing "her character, habits, education, and mental capacity for business," and she must then either obtain her husband's consent or serve him with a copy of the petition. The "unwritten law" permitting a husband to kill his wife's lover if he finds them in the act of sexual intercourse has been written into some states' laws, such as those of Texas, New Mexico, and Utah. There are no similar provisions in any of our states for a woman who finds her husband in the sexual act with another woman. In the state of Washington women are not required to undergo a premarital medical examination, although men are. Presumably this is based on the assumption that women have not had sexual experiences prior to marriage from which they might have contacted a venereal disease (Kanowitz 1969:13).

Probably the most far-sweeping legislation ever produced in the United States to help guarantee equality for women is Title VII of the 1964 Civil Rights Act. Interestingly enough, however, this bill was originally designed to protect people against economic discrimination only on the basis of "race, color, religion, and national origin." The term "sex" was probably introduced in the bill either as a joke, as some witnesses feel, or as an amendment in the attempt to assure the bill's defeat (Bird 1968:1-19; Kanowitz 1969:105). Its passage is far from a joke, however, since it provides women a broad basis for protection against economic sexual discrimination.

Not all of our laws which discriminate on a sexual basis are to the disadvantage of women, however. Some are overtly in their favor. For example, on the basis of her sex, a woman is altogether exempt from required military service. Her male counterparts can be forcibly removed from their families, occupations, and pleasures, and under the threat of duress be required to perform menial duties not to their liking, to accept various types of both physical and mental hardship and pain, to be deprived of basic rights of political activity and the expression of dissent allowed most civilians, and to be transported to nations thousands of miles from home where they are ordered to kill both combatants and noncombatants against whom they bear no personal illwill. A woman, in marked contrast, *solely on the basis of her sex,* is protected by law from such rigors.

If a woman volunteers for military duty, however, she may find sexual discrimination working against her. A married male veteran, for example, is entitled to receive a dependency benefit for his wife when he attends school under the G.I. Bill, while a married female veteran is denied this additional income unless her husband is totally disabled (*Civil Liberties, 282,* December 1971).

Sexual discrimination is also found in many aspects of education. In many school systems in the United States, boys in the seventh grade take industrial arts, while their seventh-grade female classmates are given the choice between a class in cooking or a class in sewing. In Indiana, New Jersey, and New York, female students are prohibited from participating in interscholastic sports, although legal suits have been filed to change this (*Civil Liberties, 282,* December 1971). Even in sociology, supposedly one of the more liberated disciplines in American academia, only 5 percent of female sociologists have reached our highest rank, that of full professor, while women make up 29 percent of sociologists who are instructors, our lowest rank (Jackson 1972:4).

In politics women also play a lesser role than men, and apparently the change is not going in a direction favoring women. In 1973, of our 435 Representatives, only 14, or a mere 3 percent, were women. A decade earlier, 18 were women, hardly a significant difference. Of our Senators, not a single one of the 100 was a woman, while a decade previously two women were members of the Senate (*Congressional Quarterly Weekly Report, 30,* November 11, 1972:2990). Part of the reason for low female membership in the House and Congress is perhaps not discrimination at the polls but a reluctance on the part of women to run for public office. Yet, part of this reluctance may be the perception on the part of women that the electorate, both male and female, places greater confidence in men and is more willing to vote men into public office. Part of such reluctance is probably also rooted in the early socialization women undergo into "proper" sex roles in life—of which politics is not one, as it is ordinarily considered solely the domain and prerogative of males.

Even in appointed political positions women come out on the short end. No woman has ever been appointed a Justice of the Supreme Court, and only two women have served on the President's Cabinet, the first under Franklin D. Roosevelt and the second under Eisenhower.

Sexual discrimination is also not absent in the economic sphere of American society. Women consistently average considerably less money than men. Only 1 percent of working women earn over $10,000 a year, while 28 percent of working men earn over this amount (Hole and Levine 1971:217). Where the median salary in 1970 for working men was $8,036, the median salary for working women was less than half this amount, only $3,844 (*Statistical Abstracts of the United States,* 1972, Table 536). With the exception of the professional-technical category, women are more likely than men to hold down lower-paying jobs, as is shown on Table 18.1. Even when they work at the same job, however, women consistently average considerably less than men, as Table 18.2 illustrates. This income disparity holds true even for men and women who are unemployed. The median annual income of unemployed men is $3,823, while unemployed women are again compensated at less than half this amount, only $1,686. Unemployment rates are also consistently higher year after year for women than men, as Table 18.3 illustrates. American women, along with blacks, are part of the "last hired, first fired" syndrome so commonly practiced by American business.

Of the 1,900 employers surveyed by the National Office Manager's Association, one third stated that for the same job they paid men more than women (Bird 1971:40). The largest private employer in the

Table 18.1 Sex Ratio by Type of Occupation, 1970 *

Type of Occupation	Percentage of All Female Workers	Percentage of All Male Workers
Professional, Technical	14%	14%
Proprietors, Managers	4	14
Clerical Workers	34	7
Sales Workers	7	6
Craftsmen, Foremen	1	20
Laborers	Less than 1	7
Service Workers	21	

Source: Computed from the *Statistical Abstracts of the United States,* 1972, Table 366.

Table 18.2 Median Annual Earnings by Sex and Type of Occupation, 1970

Type of Occupation	Earnings of Women	Earnings of Men
Professional, Technical	$6,675	$11,577
Proprietors, Managers	5,523	11,292
Clerical workers	4,646	7,965
Sales workers	2,279	8,321
Craftsmen, Foremen	4,276	8,833
Laborers	3,151	4,839
Service workers	2,541	5,568

Source: *Statistical Abstracts of the United States,* 1972, Table 536.

United States, the American Telephone and Telegraph Company, along with its 24 affiliated Bell System telephone companies, was brought to court by the Department of Labor because of its "pervasive and systematic employment discrimination" (*St. Louis Post-Dispatch,* January 19, 1973). In what has been described as the largest settlement in civil rights history, involving a total award of $15,000,000, ten thousand women, most of them telephone operators, were each awarded from $100 to $400 to compensate them for denial of promotional opportunities. The settlement involves a principle never before put into effect, the concept that restitution must be made to certain employees even if they never actually applied for better-paying jobs. The basis for this action was that female employees did not apply for promotion because they knew it was company policy not to promote them. In this landmark case, the negative effects of a discriminatory employment

Table 18.3 Rate of Unemployment Per Year by Sex, 1950–1972

Year	Percentage Rate for Women	Percentage Rate for Men
1950	5.7%	5.1%
1955	4.9	4.2
1960	5.9	5.4
1965	5.5	4.0
1966	4.8	3.2
1967	5.2	3.1
1968	4.8	2.9
1969	4.7	2.8
1970	5.9	4.4
1971	6.9	5.3
1972	6.2	5.1

Source: *Statistical Abstracts of the United States,* 1972, Table 340.

system upon the motivation to achieve by minority group members is at least tacitly recognized.

The movement to liberate women can also lead to greater liberation for men. A major goal of the Social-Democrat Party of Sweden, for example, is to attain the same rights, obligations, and work assignments for men and women. Leaders of this party feel that people should be able to develop their individual talents without being limited to sexually stereotyped roles. If this goal is reached, while women will play a larger role in occupational life men will play a larger role in family life. Men will especially be given greater opportunities for better contact with their children. Reaching this goal should also lessen pressure on men, which probably underlies their higher rates in such things as criminality, suicide, and even death at an earlier age (Palme 1972).

Chauvinistic attitudes by men toward women also entrap men. They prevent men from fully relating to women. One can relate fully to an equal, although even this is always accompanied by difficulty. But one cannot relate fully with persons one considers to be inferior. One can deal in various ways with persons and things one feels are beneath the self, but one does not interact in the same way as when the other is considered an equal. When women are considered sex objects, or men breadwinners, this results in some type of person-object relationship, which is quite different from the relationship persons have who are relating to one another on an equal basis. With the full liberation of both sexes, we shall have the increased possibility of equality in interaction. But we are nowhere near such equality today.

The movement to liberate women deals with all these issues: socialization into expected roles on the basis of sex, chauvinistic attitudes which lead to females being treated as inferior objects, sexual discrimination in occupational hiring and promotion policies, inequality before the law, and discrimination in the military, in education, in politics, and in other areas of social life where people are judged not on the basis of performance or relevant qualifications but on the basis of sex. Apart from the specifics, what people in this movement are protesting is the fundamental discrimination against women that is so pervasive and effective that it denigrates the concept which American women hold of themselves, a discrimination so far-reaching that women typically have less pride in their sex than do men and several times as many girls wish that they had been born boys than boys wish they had been born girls (Watson 1966:477; Broverman *et al.,* 1972). The women's liberation movement is seeking equality in a society where for so many years equality for all has been the teaching but not the practice. Should this equality be gained, it may bring with it the transformation of society as we know it.

chapter 19

Forces for Social Change: Social Movements

Groups of people poised for action—upset about something, pressing for social change, agitating for their point of view, organizing to make others aware of their grievances, actively marching, protesting, and demonstrating—are fairly common phenomena in American society. Angry women picketing Hefner's headquarters in protest against the image and role of women in *Playboy*. Grape pickers striking and millions across the nation sympathetically refusing to buy grapes. Homosexuals in mass demonstration publicly proclaiming, "Out of the closet!" Freedom riders forcefully integrating busses. White-robed and hooded night riders burning crosses under cover of darkness. Pinkerton guards busting strikers' heads at a besieged automobile plant. All are examples of social movements, specifically the women's liberation movement, the grape boycott, the gay liberation movement, the black liberation movement, the Ku Klux Klan, and the union movement of the 1920's and 30's.

A **social movement** is a group of people acting with some continuity beyond an individual community or a single event in order to systematically promote or resist some change in society (cf. Turner and Killian 1972:246). Note that there are five main elements in this definition. First of all, social movements always involve fairly large numbers of people. An individual and his friends who are protesting some issue, for example, do not make up a social movement. Second, more than one locality or a single event is involved in the protest activity; that is, the action and influence of a social movement is geographically widespread. Third, a social movement is characterized by continuity or sustained activity. An overnight event or one around which people rally for just a short period of time is not a social movement. In this way, a social movement is unlike a strike in a business or industry. Fourth, social movements always involve **social change.** Sometimes a social movement is a reactive protest against change already taking place in society, while at other times a social movement promotes social change. Fifth, a social movement is organized; that is, in some systematic fashion people are attempting through participation in group activities to achieve goals involving social change. In this way a social movement is unlike a crowd.

Social movements are of three major types: reactionary, reform, and revolutionary. When the concern of people active in a social movement is to resist change, we can call it a **reactionary social movement.** People in a reactionary social movement are reacting negatively to change occurring in society and are attempting to prevent the change from taking place or attempting to bring some aspect of society back to its prior status quo. The Ku Klux Klan of the late 1800's and the early 1900's

Reactionary, reform, and revolutionary are the three major types of social movements. People in reactionary social movements are attempting to prevent social change from taking place, or attempting to bring an aspect of society back to its prior status quo. The Ku Klux Klan is an example of a reactionary social movement. (Courtesy of Wide World Photos)

and McCarthyism of the 1950's are examples of reactionary social movements. When, in contrast, a social movement is directed at promoting social change, it can be either a reform or a revolutionary movement. In a **reform social movement** people are seeking to alter some specific or limited area of the existing social order. The grape boycott, the gay liberation movement, and the union movement are examples of reform social movements. A **revolutionary social movement** has a much broader aim: the reconstruction of the entire social order. Members of revolutionary social movements are not protesting a specific aspect of life in society, nor are they attempting to simply realign the institutions of society. They desire, rather, to replace those institutions with another social order. The movement led by Fidel Castro in Cuba is an example of a revolutionary social movement (Blumer 1969:21).

Because a reform social movement does not challenge the existence of present social institutions but their members work instead toward modifications of some particular aspect of them, persons in a reform movement are able to use those same institutions, such as schools,

While the goal of a revolutionary social movement is to replace the existing social order with another, in a reform social movement people are attempting to change some limited area of the existing social order, as in the Gay Liberation Movement. (Courtesy of Wide World Photos)

churches, the press, and even the government, in their attempt to bring about their desired social change. While others may not approve the particulars of the goals of the group, the goals themselves are based upon major cultural values, values which at least in principle are accepted by members of the society. Equality for women, for example, matches egalitarian values officially taught and commonly held in American society. This does not mean that people who disagree with the specific goals but perhaps respect the general principles on which they are based will approve the change. The changes desired by those in a reform social movement may very well challenge the vested interests of those who agree with the principles but disagree with the particulars. For example, men in dominant positions in society may feel that their security in those positions is threatened by the attempt of women to gain equality. Yet the idea of equality is probably something that they accept *in principle*.

Because people in a revolutionary social movement are challenging the existence of social institutions, along with their basic scheme of moral values, and want to replace them with an alternative set, when a movement is or becomes revolutionary it is actively confronted by representatives of the social order, especially by the police powers of the State. Because they wish to replace the social order, members of revolutionary social movements become anathema to representatives of the status quo and are forbidden to use the facilities of social institutions in their goals of social change. Consequently, revolutionary movements are usually driven underground, while reform movements are able to operate openly within the existing social structure (Blumer 1969:21).

Another major difference characterizes reform and revolutionary social movements. Although both are conflict groups, working in opposition to other groups which have contrary and competing interests, people in a reform movement seek to make changes by influencing public opinion in favor of their goals, while people in a revolutionary movement try to make converts. In this way, a revolutionary social movement operates more like a religion (Blumer 1969:22).

A single social movement can generate all three of the basic orientations which characterize social movements: reform, revolutionary, and reactionary. The women's liberation movement, to continue our example, is not composed of a single type, but consists of many specific groups holding markedly differing orientations. Some are *reform* groups: Their goal is to remove sexual inequalities from American society, to make it possible for women to be accepted on an equal footing with men. Although they assuredly wish to make changes in American social institutions, reform groups are not challenging the validity of those institutions. Members of reform groups protest the discrimination women receive, but not the social system itself. Their goal is to reform existing social arrangements in order to make things better for women, not to replace those institutions with others.

Other groups in the women's movement are more radical and have a *revolutionary* orientation. Members of these groups are not only protesting sexual discrimination, but they also stand in basic opposition to the underlying social arrangements that lead to discrimination. They are calling for the replacement of the current social system with one they feel would be amenable to equality. They feel that our current institutional arrangements are inherently evil, being based on pitting person against person in order to maintain particular groups in power. People within the women's movement who are active in groups which are revolutionary in orientation basically see capitalism as the root of intersexual problems, and they wish to restructure the means of production and distribution in order to alter basic relationships between the sexes. The abolition of capitalism and its replacement with another economic system certainly does not match the values traditionally held in the United States, and, consequently, groups within the women's movement which have this orientation are less acceptable both to members of the existing power structure and to the general public.

Not surprisingly, then, opposition to a social movement depends in part (1) on whether adherents of the movement's goals are reformist or revolutionary. Other factors in determining the amount of opposition involve (2) visibility, the extent to which others are aware of the group's goals and activities; (3) evaluation, the extent to which others feel that the goals of the movement have a chance of succeeding or the extent to which they feel the goals, if reached, would disrupt present institutional arrangements; and (4) threat, the extent to which others feel that their own position in the social order will be lessened if the movement were to succeed.

Although members of reform and revolutionary groups within the women's movement differ in many of their basic orientations, they both strongly agree that women are victims of discrimination and that change in the direction of sexual equality must take place. Working in opposition to these two types are groups of women who are *reacting against* the changes sought by the other activists. Women in these *reactionary* groups feel that men are rightfully dominant in their leadership positions and that women should play a more passive role in public life, concentrating instead on their roles in the home as mother and wife. This "petticoat and powder-puff faction," as it has been called, appears to be especially conscious of social amenities, taking the position that men should properly open doors for women, light their cigarettes, take the initiative in dating relations, and so on. They appear to be of the opinion that women in general have never had it so good and that women ought to relax in their domestic roles while the man competes for their livelihood in the world of commerce. Women in these reactionary groups are fearful of the changes sought by the women in groups with reform and revolutionary orientations: They feel that their own privileged status is threatened by the goals that others are seeking.

Social movements are frequently brought about by gradual but pervasive changes in cultural values. Such changes are called **cultural drift;** that is, a general shifting takes place in the ideas of people. These changes in basic ideas and values are not sudden, but over a long period of time they gradually "drift" in a different direction. Especially relevant for the genesis of social movements are general changes in the ideas which people have of themselves and of their rights, obligations, and privileges. Because of a variety of factors—such as technological developments, shifts in social roles of segments of the population, a changing economic base, broadening of perspectives due to exposure to contrasting information from the mass media, or changing perspectives due to travel and other forms of communication—over a period of time people can develop a different idea about what they believe they have right to expect in life. When the things they desire and the things they feel that they can legitimately hope for change sufficiently, a new set of values has emerged which then influences the way they look at their own lives, especially their relationships to others and their relative position in society.

The emergence of new values through cultural drift can provide the basic motivation for social movements. The ideas of themselves that people develop, ideas of what they can hope for, to what they can reasonably aspire, and the conditions to which they feel they have a legitimate right, can stand in marked contrast with the actual positions that they occupy in society. With their new dispositions and interests, people become sensitized in new directions. This leads them to experience dissatisfaction, whereas they previously were satisfied with their lot in life (Blumer 1969:9).

Although these dissatisfactions may at first be rather vague and indefinite, they bring with them the possibility that a focal point will develop. If leadership emerges, vague feelings of dissatisfaction which are generalized among segments of the populace can provide the nucleus for broad membership in a social movement. If the emerging leadership is able to successfully exert guidance and control, it can provide specific aims around which followers rally. For example, from the vague and general aim of the emancipation of women leaders can focus dissatisfaction onto specific issues, such as discrimination in marriage, occupations, education, or the law.

Although social movements usually begin with vague feelings and little leadership, leadership shortly develops to collectively organize these vague sentiments. Persons who turn out to be successful leaders tend to organize the membership of a social movement. A major goal in developing structure is to direct collective action toward the redress of common grievances.

Progress toward specific goals in social movements will generally be uneven, marked by steps forward and setbacks, enthusiasm and disillusionment, energy and apathy. Frequently a movement must retread the same ground that it has recently covered as the movement loses impetus or reaches what appear to be insurmountable obstacles or as new members join who must themselves be brought to points of realization about their fate in life of which others have already become conscious (Blumer 1969:10). Even attaining long sought-after goals can contribute to the uneven progress of social movements. In some cases, reaching a major goal can even be disastrous for a social movement. Rather than sparking interest, the members may very well lose interest in participating in the movement because things look so much better. Achieving an important goal can remove a major focus of dissatisfaction, and unless the leadership is able to refocus dissatisfaction and redirect the membership into battling for related specific causes, energies will tend to be spent elsewhere than in the movement. This at least appears to be part of the reason for the decline of the women's liberation movement in 1920, following the culmination of three fourths of a century's endeavors with the adoption of the Nineteenth Amendment to the Constitution. (Many other factors, however, were also involved. Cf. O'Neill 1971:89–97.)

Social movements tend to go through four main stages (Turner and Killian 1972:253). The first is a general stage of *vague uneasiness,* dissatisfaction, or restlessness. No leadership yet emerges. This is followed by a stage of *popular excitement.* During this stage, feelings and goals of those experiencing dissatisfaction are not highly specific, but more specific ideas regarding both causes of the problem and what should be done to change it are in the process of being developed. This stage is characterized by a general sharpening of objectives. Leaders in this stage are likely to be similar to prophets or reformers. The third stage is that of *formalization.* During this stage the movement becomes more clearly organized with the development of rules, policies, tactics, and discipline. The leader at this point is likely to be more of a statesman. The fourth stage is the *institutionalizing* of the movement. When this occurs, the movement has become highly organized, with a hierarchic structure of personnel differentiated into separate responsibilities to execute the movement's purposes. The leader in this last stage is likely to be an administrative type (Blumer 1969:12).

As we covered in the last chapter, not only men but also women tend to see females through the eyes of the dominant ideology, an ideology that supports the status quo of relationships between the sexes. To accept this ideology means to accept the way things are, and to lend support, at least passively, to maintaining males in their dominant position. To reject the ideology means to reject the idea of male dominance and female subservience. But there are many types of reaction to our sex role ideology, each with varying degrees of acceptance or rejection, support or nonsupport. There appear to be four main types of reaction by women to the dominant ideology of the sexes. Figure 19.1 shows one way of diagramming these reactions.

The first reaction is represented by women who experience only vague dissatisfactions with their lot in life (as do many men), feeling perhaps that something is wrong but not knowing exactly what. They do not connect their feelings of dissatisfaction with their sex role. They passively accept the ideological ordering of the sexes. The second are those who pinpoint their dissatisfactions onto their sex role, but they perceive no viable solutions to their problems. They passively reject the ideological ordering of the sexes. The third are women who feel quite satisfied with the way things are. They enjoy the security of being taken care of by men or have the hope that they will some day have a man to take care of them. They actively accept the ideological ordering of the sexes. It is from this third group of women that members of groups reacting against the women's movement are drawn. The fourth are

Figure 19.1   Reactions to Dominant Sexual Ideology

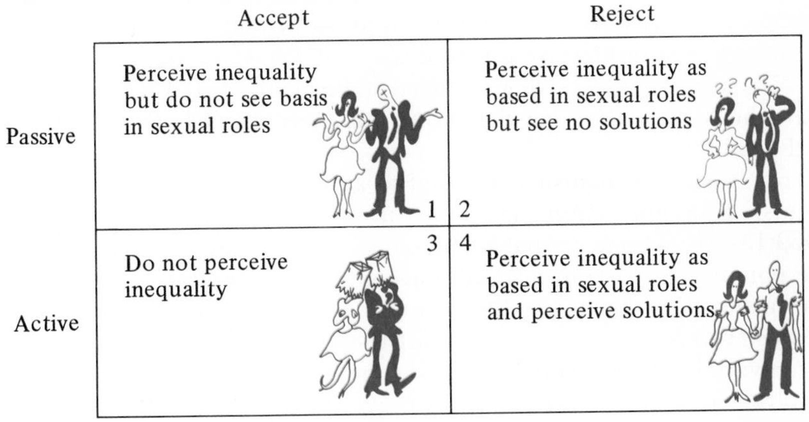

	Accept	Reject
Passive	Perceive inequality but do not see basis in sexual roles 1	Perceive inequality as based in sexual roles but see no solutions 2
Active	Do not perceive inequality 3	Perceive inequality as based in sexual roles and perceive solutions 4

those who pinpoint their dissatisfactions onto structured sex roles and feel that there are ways of solving their problems. They actively reject the ideology which supports male dominance.

Note that in this diagram we are not dealing with the extent of reaction. Cell two, for example, includes both women who feel only mildly dissatisfied with their lot in life and those who are extremely dissatisfied. It also includes both those who are trying to figure out solutions, although they see none at the present, and the apathetic who have given up hope of ever finding solutions. Although the "petticoat faction" recruits from those in cell three and the reformists and revolutionaries recruit from cell four, cells three and four also include numerous women who never become active either in the struggle for or in the opposition to social change. The vast majority of persons appear to quietly live out their lives without becoming actively involved in social movements.

From the women's liberation viewpoint, women in cells one, two, and three need to undergo "consciousness expansion." Women in cell one need to see that their feelings of dissatisfaction are based on sex role inequality. They must become conscious that their dissatisfactions result from being forced, because of their sex, to play subservient roles in society. If this occurs, they then would be categorized in cell two, with women who feel that sexual inequality is the basic reason for their problems but who do not see that viable solutions are possible or that such solutions should be actively sought out. If they come to the point of seeing solutions, they would then be part of those characterized by cell four. Many in cell four, however, fail to connect their perceptions with actions designed to solve their problems, a continued frustration and despair to activists in the women's liberation movement.

From the women's liberation viewpoint, women in cell three represent the oppressed internalizing the oppressors' ideas. From their point of view, such attitudes are the equivalent of a slave saying, "I like slavery. It's secure. I like having my needs taken care of. If I work hard all year, the Man lets me get drunk at Christmas. Mr. Charley treats me real good."

Four major mechanisms are used to attain the goals of social movements: agitation, *esprit de corps,* morale, and ideology (Blumer 1969:13–20). The *first,* that of agitation, is especially necessary when the potential activists of a social movement are complacent, when they are taking their lot in life for granted. It is then necessary to agitate people even to get the movement off the ground.

Activists in the women's liberation movement are currently heavily involved in agitation. They are working at developing what might be called a "consciousness of oppression" among women in order to re-

A major mechanism in attaining the goals of a social movement is agitation which develops a "consciousness of oppression" among a target group. In this photo are shown members of the Dutch Women's Liberation Movement who have written "Master of my own belly" on their stomachs. (Courtesy of Wide World Photos)

move what some of them call the "slave mentality" of the oppressed. They especially try to raise consciousness through disseminating information regarding differences in male and female incomes, laws which discriminate against women, negative effects of socialization into sex roles, and so forth. In order to liberate people, people must want to be liberated: otherwise they will opt for the status quo. Agitation has as its basic purpose, then, changing the ideas that people have about who they are and about their rights in life. The raising of consciousness through agitation is a basic mechanism leaders of a social movement use in their attempt to reach their goals (Blumer 1969:13–14).

The *second* mechanism for reaching the goals of a social movement is the development of *esprit de corps*. If there is merely agitation, not much will happen beyond the initial impetus. Direction must be given dissatisfactions in order to sustain a social movement. A major means of providing solidarity within a social movement is to develop **esprit de corps,** "the sense which people have of belonging together and of being identified with one another in a common undertaking" (Blumer 1969:14–15). When *esprit de corps* exists, people have the feeling that they are sharing a common experience and that they form an intimate and important part of a select group. Such feelings lead to cooperation toward mutual goals by breaking down personal competition and overcoming attitudes of aloofness.

Esprit de corps leads to the feeling that people are facing the same problems together. The individual sees himself as part of a larger group, all of whom have been faced with similar problems and are now attempting to mutually solve them as a close-working unit. This reinforces the feeling of belonging with others and gives a sense of collective support for the problems being faced. A sense of attachment grows for other people who are identified as part of the movement.

Important for the development of *esprit de corps* is the existence of an enemy. Identifying another group as a dangerous enemy threatening the goals of one's group can take advantage of basic feelings of ethnocentrism. People are then more easily able to attribute virtues and other positive characteristics to their own group, while assigning negative traits to the enemy, such as looking at them as unscrupulous, vicious, selfish, and unyielding obstructionists. An enemy provides a major symbol around which members of a social movement can rally. They can negatively identify with and react to characteristics attributed to the enemy, while positively identifying with and reacting to characteristics assigned to one's own group.

The women's liberation movement has its enemy: It is those men and women who feel that women and men *should* serve different roles in society *because* of their sex. The name commonly given to this enemy is "chauvinist pigs." Those who receive this pejorative label represent everything that the women's liberation movement opposes: superiority of males, subservient roles for women, and, in general, the total "woman's-place-is-in-the-home-and-man-is-the-aggressive-breadwinner" syndrome. Major symbols of the enemy in the early 1970's were Hugh Hefner and his *Playboy* magazine and Norman Mailer and his writings.

Esprit de corps also develops out of informal association, from such activities as singing, joking, and informal conversation. As people who are active in a social movement share with one another their experiences of dissatisfaction, they develop the ability to take one another's role. They then begin to internalize a set of attitudes, values, and a basic philosophy of life which supports the goals of the movement and encourages their continued participation. Developing and sharing such basic orientations to life leads to a sense of intimacy. Individuals who once felt lonely, alienated, and frustrated are then able to experience highly gratifying social acceptance and mutual support (Blumer

1969:16). As alienating loneliness and despair are replaced by valued feelings of belonging, and when one knows that this change is due to associating with fellow group members, one can easily develop an intense loyalty to the group and to the positions that it represents.

Esprit de corps can also be developed through formal ceremonial behavior and ritual. Mass meetings, rallies, parades, and demonstrations can lead to the feeling by a participant that he has vast support for what he experiences in life. This leads to a feeling of personal expansion, a growing sense of individual importance. Symbols used in such ceremonies and rituals, in the form of flags, slogans, signs, lapel buttons, and gestures, can become significant in developing *esprit de corps*. The symbols take on sentimental value. They come to represent shared feelings about the movement, mutual experiences, and the solution to experienced dissatisfactions. They develop in followers sentiments shared in common concerning the ultimate value of the cause in which they are participating and for which they are perhaps sacrificing. When these symbols have attained such meaning for adherents to the movement, they become a powerful force for mobilizing both action and sentiment. By skillfully using them, leaders can renew feelings of mutuality, rekindle identity with the cause, and mobilize action toward the attainment of group goals (cf. Blumer 1969:16–17).

To succeed, a social movement needs more than agitation and *esprit de corps*. This *third* mechanism utilized to reach goals is the development of morale. **Morale** can be viewed as a sense of determination in the face of adversity, and involves the feeling of collective purpose. Morale is frequently based upon the conviction that the group's goals are right because their success will lead to a better life. Morale is also frequently rooted in the belief that these goals are in line with higher moral values in the universe, and that, consequently, they will inevitably come about. Morale of this sort is closely equivalent to the belief in a sacred mission.

Especially helpful in the development of morale is being able to attach or identify the values of the group with a highly respected person. Consequently, social movements tend to develop heroes and martyrs, leaders to whom are attributed superiority in the particular values held by the group.

Also helpful in developing morale is the formulation of myths which deal with the destiny of the movement and which perhaps depict the glories of the life-to-come when the movement has finally overcome present adversity and realized its goals. Similarly, developing a creed which affirms the basic belief structure of the group can aid in the development of morale. Morale can also be nurtured by producing a literature which centers around the major goals of the group, which provides hope of attaining those goals, which demonstrates their rightness and exposes the moral bankruptcy of the enemy. Such literature can eventually take on an element of sacredness for activists in the social movement (Blumer 1969:10, 18).

Myths, creeds, and literature incorporate the ideology of the group, the *fourth* major mechanism for attaining the group's goals. Ideology contains the justification for the movement's existence, represents its values and ideals, and defines the movement by contrasting it with other social movements and institutions (King 1956:32; Toch 1965:21). This set of related beliefs, whether written into the form of a creed or merely verbally reaffirmed among the members, is a statement of what the members of the movement are together trying to achieve and what they wish to jointly affirm. Ideology "points down the road along which the social movement is moving, and specifies the principles and objectives that guide its journey" (Toch 1965:21). Ideology ultimately provides an integrated central core of values. It gives justification for the existence of the movement itself and for continued participation of the individual in the movement. The movement's ideology provides direction for future action, as well as justification for present and past action. Ideology furnishes a capstone by which one can define one's own position and maintain boundaries between one's own goals and activities relative to competing groups. Ideology also provides verbal weapons with which to defend one's own positions and to attack those of "the enemy." Finally, ideology also provides inspirational hope to the group's members and organizes sentiments into collective action. The group's ideology is often formulated by a select intelligentsia within the movement (cf. Blumer 1969:19–20).

If a social movement is to be successful, **internal tactics** must be judiciously developed, that is, tactics which are directed toward members and potential members. Internal tactics involve agitating large numbers of people. Once large numbers of people are aroused, internal tactics are then used to develop commitment to the movement by keeping members aware of the way the movement defines the sources of their problems. Internal tactics are also used to hold out the hope of solving these problems through participation in the movement. By internal tactics, leaders further strengthen the movement by developing in their followers *esprit de corps* and morale. Internal tactics are also used to socialize newcomers into the group's ideology.

External tactics are also necessary for attaining goals and must be carefully developed if a social movement is to succeed. These are tactics for dealing with persons who are not members of the group and who probably never will be members. By using the right external tactics, nonmembers can be neutralized, that is, they can be prevented from taking a stand against the group and directing their energies in opposition to the social movement. If highly successful, external tactics can do more than neutralize potential opposition: They can also enlist sympathy and tacit support from nonmembers.

External tactics are especially applied to "the enemy." If the enemy is powerful—and if he were not it probably would not be necessary for a social movement to develop in order to uproot him—it is strategic not to directly challenge the enemy while the movement has inadequate support, lest through premature action the movement be crushed. Sometimes running scrimmage with the enemy is the best tactic, fighting small battles over minor issues related to major goals. If the scrimmage is lost, the movement itself is not defeated. But whether the scrimmage is won or lost, attention by means of publicity can be focused on the movement, which can result in raising the consciousness of potential members and lead to gaining more adherents. Publicity is also an external tactic which can enlist sympathizers and neutralize potential enemies. Provoking a battle with the enemy in order to create a martyr for the movement's cause is sometimes an excellent tactic since it provides a focal symbol with which group members can strongly identify. Developing martyrs also solidifies issues, draw sharper lines between competing ideologies, and firms boundaries between conflicting groups. Martyrs can also consolidate a social movement by drawing together groups competing for similar goals. This can more easily occur when the martyr represents the general goals of the social movement and is not too firmly identified with a specific group within the movement.

Whatever tactics are used, whether they are external or internal, they must be modified to fit the goals of the social movement within its own particular historical milieu. The tactics of social movements which have proven successful in one generation, or in specific situations within one culture, can completely fail when applied to other situations and cultures. Consequently, a good part of the energies of the leaders of a social movement is directed toward the development and modification of tactics for dealing with members and nonmembers in order to further the goals of the movement.

The importance of understanding social movements is two-fold. First, social movements are a vital part of contemporary events in both the United States and in the rest of the world. Consequently, by understanding the principles involved in social movements, one gains a better understanding of many current events which affect vital aspects of our own lives. Second, contemporary life is characterized by change. We are all constantly immersed in social change, continually making adjustments in our own lives and plans in response to the swirling changes in society which so vitally affect us. There are many sources of these changes. Social change occurs in response to technological developments, competing ideologies, competition and conflict between social groups, violence within society, war between societies, modernization, industrialization, urbanization, and contacts between different cultures (cf. Lauer 1973). Social movements are one of these major means by which change is brought about in society. There is no indication that social movements will disappear from the social scene, and in the years to come we will find ourselves at least continuing to read about them in the mass media, if not actively participating in them ourselves.

5

The Social Fabric

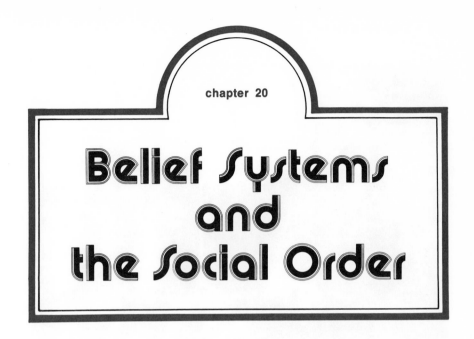

chapter 20

Belief Systems and the Social Order

What holds society together? With modern society's many competing interest groups, with all their potential and actual disruptions and conflicts, what keeps society from being torn apart? How does a society manage to remain as a unit and not break up into warring factions, with each splinter group claiming territory and proclaiming itself a nation? In answering this question, we shall build on major points and principles which we have examined in the preceding chapters.

Underlying any such answer is **power,** the ability to get what you want even though others oppose what you desire. Power in modern nation-states is not diffuse. Power is not distributed evenly among the people of a nation. Rather, power is concentrated. Some groups or individuals hold much more power than do other groups or individuals. In each modern society the naked instruments of power are the police and the armed services. It is they who are permitted to wield the weapons of violence and who are skillfully schooled in their use. These instruments of power are not responsive to the whims or the will of just anyone. The police and the armed services respond to only a limited number of persons, primarily to select officials from whom they receive their legitimation, from whom they receive their directions or orders, and to whom they are responsible.

Those who hold power in society are the legislators who make laws and the officials who administer those laws. Power is concentrated in the hands of those who possess the authority to give orders to those who bear arms. In a nation where the military and the police are under civilian authority, it is civilian authorities who wield the power. But the

The maintenance of order in modern society is ultimately rooted in physical violence. Because of effective socialization into the established ways of doing things, however, most people conform to societal dictates for less dramatic reasons.   (Photo by Laima Turnley)

legislators, officials, and various administrative authorities of a nation are also more responsive to the will of some than to others. In countries with elective processes these officials do not respond solely to the ballot box, but are also heavily influenced by various interest groups and by individuals who are either able to muster significant support for or against the officials or who are able and willing to make large campaign contributions. These persons who influence, and in some cases even direct, such civilian authorities are also power holders. Many times they wield power only behind-the-scenes, and are content to remain but faceless unknowns to the general public.

The maintenance of order in modern society and the maintenance of status quo power positions are ultimately rooted in physical violence. By either threatening to use or by actually using physical violence, those who hold elite power positions in society attempt to consolidate and maintain their positions. As has been astutely observed, even though the policeman writing a ticket for a traffic violation may courteously smile as he hands the offender his summons, the gun riding so openly at his hip is far from being merely decorative. Physical violence is the policeman's ultimate basis for enforcing the rules he is carrying out (Berger 1963:69). Even though the leaders of a huge territory secede from a nation whose policies they disagree with, as prior to our

Civil War, it is the wielding of power through massive physical violence which ultimately decides whether a separate nation shall in fact exist. The leaders of a nation do not take lightly such a threat to the social order, and if it takes physical violence to maintain that order, physical violence will be used.

As we covered in Chapter 11, the maintenance of a social order depends on making people predictable, on bringing their behavior in line with the expectations of others. For society to hang together, people must be able to know what to expect from others, and they must be able to depend on those expectations. Failure to meet those expectations brings sanctions designed to bring their behavior back into line. If, on the one hand, their violations are covered by law, they will be arrested, fined, or jailed. If, on the other hand, their violations involve severe or repetitive breaking of background expectancies, they come under a related system of social control, that of the mental health establishment. In either case, as the social order depends on people conforming to expectations, when physical constraints are felt necessary to elicit this conformance, physical constraint will be used.

But power, and its corollary of physical violence, are by no means the only bases of order in society. Although the threat of physical violence is ominously and continuously present, menacingly underlying the social order and buttressing the status quo, the use of physical violence itself is seldom necessary. As we covered in Chapters 9 and 14, to elicit conformance force is ordinarily used only as a last resort. Most of us most of the time do not do what others desire because of the threat of physical violence hanging over our heads. Conformity usually flows from a different basis. That basis is socialization into a belief system.

When we enter this life, we are joining an ongoing social group. Essential to our socialization as new members of this group is learning the group's symbols. These symbols teach us how members of our group mark out their world, what they consider important in the world, and what they feel a member of their group should be like. To learn a group's symbols, especially its language, is to receive a picture of the world; that is, language and other group symbols help to teach us what the world is like from the point of view of our group. Through its symbols, the group imparts to us a picture of reality; and it is this picture of reality which forms the major basis of our behavior.

Language, as we covered in an earlier chapter, not only provides us words with which we can describe the world, but the particular words which we are provided impart to us highly specialized ways of perceiving the world and ways of evaluating the world. As we learn language, we are being socialized into the group's norms and values (Mills 1967b:433).

It is not simply that learning a particular language, such as English, carries with it certain built-in ways of perceiving the world, although each language does this. Equally significant for understanding social relationships is that in a large pluralistic society the language we learn differs according to subgroup membership. Even though everyone may be learning the same formal language, which words one learns to apply to particular situations depends to a large extent on the subculture in society into which one is being socialized. The significance of this is that the words one learns to apply to a situation or event determine to a large extent what one perceives and how one learns to evaluatively react to those situations and events.

To use a crude but relevant example, although two children are both in the process of being Americanized, one's family is located in the social structure where people apply the word "dirty" to socks after a single day's wear. The other's family is located in the social structure where people do not describe socks as dirty until after three or four days' wear. Applying the word "dirty" to socks does not at all depend solely on objective factors. In this case, for example, such objectivity becomes irrelevant, as the first child's father works in an office and is seldom on his feet, while the father of the second child works heavy construction. The physical factors may be objectively one thing, but the perception of those factors is at least in large part linguistically based. Language is not learned in a social vacuum, and learning a language carries with it some group's set of values and their expectations of behavior.

Central to the picture of reality which our group gives us is a view of how the world *should* be. We learn that we should be a particular type of person—essentially the type of person our parents, our peers, and our teachers desire. We learn *what* we ought to do: We should obey our parents, act like a friend, do our studies conscientiously, and so on. As we are socialized into a group and are given its picture of reality, we learn what we should be like in general and we are taught the particulars concerning what we should do in various situations in our relationships with others.

In addition, we are also taught reasons which are said to underlie these "shoulds." We learn not only the rules, that is what is expected of us by others, but we are also provided a set of beliefs on which those rules are supposedly based. The rules and their matching reasons are generally tautologous, that is, the reason given for following a rule is generally some form of repetition of the rule itself, such as, "If you do that, you are bad," which means that "being good" is equated with the initial obedience which was itself demanded.

These basic rules comprise a central part of the picture of reality which we learn as children, and they ordinarily become an essential part of the unquestioned assumptions upon which we live our lives. Although we may question and modify particulars from time to time, especially as we undergo contrary learning experiences, our childhood learning yields a basic framework from which we interpret life. In both early and continuing socialization, we learn a symbolic representation of the way the world is perceived and how people in the world should be.

In our society today, for example, we learn a set of beliefs concerning childhood and a matched set of beliefs centering around parenthood. These integrated beliefs, centering around obedience and rights, form a picture of the way people "ought" to be in life. They give us a view of what is "right" and "wrong." We learn, for example, that children should be obedient, that they should do what their parents say. And we also learn that children have certain basic rights, such as the right to food, shelter, clothing, education, and, increasingly in contemporary society, the right to recreation and to self-expression. As we learn ideas about what is right for children, we also learn matching beliefs centering around expected parental roles. Specifically, we learn that parents should provide those things to which their children have rights, in return for which parents have the right to expect obedience and respect.

Although such teachings are basic in contemporary society, they are far from simple. They are part of an intermeshed system of beliefs which are of fundamental importance for social control: They both impart identity to the individual and unite him with his larger society. Through such beliefs we learn our place in society. We learn who we are and what we *ought* to be like. We learn to view ourselves as having a particular place in the world. We learn that we are children of a particular family, that we are of a particular age and that as we grow older we can expect certain changes to occur in our roles or our place in society, such as that later we will go to school, someday get married, work at a job, have more responsibilities, more rights, and so on. Such aspects of early socialization provide us a picture of ourselves in relation to others, however inaccurate the picture may be. We then perceive interconnections between our developing concept of self and our developing ideas of others (cf. Apter 1964:18).

As we relate to others within our assigned roles, we also learn what our role partners, such as our friends, our teachers, and so on, should be like. For example, we learn that **particularistic criteria** should apply to parent-child relations. That is, we learn that parents should love their children because of who they are: Parents should show favors, bestow gifts, and otherwise give deferential treatment to their children because they are their children, not because they possess certain abilities or other characteristics found favorable by the parents. When we are socialized into these early roles, we also learn that different criteria apply to other relationships. For example, we learn that teachers should deal with pupils according to **universalistic criteria.** That is, we learn that teachers should not act toward students on the basis of their being certain persons, such as the sons or daughters of particular parents, but they should be judged according to criteria that are to be equally applied to everyone. For example, as he or she awards grades, a teacher is expected to disregard parental power, wealth, or status to disregard his or her own affective reactions to personalities, and to utilize for all the same criteria of accomplishment.

As we learn such belief systems, we are learning a **system of morality,** intermeshed expectations of right and wrong. We learn what is expected of people in relationship to others, including what is expected of ourselves in relationships. We then learn to evaluate others and ourselves according to how they and we measure up to the belief system. Such belief systems become incorporated into the picture which we gain of the world.

As our experiences with others expand, that is, as we deal directly with a greater variety of people and as we are exposed to contrasting ideas from the mass media, our picture of the world also expands. We gain an idea of what society is like based on the parts of society which we experience. Thus, ways in which we view society depend upon where we are located within the social structure. As we covered in Chapters 2 and 3, quite contrasting pictures of the world are given to a child growing up in the ghetto where the resources necessary to sustain life are scarce and a child whose father is a high government official or the president of a large corporation. These are, literally, different worlds; and children growing up in such different life situations gain quite contrasting views of what the world is like.

Although the pictures gained of the world vary so greatly from one person to another depending upon the particulars of the socialization experience, they have certain features in common which unite people. For example, each child at some point learns that he is an American, that he is expected to go to school, and that males are dominant. Especially important, each learns that he or she occupies a certain place within an *authority* system. Each person learns that he or she is a child and that others are older and more powerful. Although the particulars differ markedly with the individual situation, each newcomer to society learns that these older, more powerful persons have certain expectations which must be met or punishment will follow. Thus, in spite of the wide variance of the particulars, we all learn that we occupy a smaller, more subservient place within a larger social system. We all learn that we must play certain roles in order to survive within that larger system. This is the *political significance of childhood socialization:* Authority of some sort is legitimated.

Early childhood experiences in the family aid what is called **anticipatory socialization,** that is, the newcomer to society learns how to play a role or how to be a certain kind of person before he is called on to play that role. For example, as we learn in our childhood experiences what parents should be like, we are not limited to the parental roles played by our own parents. We also see how other parents treat their children, and we become exposed to a generalized belief system concerning familial roles. We thus develop ideas of what parents in general should be like. We learn aspects of this role in advance of the actual need: We are able to anticipate how we ourselves will or should act when we become parents.

The "when" of the preceding statement is highly significant. In American culture there is the general expectation that people should marry and produce children. When we learn the dominant belief system, we also learn that we shall one day become parents.

The basic elements of these belief systems are not ordinarily isolated, but they intermesh. For example, we not only learn how we *ought* to act toward our own parents, but we also learn the roles we are expected to play toward our friends and relatives, our teachers and employers, and various authorities. Thus we learn not only that we should be good children, *whatever the particulars are at that historical moment which define "good" for us,* but we also learn that we should be good friends and good students, with these expectations later becoming extended to being good workers and good citizens. We ordinarily learn some of these expectations at home, but whatever we learn at home is modified through our exposure to other experiences. In the public school system especially, but also in other institutions such as the church, teaching "good" citizenship is a major endeavor. The institutions of society combinatively reinforce the dominant belief system. (Cf., Reynolds and Henslin 1973).

The social control aspect of the belief systems into which we are socialized should readily be apparent. When, for example, we learn that we should marry a person of the opposite sex and reproduce, we are also learning that we have the obligation to support the children that we shall one day bring into the world, which ordinarily requires working at some occupation. At an early age we learn that we are expected to exchange our labor for money. To make this exchange usually requires subordinating our personal desires to the will of an employer. To survive economically and socially almost always requires that we place ourselves within the authority system represented by occupations. Our early socialization into accepting authority and our intensive socialization into desiring material things greatly aids our entry into and continued participation in this control system, while our socialization into parental roles almost guarantees our acquiescence.

The belief systems which we learn expand, intermeshing with belief systems of larger scope. We become encapsulated further and further into these encompassing belief systems, being continually taught expected roles and being provided an *underlying rationale* for what is expected of us. One fascinating aspect of this symbolic system which provides ready-made interpretations of our experiences is that these images of the world are for the most part legacies from strangers and from persons who have already departed from our society. They are given us by "crowds of witnesses" whom we have "never met and never shall meet. Yet for every man these images—provided by strangers and dead men—are the very basis of (our) life as human being(s)" (Mills 1967b:405).

Symbolic systems are a necessary characteristic of human beings. What happens in life is meaningless by itself. It is when people interpret events that events take on meaning for them. The interpretation or meaning is not built into the event itself, but people provide meaning for what happens in life. The categories of thought prevailing in a particular culture provide meaning to events by providing a means for classifying what occurs. When events are classified, that is, when they are placed within the categories of a symbolic system, a particular framework is given for viewing the event. In the example previously cited, socks are not seen as dirty because some objective standard of "cleanliness" or "dirtiness" is built into the socks themselves. Socks are given the meaning of "dirty" or "clean" according to the way they are classified, not because their objective characteristics force themselves upon people—although there certainly are times when we smell some socks that it may appear to us that the characteristic is dependent on the condition of the socks.

Belief systems are frameworks of thought which serve to symbolically integrate or interpret what happens in life. To clarify this point, let us take the example of university students barricading themselves in a building. What does such an event mean? The meaning of the event is not built into the event itself, but the meaning depends upon how the event is classified. Classifying the event means to place the event into a conceptual framework which provides an interpretation for the event. Large-scale, all-encompassing belief systems which provide an overarching picture of the world are called *ideologies* (cf. Apter 1964; Converse 1964; Minar 1961). The meaning of such an event as students

Contemporary society is characterized by the competition of conflicting belief systems. At times, proponents of action on these belief systems directly challenge those in power, as with the widespread student demonstrations of the late 1960's and early 1970's. (Photo by J. Paul Kirouac)

barricading themselves in a campus building depends upon the ideological framework from which the event is viewed. From an ideology of conservativism, for example, this event might mean the communistic influence of radical professors being acted out on the part of their students. From the ideology of radicalism, in contrast, this event might mean a blow toward freeing the university from repressive imperialism. From the ideology of law and order, this event might mean another of unfortunately endless examples of the breakdown of traditional authority in modern society. From a fundamentalist religious ideology, it might represent demonic forces at work. And so on.

Because meaning is not inherent in an act, but is given an act according to the symbolic system from which it is viewed, different ideological frameworks lead to different interpretations, even though the same event is being experienced. We interpret the world through the symbols we have learned to apply to events, and it is through these symbols that we actually see events. To use another example, a black being promoted over whites can be any and all of the following, depending upon the ideological symbolic system within which it is placed: recognition of the rightful place of blacks, minority tokenism, black uppitiness, going too far, doomed failure, time for revolution, favoritism, discrimination, pacification, or a just reward for untiring effort in the face of severe obstacles.

Because the world is without meaning until human beings superimpose meaning upon it, people are in continual need of some form of "logic" for ordering the world. This applies to both the world of things and the world of people, the material and social worlds (cf. Polanyi 1958: 4). The particular "logic," framework, or conceptual scheme applied to experiences in life, from which the experiences take on meaning, varies from culture to culture and from group to group within the same culture. Although the frameworks vary, as we become members of a culture each of us learns some particular framework within which to view events in life. To the degree that politicians, rulers, or anyone else in a position of authority is able to control this "logic" or framework, to that degree they are able to muster support to stabilize their own positions in power; to that degree they are able to manipulate ideological frameworks in controlling the populace; to that degree they are able to rule or control people without recourse to physical violence or to other coercive measures. To the degree that the people who are in such positions of authority also interpret events from the framework they themselves promulgate, to that degree they are themselves controlled by the belief system. Although the leaders of a society have a certain amount of power to manipulate symbols, they are in good part also captive to the symbolic system they manipulate—and thus to the limitations built into it for interpreting reality.

Contemporary social life is marked by a system of **superordination** (people in positions of power and authority) and **subordination** (people who are ruled or who are in positions of less power). To get people to subordinate personal desires in order to fulfill expectations of participation in this authority system is a major goal of the intensive socialization we undergo from childhood on. We learn to accept the principle that social rewards in the form of recognition, prestige, and privileges, and material rewards in the form of cash and credit, are tied to roles or positions in the social structure. We learn to take for granted that certain positions bring few social and material rewards, while others bring them in abundance. We learn not to question the granting of rewards on the basis of position in the social structure, even though these rewards greatly determine our welfare. In this way we learn to accept inequality as a natural human condition.

If our socialization is effective, we learn to define differential access to positions in the social structure, and its resulting inequalities, as due to characteristics of the individual. It is an individual's fault if he has not succeeded: He didn't try hard enough, didn't take proper advantage of his opportunities, and so on. Being a basic part of our lives from birth, we may come to unquestioningly take for granted such differential access to the value things available in society. Not questioning the way things are set up greatly helps to stabilize any social system.

Persons who are in controlling positions typically select and manipulate elements from the symbolic system of their people in order to construct a reality which supports the status quo of the system of superordination-subordination. These symbols can become not only major means by which people interpret experience, but they can also become rallying cries for maintaining order and promoting allegiance. Rituals and myths, flags and slogans, appearance and manner, gestures and other symbols are regularly utilized for such purposes by those in power. When successfully used, such "rhetoric of leadership" instills in those who are being controlled the belief that the particular political group in power represents major cultural values and the welfare of the members of society. Such symbols and their manipulation then become instrumental in teaching that loyalty and obedience should flow from the followers to the leaders. By means of such rhetoric, leaders attempt to establish a common definition of the political situation which favors the maintenance of their own positions of power in the status quo. Both by wielding power and by manipulating symbols, persons in power legitimize what they do and attempt to maintain control.

Some symbols eventually become both popular and powerful. These are symbols which represent dominant social values and reflect the major hopes of a people. Leaders are quick to manipulate these "master symbols" in order to justify the present arrangement of power and the positions of the powerful within that arrangement. Such **master symbols of legitimation** are regularly manipulated in order to rouse support for the existing social order and provide justification for the status quo (Mills 1959b:36-37).

In order to rally followers behind them, leaders frequently single out for dramatic presentation social themes relevant to dominant ideologies. On the United States political scene such dramatic presentations have centered around the immorality of hippies, the "yellow peril," the snobbery of intellectuals, the immorality of the urban poor, welfare chiseling, the need for law and order because of crime in the streets, and so on. Although such themes rapidly tend to become clichés, by dramatizing such images politicains attempt to further their own positions in the political power structure. In doing so, they unfailingly present themselves as the virtuous representatives of democracy, while the particular subgroup (hippies, Orientals, intellectuals, the poor, and law violators in the cited examples) is purposely associated with things negatively valued.

Symbol manipulation, properly carried out, can be thought manipulation. The goal of such dramatic presentations of ideologies and the manipulation of master symbols of legitimation ultimately involves thought control for the purpose of the maintenance of the social order. Because placing events into categories leads to particularized ways of interpreting an event, to get people to negatively apply dominant ideologies and master symbols to social themes is to provide a readymade interpretation of events, an interpretation which in this case is in line with maintaining the current social order.

One of the most effective ways to maintain social order and one's own dominant place within that order is to develop an **absolutist perspective,** that is, to present social rules as originating external to the social system. Rules are almost impossible to challenge if they are believed to have been directly given by God. Sometimes rules are said to appear in mysterious circumstances, such as being given in a whirlwind on top of a mountain and written on stone. Basic societal rules are also made extremely effective by being taught from infancy by means of endless repetition and being connected with promises of extreme bliss in the afterworld for following them and extreme suffering for violating them. Their effectiveness is further increased when their violation in this life is surrounded by extreme sanctions, such as ostracism, excommunication, or death (Douglas 1972:192). Sometimes, as with the ancient Hebrews, conformity to the basic societal rules, in this case the Ten Commandments, was equated with the welfare of the whole people. The various "captivities" of the Hebrews were in this way pronounced by the Old Testament prophets to be a direct retaliatory act by God because of the people's violation of these rules.

In societies with such an absolutist perspective people are taught to believe that (1) these rules apply to all individuals, (2) their meanings are always clear, (3) they cover all of life, (4) they are universal and absolute as they apply to situations in life, (5) they are unchanging, and (6) they do not originate with any particular member of society but they are given by God himself. Such rules are able to dominate the commonsense thought of a people, and on them a social order can be created which demands and commands obedience. In no way is it left up to the individual whether he wants to follow such rules or not. As each individual is a part of the particular social order, the social rules govern him just as they do every other member of the society (Douglas 1972:192).

In absolutist societies people are bound together in a social structure which provides them shared meanings, clear social relations and roles, and an integrated view of the world. Their ideology links the populace

Thought control of a populace centers around manipulating key cultural symbols in the goal of providing a framework for interpreting events in a way which supports the view of those in power. (Courtesy of Wide World Photos)

together through common history, that is, the ideology provides a framework for interpreting past events, which in traditional societies may be unquestioningly accepted by almost every member. Such ideology also develops *mutual* expectations of behavior: High agreement exists on what to expect when dealing with other members of the society, whether the others are members of one's own or differing social statuses. Because such expectations are widely shared by the members of a traditional society, they are regularly reinforced in everyday life. Because agreed-upon interpretations are provided for almost every event, a highly integrated view of the world is given members of such cultures. Such shared meanings and expectations are thought to make for high solidarity, emotional attachment, and, supposedly at least, a low rate of **deviance** or deviations from expectations.

In traditional Japan, for example, an ideology centering around the Emperor was the mainstay of the social order. A mythical history (the will of the Emperor in administering the nation) was connected with religious ceremony (the Emperor venerates the divine spirits and increasingly becomes one with the essence of Imperial Ancestry) which led to loyalty (the obligation to revere the Emperor and follow him implicitly) and to familial and national harmony (when people fulfill their duties to members of their family, national harmony results). In this ideology the nation is viewed as being similar to a large family, with the Emperor being the father of the nation and the citizens the children. When people do their duty toward their own family and to the Emperor, then "higher purposes" are realized. The individual receives personal identity through his service to the State and Emperor, while solidarity between members of the nation is brought about through the intricate network of familial obligations, including those owed and given to the royal family (Apter 1964:25–26).

When people are thoroughly caught up in a dominant belief system regarding "proper" social relationships, as in this example, they appear to be in remarkable agreement on how they should relate to one another. They hold mutual expectations of rights and duties because of their shared perspective of the world. Such agreement on what the world is like appears to characterize both primitive and traditional societies since each member is taught to view the world either in the same way or in a way very similar to that of his fellow members. In such societies there is little ideological competition. Members appear to be marked by a high degree of social solidarity and to possess personal identities strongly rooted in approved cultural orientations.

Increasing social complexity frequently leads to less certain guides to both social and political practice (Apter 1964:30). In contrast with homogeneous societies, complex pluralistic societies are marked by vast cultural distances between some social groups, by both competing and conflicting symbolic worlds, by ambiguity of rules and relationships, and by a high degree of anonymity in social relationships. No single over-arching meaning system dominates the culture. Though there are many things with which the "majority" may strongly agree, a comparative lack of agreement on how to interpret life occurs. Not everyone views what is happening in even roughly similar ways. Although external differences may be minimized due to mass marketing, no single symbolic system governs all. With vast differences in life experiences and immersion in rapid and seemingly perpetual social change, different social groups attain different ideas of reality. They develop different rules accordingly. Even basic social rules in pluralistic societies come to be seen by many as *relative,* as originating within a particular sociohistorical context, and not as absolute, originating external to the social system.

When the interpretation of life experiences differs sharply, they can lead to conflict, a situation which appears to characterize industrialized nations. In the political sphere, the ideology of capitalism and the ideology of communism frequently clash with one another, both within the same nation and between nations. Conflict also centers around beliefs of personal morality, such as free love versus the desirability of virginity at marriage and beliefs centering around whether sexual fidelity in marriage is desirable or not. There is practically no limit to the listing of conflictual beliefs in modern society. In such cases, the basics of the varying belief systems conflict with each other. In some situations conflicting beliefs may coexist and merely compete with each other for followers, with adherents of each attempting to win converts from rival belief systems. At other times they may very well run headlong into each other, with adherents of each ready to die for their own particular brand of reality.

Conflict and competition between belief systems can easily lead to confusion over world views and to alienation. People can become unsure of themselves, of their roles, and of the worthwhileness of those roles. They can also become embittered against a social system which creates such anxieties for them. This can lead to negative emotions, such as hatred, which can be directed inward, against the self, or outward, against some part of the social system (cf. Apter 1964:33). This appears sometimes to be the reason for people directing hostility against themselves in the form of suicide, against minority groups in the form of discrimination, as well as the basis for aggressive acts directed against institutions or individuals, as in the form of an assassination. Alienative conflict can also result in withdrawal from participation in the social system without being accompanied by aggressive acts. An individual might, for example, retreat into drugs such as alcohol or heroin.

As reality does not come readymade from nature but must be interpreted in order to have meaning for people, as it is symbolic systems through which reality is interpreted, and as withdrawal, suicide, rebellion, and various acts of aggression against others are usually self-defeating, persons who feel alienated from the social system are frequently wide open to competing ideologies or belief systems. Within this framework one can analyze such disparate events as the attraction of communism among American workers during the Depression and its lessened attraction among the same group during the following periods of relative prosperity; participation in what is called the "radical right," such as the John Birch Society, McCarthyism, and the Christian Crusade for Freedom; membership in offbeat religions, such as flying saucer cults and groups which practice faith healing, snake handling, or speaking in tongues; participation in the occult, such as the recent upsurge in magic with its witches and warlocks; and the rise of the women's liberation and black power movements in the late sixties. It appears that such groups and activities have primarily drawn their membership from the alienated of society. It is possible that the further the particular group deviates from dominant cultural orientations, the greater its tendency to recruit the more alienated.

Note especially that the idea of the ordering of reality through symbolic systems can also be applied to the contents of the preceding paragraph. In other words, once one sees a relationship between lessened social solidarity, or alienation, and membership or activity in various groups, one is then using a highly particularized conceptual framework to view reality. Like all other conceptual frameworks, it gives order to information and interprets reality for the analyst or perceiver. Without a conceptual system which incorporates alienation of the individual from the social system with conflicting and competing belief systems in pluralistic societies, it is doubtful that one would see such interconnections between the membership of such disparate groups as American communists and John Birchers, flying saucerians and Pentecostals, magicians and activists in minority liberation groups. Since, however, at least much of what we perceive is symbolically based, whatever symbolic systems we use greatly affect what we perceive. The determining of reality by symbolic systems applies no less to a sociological framework of analysis than to any other conceptual system.

Social conflict is likely to result when official ideologies are rejected by large numbers of a populace. When people view events from a symbolic framework contrary to the official belief system, the meaning the events take on is likely to conflict with the one derived by applying the dominant ideology. For example, officials of the United States government initially attempted to justify their policy in Southeast Asia by manipulating key aspects of the symbolic system of the American people, particularly the concept of democracy and the necessity of preserving it. This official view of reality was rejected wholesale by large numbers of our citizens, particularly by our youth. Today's young people have been exposed to competing ideologies while their own belief systems were in the process of formation. This has made them more open to changing ideas, and large numbers of them refused to accept such official views of the war. The campus confrontations and street demonstrations that resulted are well known to all of us.

Meaning systems rivaling the dominant ideology can be dealt with in several ways. They can be made ideologically suspect, and the police power of the State can then be used in an attempt to isolate and crush their adherents. This confrontational technique is represented by the efforts once used to combat communism in the United States, with various legal, occupational, and other repressive measures directed against members of the Communist Party. Competing meaning systems can also be adopted or incorporated into the dominant belief system. An example of this is the ethos of pleasure being incorporated into the Protestant Ethic, even though the Protestant Ethic originally opposed pleasure. They can also be dealt with by privatization, that is, letting them remain as localized phenomena, a sort of odd cult of ideas limited to only a small minority. A current example would be that of the Rosicrucians. Their competing ideology vastly differs from the dominant one in the United States, but they attract few adherents and are not perceived as threatening the dominant order. When this is the case, competing meaning systems can be allowed to remain side by side with dominant ones.

When dominant belief systems are rejected and when their rejection results not only in disagreement but also in overt opposition, at that point the leaders of a society can no longer rely on the belief system to bring about support for the social order. They then tend to resort to that which always underlies the social order itself, physical violence. The vigilant activity of the police in the ghettos of America is certainly at least partially rooted on this basis, if not almost entirely so. The oppressive reactions of local, state, and federal governments to youth demonstrations during the Vietnam war also illustrates the maintenance of the social order by violence when ideology fails.

When ideologies or dominant belief systems are believed, however, they can greatly strengthen the social order. They can provide social solidarity by making a tie-up between the individual's personal identity and his conceptualization of the rest of society. People believing dominant ideologies can easily feel that they play a valuable role as an integrated part of a larger social system. With the social institutions largely aligned in a cooperative effort at promulgating dominant ideologies, the "correctness" of these beliefs is continually reinforced. Those who believe dominant ideologies receive legitimation for the place they occupy in the social structure. The social order, as it exists, is not brought into question by official ideologies but is continually buttressed by being given foundational support.

When an individual accepts the dominant ideologies of his society, his act of acceptance brings him into line. His behavior is then subject to extensive control through manipulating the relevant symbols. In Chapters 14 and 15 we noted how reality is distorted by the social institutions in order to enforce compliance with the will of the few and to protect the existing power relationships. With the extensivity of the mass media today, along with continued technological developments in communication, the manipulation of symbols by society's officials is probably one of the greatest threats to maintaining pluralism in contemporary society.

Quite unlike primitive and traditional societies, contemporary industrialized societies have both competing and conflicting belief systems which vie for followers. Members of industrialized societies are consequently marked by lack of agreement on even basic issues in life. But contemporary industrialized societies do have overarching orientating ideologies which provide for their members similar frameworks for interpreting events in life. Americans, for example, regardless of the particular religious, ethnic, occupational, geographical, sex, or age group to which they belong, tend to view many matters in a very similar way. People in American society, for example, generally agree on such fundamentals as the right to own material things, the value of science, the need for education, the right of medical doctors to charge patients for their services, the right to have children, the right of parents to discipline their own children, and the obligation of parents to provide economic support for their own children. Even on such basic issues, however, some disagree in one way or another and view the same matter from a differing conceptual framework. But the vast majority of persons in our culture learn a general orientating symbolic system which makes such things, for them, appear not only correct but natural, appearing to them as something which should be similarly understood by all.

It is not only difficult to understand life in society without knowledge of the symbolic systems of the people involved, it is impossible. A shared symbolic system is the cement of society. It elicits conformity, it helps maintain positions between superordinates and subordinates, and it creates unifying sentiments. Symbolic systems are essential for holding people in a society together, except where brute force is the element used to bind people together into a social system. *No* society, however, with which I am familiar depends solely on brute force, although in *all* societies physical violence is used when belief systems, persuasion, and other nonphysical coercive techniques fail.

Bibliography

ADAMS, JAMES T. *Provincial Society: 1690 to 1763*. Edited by Arthur M. Schlesinger and Dixon R. Fox. New York: Watts, Franklin, Inc., 1971.

AIR FORCE ROTC. *Initial Active Duty*. Air University, Maxwell Air Force Base, Alabama, 1970.

The Air Officer's Guide. Harrisburg, Pennsylvania: The Stackpole Company, Military Service Division, 1963.

ALBERT, ETHEL M. "Women of Burundi: A Study of Social Values," in *Women of Tropical Africa*. Denise Paulme, ed., Berkeley: University of California Press, 1963, pp. 179–215 (Translation of "La Femme en Urundi," in *Femmes d'Afrique Noire*. Denise Paulme, ed., Paris: Mouton and Company, 1960, pp. 173–205).

ANDERSON, CHARLES H. *Toward a New Sociology: A Critical View*. Homewood, Illinois: The Dorsey Press, 1971.

ANDERSON, NELS. *Desert Saints: The Mormon Frontier in Utah*. Chicago: University of Chicago Press, 1966 (first published in 1942).

———. *The Hobo: The Sociology of the Homeless Man*. Chicago: The University of Chicago Press, 1923.

APTER, DAVID E. "Ideology and Discontent," in *Ideology and Discontent*. David E. Apter, ed., New York: The Free Press, 1964, pp. 16–46.

ARCHIBALD, JOHN. "Documentary Humor," *St. Louis Post-Dispatch*, October 18, 1973.

ARIES, PHILIPPE. *Centuries of Childhood: A Social History of Family Life*. New York: Alfred A. Knopf, Inc., 1962.

ARISTOTLE. *Metaphysics, Books X–XV*. Hugh Tredennick, translator. *Oeconomica and Magna Moralia*. G. Cyril Armstrong, translator. Cambridge, Mass.: Harvard University Press, 1962.

ARNOLD, DAVID O., ed. *The Sociology of Subcultures.* Berkeley, California: The Glendessary Press, 1970.

AXELROD, SIDNEY. "Negro and White Institutionalized Delinquents," *American Journal of Sociology, 57,* 1952, pp. 569–574.

BARDWICK, J. *The Psychology of Women.* New York: Harper and Row, 1971.

BARTELL, GILBERT D. *Group Sex: A Scientist's Eye Witness Report on the American Way of Swinging.* New York: Peter H. Wyden, Inc., Publisher, 1971.

BARTLETT, RANDALL. *Economic Foundations of Political Power.* New York: The Free Press, 1973.

BEALS, RALPH L., and HARRY HOIJER. *An Introduction to Anthropology.* Third Edition. New York: The Macmillan Company, 1965.

BECKER, HOWARD S. "History, Culture, and Subjective Experience: An Exploration of the Social Bases of Drug-Induced Experiences," *Journal of Health and Social Behavior, 8,* 1967, pp. 163–176.

————. *Outsiders: Studies in the Sociology of Deviance.* New York: The Free Press, 1973.

BEM, SANDRA L., and DARYL J. BEM. "We're All Nonconscious Sexists," *Psychology Today, 4,* 1970, pp. 22, 24, 26, 115.

BENEDICT, RUTH. "Continuities and Discontinuities in Cultural Conditioning," *Psychiatry, 1,* 1938, pp. 161–167.

————. *Patterns of Culture.* Boston: Houghton Mifflin Company, 1934.

————. "Sex in Primitive Society," in *American Journal of Orthopsychiatry, 9,* 1939, pp. 570–574.

BENNETT, LERONE, JR. *Confrontation Black and White.* Chicago: Johnson Publishing Company, 1965.

BERGER, BENNETT M. "Hippie Morality—More Old Than New," *Transaction, 5,* 1967, pp. 19–22.

BERGER, PETER. *Invitation to Sociology.* Garden City, New York: Doubleday and Company, 1963.

BERNARD, JESSIE. *The Sex Game.* New York: Atheneum, 1972.

BERNE, ERIC. *Games People Play: The Psychology of Human Relationships.* New York: Grove Press, Inc., 1964.

BERRETT, WILLIAM EDWIN. *The Restored Church: A Brief History of the Growth and Doctrines of the Church of Jesus Christ of Latter-day Saints.* Fourth Edition. Salt Lake City, Utah: Deseret Book Company, 1944.

BIRD, CAROLINE. *Born Female: The High Cost of Keeping Women Down.* New York: David McKay Company, Inc., 1968.

————. "The Sex Map of the Work World," in *Roles Women Play: Readings Toward Women's Liberation.* Michelle Hoffnung Garskof, ed., Belmont, Cal.: Brooks/Cole Publishing Company, 1971, pp. 39–57.

BLACKSTONE, SIR WILLIAM *Commentaries on the Laws of England.* Thomas M. Cooley, ed. (Fourth Edition edited by James DeWitt Andrews), Vol. I, Chicago: Callaghan and Company, 1899.

BLAU, PETER M. *The Dynamics of Bureaucracy.* Chicago: University of Chicago Press, 1955.

———. *Exchange and Power in Social Life.* New York: John Wiley and Sons, 1964.

BLUMBERG, ABRAHAM S. "The Practice of Law as Confidence Game: Organizational Cooptation of a Profession," *Law and Society Review, 1,* 1967, pp. 15–39.

BLUMER, HERBERT. "Social Movements," in *Studies in Social Movements: A Social Psychological Perspective.* Barry McLaughlin, ed., New York: The Free Press, 1969, pp. 8–29 (Originally published in *New Outline of the Principles of Sociology.* A. M. Lee, ed., New York: Barnes and Noble, Inc., 1951, pp. 199–220).

———. "Society as Symbolic Interaction," in *Human Behavior and Social Processes: An Interactionist Approach.* Arnold M. Rose, ed., Boston: Houghton Mifflin Company, 1962, pp. 179–192.

———. "Sociological Implications of the Thought of George Herbert Mead," *American Journal of Sociology, 71,* 1966, pp. 535–544.

———. *Symbolic Interactionism: Perspective and Method.* Englewood Cliffs, New Jersey: Prentice-Hall, Inc., 1969.

BOSKIN, JOSEPH. "The Revolt of the Urban Ghettos, 1964–67," *The Annals of the American Academy of Political and Social Science, 382,* 1969, pp. 1–14.

BOTTOMORE, T. B. *Classes in Modern Society.* New York: Vintage Books, 1966.

BRONFENBRENNER, URIE. "Socialization and Social Class Through Time and Space," in *Readings in Social Psychology.* Eleanor E. Maccoby, Theodore M. Newcomb, and Eugene L. Hartley, eds., New York: Holt, Rinehart and Winston, 1958, pp. 400–425.

BROVERMAN, INGE K., SUSAN RAYMOND VOGEL, DONALD M. BROVERMAN, FRANK E. CLARKSON, and PAUL S. ROSENKRANTZ. "Sex-Role Stereotypes: A Current Appraisal," *Journal of Social Issues, 28,* 1972, pp. 59–78.

BROWN, ROGER. *Psycholinguistics: Selected Papers.* New York: The Free Press, 1970.

———. *Social Psychology.* New York: The Free Press, 1965.

BROWN, WARREN. "The Doctor Who Call the A.M.A. the American Murder Association," *Avant Garde, 10,* 1970, pp. 2–7.

BURGESS, ROBERT L., and RONALD L. AKERS. "A Differential-Reinforcement Theory of Criminal Behavior," *Social Problems, 14,* 1966, pp. 128–147.

CAMPBELL, DONALD T. "Herskovits, Cultural Relativism, and Metascience," in *Cultural Relativism: Perspectives in Cultural Pluralism.* Frances Herskovits, ed., New York: Random House, 1972, pp. v–xxiii.

CAPRIO, FRANK S. *Variations in Sexual Behavior.* New York: Citadel Press, 1955.

CATT, CARRIE CHAPMAN, and NETTIE ROGERS SCHULER. *Woman Suffrage and Politics: The Inner Story of the Suffrage Movement.* New York: Charles Scribner's Sons, 1923.

CHEEK, WILLIAM F. *Black Resistance Before the Civil War.* Beverly Hills, California: Glencoe Press, 1970.

CICOUREL, AARON. *The Social Organization of Juvenile Justice*. New York: John Wiley and Sons, 1968.

CLOWARD, RICHARD A., and LLOYD OHLIN. *Delinquency and Opportunity: A Theory of Delinquent Gangs*. New York: The Free Press, 1960.

COHEN, ALBERT K. *Delinquent Boys: The Culture of the Gang*. New York: The Free Press, 1955.

COLEMAN, JAMES F. "In Defense of Games," *Behavioral Scientist, 10,* 1966, pp. 3–4.

COLEMAN, JAMES S., and ERNEST Q. CAMPBELL. *Equality of Educational Opportunity.* Washington, D.C.: Government Printing Office, 1966.

COLEMAN, RICHARD F., and BERNICE L. NEUGARTEN. *Social Status in the City.* San Francisco: Jossey-Bass, 1971.

CONVERSE, PHILIP E. "The Nature of Belief Systems in Mass Publics," in *Ideology and Discontent.* David E. Apter, ed., New York: The Free Press, 1964, pp. 206–261.

COOK, THOMAS J. "Benign Neglect: Minimal Feasible Understanding," *Social Problems, 18,* 1970, pp. 145–152.

COOLEY, CHARLES HORTON. *Human Nature and the Social Order.* New York: The Free Press, 1956.

———. *Social Organization.* New York: Schocken Books, Inc., 1962.

COSER, LEWIS A. *Greedy Institutions.* New York: The Free Press, 1974.

DANK, BARRY M. "Coming Out in the Gay World," *Psychiatry, 34,* 1971, pp. 180–197.

DAVIS, DAVID BRION. *The Problem of Slavery in Western Culture.* Ithaca, New York: Cornell University Press, 1966.

DAVIS, FRED. "Why All of Us May Be Hippies Someday," *Transaction, 5,* 1967, pp. 10–18.

DAVIS, KINGSLEY. "Final Note on a Case of Extreme Isolation," *American Journal of Sociology, 52,* 1947, pp. 432–437.

DECK, LELAND P. "Buying Brains by the Inch," *The Journal of the College and University Personnel Association, 19,* 1968, pp. 33–37.

DEMERATH, N. J., III. *Social Class in American Protestantism.* Chicago: Rand McNally and Company, 1965.

DEXTER, LEWIS A. *Tyranny in Schooling: An Inquiry Into the Problem of "Stupidity."* New York: Basic Books, 1964.

DIAMOND, M. and W. YOUNG. "Differential Responsiveness of Pregnant and Nonpregnant Guinea Pigs to the Masculinizing Action of Testesterone Propianate," *Endocrinology, 72,* 1963, pp. 429–438.

DOBRINER, WILLIAM M. *Social Structures and Systems: A Sociological Overview.* Pacific Palisades, California: Goodyear Publishing Company, Inc., 1969.

DOMHOFF, G. WILLIAM. *The Higher Circles: The Governing Class in America.* New York: Vintage Books, 1971.

DOUGLAS, JACK D. "The Experience of the Absurd and the Problem of Social Order," in *Theoretical Perspectives on Deviance*. Robert A. Scott and Jack D. Douglas, eds., New York: Basic Books, Inc., 1972, pp. 189–214.

———. *The Social Meanings of Suicide*. Princeton, N.J.: Princeton University Press, 1967.

DRAKEFORD, JOHN W. *Games Husbands and Wives Play*. Nashville, Tenn.: Broadman Press, 1971.

DROTNING, PHILLIP. *Black Heroes in Our Nation's History*. New York: Cowles Book Co., Inc. 1969.

EISENSTEIN, LOUIS. *The Ideologies of Taxation*. New York: The Ronald Press, 1961.

ELKINS, STANLEY M. *Slavery: A Problem in American Institutional and Intellectual Life*. New York: Grosset and Dunlap, 1963.

ENGLAND, RALPH W., JR. "A Theory of Middle Class Juvenile Delinquency," *Journal of Criminal Law, Criminology and Political Science, 50,* 1960, pp. 535–540.

EQUIANO, OLAUDAH. *Equiano's Travels: The Interesting Narrative of the Life of Olaudah Equiano or Gustavus Vassa the African* (abridged and edited by Paul Edwards). New York: 1967 (first published 1789) (as cited in Cheek, 1970:41).

ERIKSON, KAI T. *Wayward Puritans: A Study in the Sociology of Deviance*. New York: John Wiley and Sons, Inc., 1966.

EVANS-PRITCHARD, E. E. *Witchcraft Oracles and Magic Among the Azandi*. Oxford, England: Clarendon Press, 1937.

EYSENCK, HANS J. *The Effects of Psychotherapy*. New York: International Science, 1966.

FELDMAN, SAUL D. "The Presentation of Shortness in Everyday Life—Height and Heightism in American Society: Toward a Sociology of Stature," unpublished paper presented at the 1972 meetings of the American Sociological Association.

FERDINAND, THEODORE N., and ELMER LUCHTERHAND. "Inner-City Youth, Police, The Juvenile Court, and Justice," *Social Problems, 17,* 1970, pp. 510–527.

FERRIS, ROBERT G. *The American West: An Appraisal*. Sante Fe, New Mexico: Museum of New Mexico Press, 1963.

FORD, C. S., and F. A. BEACH. *Patterns of Sexual Behaviour*. London: Eyre and Spottiswoode, 1952.

FRAKE, CHARLES O. "The Diagnosis of Disease among the Subanum of Mindanao," *American Anthropologist, 63,* 1961, pp. 113–132.

FRANKLIN, JOHN HOPE. *From Slavery to Freedom: A History of Negro Americans*. Third Edition. New York: Alfred A. Knopf, 1967.

FREEMAN, HOWARD E., and OZZIE G. SIMMONS. *The Mental Patient Comes Home*. New York: John Wiley and Sons, 1963.

FREUCHEN, PETER. *Peter Freuchen's Book of the Eskimos*. Dagmar Freuchen, ed., Cleveland, Ohio: The World Publishing Company, 1961.

FRIEDENBERG, EDGAR Z. *Coming of Age in America.* New York: Random House, Inc., 1963.

FRIEDMAN, JUDITH J. "Structural Constraints on Community Action: The Case of Infant Mortality Rates," *Social Problems, 21,* Fall 1973, pp. 230–245.

FRUMKIN, ROBERT M. "English and American Sex Customs, Early," in *The Encyclopedia of Sexual Behavior, I.* New York: Hawthorne Books, Inc., 1961, pp. 350–365.

GAGNON, JOHN H., and WILLIAM SIMON. "Femininity in the Lesbian Community," *Social Problems, 15,* 1967, pp. 212–221.

GANN, LEWIS H., and PETER DUIGNAN. *Africa and the World: An Introduction to the History of Sub-Saharan Africa from Antiquity to 1840.* San Francisco: Chandler Publishing Company, 1972.

GANS, HERBERT J. *The Urban Villagers.* New York: The Free Press, 1962.

GARBUS, MARTIN. *Ready for the Defense.* New York: Farrar, Straus and Giroux, 1971.

GELLEN, MARTIN M. "The Making of a Pollution-Industrial Complex," *Ramparts, 8,* 1970, pp. 22–27.

GERASSI, JOHN. *The Boys of Boise: Furor, Vice and Folly in an American City.* New York: Collier Books, 1968.

GERTH, HANS, and C. WRIGHT MILLS. *Character and Social Structure.* New York: Harbinger Books, 1964. (First published in 1953.)

GIBBONS, DON C. "Observations on the Study of Crime Causation," *American Journal of Sociology, 77,* 1971, pp. 262–278.

GLAZER, NATHAN. "Introduction" to Stanley M. Elkins, *Slavery: A Problem in American Institutional and Intellectual Life.* New York: Grosset and Dunlap, 1963, pp. ix–xvi.

GLEESON, GERALDINE A., and ELIJAH L. WHITE. "Disability and Medical Care Among Whites and Nonwhites in the United States," in *Health, Education and Welfare Indicators.* Washington, D.C.: U.S. Department of Health, Education and Welfare, October, 1965, pp. 1–10.

GOFFMAN, ERVING. "On Cooling the Mark Out: Some Aspects of Adaptation to Failure," *Psychiatry: Journal for the Study of Interpersonal Relations, 15,* 1952, pp. 451–463.

———. *The Presentation of Self in Everyday Life.* Garden City, New York: Doubleday Anchor, 1959.

GOLDBERG, PHILIP. "Are Women Prejudiced Against Women?" *Transaction, 5,* 1968, pp. 28–30.

GOLDBERG, SUSAN, and MICHAEL LEWIS. "Play Behavior in the Year-Old Infant: Early Sex Differences," *Child Development, 40,* 1969, pp. 21–31.

GOLDMAN, NATHAN. *The Differential Selection of Juvenile Offenders for Court Appearance.* New York: National Council on Crime and Delinquency, 1963.

GORDON, MILTON, M. *Assimilation in American Life.* New York: Oxford University Press, 1964.

————. "The Concept of the Sub-Culture and its Application," *Social Forces, 26,* 1947, pp. 40–42.

GOUGH, KATHLEEN E. "The Nayars and the Definition of Marriage," *Journal of the Royal Anthropological Institute, 89,* 1959, pp. 23–34.

GURALNICK, LILLIAN. *Vital Statistics–Special Reports, 53* (2), September 1962, "Mortality by Occupation and Industry among Men 20 to 64 Years of Age: United States, 1950."

————. *Vital Statistics–Special Reports, 53* (3), September 1963a, "Mortality by Occupation and Cause of Death among Men 20 to 64 Years of Age: United States, 1950."

————. *Vital Statistics–Special Reports, 53* (4), September 1963b, "Mortality by Industry and Cause of Death among Men 20 to 64 Years of Age: United States, 1950."

————. *Vital Statistics–Special Reports, 53* (5), September 1963c, "Mortality by Occupation Level and Cause of Death among Men 20 to 64 Years of Age: United States, 1950."

GUZMAN, JESSE PARKHORST. "Lynching," in *Racial Violence in the United States.* Allen D. Grimshaw, ed., Chicago: Aldine Publishing Co., 1969.

HALL, EDWARD T. *The Hidden Dimension.* Garden City, New York: Anchor Books, 1969.

HALL, RICHARD. "Dilemma of the Black Cop," *Life, 69,* 1970, pp. 60–70.

HAMMOND, BOONE EDWARD. "The Contest System: A Survival Technique," unpublished M.A. paper, Washington University, 1965.

HARRIS, MARVIN. *Culture, Man, and Nature: An Introduction to General Anthropology.* New York: Thomas Y. Crowell Company, 1971.

HART, C. W. M., and ARNOLD R. PILLING. *The Tiwi of North Australia.* New York: Holt, Rinehart, and Winston, 1960.

HARTMAN, WILLIAM E., MARILYN FITHIAN, and DONALD JOHNSON. *Nudist Society: An Authoritative, Complete Study of Nudism in America.* New York: Crown Publishers, Inc., 1970.

HASKINS, JIM, and HUGH F. BUTTS. *The Psychology of Black Language.* New York: Barnes and Noble Books, 1973.

HENRY, JULES. "American Schoolrooms: Learning the Nightmare," *Columbia University Forum, 6–7,* 1963, pp. 24–30.

————. *Culture Against Man.* New York: Vintage Books, 1965.

————. *Jungle People: A Kaingáng Tribe of the Highlands of Brazil.* New York: Vintage Books, 1964. (First published in 1941.)

HENSLIN, JAMES M. "Abortion and Male Chauvinism," in *Social Problems in American Society.* James M. Henslin and Larry T. Reynolds, eds., Boston: Holbrook Press, 1973, pp. 140–152.

————. "The Cab Driver: An Interactional Analysis of an Occupational Culture," unpublished Ph.D. dissertation, St. Louis: Washington University, 1967.

HENSLIN, JAMES M. "Guilt and Guilt Neutralization: Response and Adjustment to Suicide," in *Deviance and Respectability: The Social Construction of Moral Meanings.* New York: Basic Books, 1970, pp. 192–228.

————. "Strategies of Adjustment: An Ethnomethodological Approach to the Study of Guilt and Suicide," in *Survivors of Suicide.* Albert C. Cain, ed., Springfield, Illinois: Charles C. Thomas, Publisher, 1972a, pp. 215–227.

————. *Studies in the Sociology of Sex.* James M. Henslin, ed., New York: Appleton-Century-Crofts, 1971.

————. "What Makes for Trust?" in *Down to Earth Sociology: Introductory Readings.* James M. Henslin, ed., New York: The Free Press, 1972b, pp. 20–32.

————, and HUGH BARLOW. "Drugs as a Social Problem," in *Social Problems,* Englewood Cliffs, N.J.: Prentice-Hall, forthcoming.

————, and MAE A. BIGGS. "Dramaturgical Desexualization: The Sociology of the Vaginal Examination," in *Studies in the Sociology of Sex.* James M. Henslin, ed., New York: Appleton-Century-Crofts, 1971, pp. 243–272.

————, and LARRY T. REYNOLDS, eds. *Social Problems in American Society.* Boston: Holbrook Press, 1973.

HERSKOVITS, MELVILLE J. *Cultural Relativism: Perspectives in Cultural Pluralism.* Frances Herskovits, ed., New York: Random House, 1972.

HERTZLER, JOYCE O. *A Sociology of Language.* New York: Random House, 1965.

HINDELANG, MICHAEL J. "The Commitment of Delinquents to their Misdeeds: Do Delinquents Drift?" *Social Problems, 17,* 1970, pp. 502–509.

HOEBEL, E. ADAMSON. *Anthropology: The Study of Man.* Third Edition. New York: McGraw-Hill Book Company, 1966.

HOIJER, HARRY. "The Sapir-Whorf Hypothesis," in *Language in Culture.* Harry Hoijer, ed., Chicago: University of Chicago Press, 1954.

HOLE, JUDITH, and ELLEN LEVINE. *Rebirth of Feminism.* New York: Quadrangle Books, 1971.

HOLLINGSHEAD, AUGUST B. "Class Differences in Family Stability," *Annals of the American Academy of Political and Social Science, 272,* 1950, pp. 39–46.

————. "Cultural Factors in the Selection of Marriage Mates," *American Sociological Review, 15,* 1950, pp. 619–627.

————. *Elmtown's Youth.* New York: John Wiley and Sons, Inc., 1947.

HOMANS, GEORGE C. "Fundamental Social Processes," in *Sociology: An Introduction.* Neil J. Smelser, ed., New York: John Wiley and Sons, Inc., 1967, pp. 30–78.

HONIGMANN, JOHN J. *Personality in Culture.* New York: Harper and Row Publishers, 1967.

HOSTETLER, JOHN A. *Amish Society.* Second Edition. Baltimore: The Johns Hopkins Press, 1970.

HUBER, JOAN, and WILLIAM FORCE. *Income and Ideology: An Analysis of the American Political Formula.* New York: The Free Press, 1973.

HUMPHREYS, LAUD. "New Styles in Homosexual Manliness," *Transaction, 8,* 1971, pp. 38–46.

———. "Tearoom Trade: Impersonal Sex in Public Places," *Transaction, 7,* 1970a, pp. 11–25.

———. *Tearoom Trade: Impersonal Sex in Public Places.* Chicago: Aldine Publishing Co., 1970b.

HUNT, MORTON. "Sexual Behavior in the 1970s," *Playboy, 20,* October 1973, pp. 85–88, 194, 197–202, 204, 206–207.

JACKSON, MAURICE B. "Minorities and Women in Sociology: Are Opportunities Changing?" *The American Sociologist, 7,* 1972, pp. 3–5.

JENCKS, CHRISTOPHER, and DAVID RIESMAN. *The Academic Revolution.* New York: Doubleday and Company, Inc., 1968.

———. "Higher Education as a Social Sieve," in *Down to Earth Sociology: Introductory Readings.* James M. Henslin, ed., New York: The Free Press, 1972, pp. 216–225.

JOHNSON, KENNETH R. "White Racial Attitudes as a Factor in the Arguments Against the Nineteenth Amendment," *Phylon, 31,* 1970, pp. 31–37.

KAHL, JOSEPH A. *The American Class Structure.* New York: Holt, Rinehart, and Winston, 1957.

KANE, MICHAEL B. *Minorities in Textbooks: A Study of Their Treatment in Social Studies Texts.* Chicago: Quadrangle Books, 1970.

KANOWITZ, LEO. *Women and the Law: The Unfinished Revolution.* Albuquerque: University of New Mexico Press, 1969.

KARPMAN, BENJAMIN. *The Sexual Offender and His Offenses.* New York: Julian Press, 1954.

KELLER, HELEN. *The Story of My Life.* New York: Doubleday and Company, Inc., 1917.

KING, C. WENDELL. *Social Movements in the United States.* New York: Random House, 1956.

KINSEY, ALFRED C., WARDELL B. POMEROY, and CLYDE E. MARTIN. *Sexual Behavior in the Human Male.* Philadelphia: W. B. Saunders Company, 1948.

KINSEY, ALFRED C., WARDELL B. POMEROY, CLYDE E. MARTIN, and PAUL H. GEBHART. *Sexual Behavior in the Human Female.* New York: Pocket Books, 1965. (First printed in 1953 by W. B. Saunders Company.)

KIRKHAM, GEORGE L. "Homosexuality in Prison," in *Studies in the Sociology of Sex.* James M. Henslin, ed., New York: Appleton-Century-Crofts, 1971, pp. 325–349.

KITAGAWA, EVELYN M., and PHILIP M. HAUSER. "Education Differentials in Mortality by Cause of Death: United States, 1960," *Demography, 5* (1), 1968, pp. 318–353.

———. *Social and Economic Differences in Mortality.* Vital and Health Statistics Monographs. Cambridge: Harvard University Press, 1971.

KLEINBERG, O. *Social Psychology.* New York: Holt, Rinehart and Winston, Inc., 1954.

KOMAROVSKY, MIRRA, and S. S. SARGENT. "Research into Subcultural Influences Upon Personality," in *Culture and Personalities.* S. S. Sargent and M. W. Smith, eds., New York: The Viking Fund, 1949, pp. 143–159.

The Koran. GEORGE SALE, translator. London: Frederick Warne and Company, 1887.

KOZOL, JONATHAN. *Death at an Early Age.* Boston: Houghton Mifflin Company, 1967.

KUCZYNSKI, JÜRGEN. *A Short History of Labour Conditions Under Industrial Capitalism in the United States of America, 1789–1946.* Second Edition. New York: Barnes and Noble, 1946.

KUCZYNSKI, ROBERT. *Population Movements.* New York: Oxford University Press, 1936.

KUHN, MANFORD H. "The Reference Group Reconsidered," *Sociological Quarterly,* 5, 1964, pp. 5–21.

———, and THOMAS S. MCPARTLAND. "An Empirical Investigation of Self-Attitudes," *American Sociological Review, 19,* 1954, pp. 68–76.

LA BARRE, WESTON. *The Human Animal.* Chicago: The University of Chicago Press, 1954.

LAING, RONALD D., and A. ESTERSON. *Sanity, Madness, and the Family.* London: Tavistock, 1964.

LASWELL, THOMAS. *Class and Stratum.* Boston: Houghton Mifflin, 1965.

LAUER, ROBERT H. *Perspectives on Social Change.* Boston: Allyn and Bacon, Inc., 1973.

LEE, DOROTHY. *Freedom and Culture.* Englewood Cliffs, New Jersey: Prentice-Hall, Inc., 1959.

LEGGETT, JOHN C. *Race, Class, and Political Consciousness.* Cambridge, Mass.: Schenkman Publishing Company, Inc., 1972.

———. *Taking State Power: The Sources and Consequences of Political Challenge.* New York: Harper and Row, 1973.

———, and CLAUDETTE CERVINKA. "Countdown: How to Lie with Statistics," in *Social Problems in American Society.* James M. Henslin and Larry T. Reynolds, eds., Boston: Holbrook Press, 1973, pp. 234–257.

LEMERT, EDWIN M. "Paranoia and the Dynamics of Exclusion," *Sociometry, 25,* 1962, pp. 2–20.

———. *Social Pathology: A Systematic Approach To The Theory of Sociopathic Behavior.* New York: McGraw-Hill Book Company, Inc., 1951.

LENSKI, GERHARD. *The Religious Factor: A Sociological Study of Religion's Impact on Politics, Economics, and Family Life.* Garden City, New York: Anchor Books, 1963.

LÉVI-STRAUSS, CLAUDE. "The Family," in *Man, Culture, and Society.* Harry L. Shapiro, ed., New York: Oxford University Press, 1956, pp. 261–285.

LEVINE, S. N., and R. F. MULLINS. "Hormonal Influences on Brain Organization in Infant Rats," *Science, 152,* 1966, pp. 1585–1592.

LEWIS, OSCAR. *Children of Sanchez.* New York: Random House, 1961.

LEZNOFF, MAURICE, and WILLIAM WESTLEY. "The Homosexual Community," *Social Problems, 3,* 1956, pp. 257–263.

LICHT, H. *Sexual Life in Ancient Greece.* New York: Barnes and Noble, 1952 (first published in 1926 as *Das Liebesleben der Griechen.* Dresden: P. Aretz).

LIEBOW, ELLIOTT. *Tally's Corner: A Study of Negro Streetcorner Men.* Boston: Little, Brown, and Company, 1967.

LINDESMITH, ALFRED, and ANSELM L. STRAUSS. *Social Psychology.* Third Edition. New York: Holt, Rinehart, and Winston, Inc., 1968.

LINDZEY, GARDNER. "Some Remarks Concerning Incest, the Incest Taboo, and Psychoanalytic Theory," *American Psychologist, 22,* 1967, pp. 1051–1059.

LINTON, RALPH. *The Study of Man.* New York: Appleton-Century-Crofts, 1936.

LLOYD, P. C. *Africa in Social Change.* Baltimore: Penguin Books, Inc., 1967.

LOGAN, W. P. D. "Social Class Variations in Mortality," *Public Health Reports, 64,* 1954, pp. 1217–1223.

LOWENTHAL, M. F. *Lives in Distress: Paths of the Elderly to the Psychiatric Ward.* New York: Basic Books, 1964.

LUNDBERG, FERDINAND. *The Rich and the Super-Rich: A Study in the Power of Money Today.* New York: Bantam Books, Inc., 1968.

LUNDMAN, RICHARD J., JAMES C. FOX, RICHARD E. SYKES, and JOHN P. CLARK. "Drunkenness in Police-Citizen Encounters," in *Observations 2,* Minneapolis: University of Minnesota, 1971, unpaged.

LUTZ, ALMA. *Crusade For Freedom: Women of the Antislavery Movement.* Boston: Beacon Press, 1968.

MAIN, JACKSON T. *Social Structure of Revolutionary America.* Princeton, New Jersey: Princeton University Press, 1965.

MAISEL, ROBERT. "The Ex-Mental Patient and Rehospitalization: Some Research Findings," *Social Problems, 15,* 1967, pp. 18–24.

MALINOWSKI, BRONISLAW. "Culture," in *Encyclopedia of the Social Sciences, 4,* New York: The Macmillan Company, 1930, pp. 621–646.

———. *The Dynamics of Culture Change.* New Haven: Yale University Press, 1945.

———. *Sex and Repression in Savage Society.* Cleveland, Ohio: The World Publishing Company (Meridian Books), 1955. (First published in 1927.)

MAYER, JOHN E. "The Self-Restraint of Friends: A Mechanism in Family Transition," *Social Forces, 35,* 1957, pp. 230–238.

MCCART, CAROL. "The Study of a Public Defender's Office," unpublished paper, 1970.

MCGOVERN, JAMES R. "The American Women's Pre-World War I: Freedom in Manners and Morals," *The Journal of American History, 55,* 1968–69, pp. 315–333.

MCILWRAITH, T. F. "Facts and their Recognition Among the Bella Coola," in *Fact and Theory in Social Science*. Earl W. Count and Gordon T. Bowles, eds. Syracuse, New York: Syracuse University Press, 1964, pp. 183–200.

MCINTOSH, MARY. "The Homosexual Role," *Social Problems, 16,* 1968, pp. 182–192.

MEAD, GEORGE HERBERT. *Mind, Self, and Society*. Chicago: University of Chicago Press, 1934.

MEAD, MARGARET. *Sex and Temperament in Three Primitive Societies*. New York: The New American Library, 1950. (A Mentor Book.) (First published in 1935.)

MEIER, AUGUST, and ELLIOTT RUDWICK. *From Plantation to Ghetto*. Revised Edition. New York: Hill & Wang, 1970.

MERTON, ROBERT K. *Social Theory and Social Structure*. Enlarged Edition. New York: The Free Press, 1968.

MILLER, DOROTHY, and MICHAEL SCHWARTZ. "County Lunacy Commission Hearings: Some Observations of Commitments to a State Mental Hospital," *Social Problems, 14,* 1966, pp. 26–35.

MILLER, G. A. *Language and Communication*. New York: McGraw-Hill, 1951.

MILLER, WALTER B. "Lower Class Culture as a Generating Milieu of Gang Delinquency," *Journal of Social Issues, 14,* 1958, pp. 5–19.

MILLETT, KATE. *Sexual Politics*. Garden City, New York: Doubleday and Company, Inc., 1970.

MILLS, C. WRIGHT. "The Cultural Apparatus," in *Power, Politics and People: The Collected Essays of C. Wright Mills,* Irving Louis Horowitz, ed., London: Oxford University Press, 1967, pp. 405–422.

————. "Language, Logic, and Culture," in *Power, Politics and People: The Collected Essays of C. Wright Mills,* Irving Louis Horowitz, ed., London: Oxford University Press, 1967, pp. 423–438.

————. *The Power Elite*. New York: Oxford University Press, 1959a.

————. *The Sociological Imagination*. New York: Oxford University Press, 1959b.

————. "The Structure of Power in American Society," in *Power, Politics and People: The Collected Essays of C. Wright Mills,* Irving Louis Horowitz, ed., New York: Oxford University Press, Ballantine Books, 1963, pp. 23–38.

MINAR, DAVID W. "Ideology and Political Behavior," *Midwest Journal of Political Science, 5,* 1961, pp. 317–331.

MONEY, J. "Sex Hormones and Other Variables in Human Eroticism," in *Sex and Internal Secretions,* William C. Young, ed., Baltimore: Williams and Wilkins, 1961, pp. 1383–1400.

MULLIGAN, RAYMOND A. "Socio-Economic Background and College Enrollment," *American Sociological Review, 16,* 1951, pp. 188–196.

MURDOCK, GEORGE PETER. *Social Structure*. New York: The Macmillan Company, 1949.

MURTAGH, JOHN M., and SARA HARRIS. *Cast the First Stone*. New York: McGraw-Hill Book Company, Inc., 1957.

NEFF, WANDA. *Victorian Working Women*. New York: Columbia University Press, 1929.

NETTLES, CURTIS P. *Roots of American Civilization*. Second Edition. New York: Appleton-Century-Crofts, 1963.

NEWTON, ESTHER. *Mother Camp: Female Impersonators in America*. Englewood Cliffs, New Jersey: Prentice-Hall, Inc., 1972.

O'CONNELL, JEFFREY. "Lambs to Slaughter," *Columbia Journalism Review, 6,* 1967, pp. 21–28.

O'CONNOR, GERALD G. "The Impact of Initial Detention on Male Delinquents," *Social Problems, 18,* 1970, pp. 194–199.

OLIVER, BERNARD J., JR. *Sexual Deviation in American Society: A Social Psychological Study of Sexual Non-Conformity*. New Haven, Conn.: College and University Press, Publishers, 1967.

O'NEILL, WILLIAM L. *The Woman Movement: Feminism in the United States and England*. Chicago: Quadrangle Books, 1971.

PALME, OLOF. "The Emancipation of Man," *Journal of Social Issues, 28,* 1972, pp. 237–246.

PHELPS, ORME WHEELOCK. *The Legislative Background of the Fair Labor Standards Act: A Study of the Growth of National Sentiment in Favor of Governmental Regulation of Wages, Hours and Child Labor*. Chicago: The University of Chicago Press, 1939.

PILIAVIN, IRVING, and SCOTT BRIAR. "Police Encounters with Juveniles," *American Journal of Sociology, 70,* 1964, pp. 206–214.

PITTMAN, DAVID J. "The Male House of Prostitution," *Trans-Action, 8,* 1971, pp. 21–27.

PLATO. *The Republic of Plato,* John Llewelyn Davies and David James Vaughan, translators. London: Macmillan and Company, Ltd., 1950.

POLANYI, MICHAEL. *The Logic of Liberty*. Chicago: The University of Chicago Press, 1958.

POLSKY, NED. *Hustlers, Beats, and Others*. Garden City, New York: Doubleday and Company, Inc., 1969.

PULLIAM, ALVIN M. "The Numbers," unpublished paper, 1970.

QUERLIN, MAURISE. *Women Without Men*. London: Mayflower Books, 1965.

RAWICK, GEORGE P. *The American Slave: A Composite Autobiography,* Volume 1, *From Sundown to Sunup, The Making of the Black Community*. Westport, Connecticut: Greenwood Publishing Company, 1972.

REDDING, SAUNDERS. *They Came in Chains: Americans from Africa*. Philadelphia: J. B. Lippincott Company, 1969. (First published in 1950.)

REYNOLDS, LARRY T. "Southeast Asia and the Corporate State: Warfare as Economic Consumption," in *Down to Earth Sociology*. James M. Henslin, ed., New York: The Free Press, 1972, pp. 362–374.

———, and JAMES M. HENSLIN, eds., *American Society: A Critical Analysis*. New York: David McKay Company, 1973.

ROCHE, PHILLIP Q. *The Criminal Mind: A Study of Communication Between Criminal Law and Psychiatry.* New York: Farrar, Strauss, and Cudahy, 1958.

ROHNER, RONALD P., and EVELYN C. ROHNER. *The Kwakiutl: Indians of British Columbia.* New York: Holt, Rinehart and Winston, 1970.

ROKEACH, MILTON. *The Nature of Human Values.* New York: The Free Press, 1973.

ROSEN, EPHIAM, and IAN GREGORY. *Abnormal Psychology.* Philadelphia: W. B. Saunders and Company, 1965.

ROSENHAN, D. L. "On Being Sane in Insane Places," *Science, 179,* January 19, 1973, pp. 250–258.

ROSMAN, ABRAHAM, and PAULA G. RUBEL. *Feasting With Mine Enemey: Rank and Exchange Among Northwest Coast Societies.* New York: Columbia University Press, 1971.

ROSZAK, THEODORE. *The Making of A Counter Culture.* New York: Doubleday and Company, Inc., 1969.

ROWAN, CARL T. "Pentagon Moves against Race Bias," *St. Louis Globe-Democrat,* June 4, 1971.

ROYKO, MIKE. "Agnew, Aristotle and Aid," *Chicago Daily News,* November 27, 1971.

RUESCH, HANS. *Top of the World.* New York: Permabooks, 1959.

SAFFOLD, HOWARD. "An Open Letter to Mayor Daley," in *Social Problems in American Society.* James M. Henslin and Larry T. Reynolds, eds., Boston: Holbrook Press, 1973, pp. 82–85.

SAGARIN, EDWARD. *Odd Man In: Societies of Deviants in America.* Chicago: Quadrangle Books, 1969.

SCHALL, JAMES. *Play On.* Philadelphia, Pa.: Fortress Press, 1971.

SCHATZKI, GEORGE. "The Sodomy Laws Must Go: Origins, Effects, Prospects," *Civil Liberties, 277,* 1971, pp. 2 and 4.

SCHEFF, THOMAS J. *Being Mentally Ill: A Sociological Theory.* Chicago: Aldine Publishing Company, 1966.

SCHNEIR, MIRIAM. *Feminism.* New York: Random House, 1972.

SCHULTZE, CHARLES. *The Distribution of Farm Subsidies: Who Gets the Benefits.* Washington, D.C.: The Brookings Institute, 1971.

SCHUR, EDWIN M. *Crimes without Victims: Deviant Behavior and Public Policy: Abortion, Homosexuality, Drug Addiction.* Englewood Cliffs, New Jersey: Prentice-Hall, Inc., 1965.

———. *Law and Society.* New York: Random House, Inc., 1968.

SERVICE, ELMAN R. *A Profile of Primitive Culture.* New York: Harper and Row, 1958.

SEVERO, RICHARD. "The Lost Tribe of Alabama," *Scanlan's Monthly, 1,* 1970, pp. 81–88.

SEWALL, WILLIAM, and VINAL P. SHAH. "Socioeconomic Status, Intelligence, and the Attainment of Higher Education," *Sociology of Education, 40,* 1967, pp. 1–23.

SHAW, CLIFFORD. *The Jack Roller: A Delinquent Boy's Own Story*. Chicago: The University of Chicago Press, 1930.

SIMON, WILLIAM, and JOHN H. GAGNON. "Homosexuality: The Formulation of a Sociological Perspective," *Journal of Health and Social Behavior, 8*, 1967, pp. 177–185.

SIMPSON, GEORGE E., and MILTON YINGER. *Racial and Cultural Minorities*. New York: Harper and Row, 1965.

SIMPSON, RICHARD L. "Theories of Social Exchange." Morristown, New Jersey: General Learning Press, 1972. (A learning module.)

SINGLEMANN, PETER. "Exchange as Symbolic Interaction: Convergences between Two Theoretical Perspectives," *American Sociological Review, 37*, 1972, pp. 414–424.

SJOBERG, GIDEON. *The Preindustrial City: Past and Present*. New York: The Free Press, 1963.

SKINNER, B. F. *Science and Human Behavior*. New York: The Macmillan Company, 1953.

SMITH, FRANK E. *Congressman from Mississippi*. New York: Capricorn Books, 1967.

SPIEGELMAN, MORTIMER. "The Changing Demographic Spectrum and Its Implications for Health," *Eugenics Quarterly, 10*, December 1963, pp. 161–175.

———. *Introduction to Demography*. Revised Edition. Cambridge: Harvard University Press, 1968.

SPRADLEY, JAMES P. "The Moral Career of a Bum," *Trans-Action, 7*, 1970, pp. 17–29.

SROLE, LEO, T. S. LANGER, S. T. MICHAEL, M. K. OPLER, and T. A. C. RENNIE. *Mental Health in the Metropolis: Midtown Manhattan Study*. New York: McGraw-Hill Book Company, 1962.

STEELE, MARION, and JAY PARKER. "A Social Psychological Theory of Homosexuality," unpublished paper, 1969.

STERN, BERNHARD J. *Medicine in Industry*. New York: Commonwealth Fund, 1946.

STEINER, CLAUDE. *Games Alcoholics Play: The Analysis of Life Scripts*. New York: Grove Press, 1971.

SUDNOW, DAVID. "Normal Crimes: Sociological Features of the Penal Code in a Public Defender Office," *Social Problems, 12*, 1965, pp. 255–276.

SUTHERLAND, EDWIN H., and DONALD K. CRESSEY. *Principles of Criminology*. Sixth Edition. Chicago: J. B. Lippincott Company, 1960.

SUTTLES, GERALD D. *The Social Order of the Slum*. Chicago: University of Chicago Press, 1968.

SYKES, GRESHAM M., and DAVID MATZA. "Techniques of Neutralization: A Theory of Delinquency," *The American Sociological Review, 22*, 1957, pp. 664–670.

SZASZ, THOMAS S. "The Crime of Commitment," *Psychology Today, 2*, 1969, pp. 55–57.

SZASZ, THOMAS S. *The Manufacture of Madness: A Comparative Study of the Inquisition and the Mental Health Movement.* New York: Harper and Row, 1970.

TABER, MERLIN, HERBERT C. QUAY, HAROLD MARK, and VICKI NEALEY. "Disease Ideology and Mental Health Research," *Social Problems, 16,* 1969, pp. 349–357.

TOCH, HANS. *The Social Psychology of Social Movements.* Indianapolis: The Bobbs-Merrill Co., Inc., 1965.

DE TOCQUEVILLE, ALEXIS. *Democracy in America,* Volume 1. New York: Vintage Books, 1957.

TURNER, RALPH H., and LEWIS M. KILLIAN. *Collective Behavior.* Second Edition. Englewood Cliffs, New Jersey: Prentice-Hall, Inc., 1972.

VAN DEN BERGHE, PIERRE L. *Academic Gamesmanship: How to Make a Ph.D. Pay.* New York: Abelard-Schuman, 1970.

WALLER, WILLARD, and REUBEN HILL. *The Family.* New York: Dryden Press, 1951.

WATSON, GOODWIN. "Psychological Aspects of Sex Roles," *Social Psychology: Issues and Insights.* Philadelphia: Lippincott, 1966, pp. 427–459.

WEBER, MAX. *The Protestant Ethic and the Spirit of Capitalism.* New York: Charles Scribner's Sons, 1958.

WEINBERG, S. KIRSON. *Social Problems in Modern Urban Society.* Second Edition. Englewood Cliffs, New Jersey: Prentice-Hall, Inc., 1970.

WEINER, NORMAN L. "The Teen-Age Shoplifter: A Microcosmic View of Middle-Class Delinquency," in *Observations of Deviance.* Jack D. Douglas, ed., New York: Random House, 1970, pp. 213–217.

WELLS, THEODORA. "Woman—Which Includes Man, Of Course: An Experience in Awareness," in *Social Problems in American Society.* James M. Henslin and Larry T. Reynolds, eds., Boston: Holbrook Press, 1973, pp. 128–130.

WERTHMAN, CARL. "The Function of Social Definitions in the Development of Delinquent Careers," in *Task Force Report: Juvenile Delinquency and Youth Crime.* The President's Commission on Law Enforcement and Administration of Justice, Washington, D.C.: U.S. Government Printing Office, 1967, pp. 155–170.

WEST, D. J. *Homosexuality.* Chicago: Aldine Publishing Company, 1967.

WESTLEY, WILLIAM A. "Violence and the Police," *American Journal of Sociology, 59,* 1953, pp. 34–41.

WHORF, BENJAMIN. *Language, Thought and Reality.* Cambridge, Massachusetts: MIT Press, 1956.

WHYTE, WILLIAM H., JR. "The Wife Problem," in *Selected Studies in Marriage and the Family.* Third Edition. Robert F. Winch and Louis Wolf Goodman, eds., New York: Holt, Rinehart and Winston, Inc., 1968, pp. 177–188.

WILLHELM, SIDNEY M. *Who Needs the Negro?* Cambridge, Massachusetts: Schenkman Publishing Company, Inc., 1970.

WILLIAMS, ERIC. *Capitalism and Slavery.* New York: Capricorn Books, 1966. (First published 1944 by The University of North Carolina Press.)

WINICK, CHARLES, and PAUL M. KINSIE. *The Lively Commerce: Prostitution in the United States.* Chicago: Quadrangle Books, 1971.

WITKIN, HERMAN A. *Psychological Differentiation.* New York: John Wiley, 1962.

WOODBURY, ROBERT M. "Infant Mortality in the United States," *Annals of the American Academy of Political and Social Science, 188,* 1936, pp. 102–104.

WYMAN, WALKER D., and CLIFTON B. KROEBER, eds., *The Frontier in Perspective.* Madison, Wisconsin: The University of Wisconsin Press, 1957.

WYNNE-EDWARDS, V. C. *Animal Dispersion in Relation to Social Behaviour.* Edinburgh: Oliver and Boyd, 1962.

YABLONSKY, LEWIS. *Synanon: The Tunnel Back.* New York: The Macmillan Company, 1965.

YINGER, J. MILTON. "Contraculture and Subculture," *American Sociological Review, 25,* 1960, pp. 625–635.

YOUNG, W. C., R. GOY and C. PHOENIX. "Hormones and Sexual Behavior," *Science, 143,* 1964, pp. 212–218.

ZELNIK, MELVIN. "Age Patterns of Mortality of American Negroes: 1900–02 to 1959–61," *Journal of the American Statistical Association, 64,* 1969, pp. 433–451.

Index